"*I had the privilege of sitting under Pastor* [Don's] *original presentation of The Reign of Grace sermon series and it changed my life. For over forty years, I have also used it in transcribed manuscript format to teach hundreds of believers world-wide. The impact on their lives has consistently been life changing too as Pastor Don opens the deep theological truths of Romans 6-8 in an easily understood and practically applied way. I cannot say enough about this series.*"

Gary Matsdorf

Global Education Coordinator
International Church of the Foursquare Gospel

"Words carry weight and when a respected leader uses them wisely, they become a foundation for life. Pastor Don Pickerill is a gifted communicator, thinker, pastor, and visionary. He doesn't just see behind what most people see, he sees it before they do, as well. Long before the word grace became a buzzword in modern Christendom, Pastor Pickerill was teaching it, living it and practicing it. His words have great meaning because they emerge from a rich life of experience and wisdom. Grace is God's platform of restoration and redemption. Don Pickerill has known that and has been a recipient of it. So have we all."

Dr. Glenn Burris

Former President of The Foursquare Church

"The Reign of Grace series opened up the love of the Father to me. Also, my husband Russ listened to the series 18+ times and then truly grasped what grace was all about, so we named our daughter, Raina Grace in honor of 'The Reign of Grace.'"

Robin McGregor-Witt

"Read this exciting book on a passage of Scripture that is unfortunately little taught and less understood, but is absolutely vital to understanding and living the Christian life as Christ means for us to live it.

It makes no difference whether you have been a believing Christian for decades or whether you just began your life with Christ last week, or whether you are seeking to understand what Christianity is all about-- there is something important and vital for everyone who is in need of a more mature faith. That's all of us.

Thank you, Pastors Don and Ron for making this little gem available to a wider audience!"

Rev. Dr. Valson Abraham
President, India Gospel Outreach &
India Bible College and Seminary

"I was a new Christian and began attending Italian Christian Assembly in Los Angeles a few months before my Uncle Don Pickerill began the "Reign of Grace" series. What a gift it was to my soul to have the grace of God taught to me as I began my journey of faith. A life changing foundational teaching that helped me trust in the goodness of the Lord through every storm and trial, but also gave me the confidence to "enter the throne of grace" knowing He loved me as a son in spite of my many failures as a new Christian. These truths have fueled spiritual balance and growth in my life over and over through the years."

Mike McGregor

THE REIGN OF
Grace

DONALD R. PICKERILL
WITH RON ISAM

Quantity sales and special discounts are available on quantity purchases by corporations, associations, and others. For details, contact the publisher at the address above.

Orders by U.S. trade bookstores and wholesalers. Email info@BeyondPublishing.net

The Beyond Publishing Speakers Bureau can bring authors to your live event. For more information or to book an event contact the Beyond Publishing Speakers Bureau speak@BeyondPublishing.net

Scripture quotations from the Revised Standard Version (RSV) of the Bible, copyright © 1946, 1952, and 1971 the Division of Christian Education of the National Council of the Churches of Christ in the United States of America. Used by permission. All rights reserved.

Scripture quotations taken from the Amplified® Bible Classic (AMPC), Copyright © 1954, 1958, 1962, 1964, 1965, 1987 by The Lockman Foundation. Used by permission." (www.Lockman.org)

Scripture quotations taken from the King James Version (KJV) were copied from the Bible Gateway matches the 1987 printing. The KJV is public domain in the United States.

Scripture quotations taken from the American Standard Version (ASV) were copied from the Bible Gateway and were the basis of four revisions. They were the Revised Standard Version, 1971, the Amplified Bible, 1965, the New American Standard Bible, 1995, and the Recovery Version, 1999. A fifth revision, known as the World English Bible, was published in 2000 and was placed in the public domain. The ASV was also the basis for Kenneth N. Taylor's Bible paraphrase, The Living Bible, 1971. This Bible is in the public domain in the United States.

The Author can be reached directly at BeyondPublishing.net

Manufactured and printed in the United States of America distributed globally by BeyondPublishing.net

BEYOND

New York | Los Angeles | London | Sydney

Library Of Congress Control Number: 2022916193

ISBN Softcover: 978-1-63792-358-0
ISBN Hardcover: 978-1-63792-357-3

"The Reign of Grace has been the most transforming study of my life, and my ministry life. I have taught it and preached it... I wholeheartedly endorse this book. While attending L.I.F.E. Bible College in LA, presently called Life Pacific University in San Dimas, CA, I was honored to attend Christian Assembly (CA) with Don as my pastor for 9 years as a student and beyond. Everything he taught from God's Word was of great import. Later, I simply called him the best preacher of theology I have ever known or heard. After more than 40 years in ministry, I remain in contact with Don, and each time I visit, he "blesses my socks off." At the most recent visit, Don had put out a whole treasure of his works, and offered I take anything I could use. I took much. That is the enduring character of Don Pickerill, that anything he has written or said is simply to be given away."

In Grace, Jim Cosby

ACKNOWLEDGMENTS

I cannot say thank you enough to the ministry team of Anchor of Grace in Moore, Oklahoma for completing this great task of putting the Reign of Grace in book format. I thank Pastor Ron Isam, my friend, and founder of AOG, for having the vision and fortitude to put these audio sermons into a written format. My thanks also go to Johnny Fowler, Ron's right hand man, who transcribed the first drafts to get the words in a text format. Finally, I thank Ron's wife, Diane, who took on the challenge to get the final draft as close to the audio sermons as possible. I am amazed at this great accomplishment.

Pastor Don Pickerill

PREFACE

The following pages contain transcribed sermons I preached nearly 50 years ago at Christian Assembly in Eagle Rock, California. They contain one of the most profound sections of the Bible and that is Paul's observations and commentaries in Romans chapters 6, 7 and 8 on the meaning of being under grace. These chapters are looked at in length and in detail in these sermons and the main theological truth are the words, "You are not under law, but you are under grace." The reign of grace. The abundance of grace. King Grace.

In these 25 sermons we are going to read some of the most loved and famous words in all the New Testament. I'm not talking about something merely on the pages of the Bible. I'm talking about a life, a doctrine, a truth that sets you free into the glorious liberty of the children of God. This truth will work in our lives, in our marriages, in our families, and in our relationships with one another.

You will never fully enter into life until you discover how to be free from the law. The consequences of that, are that we might be super conquerors, more than conquerors, through Him that loved us. It is wonderful to know what Jesus Christ can do and to rest in His grace. I thank God for the good news of the grace of God that I can be freed from sin, its guilt and its power, by the marvelous work of the Lord Jesus Christ.

My prayer is that you will let this marvelous knowledge, this word of grace come home to your life, that you will receive this message down deep in your soul. Come to Jesus, just as you are and believe the message of grace.

Pastor Don Pickerill

WHY THE BOLD?

The words in this book contain 25 transcribed sermons preached by Pastor Don Pickerill in 1973. Transcribing sermons into a written format has its challenges. There are software programs that can help with the busy work of taking an audio recording and typing it out to become words on a page. However, the personality of the speaker and the meaning he is trying to get across can sometimes get lost to the reader. As scriptures are being explored and meanings are being defined, sentence structure, word choice, and punctuation can be disarrayed through transcribing. The speaker so wanted for the congregation to understand having grace reign in their lives that he accentuates words, statements, and sometimes paragraphs. In order to feel the emphasis that Pastor Don's voice and cadence placed on these words throughout the teaching, we chose to put those words in **bold**. Often times when he used even more volume, we put the words in **<u>bold and underlined them</u>**. When Pastor Don shouted, for extreme emphasis, we not only put the words in **bold** and **<u>underlined</u>** them, but we also put the words in **<u>ALL CAPS</u>**.

Long dashes are used throughout the sermons to join several statements or thoughts that may or may not be a complete sentence on their own. By combining multiple statements with dashes, the reader can pick up on the passion and enthusiasm of the speaker. Long dashes were also used to represent a pause Pastor Don used between words and thoughts to bring emphasis. Example: You (pause) are (pause) not (pause) under (pause) the law (pause) you are (pause) under grace. Same example with long dashes: You—are—not—under—the law—you are—under grace.

Generally, in written pieces, very few contractions are used. However, in transcribing these sermons, we chose to leave the majority of the contractions Pastor Don said in the messages to keep his relaxed flow and reveal his personality. In addition we have left adjoining words he said such as "now"—"and"—"so"—and "well"—that he used quite frequently at the beginning of sentences and paragraphs to connect Biblical facts and personal illustrations to help the listener connect the various building points of each sermon.

Pastor Don primarily used the Revised Standard Version translation when he preached these sermons. Please note that there will be times when a scripture reference is given and only portions of that verse or verses are actually quoted by Pastor Don in the sermon to make various points. Many times, it appears that he was quoting portions from the King James Version or New American Standard Version most likely because he had memorized it from those versions. For your reference we have placed all of the scriptures that were studied in each message, entered word for word, in the version that he was quoting, at the end of each corresponding sermon.

The ministry team from Anchor of Grace has worked hundreds of hours to try to bring the reader into the live service, to experience the anointing of the Holy Spirit on Pastor Don and to understand what he is teaching through the words typed on the following pages. We pray that you will enjoy these messages and grow in grace as you learn about *The Reign of Grace*.

The Ministry Team @ Anchor of Grace

INTRODUCTION

It was 1974 when I became introduced to the truth found in this great book you are holding. I had just arrived at Bible College and began to attend services at a growing, exciting, and vibrant church. To be completely honest, I had never experienced church like this before. This church was growing quickly in a little building on Avenue 22 in Los Angeles, California. As I got more acquainted with people there, I couldn't help but ask what is happening to make this church so exciting that so many people would want to crowd in here. The person I asked, introduced me to the series of sermons that were given just the year before called "The Reign of Grace."

It is a real joy to introduce Don Pickerill, the Senior Pastor of the church I was just describing and the author of the book you are looking at today. Pastor Don was one of the favorite professors at LIFE Bible College, now called Life Pacific University, where I attended. He is an incredible man of God and a master teacher of the Word of God. If you were to actually meet him in person today, you would find a spiritual giant. He is one who walks deeply in the Spirit and has profoundly touched the lives of so many men and women who attended the college as well as the churches where he served. He is the most gracious, loving and humble man of God.

I would really miss my assignment here, if I didn't also introduce, Pastor Don's lovely wife, Maurine, who is also a great teacher of the Word. Now in their senior years, their bodies are not as able, but their minds and hearts are still very clear and powerful as they walk in the Holy Spirit. I have been so blessed to have Pastor Don and Maurine in my life all of these years. While they are retired from full-time ministry, I still get incredible papers written by Pastor Don, emailed to me by Maurine, as he studies the Bible every day.

When I have a question from my studies of the Word, where I cannot get something straight in my mind, I can call and ask Don my questions. If I didn't know him like I have had the privilege to know him, I would have thought by his comments on my questions that he, too, was studying the very same scripture. What a wonderful blessing to have Don Pickerill as my pastor/mentor and a living commentary.

Though the teachings that are given in this book were given in 1973, I did not hear the sermons until 1974 from cassette tapes. I can only say to you that when I was a freshman in college, you could find me in a small prayer room in the men's dorm, listening to these messages over and over. I listened to them there because I was fairly certain I would not be interrupted much.

This teaching literally changed my life in incredible ways. These words of grace were breaking down the chains of bondage to the law. These truths were building me up in ways that I could not explain at that time. I can tell you now that this is the most life transforming truth I have ever heard. It profoundly touched the lives of the people who were a part of the congregation at Christian Assembly Foursquare Church, in Eagle Rock, California. It changed the entire culture of this church family. Grace was literally reigning in the lives of those precious people, and it still is to this day.

Many of the people who were transformed through these truths were experiencing, "The glorious liberty of the children of God." This message, as well as other messages of Pastor Don, were sent through recordings made by Christian Assembly to people around the world, but the message was also spread by the people in the congregation who heard this teaching and allowed the Holy Spirit to transform them. It has been taught through many, but honestly, the most powerful thing that was happening was people in the body touching others by the grace of God. Many who heard this message have taught it in almost every ministry assignment where God has led them. I know I have.

One interesting story about the Reign of Grace series is that there was a married couple by the name of Russ & Robin Witt who were deeply touched by these teachings. Russ listened to these messages over and over. It affected this couple so deeply that when their daughter was born, they named her Raina Grace. Incidentally, Robin is Don Pickerill's niece.

My prayer is that you will use this book as a resource for your study of Romans, 6, 7 and 8. It will take a while to get through it, but I can assure you, as you stay devoted, it will be the most life transforming truth you will ever experience.

Pastor Ron Isam
Anchor of Grace

TABLE OF CONTENTS

SERMON 1

THE INTRODUCTION

"God knows what we need, and that's His marvelous grace!"

This morning I want to begin a series of sermons that in my opinion will be the most important that I'll ever preach to you from a practical viewpoint. The **most significant** part of our Bible is the book of **Romans.** Romans is the **key** to the **gospel.** And anyone who tries to understand what Jesus Christ has **done**, you **must grapple with Romans. And**, I would say the mos*t* **profound** and again the most significant part of **Romans,** if there were such a thing, would be Romans chapters 6, 7 and 8—those three chapters. So, we're going to concentrate on them for a few weeks and pray that the Lord Jesus will give us **courage**, and **insight** and **wisdom** into His word.

Now I have read these repeatedly. I have studied them intently. As a matter of fact, I've diagrammed every Greek sentence and gone back again to work through those diagrams and I'm praying that the Lord is going to **help us.** But I must tell you that there are great aspects of this which seemingly escape you, even when you read it, you wonder, "Am I grasping what the Apostle was saying?"

And I have the feeling when I come to Romans 6, 7 and 8, like the day or two trip I made through Switzerland one time—and we were on a little road and I could see the great valleys and the beautiful hills and mountains off to a distance—but I felt they were **unexplored,** and they had **depths** to them and **heights** to them that I couldn't comprehend. Well, that's certainly true of Romans chapters 6, 7 and 8. But we're praying that the Lord Jesus will help us.

Today our task will simply be to **introduce** to you, in a **summary way,** what the **salient** or the **main features** are of these three chapters, and it will be up to the rest of the series to detail it. I do pray that you will not miss a one. It's not often I think my sermons are all that important, but I think this series is absolutely the **most vital** that I'll ever preach to you. I'm sure that I'm going to say some things that will be, maybe, misunderstood. As a matter of fact, if you don't flirt with Antinomianism, A you haven't followed **the Apostle Paul.** You don't begin yet to comprehend the **tremendous depths** that he's taking us to in these chapters.

If there was a **verse** that introduces these three chapters, it would be the **closing** verse of chapter **5.** And I would regard this as a good **title,** really, for Romans chapters 6, 7 and 8. Would you look please at the **last verse** of Romans chapter 5, and pray the Lord will give you understanding, give me utterance and give us all courage and wisdom. Chapter 5, verse 21, *"...as <u>sin</u>—<u>reigned</u>—in <u>death</u>—<u>grace</u> also—might <u>reign</u>—<u>through righteousness</u>—to eternal life—through Jesus Christ our Lord."* [1] And so, you have a **comparison,** *"as sin—<u>reigned in death</u>—so <u>grace</u>—might reign—in <u>life</u>."* Now, that's what that amounts to. If you were to write a caption or a title over Romans chapters 6, 7 and 8, it would be **that: That grace—might reign—in life—through Jesus Christ.** So, I regard these three chapters as an exposition of **The Reign of Grace—King Grace— Grace on the Throne—Grace Properly Understood.** It's the great **key** to the human **solution.** These chapters are an exposition of **The <u>Reign</u> of <u>Grace</u>** and the consequences of it when grace dominates your life and sits on the throne of your universe.

I think there are really three summary things to be said about these chapters, by way of an introduction. I want to underscore the **key theological truth.** I want to point out the **main practical truth** and **finally** we'll close with the **main exhortation**—the key exhortation. So, we're talking about the key truth, the key practical point, and the key exhortation to these three chapters.

We have said that the whole thing has to do with the **reign of grace**—grace reigning _in_ life. The main formulation of that is given in chapter 6, verse 14. Would you look please at this statement, and this is the **main theological truth** that Paul is trying to convey. Romans chapter 6, verse 14, here it is, _"sin will have no dominion **over** you, **since** you are not under **law** but under **grace**."_ ² Now, it's **very** important that we grasp the implications of that theological truth. It is not my purpose this morning to exegete that for you, nor to talk about that. We'll probably get around to that next week, but I simply want to introduce to you the **main thought.** All of us want to live a life that is **free.** We've been set free without bondage. We don't want to be under **dominion.** We want to be freed from sin, but how easily we get **deceived!** And I don't want to be overbearing with you, but I can honestly say that **90%** of the people that I know, even in the church, are **still under the law.**

I know the depths of my own heart and I know the tendency constantly to, quote, "be under the _law._" Now I don't have time again to tell all the details of this but let me explain **briefly—that to be under the _law_, means basically to be on your own and in some way to be _down_ on yourself.** Anybody who's under the law is, in a sense, **down** on themselves—they have a **judgment** against themselves. **All I can say is 9 out of 10 people that I know, in some way, are _down_ on themselves. And the whole modern psychological insights are simply a broad commentary, in _my_ opinion, of what it means to be _laboring_ under that kind of an attitude. We call it guilt—condemnation—this is _very,_**

very, far-reaching. The Apostle Paul is going to work all this <u>out</u>. If you are the <u>slightest bit</u> down on yourself, you don't stand a ghost of a chance to enter into life. You are under law. That's what that means. That's one of the **parts** of it.

What an amazing thing to know that you are under nothing— but—grace! It's the <u>only way</u> to be delivered from sin. And I'll show you how all that works out in days ahead. **There is only <u>one way</u> to enter into life and that's to enthrone <u>grace</u>! If grace <u>reigns</u>, it's then** that you enter into life. If it does **not,** you're going to find just phases of **death** in all of its various **ways.** So that's the **main truth** of these three chapters. **You—are—not—under— law. No law, of any kind.**

And again, let me repeat, if you don't come **dangerously** close to Antinomianism ^A you have **not** followed the Apostle Paul. **We're not under law! <u>No law</u>! There is no claim upon me! <u>There is no claim upon me</u>! I'm not under law.** May the **Holy Spirit** even **faintly** begin to reveal to us the implications of that. Most of us just **gasp** at the very thought of it—we can't even believe it. Let's go back and **read our Bibles once again. You are not under law. You are under grace and that's <u>all</u> you are under. That is <u>ALL</u> you are under!** If that ever **faintly** dawned upon our consciousness, it would be such an emancipation and such a liberation, that few of us could stand it.

So that's the main point to these three chapters. It's to get that theological truth across. You are not under **law;** you are **under grace,** and may Jesus Christ give us comprehension of what that means.

The <u>main</u> practical part to this, is also suggested in Romans 5:21, "...that grace might reign to eternal life." [1] So again, this is all about **life.** And I don't care how much theology you've gotten; you're going to bump into **reality.** You're going to bump into **your nature.** You're going to bump into **life.** You're going to bump into your person and you're going to bump into other people. You're going to bump into circumstances and **that's called life.**

So, we want **life!** And I would say that the **key passage** dealing with this is Romans chapter 8, verse 21. Now, there are **seven aspects** of **life** described in these three chapters. I'll only quickly read them for you, but this is the summary. This I believe is what we want more than anything else. Paul writes in Romans 8:21, he says, *"...creation itself will be set free from it's **bondage to decay and obtain"**—* **this**, and here it is—*"the glorious liberty of the children of God."* [3]

I was impressed by the release of our POWs, [B] and I remember one of the colonels said, **"Next to life,** the greatest thing in the world is **freedom."** And wasn't it **wonderful** to watch all those boys come home with **freedom. More than anything else we long to be set free! We long to enter into glorious liberty. And if life has bondage**—if you're **under the dominion of something—you can't have life. We long for this freedom—we long for glorious freedom—the glorious freedom of the children of God.** Now, that basically is the **main point** to these chapters—**is glorious freedom! An emancipation proclamation— where we're utterly and absolutely free. Utterly and absolutely—free!** So, we're longing for the **glorious liberty** of the children of God.

"But thanks be to God, that you who were once slaves of sin have become obedient from the heart to the standard of teaching to which you were committed. - Romans 6:17 RSV

Now there are seven characteristics to this life, and I only have time to point them out this morning. The first is found in chapter 6, verse 17, where Paul says, *"...thanks be to God, that you who were once **slaves*** *of sin have become obedient from the **heart** to the standard of teaching to which you were committed."* ⁴ So, the first thing that **happens** in this kind of life is a heartfelt obedience. You have **obedience from the heart.** Now, it's a very difficult thing to have a spontaneous obedience. There's a very subtle **rebellion** that works in all of us, anytime we get crossed. It's an amazing **thing,** when it goes from **duty** to **delight,** and you have a **heartfelt obedience. That's** a work of **grace.** That's the grace of God, bringing you to this **kind** of obedience. A heartfelt obedience, where you spontaneously **long** to do it. You do it now **not** out of threat, **not** out of law, but with a **heartfelt** obedience.

The second, is found in chapter 6, verse 22, *"But **now** that you have been **set free** from **sin** and have become **slaves of God,** the return you get is—**sanctification,"*** ⁵ and that issues into eternal life. Sanctification is a misunderstood word. It's kind of a church term almost—it doesn't fit into our modern vocabulary. But let me just explain to you that sanctification has the heart, the thought of being whole—or wholesomeness. That which is wholesome and **made whole.** Anybody who has an **integrity** and a **wholeness** to them, **that's sanctification.** So, we're longing for this **wholeness.** That's the **second benefit** that comes out of this life of glorious freedom.

Now the **next** is found in chapter 7, verse 4, where Paul says, *"Likewise, my brethren, you have **died** to the **law,"*** and all of its claims—all gone—**dead** to us, *"through the body of Christ, so that you may belong to another, to him who has been raised from the dead in order that you may **bear fruit** for God."* ⁶ And so the **third benefit** of this life is fruit for God or fruitfulness.

The fourth is found in chapter 8, verse 6, and here are **two things,** *"To set your mind on the flesh,"*—the attitude of the flesh—*"is **death"***—and Paul means physical death but he's talking about all the **misery** and all the **confusion** and all the **corruption** that comes this **side** of **death.**

To live in a kind of a **lethal** to wish for death—to wish you were **dead** more than **alive.** So, *"To set the mind on the flesh is death, but to set the mind on the Spirit—is—life."* [7] This "life" here, is talking about a **kind** of life and really it means to enjoy life. It has the thought of really **enjoying life** and **enjoying God.** And I said that the heart of our creed **is that** we might **glorify God** and **enjoy Him forever.** And so, God has designed life, for us to enter into it **joyfully** with **real joy.** So the fourth thing is life and the fifth thing is peace—"*is life and peace.*" [7] Well, do I need to describe that? That doesn't need definition. **All** of us know what it means to be in an attitude of **peace** and **quiet** where everything is at rest.

The sixth one is this *"glorious liberty of the children of God,"* [3] in chapter 8, verse 21. And the **seventh** thing, the **seventh benefit** of this life is in chapter 8, verse 29, that you might "*...be conformed to the image of his Son who is the first-born among many brethren.*" [8] And so the **seven things** that come to us when we're under grace are willful obedience, a wholeness, fruitfulness, the enjoyment of life, peace, Christlikeness and freedom.

Now, if you were to ask the average person what's keeping them out of life and freedom? What's keeping them from enjoying life? I'm sure most of us would say something like this: "Well, it's my set of circumstances. It's the problems I'm in. I've got problems. That's why." Can you live in this **life** and not have problems? Can you live in this life and **not suffer?** Well, that can be like a **bondage. It can be like a dominion. Things,** things that would want to drive us into the **ground** as it were and **destroy** us. This set of circumstances round about us can be **very lethal indeed, full of all kinds of bondages.**

Well, the Apostle Paul is going to address himself to that very real problem in Romans chapter 8. His circumstances—how does one face them? What do they really mean? What's really going on in

these trying circumstances? Is Romans 8:28 <u>really</u> <u>true</u>? Do all things <u>really</u> work together for good? Most of us have difficulty believing that. We're going to have to take a **close** look again at Romans chapter 8. But we're going to see that you're going to meet a **very terrifying reality**—tribulation—distress—nakedness—famine—perils—swords. Thanks be unto God, there is a **way** that one can face all of these things and **find deliverance** from them so that you're not under their **bondage.** **Deliverance** from the **bondage** of circumstances.

Then secondly, I'm sure that most of us would say, "Well, my problem is me. If I had a different personality. If I were a different kind of person, then I'd be able to enter into life." Well, you're on the right track. You're the problem. But you see, you know what the difficulty is with most of us? Most of us do not know how **deadly** we are in that problem.

Now I urge you **strongly** to be here tonight when I talk about "The Reign of Sin." I'm going to say some things that may utterly surprise you. You've **got** to hear this message. It **has** to be heard. It's the only way I **know** to help us see aright the truth of our nature. And I'll just anticipate that briefly by saying, "**You can do nothing <u>but</u> sin.**" That's all you **can** do. **I sin even when I "will" against it. I don't want to sin, and <u>I do</u>.** And you're not kidding me, you're **exactly** like I am and most of you just haven't admitted it.

We're going to **look at** that tonight—<u>**head-on**</u>! As the great Apostle Paul, like open-heart surgery, opens up his heart and <u>**our hearts**</u> **as he uses that great rhetorical, "I" describing <u>all</u> people. And his verdict is sew them back up, they're beyond hope. They're dead.** They **cannot** perform righteousness. <u>**Impossible**</u>! But most of us **won't believe that!** So, I tell you, **we are** the problem. **Now, Paul is going to look at that in Romans chapter 6. That's why you've got to be <u>only under grace</u>! If <u>you're only under one inch of the law you're doomed!</u> If it's not grace** and anything but grace there is no deliverance for the human heart—if there's any demand on you whatever any slightest demand. I know how easily it is for us as parents and for preachers to get that all mixed up. We just do it constantly, as we meet one another constantly with the spirit of law and expectation. So, Romans chapter 6 is going to take a look at the "self."

But now there's a third thing that most of us would not know anything about. Here's where you need an apostle. This is where we need the great Apostle Paul to help us see what the problem is. Now, if you were to go to a doctor, you may have some problem. You may have a headache and you say, "Doctor, my head aches," and he responds, "Oh, you see the problem with you is you've got this pinched nerve in your spine." You would not have known that. Would we know that the connection between sin was the law? Most of us would not. And most of us don't understand that. I want to, in very clear terms, tie that together and show you how that works—what the connection is between the law and sin. And so, Romans chapter 7, is freedom from the law.

There are the three great things that keep us out of life—our trying circumstances, the reality that we're in that overwhelm us and make us suffer—our own natures—and finally the connections with the law. Now, we'll have to go into that as the Lord enables us to. But this is the great practical point—"that we can have the glorious liberty of the children of God." [3] And let me tell you, I don't take it for granted that any of you have ever yet heard the gospel. It's amazing to me what people can say who have been in the church all of their lives and like the Apostle Paul, was the best religionist on the face of the earth. He kept the law perfectly, and he turned around and put the Son of God to death. It's very easy for us to be caught up in a self-righteousness of which we are not aware of whatever. And so may the Lord Jesus

Christ help us to see how we can come into the glorious liberty of the children of God.

 "For if you live according to the flesh you will die, but if by the Spirit you put to death the deeds of the body you will live."
- *Romans 8:13 RSV*

And **now** for the **third great exhortation,** and that would be the main exhortation. There are two primary exhortations in these three chapters. You'll find them in chapter 6, verses 12 and 13 and you'll find it in chapter 8, verses 12 and 13. Verse 13 of chapter 8, I think **best states it** when it says, *"That if you live according to the flesh you will **die,"***—and death here means, eventually physical death, but it means the **death** of the **misery of life**—*"but if by the Spirit you put to death the deeds of the body you **will live."** *[9] Now that's the exhortation. Now I'd like to go over those one more time. The **main theological truth** of Romans 6, 7 and 8 is that you are <u>not</u> under the <u>law</u>. You are <u>under grace</u>. And that's all you're under. <u>Grace reigns!</u> <u>And let me tell you this, that grace is greater than your sin. Where sin abounds, grace does much more ABOUND.</u>

What's the answer to sin? It's <u>grace</u>! And if the medication isn't working just increase the <u>dosage</u>. But most of us try to <u>turn that around</u>. We try to use the law in some way to control sin. It will not work. There's only <u>one</u> answer to it, and that's the grace of God. Mankind had one thousand five hundred years to experiment under the law, to <u>show</u> that it brings <u>nothing</u> but rebellion and winds up crucifying the Son of God. And I wonder <u>when</u> we'll ever learn this lesson? <u>When</u> will it ever come to our hearts individually and then show up in our relationships? Again, let me tell you that <u>most </u>people I know, including myself, <u>labor</u> under a spirit of the law. You are—not—under—the law—you are—under grace. There is no demand upon you whatsoever, **not one. Not one.** "Oh," you say, "Pastor, then let's sin that grace may abound!" **Well, let me tell you this if you <u>do</u> sin, grace will abound all the more. I'm not making that up. That's Paul's words. Now <u>obviously</u>, that brings us to a certain problem. Paul's going to answer that in Romans 6, 7 and 8. But if you don't come close to that doctrine, you have not understood the grace of God.**

You are not under <u>LAW</u>! It's <u>all</u> over. There is no obligation. You couldn't do anything if there were on you but <u>rebel</u> and sin all the more. If it's not grace, then we're of all men most miserable. **And the main point is <u>life</u>! And that's this <u>glorious liberty</u> where I'm as free as a bird. Now <u>you</u> and <u>my conscience</u>, and the <u>devil</u> and <u>everybody else</u>, would like to get me <u>all</u> bound up** (*Don speaking with annoyance*)—**like to get me in all kinds of little bondages. Well, I'm not going to let you do it. I was made for freedom brother! I was made for glorious liberty and that's why I want to be set free from the law of sin and death. I— want—to be—free! I want the <u>glorious liberty</u>!** I don't want to tip toe around through life here—**hung up** and under **dominions** and **all bent out of shape** (*Don speaking with displeasure*). **Forget about it.** There's only one life and it's soon going to be over. **I want to live.** Give me plenty of elbow room brother (*Don chuckles*).

We've found the formula though, *"And if by the Spirit, I can put to death the deeds of the body I'm going to live,"* [9]—**by the Spirit. So, here's this great chapter here's this great section, dealing with life. The grace of God.**

Well, marvelous, infinite, matchless grace—grace that is greater than all of our sins.[C] **Did you come in here this morning down on yourself? I'll bet half of you did. I'll bet half of you came in here like whipped dogs, barely feeling you had the right to face the light of day. Well, you're under the law. Because all I can say,** "Lord, just open up the heavens and pour massive doses of grace down on this people—

Grace that is greater than your sin." You say, "Oh, Brother Don, wait a minute, I've got to do some atoning for <u>my sin</u>." <u>JESUS CHRIST DIED FOR YOUR SINS! EVERY ONE OF THEM! IT'S NOT SINS! It's the grace of God. Sin has been settled. The sin question—He died for sin ONCE! It's all over! There's NOTHING against you! NO CONDEMNATION! And let God be true and every man a liar. If God is FOR you, who can be against you?</u> You say, "Brother Don, you don't know what I did this week." I say, "If <u>GOD</u> can be for you, who can be against you?" And God is <u>nothing</u> but for you. <u>Grace reigns! It's the reign of grace</u>! Can anything separate you from the love of God? <u>Nothing in creation</u> can separate you from the love of God. Sin has been put away. There is nothing but grace that reigns! Marvelous, infinite, matchless grace.

Well, some of you are about ready to stick your tongues out at me. You don't believe it. I tell you it's true! It's true. It's just the gospel. And if that doesn't bring you glorious liberty, I don't know what does. "*The glorious liberty of the children of God.*" [3] No condemnation. Not a bit.

You're under nothing but grace—that's all. Now, you can get hoodwinked and go back under the law, with all of that down on yourself business, and I can tell you how lethal that is. Oh, that is devastating to the human heart. You weren't made for that, you see. And what that does to human relations is something frightening. Because all I can say this is, I've been in the religious world now with the very best of them. I've trained ministers, and I know their hearts and they're just like mine and I know they desperately need grace. That's all we need is nothing but grace.

And I found this too, that some people, as I say in a humorous way, "They want grace for themselves and law for everybody else." But you let them get in a bind. Do they want love and understanding and forgiveness? Of course, they do. Well, is anybody different than you? Well, God knows what we need, and that's His marvelous grace.

SERMON 1 ENDNOTES:

A Antinomianism, a doctrine of lawlessness, of living by one's own opinions and deciding for themselves what is right and wrong instead of living under the law of Jesus Christ which is Matthew 22:37 & 39, "37You shall love the Lord your God with all your heart, and with all your soul, and with all your mind. 39You shall love your neighbor as yourself." Living with a moral "ought," you ought to be good. Don Pickerill November 2020.

B POWs, is an acronym for Prisoners of War. On February 12, 1973 the first 591 U.S. military and civilian prisoners of war were released in Hanoi (the capital of Vietnam and located in northern Vietnam) and flown directly to Clark Air Force Base in the Philippines. www. britannica.com

C "Marvelous, infinite, matchless grace—grace that is greater than all our sins." These are excerpts from the hymn, Grace Greater Than Our Sin.

SERMON 1 SCRIPTURE REFERENCES:

1 Romans 5:21 (RSV)

so that, as sin reigned in death, grace also might reign through righteousness to eternal life through Jesus Christ our Lord.

2 Romans 6:14 (RSV)

For sin will have no dominion over you, since you are not under law but under grace.

[3] Romans 8:21 (RSV)

because the creation itself will be set free from its bondage to decay and obtain the glorious liberty of the children of God.

[4] Romans 6:17 (RSV)

But thanks be to God, that you who were once slaves of sin have become obedient from the heart to the standard of teaching to which you were committed,

[5] Romans 6:22 (RSV)

But now that you have been set free from sin and have become slaves of God, the return you get is sanctification and its end, eternal life.

[6] Romans 7:4 (RSV)

Likewise, my brethren, you have died to the law through the body of Christ, so that you may belong to another, to him who has been raised from the dead in order that we may bear fruit for God.

[7] Romans 8:6 (RSV)

To set the mind on the flesh is death, but to set the mind on the Spirit is life and peace.

[8] Romans 8:29 (RSV)

For those whom he foreknew he also predestined to be conformed to the image of his Son, in order that he might be the first-born among many brethren.

[9] Romans 8:13 (RSV)

for if you live according to the flesh you will die, but if by the Spirit you put to death the deeds of the body you will live.

SERMON 2

THE REIGN OF SIN

"You have no hope, unless it's by the total grace of God!"

We began a series of sermons this morning based upon one of the most significant parts of the Bible—that is Romans chapters 6, 7 and 8. Perhaps you'll recall for those of you who were here this morning, we said that there are **three** main aspects to these three chapters. The main truth is in 6:14, *"...you are not under **law** but under **grace**."* [1] This is a **commentary** on **law and grace.** As a matter of fact, a good title for these three chapters would be **"The Reign of Grace"** or "How Grace Reigns in Life". Then we saw that the **main practical point** to this was chapter 8, verse 21, *"...that we are not to be in **dominion** but to have the **glorious liberty** of the children of God."* [2] The main exhortation was chapter 8, verse 13, *"...if by the Spirit you put to death the deeds of the body you will live".* [3]

"Because the creation itself will be set free from its bondage to decay and obtain the glorious liberty of the children of God." - Romans 8:21 RSV

We're beginning to **expound** what it means to be **under grace** because that's the key to these chapters. You are not under **law** you are under **grace.** We suggested that the most important verse to understand these three chapters, is Romans chapter 5, verse 21. Here's what the apostle says *"...as _sin_ reigned in _death,_ grace also might reign through righteousness to eternal life through Jesus Christ our Lord."* [4] So, we want to talk about the **reign of grace.** But in order to do that, and understand this, to understand "King Grace," you're going to have to understand what it means to be **under sin,** *"as _sin_ reigned in _death_ so grace reigns in _life."_* [4]

Let's talk about the **reign of _death,_** and the purpose of this sermon is to show us why we **must** be under grace. It's the only way when you see what it means to be under **sin.** Now I'd really like, in a summary fashion, to point out some of the more **significant parts** of these three chapters. We're not going to begin our verse-by-verse exegesis yet, but I'd like to talk about this, still in a general fashion, what it means for **sin** to **reign.**

I believe that our biggest **problem** is that we don't do an adequate **diagnosis** in understanding how **lethal** is our problem. I'm quite persuaded that when people are helped emotionally, psychologically, and personally, there must be an adequate **diagnosis.** Certainly, that's true biologically and physiologically. A doctor **must** adequately diagnose the **problem.**

The Apostle Paul is doing open-heart surgery in these three chapters. He's revealing **his** heart. It's an amazing autobiography. It's also what we call a rhetorical—"I." I'll show that to you later, as he's talking about the heart of **every** man. And so, the Apostle Paul opens up his **nature** and he looks by the enablement of the Holy Spirit, and he says **in effect,** "It's beyond hope. It is beyond redemption." Like a doctor would open up a person and say, "Sew him back up, he's too far gone, he only has **death** at work in **him.**"

Now I'm ready to make **this** statement and I want you all to listen very carefully. This is a great deal of our problem. **One reason we do not prosper under grace is because we do not see the depth of our depravity and our nature. So, one of the most important truths in chapter 5, is that you have a part of your personality that is underdeemable.** Now notice what I said. **You have a part of your personality that cannot be redeemed. It cannot be changed. You are—too—far—gone!** Now this is what confuses many people. **They are quite persuaded that in conversion, they become better.** Now there is nothing more alien to the spirit of these chapters (Romans 6, 7 & 8). **Paul is very clear in describing what this is in his personality, and he is very clear in describing it as being unredeemable. It is beyond change. It—can—not—be changed!**

And so many people are trying to change! And even when they are converted, even when they have the spirit of grace, then they think surely some goodness has come to me! In a very subtle way, they are thrown back—on—that—goodness that they're seeking for in themselves. And that's the devastating thing of converging law and grace. And so, most of us wind up to be **Galatian Christians.** A You have got to know that there is a **part of you,** there is a **factor** in you, that is unredeemable. It—can—not—be redeemed. It is beyond redemption. How **important** to understand this truth.

The Apostle Paul has three names for it in these chapters and his more famous one is "the flesh." Now you'll find the flesh referred to time and again in these chapters. And there are three things said about the **flesh.** I'd like you to find them. In chapter 7, verse 18, the Apostle Paul says, **I know that in me, in my flesh, dwells—no—good—thing.** Romans 7:18, *"I know that nothing good dwells within me, that is, in my flesh. I can will what is right, I cannot do it."* [5] So the first thing to learn about the flesh: **It is utterly evil.** It cannot be made good. It is

beyond redemption. In <u>my</u> flesh dwells <u>no</u> good thing! Now that's very difficult for us to admit. Few of us understand that or admit that.

The second thing he says about his flesh, is that it is totally captive. He says in chapter 7, verse 25, that the **only thing** the flesh can do is *"serve the law of sin."* [6] It's in **bondage** to sin. It is captive to sin. And it can **only sin.** That's all. And me, Don Pickerill, is all I can do is **sin.** Me outside grace, I can only sin. And so he **concludes,** and how important to see the conclusion of chapter 7, verse 25, *"**So then,** I of myself I serve the law of God with"*—my reason—*"with my mind,"*—my rationality tells me to serve the law of God—*"but with my flesh—I serve the law of sin."* [6] That's all your flesh can do is serve the law of sin. It is **never** changed. It is **unredeemable! It ca<u>nnot</u> be converted! Your flesh alone can serve the law of sin.**

Now the third thing about your **flesh** is in chapter 8, verse 7, and the Apostle explains here that it is nothing but **rebellion.** It **ca<u>nnot</u>** be subject to the law of God. It is **impossible.** Listen to Romans chapter 8, verse 7, *"...the **mind** that is set on the flesh is hostile to God; it does **not** submit to the law of God, indeed it <u>cannot</u>."* [7] **Now so many people are trying to consecrate their flesh. They're always trying to bring this under the law of God. You can't do it! It's impossible! <u>It will not go there!</u>**

There are three things about the flesh: It is totally **evil**—it cannot do good. It is **captive**—it can **only** serve the law of sin. And third, it **cannot** be subject to the law of God—it is rebellious. The **flesh** is that **bent** in our personality that drives us to sin. The flesh is really **man** outside redeeming grace. <u>**You,**</u> taken alone, **you—by—your—self—are** flesh! I, Don Pickerill—me—my ego—is nothing but flesh. I am evil. I am captive to a power at work in my nature. And I am rebellious. I cannot change that.

So many people are trying to restore that. Trying to convert that. Trying to change that. Trying to consecrate that. No wonders we get nowhere because we haven't adequately diagnosed our problem. You've got to go very deep and see that there is an unredeemable part of your personality. You've got to accept that. You're never going to go anywhere until you see how utterly depraved you are. And if it's not for outside redemptive grace that comes into your life, there is no hope. And so, the flesh is unredeemable.

Secondly, it is called *"the old man,"* [8] in chapter 6, verse 6. This is the *palaios anthropos*, this old way—the old way of thinking. Paul refers to it as the old man. Now here is man before grace comes to him. Here is what I think we would call the ego. Have you met your ego lately? It is a very delicate fragile thing—your dainty little ego. You just let somebody cross your ego and watch what happens. You'll find out whether the old man is redeemed or not. It's unredeemable! Your ego is beyond redemption—your "self"—"you"—outside grace.

It is also called, in chapter 6, verse 6, *"the sinful body."* I'd like to read that verse please, Romans 6:6, *"We know that our old self"*—the old man—*"was crucified with him so that the sinful body might be destroyed."* [9] Now then, I must carry us one step farther to explain the balance between the flesh and the body. Now when Paul refers to the flesh, he is not basically talking about the human body, but there is a very close connection between them. There is an affinity between your flesh and your body. Now the Bible nowhere says that our bodies, as such, are sinful. We do have this passage that talks about our *"sinful body."* [9] And if you look very carefully at Romans chapters 6, 7 and 8 you'll find an amazing commentary on the body. Now let me, in essence, tell you what the role of the body is, in these chapters.

There are really three things said about the body. I've said that the flesh is unredeemable. And now we'll make this statement about the body: **The body is unredeemed but redeemable.** Now it's **important** that you understand that. The **flesh—**the **old man—**the **sin nature—** the **ego—you—**outside grace, are unredeemable. There's no hope for you. Sew it back up. It's dead. It's gone. **No hope!** But your **body also is unredeemed. You are living in an unredeemed body, but a body that has the possibility of redemption. It can be changed, and it will be changed. But in this age your body is dead.** It is **dying** because of **sin.**

There are **three things** to be said about this body. **Chapter 8, verse 10, I want you to note these verses please, they're very important to understand our condition.** *"Now if Christ is in you,"* and He is, **since Christ is in us, we have the** reality of the indwelling Christ. But notice what happens—**even—with—Christ—in us, with Jesus Christ indwelling us, the—** *"body—is—dead."* **Your bodies are dead because of sin; although,** *"your spirits are alive because of righteousness."* [10]

I don't have time to exegete that in detail, except to say this: **Our bodies,** we probably should say, **are dying. There is a principle of death at work in my body—**I'm **seized** all around—**my body is a prey of death—I cannot change that. The only thing that's certain, they say, is taxes and death. Death is claiming my body. Death is at work in my body.** It's like a **dead** thing. **And it becomes a natural ally for sin** because it has **death** at work in it. My body does not have life at work in it. My **spirit** is alive. The Holy Spirit **in me** is alive because of redemption or righteousness. But my **body,** in this dispensation, is **dead.** It has a principle of death in it. So, I have an **unredeemable flesh,** and I have an **unredeemed body.**

 "And not only the creation, but we ourselves, who have the first fruits of the Spirit, groan inwardly as we wait for adoption as sons, the redemption of our bodies."
- Romans 8:23 RSV

The second thing that's said about our body is that it can be redeemed. Chapter 8, verse 23, and this is the way the Apostle describes it. He says that our bodies **can** be redeemed, "*We know that the whole creation has been **groaning** in travail,*" in birth pangs really, "*until now; and **not only all creation**, but ourselves we who have the first fruits of the Spirit **we groan inwardly, as we wait for the adoption**" that is "the redemption of our bodies.*" [11]

Now the "adoption of sons" is talking about the manifestation of the sons of God. In this age there are many people who **do not know** that we are **God's sons.** I like to say, in a facetious way, "We've got our dark glasses on—nobody recognizes us." Our spirits are alive because of righteousness or redemption, **but our bodies are just like anybody else's body! They're subject to the same thing. They're going to <u>die</u>! And so, we <u>groan</u>—we have these awful <u>problems</u> that we experience in our <u>bodies,</u> and we have all kinds of <u>problems</u> that come to us because of the <u>weakness</u> of our body. But Paul is saying that our <u>bodies</u> can be redeemed and <u>will</u> be redeemed. They are redeemable,** the flesh cannot.

The third thing he says about the body, and this is very important for us to see, is that there is a **definite** connection **between the flesh,** and that is this **ethical principle of sin, this evil bent of your disposition <u>and</u>—<u>your</u>—<u>body</u>! They are a natural ally because your body is dead or dying. It has a natural affinity for the flesh. And so, <u>sin</u> embodies itself in your <u>body</u> and makes up what we call the <u>sinful body</u>.** This was the way Paul describes **that** in chapter 6, verses 12 and 13. **Notice how the sin <u>seizes</u> the members of the body and works itself out in that fashion. "*Let not sin therefore <u>reign</u> in your mortal <u>bodies</u>, to make you obey their passions.*"** [12]

Now the body has its appetites. It has its passions and its desires. I have certain hungers within me. I hunger, for example, for food and how easy it is for that to become gluttonous. How easy it is to lose all discipline and become inordinate so that I'm constantly just feeding my body. I have a need to sleep, but how easy it is for me to become lazy and just spend all my time goofing off, as it were, because of these things that arise through my body. We reach out to touch one another. We have our sexual desires that come through our bodies, and they are very difficult to control. *"Let not sin therefore reign in your mortal bodies, to make you obey their passions. Do not yield your members to sin as instruments of wickedness but yield yourselves to God as men who have been brought from death to life, and your members to God as instruments of righteousness."* [12]

We're going to touch on this further. But I want us to see this: That in and of ourselves there is no hope! I have a power at work in my nature! It's the sin principle! It's my old nature, and it's greater than I am! I can't control it! I'm captive! I'm in bondage to that, and furthermore, I have a body that's dying. Now where is there any hope? I don't know if there's any hope at that level. But our big problem is that so many of us look for hope at this level—*at* this horizontal level. We come and hope that some way we can get better. Something can change in me. I want to tell you that you are beyond repair! Unless something is going to come from without and give us a transplanted heart— unless there's going to be a new life—some new disposition—*some new life—some* new *nature—*I'm undone!

And so, I'm here to tell you, that in and of ourselves we are unredeemable. It's going to take the grace of God to bring a **whole new** nature—a whole new disposition. And this is where I think so many Christians **go off.** They think there's something good in **them.**

Take a man for example that has a heart transplant. That would be a good illustration. Here's a man who's got a heart that he has **no hope.** The only thing is to take that man's heart out and put a **new** heart in him. Now where is his life? In his old life? **It's dead.** He's gone. He can only live by the **beat** of that **new** heart. And if that life of the Spirit will **beat** in him, then he can have righteousness and life. It's your **only** hope. **Dare—you—glory—in your—old—heart? I tell you it's beyond repair!** It has to be that new nature that comes down through Jesus Christ and begins to beat within me.** That's my only hope—is that new nature—*t*hat new man—*t*hat new heart. In **myself** I am beyond repair.

I write notes to myself in my Bible. And in the margin of my Bible, I wrote four things. I don't like to forget them. And here's what I put down about my **self** and my **sin nature.** Now you may not **like** your pastor after I tell you this, but I tell you **this is the truth,** this is **what I am.** And if you thought I was all some kind of a **holy Joe,** forget all about it. You've got something else on your hands. Here is who I am.

"I sin—even when I 'will' not to." I sin—even—when—I—will—not—to. I "will" not to sin, and I turn around sinning. Oh, you say, "Brother Don, how could you?" You're **just** as bad as I am, and I'm going to point my finger right at you and tell you. None of you are any **better** than I am. I know what you're like. *(Congregation chuckles)* You've got that same Adamic blood in you that **I've got.** You've got the **same problem I've got.**

And so, number two, "A part of me is unredeemable and unchanging." I can do nothing but sin, even after my conversion. My flesh cannot be changed. There's only **one** possibility. If someway it can get **crucified,** and I can go **dead** to that. If I can get a **new** heart, a **new** life, then I've got a chance. But a part of me is unredeemable and unchangeable. You didn't get patched up when you got converted.**

Conversion didn't have anything to do with your old heart. The only way is to take that out totally and completely. And this throws more people off in the Christian gospel. This has been the <u>devastating</u> news that has come to so many that have tried to live at that level. And no wonders they've never got into grace because they're <u>still</u> under that spirit of hoping that something can happen to them.

Thank God, number three, "The grace of Jesus supersedes my sin." The grace of Jesus supersedes my sin and I said it this morning and I'm going get repeating it. I'm going to skirt very close to Antinomianism. [B] If your pastor doesn't have to defend himself against Antinomianism, you'd better get another pastor, because it's only the grace of God that's going to work. The Apostle Paul has to **defend** himself against **Antinomianism,** and that's what these three chapters are. That means such amazing freedom that you almost **exemplify grace** to the point of **sin.** Paul has to **defend** himself with that point. And I'm going to tell you this, that *"where sin abounds—grace—does—much—more—<u>abound!</u>"* [13] **You can't sin fast enough for God's grace! You can't keep up with it! <u>The more you sin, the more God's going to throw His grace at you</u>!**

We're going to take a close look at these chapters but let's <u>get—that—truth—straight</u>! <u>If you don't START from there</u>, you're <u>never</u> going to go into grace. **You can—not—out—sin—grace! For where sin abounds, grace does much more abound.** Well, a lot of people say, "My goodness, how can this be? This is so risqué to talk this way." You wait until we get into Romans 6, 7 and 8 and you'll see how God does it without the **law.**

But folks we've <u>got</u> to get this message <u>straight</u>. You've <u>got</u> to understand this—**pure—un—mitigated—grace of God.** Or I tell you it's nothing but <u>striving</u> and <u>straining</u> and <u>confusion</u> and back to the old nature and the old way. **We're beyond repair.** It has to be total grace or there is **no hope** for me and no hope for you. The grace of God supersedes my sin, and that keeps me **constantly** at peace.

And so, number four, "By grace <u>alone</u>, my flesh does not dominate me, even though it is always with me." I'm going to repeat that one more time. "By grace alone, my flesh does not dominate me, even though it is always with me." At any given moment, Don Pickerill is Don Pickerill. But **thank God** there's been a **heart transplant** and I can **live** in the **power** of that new heart. But you see we ought to understand then how **unthinkable** it would be that we would try any kind of self-reformation or self-**salvation**. And I'm going to tell you the best I know how, **much preaching that I hear is a subtle form of self-salvation. It's an appeal to the human will. Do better! Buck up! Do this! <u>We're dead! We're unredeemable! Don't APPEAL to my will! My will is in bondage! If you won't give me another message, I'm undone!</u> And my only hope is to become a hypocrite and pray that you won't know what really goes on in the <u>depths</u> of my heart, and just become a classical Pharisee. But I tell you when you open up my heart, and when I open up your heart and look at the <u>depths</u> of your heart, I say, sew it back up. It's a mess of cancer. It's dead. It's too far gone.**

This is what the Apostle Paul said **early** in Romans chapter 3. He says in Romans 3:9, "*I have charged that <u>all</u> men, both Jews and Greeks, are <u>under the power of sin.</u>*" Now you may not <u>like</u> this list but if I opened up <u>your</u> heart and saw <u>your</u> dream life—and saw <u>your</u> emotions—and saw <u>your</u> thoughts—it would be <u>just</u> like this: " '*None is righteous, <u>no, not one</u>; <u>no one</u> understands, <u>no one</u> seeks God. <u>All</u> have turned aside, <u>together</u> they have gone wrong. <u>Their throat is an open sepulcher.</u>*' " *And* it's <u>amazing</u> what people can <u>say</u> and <u>do</u> with their tongue. " '*Their throat is an open sepulcher they use their tongues to deceive. The venom of <u>asps</u> is under their lips. Their mouth is full of curses and <u>bitterness</u>. Their feet are swift to shed blood, in their paths* *are ruin and misery, and the <u>way</u> of peace they do not know. There is no fear of God before their eyes.' "* [14] **And the prophet Isaiah discerned very rightly human nature in the nation of Israel when Isaiah said in Isaiah 1:5,** *"The whole head is <u>sick</u>. The whole heart is <u>faint</u>. From the sole of your foot even to the head, there is no <u>soundness</u> in it, but <u>bruises</u> and <u>sores</u> and <u>bleeding wounds</u>."* [15]

Well, that's the picture of human nature. That's the flesh. That's you. Now you may have not seen <u>all</u> the potential of your flesh yet. Some people see it more **readily** than others. **But I'm going to tell you this— I'm praying that God will let you see your <u>wretchedness</u>. Why? When you say, "Oh wretched man is me," <u>it's THEN and THEN only that you're ready for pure grace</u>! <u>And until you see the depths of your sin, you don't want another heart plant</u>. <u>You don't want a transplant</u>. You want to trust your own way and your own goodness. And I tell you that's a very subtle thing that creeps into the Christian life,** and just makes us a seeming mass of religious Pharisees.

But if **God** by His **grace** will first of all show us our sin. And I tell you when sin reigns there is **nothing** but **death.** Now this is the Divine **Doctor's diagnosis** of **your** nature. That's what the Lord Jesus Christ has said through the Apostle Paul, that in and of ourselves, we are **unredeemable.** Our flesh **cannot** be changed—**it will not**—it **cannot** be subject to the law of God. You are living in a body that is **unredeemed, but** redeemable. But in **this age,** there is an actual affinity with sin, and **sin** comes up through **your body**—and through its **members**—and through its **appetites**—through your **eye**—through your **tongue**— through your **hands**—through your **feet**—through your **feelings**— through your **sentient life.** This is the way **sin seizes** upon your body you see and brings you into captivity.

And so, there is only **one hope** and **that is** that the **grace of God** will come along and do something absolutely and completely **for us.** It is

unthinkable that you would try to reform yourself and do better. **Self-salvation is <u>unthinkable</u>.** It's not even in the picture. **You have no hope unless it's by the total grace of God.**

SERMON 2 ENDNOTES:

A Galatian Christians: The book of Galatians is the letter that the Apostle Paul wrote to the believers in Galatia. These new believers embraced Paul's message of grace but found it almost impossible for them to not attach the law to it. They kept struggling with legalism. They were still trying to become righteous by the law or by works. Don Pickerill 2020

B *Antinomianism, a doctrine of lawlessness, of living by one's own opinions and deciding for themselves what is right and wrong **instead of** living under the law of Jesus Christ which is Matthew 22:37 & 39, "37You shall love the Lord your God with all your heart, and with all your soul, and with all your mind. 39You shall love your neighbor as yourself." Living with a moral "ought", you ought to be good. Don Pickerill November 2020*

SERMON 2 SCRIPTURE REFERENCES:

1 Romans 6:14 (RSV)
For sin will have no dominion over you, since you are not under law but under grace.

2 Romans 8:21 (RSV)
because the creation itself will be set free from its bondage to decay and obtain the glorious liberty of the children of God.

3 Romans 8:13 (RSV)
for if you live according to the flesh you will die, but if by the Spirit you put to death the deeds of the body you will live.

[4] Romans 5:21 (RSV)

so that, as sin reigned in death, grace also might reign through righteousness to eternal life through Jesus Christ our Lord.

[5] Romans 7:18 *(RSV)*

For I know that nothing good dwells within me, that is, in my flesh. I can will what is right but I cannot do it.

[6] Romans 7:25 *(RSV)*

Thanks be to God through Jesus Christ our Lord! So then, I of myself serve the law of God with my mind, but with my flesh I serve the law of sin.

[7] Romans 8:7 (RSV)

For the mind that is set on the flesh is hostile to God; it does not submit to God's law, indeed it cannot.

[8] Romans 6:6 (KJV)

Knowing this, that our old man is crucified with him, that the body of sin might be destroyed, that henceforth we should not serve sin.

[9] Romans 6:6 *(RSV)*

We know that our old self was crucified with him so that the sinful body might be destroyed, and we might no longer be enslaved to sin.

[10] Romans 8:10 (RSV)

But if Christ is in you, although your bodies are dead because of sin, your spirits are alive because of righteousness.

[11] Romans 8:22-23 (RSV)

22 We know that the whole creation has been groaning in travail together until now; 23 and not only the creation, but we ourselves, who have the first fruits of the Spirit, groan inwardly as we wait for adoption as sons, the redemption of our bodies.

[12] Romans 6:12-13 (RSV)

12 Let not sin therefore reign in your mortal bodies, to make you obey their passions. 13 Do not yield your members to sin as in-

struments of wickedness, but yield yourselves to God as men who have been brought from death to life, and your members to God as instruments of righteousness.

[13] Romans 5:20 (KJV)

Moreover the law entered, that the offence might abound. But where sin abounded, grace did much more abound:

[14] Romans 3:9-18 (RSV)

9 Law came in, to increase the trespass; but where sin increased, grace abounded all the more, What then? Are we Jews any better off? No, not at all; for I have already charged that all men, both Jews and Greeks, are under the power of sin, 10 as it is written: "None is righteous, no, not one; 11 no one understands, no one seeks for God. 12 All have turned aside, together they have gone wrong; no one does good, not even one." 13 "Their throat is an open grave, they use their tongues to deceive." "The venom of asps is under their lips." 14 "Their mouth is full of curses and bitterness." 15 "Their feet are swift to shed blood, 16 in their paths are ruin and misery, 17 and the way of peace they do not know." 18 "There is no fear of God before their eyes."

[15] Isaiah 1:5-6 (RSV)

5 Why will you still be smitten, that you continue to rebel? The whole head is sick, and the whole heart faint. 6 From the sole of the foot even to the head, there is no soundness in it, but bruises and sores and bleeding wounds; they are not pressed out, or bound up, or softened with oil.

SERMON 3

WHAT IT MEANS TO NOT BE
UNDER THE LAW

*"It's amazing how people want grace
for themselves and law for everybody else!"*

We have begun a series of sermons based upon Romans chapters 6, 7 and 8. Today, I want to return **to that** and underscore the most **significant theological truth** in these three chapters. Now you will recall that we have suggested that Paul is giving a remarkable commentary on the closing words of chapter 5, verse 21, where he says, **"...as <u>sin reigned</u> in <u>death,</u> grace also might <u>reign</u> through righteousness to eternal life through Jesus Christ our Lord."** [1] So, you might write over Romans chapters 6, 7 and 8, the **"Reign of Grace,"** or **"King Grace."**

*"For sin will have no dominion over you, since you
are not under law but under grace." - Romans 6:14 RSV*

The leading theological truth is given in chapter 6, verse 14. Paul is trying to establish, more than anything else, this important **truth.** Romans 6:14, **"...<u>sin will have <u>no dominion</u> over you, <u>since</u> you are not under <u>law</u> <u>but</u> under <u>grace</u>."** [2] And so today, in both of the services, this morning and tonight, we're going to underscore **that** great truth and it really has two **parts** that we must consider. The first would be a thorough understanding of what it means **not** to be **under <u>law</u>, but to be under grace.** Now we've already done a couple of introductory things. You remember we underscored what it means to be under **sin.** One can hardly understand what it means to be under **grace** if you can't quite grasp some of **those** things. So today we're going to talk about what it means **not** to be **under the law.**

Anytime you move into this area—we're facing some very, very profound thinking. Those who study ardently Romans chapters 6, 7 and 8, readily **admit** that **here** are some of the most **profound** insights to scripture. And you have to come **back** to them **repeatedly** as they **grow** in your **mind** and your **understanding.** And so, I don't know how to do this except in a way to **teach.** I don't know how to **preach** on the subject that you are **not** under law. But I do know what it's all **about.** So, I'm going to give you a lesson this morning.

I have proposed ten questions that I'm going to **answer** relative to this subject. Ten **key** questions on what it means **not** to be **under the law.** And so, I hope that will be meaningful for us. Sometimes we need **great** inspiration and sometimes we need **insight.** We need to <u>know</u>. Paul keeps saying over and over, **"Don't you <u>know</u>—<u>know</u> you not—aren't you <u>aware</u> of certain things?"** And so, you'll regard this, this morning, as an attempt to understand **clearly** what **all** this is about.

The most simple question we can ask, and our starting point will be simply this: **<u>What is the law</u>? What does it mean to be under law?** What is law? There are really three **elements** that enter into that definition. Anytime you're talking about **law,** you're talking about three **elements.** The first and the most **obvious** is **any kind of an external code. Law** refers to a code. Now that may be **written** or **not written.** It can be **expressed** or **unexpressed.** But there is a **code** that has reference to human **conduct** and human behavior. Man can't live without making **laws** and attempts to **conceptualize** human conduct. Now we have laws down in **City**

Hall, and we also have laws in our **Bible.** The most significant of course would be the **Law of Moses.** But anytime you're talking about law you're talking about an **external code or standard.** Now, that becomes, at the same time, an **authority.** So, you cannot talk about law without talking about an **authority.** So here is an external **claim** upon me in terms of an **authority**—this **standard** of my behavior—that's what we mean by law.

Now of course, **embedded** in that is the <u>response</u> that I have **to** that external code. **Or** the **internal claim** that I feel with reference to that authority. Notice I can't talk about an **external authority** without an <u>internal</u> **obligation to meet that claim.** When we're defining law, we're not only talking about **what** is there, we're talking about **how** you get there. And **that's** an **integral part** of the law as defining this external **code.** And so here is this <u>claim</u> upon me, this inner <u>claim</u> that ought to <u>meet</u> that standard of **goodness or right.**

And then **thirdly,** you cannot talk about law without talking about the **consequences** of all that. Or, using a negative term, condemnation. And so, I really have **three things.** I have a **code,** I have a **condition,** and I have **condemnation.** Those three things are tied in, to what we mean by the law. So, here's an **external authority,** here's an **internal claim** that I'm **feeling** toward that, and the **consequences** if I do not meet that claim.

Here's a rather **basic** question. Is **there anything wrong with that?** <u>**What's wrong with the law?**</u> **Is there anything wrong with the law as such? No!** No, there isn't anything wrong with **that.** What's wrong with having standards? What's wrong with **knowing** that you ought to do good? And what's **wrong** with being punished if you're **not** good? If you break the law. You run red lights. Should you get tickets? Of course. **It is just.** So, the Apostle Paul at **no point** in our discussion will permit us to say that there is anything intrinsically, "per se," **wrong** with **law** or with the law of God—the Law of Moses. As a matter of fact, he has four definitive **statements** for the law. He says that it is <u>**holy**</u>. He says that it is <u>**just**</u>. It's entirely fair. He says that it is <u>**good**</u>. It's a **positive thing** and he says it's <u>**spiritual**</u>. And by that he probably means that it comes from **God** or comes from the divine origin of the law. So, you're **not** to imagine that there's anything **wrong** with the law, as such.

The third question then, is **why the problem? Why the issue? Why is this such a problem?** You have two answers. <u>What's the problem in the law?</u> It has **two basic problems.** And the first is very **graphically** stated in Romans chapter 7, verse 14: *"The law is spiritual, <u>but</u>"*—and **this** is what begins our **problem**—*"but—I."* Now if you could have kept that out of it, it would have been alright. *"The law is spiritual, **but I**—*and **this** is where we meet our problem. *"The law is spiritual, <u>but I</u>—am— carnal, I am sold under sin."* [3] And so, the problem is not the law. The problem is the **human nature** that **meets** the law. The problem is **you and me** trying to **keep** that law. Here's where we get into difficulty. The Apostle in Romans chapter 7 is telling us that he acknowledges that the law of God, that standard, is very good. But the problem is he just can't **keep it.** Now have you found that out yet? Well, you're due for a surprise if you haven't. What a <u>**shock**</u> when you begin to see something about your **nature**—that you're unable to **keep that law.** You're unable frankly to **do good,** and to **do right.** Just give it a try. Try to love God with all your heart and your neighbor as yourself and let me know how you get along. As a matter of fact, you're going to find that you just do the reverse of that. So **that's** the problem of the law, is it is addressed to people **like us.** So, we're not to **imagine,** we're not going to impugn the law in any way.

Secondly, there is another problem. And I suppose we would **have** to say there **is** a **weakness** in the law as such. Paul makes that very clear in Romans when he says in Romans 8:3, *"**God has done what the <u>law</u>, weakened by the flesh—<u>could</u>—<u>not</u>—<u>do</u>."*** [4] What the **law—could—**

not—do. Now, what can**not** the law do? It can't give you any **power.** I can see that it's **good,** but I don't have any power. It's an **external code** to me. I have no way of getting a **dynamic** or an **energizing** to **keep** that law. And so, **the law** has **absolutely no power.**

The **problem** with the law is that it's addressed to **human nature** and that the law in and of itself cannot give us any **energizing** or enablement to perform. I might add by the way, just in a practical word, how that we ought to really learn that. We're very slow learning that. So often we think this is just a nice high blown theology written in the pages of a book here. We're talking about the spirit of **life.** We're talking about how **life** works. You try to run your family, for example, by **law.** Let me know how far you get. But it's amazing how we try it. How we come back to it again and again hoping that a spirit or a principle of **law** will work. And the Bible makes it very clear, *"The **law** made **nothing** perfect!"* [5] Now then, we suggested something wrong with **us** and that leads us to the fourth question.

<u>**What is the real connection between the law and sin?**</u> The Apostle Paul tells us that there is a three-fold connection between the law and sin, and he describes it in chapter 7, verses 7 through 12. *"What then shall we say? That the law is **sin?** By no means! **Yet,** if it had **not** been for the **law,"**—* number one—*"I should not have **known** sin. I should not,"* for example, *"have known what it is to **covet"**—to **desire,** to **lust**—"if the law had not said,"—*you shall not do that—*"You **shall not** covet."* **Furthermore,** *"But sin, finding **opportunity** in the commandment, <u>wrought</u> in me all <u>kinds</u> of covetousness. Apart from the law, sin lies dead. I was once **alive** apart from the **law,** but when the commandment came, **sin revived** and **I died."**—*as it were. And—*"the **very commandment** which promised life proved to be **death** to me. For **sin,** finding **opportunity** <u>in</u> the commandment deceived me and by it killed me."* That's all you can say. *"So the law is holy, and the commandment is holy, just and good."* [6]

Paul said three things about the **law** in his connection to sin there. The **first** thing he says is that **the law shows up sin.** It shows us what sin **is. See,** you might take any of your natural appetites. You might imagine you have a desire for **food.** What's wrong with that? Nothing. But here's a law that says you're **not** to **covet. You are not** to desire certain things and it describes what they are. **Now then,** you **see** that that is **wrong. So, the law simply <u>reveals</u> to us. It**—shows—up—sin. It tells us what's right and wrong, in other words. And we see it. So, we're able to have a knowledge now of what's right or wrong **by** the law.

Secondly it does more than that, however. **It not only <u>shows</u> us what sin is,** but **here's** the **surprising thing,** and this is going to **amaze** you, wouldn't you **think** that God gave the law so that men could **keep it,** and that they would be **good?** Well, that's not the reason at all. The law was **not given** to be **kept.** The law was **given** to **be broken.** He says the law came **in** that the trespass might **abound. And so, the <u>law</u>, if you're under <u>law</u>, it really <u>stirs up sin</u>. Sin is like a general and it seizes an opportunity, a <u>base</u> of operation if you please, and it finds that through the commandment or through the law.**

Let me show you how a good thing can do that. I don't know if this is a very appropriate illustration, but I'll **use it** anyway. Suppose you have some **garbage** outside your house. Now it's **nighttime.** You don't see it. It's **there,** but the good sun comes up you might be smelling something all the while, by the way *(Pastor Don chuckling).* But the good sun comes up and you **see** that. It **reveals** the **garbage.** Should you do something about it? Yes, you see it. But that sun, **also** with its **heat,** begins to make the garbage dump **smell** all the more. And so that **good law** addressed as human nature has a way of just **stirring up the rebellion** that's in our heart. That's all you've got to do is just have somebody start putting **pressure** on you and ordering you around and telling you what to do. And **instantly,** I'll tell you what you'll find in your nature. Does the **law** provoke our rebelliousness and make sin exceedingly sinful? **It does!** And so, for a person to be under **that** principle, though they may disguise it outwardly, they're still finding more and more that the law stirs up sin.

Thirdly, it kills you. It slays you. Now that works two ways. Paul's **really** talking about death as such, because anybody under the **law** is subject to **death** and **should** be punished. Under the wrath of God that would be **nothing but <u>death</u>. Justly so.** But all the experiences that we are having **this side** of physical **death**—of the **misery** and the **agony**—is also the work of the **law.** Anybody who has a conscience **under the law** is going to go through this disturbance, through this **misery.** The only word you can call it is **death,** that's all. It's a **deathlike existence.** It's the very opposite of **life.** And so, the law is connected to sin in **that** way. It shows sin up, it stirs sin up and in turn it **slays** the sinner. It kills you. It puts you to **death.**

Question number five—<u>What's the relationship between law and works?</u> Now you really cannot separate these two. They go **together.** **Works** has reference to the **second phase** of what I was talking about in **defining law.** You have a **standard here** but now the question is how are you going to get up there to meet that standard? How am I going to **keep** that law? That's this **condition. Now, <u>works</u> is the <u>striving</u> or the <u>effort</u> that I'm <u>expending</u> to meet this <u>claim upon my life</u>.** And so, I'm under this **strain** with this **unaided obligation.** I'm trying to satisfy this claim so I can feel good about myself and feel that I'm pleasing God. **Works** has reference to that **striving** to **meet this claim** upon your life, the moral claim that all of us are feeling.

Now, if you're caught up under that, it will either lead you to one of two things. It will lead you to **pride.** Imagine that you have done that and lifted yourself up. Or it will lead you to this form of **death** where you utterly **despair** and you realize, **"I can't do it."** And you feel all this **confusion** and all this **guilt** and all this **pain.** And that can make you to be a hypocrite, by the way. You don't **dare** tell anybody what your inside systems are **really** like. So, you go around **feigning** and **playacting** the whole Christian life and it has no **life** in it at all. It's just nothing but a mass of **misery.** Is that one reason so many Christians are unhappy? **Yes. By the boat load!**

Number six—**What is our relationship to the law?** It's very simple. You're not under the law. Now you see I can say that so **fast** and so **glib** that nobody will understand it. **Will you please just let that soak in for a moment? It's the most utterly shocking revelation possible! If it wasn't in the Bible, I couldn't believe it! You're not under it!** You are not—under—law. Now, that means two things. Number one: **There is— no—claim—upon you.** No claim. **If you're not under the law, you're under no claim of any kind! NONE! This is what we've never gotten straight,** and this is where a lot of people won't **go** that far. **They will not follow Paul to this logical conclusion.** They fear the Antinomian Doctrine, and they **fear** that this is going to make people **loose.** But I tell you, we're going to say it **emphatically; There is absolutely—no— claim—upon you!** That claim has ended. Now, that either means that or it means **nothing. You are—not—under—the law.** I dare some of you to believe it. You'd be so **revolutionized.** You'd be so **free.** It would utterly transform your existence. You'd start entering into the perfect liberty of the children of God. Number two: **There is NO condemnation.** If you're not under the law, how can you be condemned? See! The law alone can condemn you. No condemnation. **None! Not a bit!** *"There is therefore now NO condemnation!"* [7] Is **that** good news? Is that **gospel?** It's the only gospel I know. Now, you can be Galatian Christians [A] all you want. I say let's go **all** the route. Let's take Paul's teaching: **We—are—not— under—law—period!**

The Apostle says in Romans chapter 10, verse 4, *"...Christ is the end of the law."* [8] **How does Jesus end the law?** Question number seven.

If we're not under the law, how does it come to an **end?** How does Jesus **end** the law? Well, He does it two ways. **He satisfies the claim, and He satisfies the condemnation. Now the** Lord Jesus Christ **ends** the law **by perfectly fulfilling it. The Lord Jesus Christ is the** <u>only</u> **man that ever lived, who had no sin, and had perfect obedience to the will of God. He's the** <u>only</u> **one who** <u>ever</u> **pleased God.** And I remind you, if you don't have perfect obedience, if you're just missing one little point, have you fallen short of the glory of God? **You have! If you don't** <u>perfectly</u> **keep the law** <u>PERFECTLY</u>—<u>absolutely to the letter</u>—you have **defiled** the holiness of God, and **justly** you could be abandoned from His favor. You must **absolutely perfectly** keep the law of God. And the only one I know who did that is **Jesus.** Did He perfectly keep the law of God? **Thank God He did!** Romans 5:18 & 19, *"...as <u>one man's</u> trespass led to condemnation for all men, so <u>one man's</u> act of righteousness leads to <u>acquittal and life</u> for all men. As by one man's <u>disobedience</u> many were made sinners, so by <u>one man's</u> obedience many will be made— righteous."* [9]

Now, that's a very beautiful thing. I believe in the Doctrine of **Imputed Righteousness.** What does that mean? **That means that the righteousness of God through Jesus Christ has been** <u>put</u> **into me. It's an input—imputation—it's** <u>in me</u>**!** Why did Jesus do all that, for **Himself?** No, He did it for **me.** Why did Jesus get in John's baptismal **line** and go through the baptism for sinners, for **Himself?** He did that for **Don Pickerill.** He did that for **you.** This is what we call **imputed righteousness.** It's a **gift** through the gospel. That's shocking. It's true. That's the **good news friend!** Hebrews 10:9 and 10, Jesus says He came to do **God's will. And the conclusion is by that** <u>will</u>**, we have been** <u>sanctified</u> **through the offering of the body of Jesus Christ,** <u>once for</u> <u>all</u>**.** [10] **By** <u>His</u> **will, not** <u>my</u> **will. My will's in** <u>bondage</u>**.** I just will to **sin** that's about all. *(Don chuckles)* But thank God for **His will,** who delighted to do the will of God, and that Jesus Christ **ends the law** by perfectly fulfilling it.

But then, it's more **tragic** than that. Jesus Christ **ends** the **law,** by going to a **cross** and **suffering** under its **just** claims—**all** the condemnation that could possibly come to you and to me. The **death** of Jesus Christ **ends** the law. **Jesus Christ <u>died</u> for the law** in His death and His resurrection. And so, <u>all</u> the claims of the law have been satisfied in Jesus Christ. He perfectly **kept it,** and He **died** for the claims of the law. So, there **is** no claim. There **is** no condemnation.

Now a lot of you are looking very disturbed at me this morning and I know you're wondering; "Now, wait a minute! <u>What kind of authority are we under if we're not under law</u>? What makes us be **good?** If we are not under the law, then are we under an authority? What **guides** our lives? Are we a bunch of outlaws?" Well, you know the answer to that at once. Of course not! Of course, we are not. We are **under** what the New Testament calls, **"The Law of Christ."** Now, this is not a **subtle** way of putting you back under a principle or a spirit of law. We're not talking about a principle of law or the power of law. We're talking about being under **a person.** You see the amazing thing is once you come to Jesus Christ and His **gospel,** then He's **got you.** Because you fall in love with Him, and He falls in love with you and is that beautiful!

Now, you're **under** the *"law of Christ."* Galatians 6:2 [11] And Paul says in 1 Corinthians 9:21, *"To those who are outside the law I became as one outside the law—**not being without law toward God but under the law of Christ"*** [12] —and this is what we mean by the **new covenant.** This is what we mean by the **new disposition**—the **new dispensation**—the **whole New Testament.** We're under a **whole new system.** We're under a **new covenant.** And that leads us to this question: <u>What is the **nature** of this authority</u>?

What is the nature of this new law? According to the New Testament it's described four ways. There are **four qualities** to this new authority. And here they are. Now if you'll just remember that the **law** of Moses and any law, points after a **righteousness,** doesn't it? A rightness, a goodness or a badness, a right or a wrong. Now what was the essential **rightness** of the law aimed after? If you were to take all the law and all the prophets as Jesus did and **summarized** them in one little capsule, what would they add up to? *"You shall **love God** with all your heart **and your neighbor as yourself."** *[13]* Isn't that the **rightness** that the law was aiming at? **Exactly!** So, what did Jesus do? Well, in the upper room, the night of His betrayal when He instituted the Lord's Supper—the fulfillment of the covenant—Jesus said, *"A **new** commandment"—*a **new way,** a new **law**—*"I'm going to give unto you that you **love** one another even as I have loved you."* [14] Now, if you are **in love** with someone, do you need rules? Not really. Not if you have the true love of God in your heart. That satisfies so many things. If you love someone, would you **hurt them?** Would you **steal** from them? Would you want to **offend** them? No, you **wouldn't.** So, you see we're brought under this **principle—this way—this authority of love.** And is it authority! It's the only **life** transforming thing **I know.** And I might try to discipline my children into **subjection.** But if they don't love me, where are we? If I don't have that **relationship** with them? But if they **love me,** everything is alright.

Number two is called the **law of faith.** Romans 3:27, *"What becomes of our **boasting?** It's excluded. On what principle? On **works?** No, but by the <u>law—of faith</u>."* [15] Now, **faith** is the opposite of **striving.** Faith is trusting someone else. Faith is **resting.** And our biggest problem is most of us have not come to an **end** of ourselves where we know that we **have** to have somebody else to **enable** us—**all** of our provisions met. Somewhere in my heart I **still think** that I can do some **good.** But **faith** means that I say **no** to myself, and **yes** totally to Jesus Christ. That's the resting. Then is the strain out of life? I tell you it is. Then you're at peace. Otherwise, I've got to **work and strain. Now, that's an authority! That's a power! And when I see that, do I want to get away from that? Oh, I tell you what a law of my life that is**—**to rest** and to be at **peace** and not to strain. You go ahead and work all you want to. Gives me a nervous breakdown. **Gives me ulcers.** You can do **all** you want to. **I'm** going to **trust. My** only hope. Maybe you're a little bit better off than I am, but **I doubt it.** I know what you're like. You're no **better off** than I am.

"So speak and so act as those who are to be judged under the law of liberty." - James 2:12 RSV

Number three: It's the **law of freedom or liberty.** James chapter 2, verse 12, James says, *"Speak and act as those who are to be judged under the law of liberty."* [16] Or the law of freedom. **Now once you taste true freedom, do you want to lose it? That's an <u>authority</u>! That's a <u>power</u>! And it <u>holds</u> you like a beautiful magnet when you know what it is to be free. Oh, I tell you that's an authority, that's a power, that's a law. It's a <u>marvelous</u> thing.**

Then the **best of all,** number four, you're under **the law of life.** Romans chapter 8, verse 2, *"The <u>law</u> of the Spirit of <u>LIFE</u>,"* [17] that's what we have. Now, if you have **life** and you're really **tasting** that, is that an **authority? Is that a power? Oh, I tell you it's a power. The power of life. What <u>life</u> can do.** It's **amazing** the upsurge of **life** through **plants** and through **trees.** They can **break up** through concrete. **What a power!** A lot of people thought that **we needed** the law to keep people **straight** you know, and so on. I tell you; you need the **law of life.** You need the **law of love.** You need the **law of liberty** and **freedom.** And you need the law of **faith** and trusting. So that's the **nature** of this new authority. That's what Christ's law is like, this **law of Christ** that we're under.

Question number 10: **What part, if any, does the law still have in our lives?** Is it any value? Now that we've established what we said, do we need the law whatever? Now, my answer may surprise you. **We do.** Now **why?** Because the law **does** the very thing that I've been **hinting** at in this sermon. The Apostle Paul, for example, brings this out very **forcibly** in Romans chapter 7, but we will not go into in this sermon. But the Apostle Paul began to understand his **misery**—and his **bondage**—and his **wretchedness.** And he **cried out** and he says, *"In me dwells no good thing."* [18] **And he says, *"Who's going to <u>deliver me</u>?"* [19] How did that happen? It happened by the <u>law</u> doing its <u>work</u> to—drive—him—to—Jesus—Christ and let him know that he was absolutely a <u>sinner</u>. And that absolutely he could not <u>please</u> God unless he had an outside help. This is why we say the law is like a <u>schoolmaster</u>, to—bring—you—to Christ. Does the law still do that? <u>It does to me</u>! Now as well as I know the gospel, there are <u>still times</u> when something <u>happens</u>, I can't explain it to you. I wish that I were totally <u>beyond</u> this. I'm getting there. I'm a Christian in the making.** I'm a process person.

There **are times** when all of a sudden I get to thinking, "You know, I'm doing pretty good. You know the Lord is really doing a healing work in me. Boy, it's really getting hold! I'm just really getting holy." And about that time the Lord says "Ut-Oh, I heard that," *(Pastor Don and congregation laughing)* and sets in this whole process again. **All** these things I've been describing to you—the sense of **bondage**—the sense of **condemnation**—the sense of my **helplessness**—and my corruption, and I say, "Oh, Jesus!" And it drives me right back to Jesus. **So, the law shuts me up to <u>faith</u>,** and it does it **again** and **again.** And that's why I think you've got to hear this preaching **again** and **again** and **again.** I don't **trust** the human heart. *"It's **deceitfully desperately wicked** and who can know it."* [20] So we have to have that law, as it were, that brings us to **Jesus. And it does that.** Either that **striving** within you to meet a

moral claim, or some external law makes no difference, it's **all** the **same type** of principle we're talking about.

And then **secondly,** the **law** also **provides** what I'll call here a kind of a **definitive content** for **righteousness.** Now we said that the law **aims** at a **righteousness** which is **basically love.** But still for a lot of people just to say, "Now go love God and love your neighbor as yourself," it's **still** that we need often some **content to that. We need** a little more **definitive statement** about that, and the law **enables us—we fall** <u>**back**</u> **on that.** As Paul, at the Jerusalem counsel, they said they have Moses read every week. They had **Moses** there that **reminded them** of some of these things. And so, the law **does** that, and this is why the Apostle Paul could tell Timothy, 1 Timothy 1:8, *"The law is good, if a man used it lawfully."* [21] —and that is, properly and understand what he's talking about.

Well, church look, will you please understand? **You are** <u>**not**</u> **in any way, shape, or form under law. There is** <u>**no claim**</u> **upon your life. You have nothing to** <u>**give**</u>**. If Jesus Christ, by His grace, will not come and provide all of that, you cannot meet those claims.**

And that brings us to this **next** part of it, of what it means to be under grace. We're going to talk about that in the service tonight and may the Lord Jesus Christ quicken that great message to our hearts. What it means to be under grace and **nothing** <u>**but**</u> **grace—The Reign of Grace.**

Now how do you know whether you're under the law or not? I have suggested some of these things. Here are some of the indications when you know whether you're under the law or not:

1. <u>**When you feel you must be doing something to be accepted with God—you're under the law.**</u> **You can't** please God. Whoever thought you could? And if you feel you must be doing something to

be accepted with God, you're **under law. It's all been provided. You are righteous. You don't understand the gospel yet. It's over!**

2. <u>**When you are striving in any way to establish your own sense of worth—you're under the law.**</u> You're **struggling** to feel of **worth.** You haven't heard the judgments of the law yet that says, "There is no good **in** you." You might as well go ahead and **die.** Roll over and **die.** You know that's why Paul says that we're not only **dead** with Christ we're **buried.** Do you bury **live** people? **No,** you've got to **die** before you **bury** them. So, if some of us would get **buried,** we'd be alright. We just haven't **died** yet. We've still got one foot out of that grave somewhere *(Pastor Don chuckling)* trying to, you know, come back to life someway. Go ahead and **die** friend. The quicker you die the quicker we can **bury** you and the happier it's all going to be here *(Pastor Don Chuckling).* When you are **striving** in **any way** to establish your **own** sense of worth.

   Now this is going to surprise you. This part has some psychological implication.

3. <u>**When you feel inferior, unacceptable or unworthy, you are still under the law.**</u> You don't know what it means to be under grace. If you're under **grace,** then you're alright. You're in His favor.

4. <u>**If after confession, you still go on putting yourself down and feel guilty with the need to do penance, are you under law?**</u> **You are!** You're under the law. **If after** confession, you're still **down** on yourself, and you still feel a need to do some form of **penance,** you're under the law, that's all.

   And I would like to add **this one,** because **I believe** that this is **intently practical.** I think it makes a **heap** of difference whether your conscience is under the law or grace or whether your **life** is full of grace or law. It makes **all the difference** in the world **how you live;** and **especially,** with other people.

5. **And I would like to say that <u>when you are harsh and hard on other people with great demands, YOU are under the law</u>. That's the way it shows up. But life is now a demand and you're making those demands on other people because you're under a demand. You don't know what it is to be under grace. And so, you're out there to help the Lord out, you see, and to put everybody else under the law. And like I love to say, "It's amazing how people want grace for themselves and law for everybody else." Thank God, Romans 6:14;** *"You—are not—under—the law. You are—under—grace."* [2]

SERMON 3 ENDNOTES:

[A] Galatian Christians: The book of Galatians is the letter that the Apostle Paul wrote to the believers in Galatia. These new believers embraced Paul's message of grace but found it almost impossible for them to not attach the law to it. They kept struggling with legalism. They were still trying to become righteous by the law or by works. Don Pickerill 2020

SERMON 3 SCRIPTURE REFERENCES:

[1] Romans 5:21 (RSV)

so that, as sin reigned in death, grace also might reign through righteousness to eternal life through Jesus Christ our Lord.

[2] Romans 6:14 (RSV)

For sin will have no dominion over you, since you are not under law but under grace.

[3] Romans 7:14 (RSV)

We know that the law is spiritual; but I am carnal, sold under sin.

[4] Romans 8:3 (RSV)

For God has done what the law, weakened by the flesh, could not do: sending his own Son in the likeness of sinful flesh and for sin, he condemned sin in the flesh,

[5] Hebrews 7:19 (RSV)

(for the law made nothing perfect); on the other hand, a better hope is introduced, through which we draw near to God.

[6] Romans 7:7-12 (RSV)

7 What then shall we say? That the law is sin? By no means! Yet, if it had not been for the law, I should not have known sin. I should not have known what it is to covet if the law had not said, "You shall not covet." 8 But sin, finding opportunity in the commandment, wrought in me all kinds of covetousness. Apart from the law sin lies dead. 9 I was once alive apart from the law, but when the commandment came, sin revived and I died; 10 the very commandment which promised life proved to be death to me. 11 For sin, finding opportunity in the commandment, deceived me and by it killed me. 12 So the law is holy, and the commandment is holy and just and good.

[7] Romans 8:1 (RSV)

There is therefore now no condemnation for those who are in Christ Jesus.

[8] Romans 10:4 (RSV)

For Christ is the end of the law, that every one who has faith may be justified.

[9] Romans 5:18-19 (RSV)

18 Then as one man's trespass led to condemnation for all men, so one man's act of righteousness leads to acquittal and life for all men. 19 For as by one man's disobedience many were made sinners, so by one man's obedience many will be made righteous.

[10] Hebrews 10:9-10 (RSV)

9 then he added, "'Lo, I have come to do thy will." He abolishes the first in order to establish the second. 10 And by that will we have been sanctified through the offering of the body of Jesus Christ once for all.

[11] Galatians 6:2 (RSV)

Bear one another's burdens, and so fulfil the law of Christ.

[12] 1 Corinthians 9:21 (RSV)

To those outside the law I became as one outside the law—not being without law toward God but under the law of Christ—that I might win those outside the law.

[13] Luke 10:27 (RSV)

And he answered, "You shall love the Lord your God with all your heart, and with all your soul, and with all your strength, and with all your mind; and your neighbor as yourself."

[14] John 13:34 (RSV)

"A new commandment I give to you, that you love one another; even as I have loved you, that you also love one another."

[15] Romans 3:27 (RSV)

Then what becomes of our boasting? It is excluded. On what principle? On the principle of works? No, but on the principle of faith.

[16] James 2:12 (RSV)

So speak and so act as those who are to be judged under the law of liberty.

[17] Romans 8:2 (RSV)

For the law of the Spirit of life in Christ Jesus has set me free from the law of sin and death.

[18] Romans 7:18 (RSV)

For I know that nothing good dwells within me, that is, in my flesh. I can will what is right, but I cannot do it.

[19] Romans 7:24 (RSV)

Wretched man that I am! Who will deliver me from this body of death?

[20] Jeremiah 17:9 (RSV)

The heart is deceitful above all things, and desperately corrupt; who can understand it?

[21] 1 Timothy 1:8 (RSV)

Now we know that the law is good, if any one uses it lawfully.

SERMON 4

WHAT IT MEANS TO BE UNDER GRACE

"I want to be under nothing
—but—His—grace!"

Today we're considering the words of Paul in Romans chapter 6, verse 14, which we have **suggested** is the **key theological truth** of these three chapters. Romans chapters 6, 7 and 8 contain some of the most **profound** insights in the Bible, and also the **most practical.** These are far more than just truths to be taken off the pages of the Bible. They have to do with the very **stuff** of life—how you wake up in the morning and **regard yourself**—and how you **regard God**—and how you regard what's **happening** in your circumstances. These three chapters are extremely **penetrating,** as they seek to analyze the nature of the human **heart** and the nature of the human **need.**

The Apostle puts his finger on the **main theological truth** when he says in Romans chapter 6, verse 14, *"...that <u>sin</u> will have <u>no dominion</u> over you."* [1] Now that's what we all want is **freedom.** We don't want **sin** to have dominion over us. It's very important that we know **how.** Now, the **natural mind** would begin to say, **"Yes,** I must now have victory over **sin!"** Well, I'm going to surprise you. You know the Bible does not teach victory over sin? That's **not** the pathway to victory in the **Bible.** All that terminology is **faulty** that we have **victory** over sin. There **is** no such thing because all we do is **die to sin.** It's another way altogether. The Bible is **telling** us how we have freedom and sin does not have dominion **over** us. And here it is. It surprises you. It says, *"...sin shall not have dominion over you,"*—**because** or *"since you are <u>not</u> under law but under grace."* [1]

And so, this morning we talked about the implications of being under the **law**. What it means to be **under the law**. And now we're going to take the **positive** side and stress, what it means to be **under grace**. Now that's the **key** to these three chapters, that we are **under grace**. That's all we are under. **Grace. You are under grace!** And when a person **knows** that and **experiences** that, **then** they move into this **freedom** that their heart searches for. Otherwise, it's not available to them. It's always the struggle and it's always the condemnation. So, let's talk about that simple little subject: <u>What does it mean to be **in** and **under** the grace of God</u>?

I'd like to first of all, just to read in a mechanical way, some of the more significant scriptures **regarding grace**. You know the word **grace** appears 150 times in our New Testament. It's a very familiar word. Our word charisma, charismatic. It's the Greek word *charis*. We have these words charismatic—the idea of a **gift bestowing** element—but it occurs at least 150 times in the New Testament.

"And from his fulness have we all received, grace upon grace."- John 1:16 RSV

Here are some of the more **familiar** ones and ones that are very precious to us. John's gospel practically opens by saying in John 1:16, *"From his fullness,"* the *pleroma*, the **fullness** of Jesus Christ, *"have we all received,"* and it says, *"grace upon grace."* [2] Now we hardly know what to **make** of **that**. It's very difficult to really translate, but the thought seems to be **this; of His fullness have we all received and one grace** after another grace. Grace follows grace. In other words, you are getting nothing else <u>but</u> grace. The law was given by Moses, but <u>grace</u> and <u>truth</u> came through Jesus Christ. In other words, you never go from <u>grace to law</u>. It's true that the law can <u>lead us</u> to grace, but at no point do we then turn around and <u>need</u> the <u>law</u>. It's <u>amazing</u> how many people believe <u>that</u>, that you are saved by grace, and now it's up to <u>you</u>. <u>I've heard that preached</u>. Almost in those very <u>words</u>. <u>That's Galatian Christianity</u>. ᴬ You are <u>never</u> made perfect by the flesh. It is—grace—upon—grace. Of *"his fullness we have all received and grace <u>upon grace</u>."* ² **One pile of grace upon another.** It just continues to outdo itself.

Romans chapter 3, verses 23 and 24, *"Since all have **sinned <u>and fall short</u>**,"* I'm reading from the Revised Version Translation and please notice the **tenses.** *"**All have sinned** (aorist tense ᴮ) **and fall short** (present tense)"*—**all continually fall short**—*"**of the glory of God they are justified by his grace as a gift through the redemption which is in Christ Jesus our Lord."** ³ All have sinned **and all fall short** (present tense). Is there anybody here who does **not** fall short of the will of God? **You all do.** That means we **constantly need <u>grace</u>. We have sinned and we all fall short.**

Romans 5:17, *"...those who have received the <u>abundance</u> of grace and the <u>free gift</u> of righteousness <u>will reign</u> in life through Jesus Christ."* ⁴ And that's the only way you **will** reign is if you get an **abundance** of grace. You can't have a trickle of it. If you receive the **<u>abundance</u> of grace,** you will reign in life.

Ephesians 1:5-6 *"He **destined** us in **love** to be his sons through Jesus Christ according to the purpose of his **will** to the praise of his **glorious** grace which he <u>freely</u> bestowed on us in the Beloved."* ⁵

Ephesians 2:8-9, you can all quote it, *"**<u>By grace</u> you have been <u>saved</u> <u>through faith</u>."*** Notice you're saved by grace **not faith.** Some people think their **faith** saved them. **It does not! Grace saves you.** Your **faith** is just the empty hand that receives it. **You're not saved by your faith. You're saved by grace!** *"By grace you are saved through faith and that's not your own doing, it is a gift of God—not of works, lest any man should boast."* [6]

The Apostle Paul could summarize all that when he makes such statements in the epistles: *"…by the grace of God I am what I am."* [7] And you remember that every one of Paul's letters practically begins by—*"Grace and peace to you from God the Father and our Lord Jesus Christ"*—or something like that.

Now you'll notice then in reading of those simple scriptures that we have **nothing but grace. Grace upon grace. Grace following grace.** We have **free** grace, as through you needed to **say that** because **grace** means **a gift.** The very word **means it's free.** We have an *"abundance of grace,"* [4] we have *"glorious grace,"* [5] and we have this **"personal grace"** [6]— **out of** *"His fullness have we all received."* [2]

I would like to give you that familiar working definition of grace, but I'm not entirely satisfied with even the definition I'm about to propose. It's **very familiar** and if you ask anybody **what is** grace they generally always say **"it is unmerited favor."** Now that's not **bad.** That says **realms. Unmerited favor.** But you see you can kind of make that impersonal. Let me say this, **you cannot separate grace from the Lord Jesus Christ, because grace is just not His loving disposition or His loving attitude. Grace is Jesus Christ Himself going out in a personal way.** It's the **gift of Him! It's this emanation that's coming from God—** *"out of his fullness have we all received—and grace for grace."* [2] **So we get into this rather dry definition. I still want us to know that it's more than just God's loving attitude. It is God giving Himself. Grace is the love of God meeting you at the point of your need in the person of our Lord Jesus Christ. You see grace is not something that just floats** around in the air. It's always <u>personal</u>. It's always tied into a <u>person</u>. And when you meet Jesus, you're meeting the grace of God and that's all you meet is <u>grace</u> <u>upon</u> <u>grace</u>.

So, grace is unmerited favor. Well let's talk about it for a moment, shall we? And we'll underscore those two points. Let's stay with the word **favor** first of all. I like that. It is unmerited **favor**. As a matter of fact, six times in our New Testament, the word **grace** is translated **by** that word **favor.** You remember when Mary found **favor** with God? It's just the word grace. She found **grace with God.** Now, that's the source of our English word **favorite.** Did you know that you are one of God's favorites? That's what that means. You're under God's **favor.** It's really from a Latin word that has the idea of **a friend. Let me tell you something. God's not mad at you! He doesn't have anything <u>against</u> you.** That's what it means to be under grace. **It means that God <u>favors you</u>! He loves you! He gives His <u>grace</u> to you!** That's what we're talking about here. He has absolutely nothing against you. If you're somebody's favorite, do they **like you?** Well, folks listen; it's a very simple **thing**—but **God likes you. He likes you!**

Now so many people are **stunned** by that. Most people are quite persuaded God doesn't **like them.** They're just **quite** persuaded that God has it **in** for them. **Grace means that God is <u>for</u> you! He likes you! He doesn't have a thing against you. You are His favorite. You are under His <u>favor</u>. You are <u>always</u> under His favor. It never changes. You are <u>under</u> the grace of God. Grace reigns! You're not under <u>law</u> as we saw this morning.** And that means of course, that you are **not** under an **external code.** You are **not** under an **obligation.** God has no claims upon you. **Grace means that He <u>supplies</u> everything! He <u>gives</u> everything! He <u>provides</u> everything! That's what grace means.** So, you're constantly **under** His favor. You are not under **condemnation.** You are in a state of justification. So, you are free. You have no **external**

law. You have an internal freedom, and you have no condemnation. **You—are—in a—state of—justification. That's what it means to be under grace.**

Now you can **never** separate grace then from **goodness.** If somebody is dealing with you in grace, they **desire—good—for—you**. And this is the great key to **grace,** is that God pursues us with His **goodness.** Now this goes all the way back to the Garden of Eden. **The most subtle temptation, and Satan's <u>best strategy</u>, is to somehow make us <u>doubt</u> that God is all loving. If we can somehow get a thought in our mind that God is not totally for us—that somehow, He's <u>mad</u> at us—He's <u>against</u> us—and He wants to use us as His <u>pawns</u> someway—then we're in trouble. And that is <u>still</u> the primary fundamental temptation. I find it everywhere I go. And people who have been in <u>church</u> for years and years and years, they are <u>quite</u> persuaded someway that they are under God's judgment, that God is out to settle some scores with them. That was the <u>first temptation</u> that came and passed a shadow on the <u>absolute love</u> of God, and for man to begin to believe that God was not totally for him and to doubt His goodness.**

Let me tell you that the grace of God has been formalized in a <u>covenant</u>. God has entered into what we call the new covenant. And He has <u>solemnly sworn</u> by ratifying the new covenant that He is going to do nothing but pursue us with His goodness. Now that is given in this **great** prophecy of Jeremiah chapter 32, beginning with verse 38. I'd like you to note this, because this is prefiguring the **new covenant.** It's describing the **covenant** relationship—the **formal** basis on which God **swears** that **He's** going to pursue us only with His **goodness.** This is what the Lord said by the prophet Jeremiah, Jeremiah 32:38, *"They <u>shall</u> be my people, <u>I will</u> be their <u>God</u>. I will give them <u>one heart</u> and <u>one way</u>, that they may <u>fear me for ever</u>, for their own good."* Now, that word **fear,** by the way, means **love.** It's equivalent and it's often translated in our New

Testament by **love,** *"...that they may **love** me for ever for their **own good** and for the good of their children after **them. I will make with them an everlasting covenant; I—will—not—turn away—from doing—good—to them;"**—* I will do nothing else! I will **not** turn away from doing good to them—*"and I will put the love of me in their hearts, that they may not turn from me."* [8]

Now that's going to be how we're going to solve this subtle question of not being under **law** with no obligation, and yet still panting after **holiness** and **desiring to do good with all of our hearts. A lot of people can't stand this message of the grace of <u>God</u> because they think it leads to <u>looseness</u>. Grace <u>alone</u> is the thing that will cause your heart to fear God and to love Him. <u>Notice</u> what the new covenant says, "***I will not turn away from doing good to them; and I will put the <u>love</u> of me in their hearts, that they will not turn away from <u>me</u>. I will <u>rejoice</u> in doing them good...with all my heart and with ALL MY SOUL</u>." Oh, will you listen to that blessed verse!*** This is the new covenant promise— *"I will <u>rejoice</u> in doing them good. . .with <u>all my heart</u> and with <u>all my soul</u>."* [8] **I tell you if God is happy and rejoicing to do us good and nothing <u>but</u> good with all of His heart and with all of His soul <u>then</u> you're under grace. <u>Now that's what it means to be under the grace of God</u>. It's to know that He designs <u>nothing</u> but good <u>for</u> you. That's the new covenant promise. There can be no <u>bad</u> coming out of God from you. It couldn't be from the groundwork of creation anyway, let alone the new covenant.**

Now here's where we get into trouble though. This is where our faith begins to waiver. Because do we get in a trying set of circumstances that looks like it might be **bad?** Now that brings us to Romans chapter 8, where you have **all** of these circumstances that **look like** you have to **suffer.** And we begin to wonder, is **God** designing **good** for me here? This is where our **faith** can get **tested. But let me reassure you** church, that the Lord Jesus Christ is the <u>master</u> of every one of these circumstances and the verse is still clear; "<u>*All*</u>—*things*—<u>*are working*</u> <u>*together*</u>—<u>*for good*</u> *to them that love God and are the called according to his purpose.*" [9] I must tell you there are many things that I cannot understand. There are many things that have <u>stressed me</u> and I've gone down into the <u>darkness</u> of my own soul, too, and I've had the <u>blackness of night</u> when experiences were <u>overwhelming</u> to me, and I couldn't seem to find the goodness of <u>God</u>. But I <u>reassure</u> you by faith in Jesus' name, that He designs <u>good</u> for us and what's coming into our life is <u>working together</u> for our <u>good</u>. <u>You</u> can't see it at <u>this</u> point. But from the standpoint of eternity, <u>God</u>—designs <u>nothing</u> but <u>good</u>—<u>for</u>—<u>His</u>—<u>people</u>. That's what it means to be under grace. And even those very difficult circumstances you are in that are **testing** and **stretching** your soul, <u>God</u>—means to do <u>good</u> through that! <u>Good</u>— <u>is</u>—<u>going to</u>—<u>come out of that!</u>

When Joseph was sold in slavery, I'm sure at that moment it looked very <u>bad</u>. And when he got cast into prison, I'm sure that looked very <u>stressful</u>. He was able to look back and say, "<u>*You*</u> *meant it to me for evil, but <u>God</u> meant it to me for <u>good</u>.*" [10] To be under the grace of God then means there is <u>nothing</u> but goodness that comes into your life. <u>Nothing but goodness!</u> <u>Nothing can harm you!</u> <u>Jesus said</u> <u>so!</u> <u>NOTHING CAN HARM YOU!</u> You may be <u>hurt</u> for a moment, but <u>nothing</u> <u>evil</u> can come into your life. It's impossible! You are <u>only</u> <u>in</u> the grace of God. You are not under law. You are—**only**—**under**— **grace.** And this is what we're asked to believe.

So, grace is **unmerited <u>favor.</u>** **Favor.** That's all. God likes you did you know that? He loves you. He doesn't want to do anything but **good** for you and that's **all** He wants to do. Grace upon grace. He **never** changes His mind. That's what it means to be under grace. Now, is that

---

liberating? I tell you, if that really comes home to our heart, what **peace** that brings to the human soul. What **freedom** there is. What **joy** there is.

Now, it is **unmerited.** Now this is where it **really** gets interesting. This is **unmerited** favor. Grace of course is a gift. You couldn't **merit** it if you wanted to. You could not **earn it** and of course we saw from our early sermons on the law and **sin** that we are in and of ourselves **powerless** to do good. You **can't do good.** You, in and of yourself— **impossible** to do good. The only way you can **do good** is if God gives you a heart transplant—puts a new heart in you—and by His Holy Spirit **enables** you to **do good.** So, you see it **has** to be unmerited **because you can't merit it. It is impossible.** But you see **somewhere** along the line, we're hesitant to believe that. We somehow think that there's this **ounce of goodness** somewhere **in** us. And we somehow think that **conversion** made us over. But I hope it's clear to us now that that which is born of the flesh is flesh. The **flesh** is not changed in conversion. It is **unredeemable.** We've established that now, that you **cannot change the flesh.** That which is born of the flesh **is flesh. It will always be flesh.** And so many people tell me that they're **surprised** that they have all this in them. Why should you be **surprised?** The only thing you can do with that is crucify it. You **can't change it.** It's unchangeable. The flesh doesn't go through a process of conversion. And so, this is **unmerited,** meaning that there are **no works that you could perform to do it.**

In a discussion the other night I made a very risqué statement when I said that the more you sin the more grace you get. **Which is true by the way.** Where sin abounds, grace does much more abound. Now **obviously,** that's not the **conclusion** we want to **leave. But I want you to see that that's the truth none the less!** *"Where sin abounds grace does much more abound."* [11] **Is grace greater than our sins? Either that's true folks or it's not true. And if you fall just one little bit, if you just** sin <u>ONCE</u>, then you've <u>had it</u>! To break the law once means you're guilty of the whole law [12] and that's what James taught.

Can you be good enough to earn this? It is <u>utterly</u> <u>impossible</u>. And so, this is what Paul is trying to **tell us, that it cannot, at <u>any</u> time, be works.** Romans 11:6, *"If it is **by grace,** it is no longer on the basis of works; otherwise **grace**—would no **longer**—be—**grace.**"* [13]

We talked momentarily about the point of works this morning, but I'd just simply like to underscore that again. **Works basically** means you want to attain some **goodness.** Again, we're talking about the **standard.** You want to **do—good.** You feel the obligation upon you to do that, and so, out of **effort** now, comes the **striving,** comes the **straining** to establish your goodness or your **worth.** But the trouble of it is, is that we **can't** do that. We just simply do not have it within our power to attain that. **So, it <u>has</u> to be <u>unmerited</u>, because it's impossible to do it <u>by</u> works.** And a number of you came up to me after the service this morning and **bore that out.** You said that the message was somewhat **new** to you. But I asked several of you. I said, "Well has it worked by your striving?" And every one of you said, "No." Well then, let's find a better principle. It's obviously not working **by** your **works.** So, let's go over to some other principle, you see. And that has to be—**grace.**

It is—totally—un—merited. It comes as a free gift. You **can't** earn it. Impossible. So, you see, toss out the **whole idea** then of good or bad. This is where we get into the **problem,** is we start thinking if we're **good,** then we **merit it** some way. But you can never go into that syndrome at all. **You cannot! There's no way! You have** to accept it, **at first, and always, and constantly, this marvelous unmerited favor.** Now, does that obligate you to God? If **you** can't do it, who gets all the glory? Now can you **get** praise? Can you boast? No. Ephesians 2:8-9 says, *"...not of works, **lest—any—man—should boast.**"* [14] You can take no credit. And you know it's very important in God's sight that we come to an end of ourselves. That we are **not** filled with that. That we **truly** see who we are. But we **so deceptively** want to get **some** boast. **We want** people to pat us on the back. Doesn't it make us feel good when people say we're a great **guy?** Oh, we'd do just about anything to **get** that, you see. But there's that **subtle thing** that creeps into our hearts, and **God alone** wants to get all the glory. Therefore, it has to be by—**grace—through—faith.** The Bible is **very clear** at this point.

Now then, **does** grace really lead us to righteousness? Well, you remember what Romans 5:21 says, *"That grace—might reign— through—righteousness."* [15] Now we're very much concerned about doing the will of God. We want to **please** Him. In other words, **we really want to do good.** We want to have **good** working **in us.** But you see we think to do it on terms of the **law,** rather than realizing that it's **by grace alone** that can establish us in righteousness. And so, I would like to say that these sermons I'm preaching to you, **in no way lead people to looseness and to ungodliness,** because this is totally **just!** You see this is based upon **the justice of God.**

We need to understand that we have **righteousness** on two counts. The **first** is Romans 5:21, *"...grace reigns through righteousness."* [15] **Grace and truth came by Jesus Christ.** Romans 3:24, *"...we are justified by his grace through the redemption that is in Christ Jesus."* [3] **In other words, the death of Jesus has satisfied all these righteous claims,** you see. This is on **strict justice.** This is **reigning through righteousness. You're not to imagine that God is just doing this out of His love.** He's doing this out of strict justice. He's giving you His grace out of **strict justice** because of the death of Jesus. He is **just** and the **justifier** of them who believe in Jesus.

"They are justified by his grace as a gift, through the redemption which is in Christ Jesus." - Romans 3:24 RSV

And **now** comes this other wonderful **truth** that I **barely** touched on but now I think we're **ready** for. You see the book of Romans has two great aspects to it. Roughly chapters, say 1 to 4, or 1 to 5, are stressing **one** part. And Romans 6, 7 and 8 are stressing another **truth.** But I want to establish this first part <u>first</u>. **Otherwise, people are <u>always</u> struggling. You've got to know that Romans 1 to 4,** or 1 to 5, **are telling what Jesus has done "<u>for</u>" us. That's talking about our <u>justification</u>. That's talking about our <u>forgiveness</u>. That's talking about our <u>sins</u>. That's talking about Jesus as our <u>substitute</u>. What Jesus did on the cross by His precious blood.**

Now Romans chapters 6, 7 and 8 are talking about what Jesus does "<u>in</u>" us. This is talking about <u>sanctification</u>. This is talking about our <u>wholeness</u>. This is talking about our being <u>sinners</u>. We have our <u>sins</u> in 1 to 4. We have our <u>nature</u>, our sinner-<u>hood</u>, in chapters 6, 7 and 8. Now at some point you're going to meet your <u>nature</u>. Not only what you've <u>done</u>, but what you <u>ARE</u>! And that's where you need Jesus "<u>in</u>" you, you see. Not only Jesus "for" you but Jesus "<u>in</u>" you.

This is where the <u>grace</u> of God <u>weds us</u> to the Lord Jesus Christ. Jesus Christ is our **substitute** in 1 to 5. We are **identified <u>with</u> Him in chapters 6, 7 and 8. And the thing that precludes this being a <u>loose</u> doctrine is that we have this mystical union with the <u>Lord Jesus</u>. You see when you have faith in Jesus, for the forgiveness of your sins, then the Holy Spirit also brings you <u>into</u> <u>Christ</u> and that <u>Spirit</u> comes into <u>you</u>. And now by the miracle of regeneration you <u>long</u> to be <u>like</u> Him. Not through the old standards of the law, but by that marvelous indwelling Spirit of <u>Jesus</u> that makes you <u>hunger</u> and <u>thirst</u> and <u>pant</u> after <u>righteousness</u>. And <u>there</u>, by the <u>grace</u> of God does ten times more than the law ever could. It's the <u>grace</u> of God that teaches us. We so fall in love with <u>Jesus</u> that we want to be <u>like</u> Him. And now we see Him, and we <u>HATE</u> our sin with everything within us. Now we're**

only driven to the Lord Jesus Christ. And so, I tell you this is the <u>safest doctrine</u> I know. It's the <u>only</u> way to bring people freedom from their sins—is to on the one hand show them that they must come <u>totally</u> to an end of themselves. And you'll never come totally under <u>grace</u> until you know there is no good thing in you. You've <u>got</u> to come to an end of yourself. And when you come <u>totally</u> to an end of yourself, it's then that you turn to another and to the marvelous grace of God.

And so, this doctrine makes us **love slaves** of the Lord Jesus Christ. Just this **marvelous mystical union** with Him. And we'll begin to see what it means to be **"in"** Christ. To associate with His **death,** with His **burial,** with His **resurrection.** Thank <u>God</u> for that glorious truth. And I tell you that's real! But <u>listen,</u> your <u>self-life</u> has got to go! And I tell you it's a very subtle thing how this stays on and we keep wanting to establish it. We keep thinking there's some good in us. And so, the law has never fully done its work to bring us to total weakness and to <u>death</u>.

But I'm urging that the Lord Jesus Christ by His **Spirit** and by His **Word** will show us what it means to be **totally** under grace. That's why, when you're **totally under grace,** you are no longer under the bondage of **sin.** Because if <u>you're</u> at the <u>center,</u> if there's any of your <u>self-life</u> around, then I tell you, you're wedded to nothing but <u>sin</u>. Paul is going to use the illustration of <u>slavery</u>. He's going to use the illustration of <u>marriage</u>. And the <u>only</u> thing that can happen is to bring you into a new love-slave relationship with the Jesus Christ. If you're still in your flesh whatever, and under the bondage of that, you can do nothing <u>but</u> sin. You can do <u>nothing but SIN</u>. <u>That's all!</u> <u>It's under the power of sin</u>. But when the Lord Jesus Christ comes in and when you're totally under grace **then** you have this new Lord that sets you free into the marvelous liberty of the children of God.

So let me tell you that to be under grace means that you are **totally** under God's favor. **Sin—is—not—the problem. The problem is not sin. The problem is our relationship to God through Jesus Christ. It's always one of relationship. Would you please believe that <u>every</u> sin that has <u>ever</u> been committed—past, present and future—has been identified with Jesus Christ on the cross? The problem is not sin. The <u>problem</u> is our relationship to <u>Him</u>.** You can see that as parents. I would like my children to be **good.** I would like my children to make good grades. But I want my children **to love me.** I want them to be open to me, and to be honest with me. If I've got a relationship with them, then **that's** what I want. We can go somewhere. They can be **bad** as long as they **love me. As long as they love me! But if our relationship is broken, <u>then</u> we've got terrible problems. We've got awful problems if the relationship is gone.** But that's what we want is that **relationship** with the Lord Jesus Christ. And so, to be under grace means to be totally under His favor. **You are. You can't earn it.** So, rest in it and accept it.

Secondly, to be under grace means to have found a way to have **freedom from the bondage of your "self" and sin** and this horrible self-life that we go through. Why we can even have it in the energies, I believe, of the natural man and still just be our self-life. We have **never** come to an end of ourselves. And I'm going to tell you this: It's possible for people to be in church **all their life** and not understand this doctrine. It's possible for people to be graduates of Bible School and studied Romans and **still** not understand this doctrine. I'm praying that the Lord Jesus Christ will help us see this. It's a **whole new** way of life. It's a **whole** different concept than most people see and **all** that we generally experience in our society. I would say that much of the preaching we hear, much of the teaching we hear, is a Galatian form of Christianity. ᴬ And so no wonders we have such awful bondages. But I **long** for that glorious liberty that's available to the children of God. I want to be under nothing—but—His—grace.

SERMON 4 ENDNOTES:

A Galatian Christianity: The book of Galatians is the letter that the Apostle Paul wrote to the believers in Galatia. These new believers embraced Paul's message of grace but found it almost impossible for them to not attach the law to it. They kept struggling with legalism. They were still trying to become righteous by the law or works. Don Pickerill 2020

B Aorist tense is the Greek grammarian's term for a simple past tense. Unlike the other past tenses (imperfect and perfect), the aorist simply states the fact than an action has happened with no indication of how long it took. Aorist is like a snapshot; present is like a video. www. ezraproject.com

SERMON 4 SCRIPTURE REFERENCES:

1 Romans 6:14 *(RSV)*

For sin will have no dominion over you, since you are not under law but under grace.

2 John 1:16 (RSV)

And from his fulness have we all received, grace upon grace.

3 Romans 3:23-24 (RSV)

23 since all have sinned and fall short of the glory of God, 24 they are justified by his grace as a gift, through the redemption which is in Christ Jesus,

4 Romans 5:17 *(RSV)*

If, because of one man's trespass, death reigned through that one man, much more will those who receive the abundance of grace and the free gift of righteousness reign in life through the one man Jesus Christ.

[5] Ephesians 1:5-6 *(RSV)*

5   He destined us in love to be his sons through Jesus Christ, according to the purpose of his will, 6 to the praise of his glorious grace which he freely bestowed on us in the Beloved.

[6] Ephesians 2:8-9 *(RSV)*

8 For by grace you have been saved through faith; and this is not your own doing, it is the gift of God— 9 not because of works, lest any man should boast.

[7] 1 Corinthians 15:10 *(RSV)*

But by the grace of God I am what I am, and his grace toward me was not in vain. On the contrary, I worked harder than any of them, though it was not I, but the grace of God which is with me.

[8] Jeremiah 32:38-41 *(RSV)*

38 And they shall be my people, and I will be their God. 39 I will give them one heart and one way, that they may fear me for ever, for their own good and the good of their children after them. 40 I will make with them an everlasting covenant, that I will not turn away from doing good to them; and I will put the fear of me in their hearts, that they may not turn from me. 41 I will rejoice in doing them good, and I will plant them in this land in faithfulness, with all my heart and all my soul.

[9] Romans 8:28 *(KJV)*

And we know that all things work together for good to them that love God, to them who are the called according to his purpose.

[10] Genesis 50:20 *(RSV)*

As for you, you meant evil against me; but God meant it for good, to bring it about that many people should be kept alive, as they are today.

[11] Romans 5:20 *(KJV)*

Moreover the law entered, that the offence might abound. But where sin abounded, grace did much more abound:

[12] James 2:10 *(RSV)*

For whoever keeps the whole law but fails in one point has become guilty of all of it.

[13] Romans 11:6 *(RSV)*

But if it is by grace, it is no longer on the basis of works; otherwise grace would no longer be grace.

[14] Ephesians 2:8-9 *(RSV)*

8 For by grace you have been saved through faith; and this is not your own doing, it is the gift of God— 9 not because of works, lest any man should boast.

[15] Romans 5:21 *(RSV)*

so that, as sin reigned in death, grace also might reign through righteousness to eternal life through Jesus Christ our Lord.

SERMON 5

NEWNESS OF LIFE

"Go tell my brothers that I'm ascending to my God and their God!"

I'd like to share with you about four or five verses starting with Romans chapter 5, verse 21. We're going to look at particularly verse 4 of chapter 6. The Apostle says, *"...as **sin reigned in <u>death</u>, grace also might <u>reign</u> through** righteousness to eternal life through Jesus Christ our Lord."*—we call this the **"Reign of Grace"**—"**King Grace"** that is leading us to **life,** to eternal life— *"What shall we say then? Are we to continue in sin that grace may abound?"* [1]—because the Apostle has said, *"that where sin increases grace abounds all the more."* [2] Which is a **truth** by the way, and we perilously want to say **that.** That *"where sin abounds grace does much more abound."* [2]

"So that, as sin reigned in death, grace also might reign through righteousness to eternal life through Jesus Christ our Lord." - Romans 5:21 RSV

In other words, you cannot out sin grace—if you would like to put it in those terms. But the question comes—*"Are we to **continue** in sin that grace may abound?"*—Of course the answer is **no**—by no means—don't even **think** of such a thought. How can we **strangely,** the passage says—"How can we who **died** to sin still live in it?"—Now, that sounds strange, doesn't it?—"Don't you know that all of us who have been baptized into Christ Jesus were baptized into **His death?** We were **buried** with him by baptism into death, so that as Christ was raised from the dead by the **glory** of the Father, we too might walk in **newness of life.**" Let me repeat that, "As Christ was raised from the **dead** by the **glory of the Father,** we too might **walk in newness of life.**" [3]

What does the resurrection mean **right now?** Is there any pie with ice cream on it here and **now?** Well, I like those words and I'd like to **underscore** them today. Newness of life. I've being saying those words over and over in my mind the last couple of weeks and they're **exciting** just to **say,** that we might walk or experience or possess or have—**newness—of—life.** Now I like life, period. But I like adding that little adjective, **"newness"** of life. Oh, I like that. That we might have newness of life.

Well, what do we really have? I'd like us to look at that this morning and see what we can have in **light** of the resurrection of Jesus Christ, **here and now.** Now I'm **impressed** that this **key** verse, in verse 4 says, "that Jesus Christ was raised from the dead by the **glory of the Father.**" [4] That's interesting. I wonder why it didn't say by the **power of God.** It must have taken **great power** to resurrect Jesus Christ. And I remind you we're not simply talking about the resuscitation of a corpse. We're talking about **resurrection** which is interesting to a whole new order of **life. Never** to die again. But it says He was raised up by the **glory** of the **Father.**

I'm almost hesitant to tell you what I **think** this newness of life includes. I believe that the newness of **life** means that we can **walk** in the **glory of the Father. He was raised up by the glory of the Father, so that we might walk in newness of life in association with the glory**

of the Father. Well, that means we've got to find out what the glory of the Father is, doesn't it? So, we're not much farther ahead. I got excited thinking about that. *(Don chuckles)* But now we've got to establish what is the **glory of the Father** that we can walk in. That brings us, of course, to the **glory** of God.

What is the **glory** of God? If it's something that we can experience called newness of life, then we want to understand it very clearly. Well, let me briefly say that the **glory** of God is just the sum total of His attributes. If you were to meet God, you would meet **glory.** That's all you can say. **It would be <u>glorious</u>!**

Now there are certain qualifications before a thing can qualify as being **glorious.** The more **perfect** a thing is the more glorious it is. It's a **glorious** service. The praise song was **glorious!** The choir was **glorious!** It qualifies because it was very, very good. So, anything that's not **good,** you see, is not **glorious!** The garbage dumps aren't **glorious.** Something must be **perfect.** The more **beautiful** it is, the more **awesome** it is, the **better** it is, the more **goodness** it has, the more glory it has.

So, when we talk about the glory of God, we're talking about the **being of God,** aren't we? But notice it says, *"...that Jesus Christ was raised up by the glory of the God."* [4] The best commentary that I know, on the glory of God, is **given** when Moses asked to see it. He said, *"Lord, let me see your glory."* [5] Now you need to know the context though. This is taken from the book of Exodus back in chapters 33 and 34. And this is going on at the foot of **Mount Sinai.** The children of Israel have just received the law of **God. God's righteous standard**—denoting **His holiness.** What **God** wants **for man,** you see, spelled out in terms of His law, **the ten commandments.** Though, when Moses comes down to the foot of the mountain the children of Israel are practically breaking every one of these commandments. And so, Moses, in **despair and outrage, threw** them to the ground and **broke** them as a symbol of the way they had broken the law of God.

And then God moves in **wrath,** and He speaks in Exodus 32, *"Whoever has sinned against <u>me</u>, him will I blot out of my <u>BOOK</u>."* [6] And He tells Moses, "Now you go on up and take the children of Israel, but I'm not going **with you.**" He says in Exodus 33, *"I—will—<u>not</u>—go up among them,"*—I will **not** let my <u>presence</u> or my <u>glory</u> be among **them**—*"lest I <u>consume</u> you"*—and **have to kill you**—*"in the way, because you are a stiff-necked people."* [7] He says, *"You are a stiff-necked people."*—**If just a** <u>split-second</u>—*"for a single <u>moment</u> I should go up among you I would <u>CONSUME YOU</u>."* [8] Because God is so **perfect** and so **holy**—"that they would be **consumed** in a split-second if I were there among you with my glory or my presence."

So Moses is **disturbed** by this, and he says, "If your glory, if your presence won't go up, then **I don't want to go up**"—*"he says, 'If thy presence will not go with me, then **don't** <u>carry</u> us up into that land.'"* [9] And then he says **Lord,** and he makes this great prayer, *"Lord, show me your glory."* [10] *"And God says, 'I will make <u>all</u>—my—goodness—to pass—before you, and I will proclaim before you the <u>name</u>'"*—or the **nature, the characteristics, the being of God**—*"'I will be gracious to whom I will be gracious, and I will show mercy upon whom I will show mercy.'"* [11]

And so—*"The Lord passed before him, and <u>proclaimed</u>,"*— and these are the words in Exodus 34, *"'<u>The Lord</u>,'"*—**Adonai**—*"'the <u>Lord</u>, a God merciful <u>and</u> gracious, <u>slow</u> to anger and <u>abounding</u> in steadfast love and faithfulness, keeping steadfast love for **thousands**'"*— of generations—*"'<u>forgiving</u> iniquity and transgression and sin, <u>BUT</u> who will by no means <u>clear</u> the guilty,'"*—*"by <u>no means</u> clear the guilty."* Because God is **holy,** God is **just,** and He cannot **clear the guilty.** The

guilty must be punished—*"and so I visit the **iniquity** of the fathers upon the children to the **third and fourth** generation.'"* [12] Notice the contrast between **thousands** of generations and the **iniquity** to **three or four** generations.

And then Moses prays and says, *"Lord, if I found favor in your sight, Oh Lord, let the Lord, I pray thee, go in the midst of us, **although**'"*— **even though**—*"'we **are** a stiff-necked people; and **pardon** our iniquity and our sin, and **take us** for **your** inheritance.'"* [13]

So, the **glory of God** is the sum total of His **attributes.** Meaning on the **one hand** that God is **full** of **compassion** and **goodness** and **love.** And He is longsuffering to **thousands** of generations. That's His love, His goodness and His mercy as He made **all** of His goodness to pass before Moses. **But also, God is just, and God is holy.** Could you respect God? Could you say He was **glorious** if He winked at sin or if He didn't settle the score with imperfection? **He must!** God **must** necessarily **do that.** And so, you have these two elements merging. You have **righteousness,** and you have **mercy.** You have **truth,** and you have **peace.** How are they going to meet or kiss together as the psalmist poses the question? [14]

Now I think the most obvious thing that we have in our **experience** is that **every one** of us here without exception, *"have **sinned** and come short"*—can you finish it? *(Don and the congregation finish quoting the verse together)* —*"of the **glory of God.**" "You have **all** sinned and fallen short of the glory of God."* [15] Now if that's **so,** what must happen? If you fall **short** of the glory of God, what must take place?

I don't need to catalog all the gross things that we do. You only have to read Romans to see how we fall short. If our hearts were exposed here this morning, I'm sure that every one of us would cast ourselves down with **shame** because we have fallen short of that glory. But then we have our more sophisticated **sins** where we just want to run our own **lives** in our **pride** and our **self-will.** We want a false kind of an **autonomy, pretending there is no God, and no claim upon our lives. With our stiff-necked and our rebellious attitudes, we won't bow our knee to anybody!** In some ways that's the worst form of all is to imagine that we are independent of God and His claim upon us.

By the way, it's an interesting thing **to me** that when **we** sin, we normally think of the punishment that we ought to **get.** But in **God's mind,** when we sin, He thinks of the **glory** that we **lose.** We fall short of His glory or His goodness. And I think that's true. The **most evil** thing **about evil** is that it's a negation of the **good.** It's not the **bad** you do, but the **good** that you're missing. You're falling short of the **good.** And this is what we want is this **glory** and this **perfection.**

Now that leads us to some **very** basic truths in Romans. And I'd like to make this as clear as I possibly can this morning, remembering, however, that we will have to expound this for some weeks ahead. And I trust that everyone will hear this **entire series** as we look at the possibilities of entering into the newness of life.

The book of Romans is basically an exposition of two great thoughts. The Apostle says in Romans1:16-17, *"...I am not ashamed of the gospel"*—and that's a double negative that means I'm really proud of it. **Thank God for the gospel,** because of two reasons: Number one, *"It is the power of God unto salvation."* **It is the power of God!** Number two, in that gospel is the **revelation,** or the revealing, the making known **of a righteousness.** *"...the righteousness of God is revealed from faith to faith, as it is written, the just—shall live—by faith.* [16] Or as someone translates it, **"He who by faith is justified—shall live."**

We're wanting to walk in the **newness of life.** I tell you it's all about **life.** And so, we have these two-fold needs. We have the need for **power,** and we have the need for **righteousness.** Because, you see, man has two basic **problems.** Number one, **all of us** are **guilty.** All of us are deserving of **wrath** and punishment and condemnation. We have a **conscience** that's **uneasy.** We have this **problem** of not being **right,** not being **righteous. Especially** not righteous enough to merit the glory of **God.**

But secondly, we also have our **selves.** Now you see, **sin** is so **heinous** and so **bad,** not because of the bad things you do, but because it's an objective power that **holds** you. You see, you not only have "**sinning,**" but you have the "**sin**ner." That is, **you. You're the problem.** So many people imagine it's just these **bad things** that they do by their **will** and if they try **harder,** you know be an "Avis type Christian," ᴬ then all of a sudden, they're going to **make it.** They think that somehow if they just **try harder. Let me tell you the problem is that man is actually in bondage! He's held by a power! Now the Bible calls that sin! You can call it what you like, but there's an objective power that controls human personality and men always fall short! They try and they try, but they fall SHORT!**

And so, we've got to have two basic things: Number one, we've got to someway be able to enter into the glory of God and be accepted with Him. We've got to be righteous! I've got to be righteous! I've got to satisfy the glory of God. **And secondly, I've got to someway be free to cope with this power at work in my being and in my nature.** I've got a terrible thing in me. I'm not as good as all of you think I am. In me dwells **no** good thing. I've got a **terrible sinful nature** and unless I can someway be **free** to cope with that, I tell you, "I'm going down the **drain,**" as they say today. I've got those two basic problems. I've got **guilt** and I've got a **nature** from which I must be **redeemed.**

And now that leads us to this **glorious truth** this morning and there are two **great** solutions to this in Romans. And I'd like you to remember two words this morning. The first word **is "substitution." All** that Jesus Christ has done **for me** and **instead of me.** Romans chapters 1 to 4, sets forth Jesus Christ as my **substitute.** We believe in a substitutionary vicarious atonement. **That Jesus Christ died—for—me—for—my—sins.** I only read **one** verse, Romans 4:25, that Jesus Christ *"...was put to death—for—our—trespasses and He was raised—for—our—justification."* [17] Now will you notice the connection between the **death** and the resurrection of Jesus? He was put to death **instead of—for—my—trespasses,** but he was **raised again for our justification.**

 "Who was put to death for our trespasses and raised for our justification." - Romans 4:25 RSV

Now I told you that glory demands **perfection** but notice that Jesus Christ was **raised** by the **glory of God.** **That means that Jesus Christ had to be PERFECT! He had to be SINLESS! And that was the big question. Was that man who went to the cross, was He absolutely perfect? So perfect, that He could be raised up by the glory of God? By the holiness and the justice? And also, the love and the goodness of God?** Could he be **raised up** by the **glory** of God? Well, thank God He was **raised** by the **glory of the Father. All the holiness. All the perfection. All the justice of God looked at that dead body of the Lord Jesus Christ and said, "Glorious!" And so, that glorious person went right up into the glory of God. He was raised for my justification.**

Oh, I tell you the newness of life means that I am free from condemnation and guilt because Jesus Christ died instead of me. Don Pickerill is a sinner. I'm undone. I fall short of the glory of God within myself. But thanks be unto God, Jesus Christ is so glorious and so perfect and so sinless that He matches that glory of God. And now I do not fall short of the glory of God. I have a conscious void of offense. I'm not under guilt. I'm not under wrath. I'm not under condemnation, because I walk in newness of life. And I tell you

friends that's <u>glorious</u>! That's <u>wonderful</u> news! That's **good news** to know that Jesus Christ has made us accepted with God the Father.

Do you know the very first thing Jesus said on resurrection morning? Do you know what His first message was? Do you know what He said? He met Mary at the tomb and Jesus said to Mary, **"Go tell my brothers.** My people. My disciples. Go tell those who **denied** me. Go tell Peter, James, John. <u>**Go tell my brothers!**</u> **I want you to tell my <u>brothers</u> this message: Go tell my brothers that I am ascending to <u>my</u> God and their God."** *"I am ascending to <u>my</u> Father and to <u>their</u> Father."* [18] **Go tell my <u>brothers</u> that we have a common Father. They are my <u>brothers</u> now because what is happening to me is going to happen to <u>them</u>.**

This is why Romans says, *"...he is the <u>firstborn</u> among <u>many</u> BRETHREN."* [19] **And I tell you He is leading many sons to <u>glory</u>. I'm going right up in on the train of His glorious glory. I'm going <u>right</u> into the acceptance and the presence and the goodness of God. And I sit there in Jesus Christ this morning, <u>beyond</u> the judgment. <u>I am justified by faith</u>, and justification has reference to the <u>final</u> judgment seat of <u>God</u> and that sentence has already been handed back on me. And the sentence is: You are <u>righteous</u>! You are <u>acquitted</u>!** There is no condemnation because of the death and the resurrection of the Lord Jesus Christ.

Did He do that for His own sins? He did it for **my** sins. They were **laid** upon **Him.** And so, you must remember the word, **"substitution."** Jesus Christ did **that** for you and we are **righteous** this morning and free of all guilt and condemnation. I tell you that's good news friend. You can grub around with your seemly conscious all **you want,** and how that's going to <u>sap</u> **the very life out of you, so that you can't look <u>man</u> nor <u>life</u> square in the eye. You have to <u>sneak</u> around through life, shifty eyed. I don't want anything to do with that.** I want to be **accepted** before

God. I want to be **righteous.** Thank God, He was raised by the <u>glory</u> of the Father. **The glory of the Father raised Him up,** and I can walk in newness of life. Do you hear that **good news?** Do you thank God for that gospel?

But there's another **word** because we have this second problem. And that is **my nature. The power of sin.** The **forces** that **work** in me. And that leads us to the second word and that's the word that we're going to talk about some in the weeks ahead. I want you to remember the word, **"identification,"** because Jesus Christ not only died **for me** as **substitute,** but if it were not here, I could hardly believe it. Did you notice what is says? That, *"...we have been buried with him by baptism into death so that Christ was raised from the dead by the glory of the Father, we too might walk in newness of life"* [4] —<u>with</u> Him.

Now, this is a truth that I don't have time to develop this morning except to say Christ is not only <u>**for**</u> me, but Christ is <u>**with**</u> me, and Christ is <u>**in**</u> me. I have this **union** with Jesus Christ. I have been **incorporated.** The word later used here is like a **transplant.** We've been **transplanted** into Jesus Christ. As though you'd put an old dead stem, as it were, and transplanted into that **living body.** We were there **with** Him. We've been **engrafted** in Him. **Incorporated** into Him. So, what happened to Jesus Christ has happened **to me.** I'll explain that in the days that are ahead. **That's** the truth that many people do not know. And Paul goes on to say many times in this chapter, **"Don't you know?" "I've got to tell you this."** Many people know that Jesus died **for** them, but they know **little** about **this truth** of **incorporation,** of **identification,** of **union,** of identification with the Lord Jesus Christ. **Christ <u>with</u> me. Christ <u>in</u> me.** We'll talk about that in the days that are ahead.

Is it possible to be freed from sin? I tell you it is **possible** to be **free** from sin. Paul says in chapter 6, verse 7, *"...he who has **died** is freed from* *sin."* [20] When Jesus Christ **died,** did sin have any longer control over him? Does the **law** or sin or anything control a dead man? When a dead man dies can you **reach him?** No, he's **beyond** all the powers of this age. He may owe a million dollars. Can you collect your debt? If a man drops dead, can you collect your money from him? **He's out of it. He's dead.** (*Don chuckles*)

The Bible says you are **freed from sin,** but I want you to note it does **not** say that you are **"sinless."** It's **very** important that we understand the difference. To be **freed** from sin is **not** the same thing as being **sinless.** Let me see if I can illustrate that. We recently brought our prisoners of war home. They were held **captive** by the Viet Cong; whatever forces they were held by. Why did we bring them **home?** We got them **freed** from the Viet Cong, **but they went right back into the Army. They went right back to fight the Viet Cong.** Do you see the point? **You are freed from sin because it's an objective power. Let me tell you, you must understand, that there's this great force, this great power working within and without you that Jesus Christ broke by His death and resurrection. Jesus Christ is able to free us from sin in order that we might fight sin. In order that we might be able to cope with it.** And we'll go on to look at that in Romans chapter 6. So, to be freed from sin does not mean you are **sinless.** We have all these exhortations to **cope with sin.**

The Lord Jesus Christ is offering us **newness of life.** He was **raised** from the dead by the **glory of the Father.** By the **holiness.** By the **perfection.** By the **justice.** By the **righteousness of God,** He was raised up. What for? So that we might receive the **gift** of righteousness. You know the **best** news I know is that you can have the righteousness of God in Jesus Christ. The righteousness of God. That's a glorious thing to me. I walk in the newness of that. In and of myself, I'm undone. But thank God, what Jesus Christ has done. He has lifted me up beyond condemnation and guilt and wrath and punishment. **That is newness of life.**

Secondly, Jesus Christ, by His identification with me, incorporating me **with Him,** and indwelling me by His Spirit, **frees me** to be able to **fight and cope with** these powers that would squeeze the life out of me. And is **that** good news? I tell you men have got to have some good news someway because of these **terrific** things that come. There may be many Christians here who have never understood that. Again, I urge you to hear this entire series as we see how an incorporation with Jesus Christ frees us from the power of sin.

And so, I have this **glorious** freedom. Do you want to know what this newness of life is? One word, **"freedom."** To **really truly** be free. The **glorious liberty** of the children of God. That's what we're talking about, and that's what we want to experience. This is called the **glory** of the Father.

Well, I tell you, I want some pie right now with ice cream on it. I want my pie in the sky by and by too! **The resurrection will bring up my dead body. My body is dying right now because of sin but my spirit is alive right now because of righteousness. My pie and ice cream here and now is the spirit that's alive. That's freed from condemnation and can enter into glorious freedom. My pie in the sky is when my body is going to get caught up with my spirit, and I am going to be transformed and transfigured by the resurrection of the Lord Jesus Christ.**

But I've got something right now. I've got this glorious freedom! Wonderful freedom! Because of what Jesus Christ has given. And I tell you friend, it's yours too. *"Go tell my brothers that I'm ascending to my God and their God."* [18] Well that's Jesus Christ's resurrection message to you this morning. That for **all** of the brothers, He is leading **many sons**

to glory. He's taking us right on up into the glory of God. Well, I want to go. **I am glory bound!** I'm **headed** for the presence and the glory of God.

SERMON 5 ENDNOTES:

A   Avis type Christians is a reference to the Avis Car Rental company that had the tag line: "We Try Harder" as part of their advertising.

SERMON 5 SCRIPTURE REFERENCES:

1   Romans 5:21 (RSV)

so that, as sin reigned in death, grace also might reign through righteousness to eternal life through Jesus Christ our Lord.

2   Romans 5:20 (KJV)

Moreover the law entered, that the offence might abound. But where sin abounded, grace did much more abound:

3   Romans 6:1-4 (RSV)

1 What shall we say then? Are we to continue in sin that grace may abound? 2 By no means! How can we who died to sin still live in it? 3 Do you not know that all of us who have been baptized into Christ Jesus were baptized into his death? 4 We were buried therefore with him by baptism into death, so that as Christ was raised from the dead by the glory of the Father, we too might walk in newness of life.

4   Romans 6:4 (RSV)

We were buried therefore with him by baptism into death, so that as Christ was raised from the dead by the glory of the Father, we too might walk in newness of life.

5   Exodus 33:18 (RSV)

Moses said, "I pray thee, show me thy glory."

⁶ Exodus 32:33 (RSV)

But the Lord said to Moses, "Whoever has sinned against me, him will I blot out of my book."

⁷ Exodus 33:3 (RSV)

Go up to a land flowing with milk and honey; but I will not go up among you, lest I consume you in the way, for you are a stiff-necked people."

⁸ Exodus 33:5 (RSV)

For the Lord had said to Moses, "Say to the people of Israel, 'You are a stiff-necked people; if for a single moment I should go up among you, I would consume you. So now put off your ornaments from you, that I may know what to do with you.'"

⁹ Exodus 33:15 (RSV)

And he said to him, "If thy presence will not go with me, do not carry us up from here."

¹⁰ Exodus 33:18 (RSV)

Moses said, "I pray thee, show me thy glory."

¹¹ Exodus 33:19 (RSV)

And he said, "I will make all my goodness pass before you, and will proclaim before you my name 'The Lord'; and I will be gracious to whom I will be gracious, and will show mercy on whom I will show mercy."

¹² Exodus 34:6-7 (RSV)

6 The Lord passed before him, and proclaimed, "The Lord, the Lord, a God merciful and gracious, slow to anger, and abounding in steadfast love and faithfulness, 7 keeping steadfast love for thousands, forgiving iniquity and transgression and sin, but who will by no means clear the guilty, visiting the iniquity of the fathers upon the children and the children's children, to the third and the fourth generation."

[13] Exodus 34:9 (RSV)

And he said, "If now I have found favor in thy sight, O Lord, let the Lord, I pray thee, go in the midst of us, although it is a stiff-necked people; and pardon our iniquity and our sin, and take us for thy inheritance."

[14] Psalm 85:10-11 (RSV)

10 Steadfast love and faithfulness will meet; righteousness and peace will kiss each other.11 Faithfulness will spring up from the ground, and righteousness will look down from the sky.

[15] Romans 3:23 (KJV)

For all have sinned, and come short of the glory of God

[16] Romans 1:16-17 (KJV)

16 For I am not ashamed of the gospel of Christ: for it is the power of God unto salvation to every one that believeth; to the Jew first, and also to the Greek. 17 For therein is the righteousness of God revealed from faith to faith: as it is written, The just shall live by faith.

[17] Romans 4:25 (RSV)

who was put to death for our trespasses and raised for our justification.

[18] John 20:17 (RSV)

Jesus said to her, "Do not hold me, for I have not yet ascended to the Father; but go to my brethren and say to them, I am ascending to my Father and your Father, to my God and your God."

[19] Romans 8:29 (RSV)

For those whom he foreknew he also predestined to be conformed to the image of his Son, in order that he might be the first-born among many brethren.

[20] Romans 6:7 (RSV)

For he who has died is freed from sin.

SERMON 6

IDENTIFICATION

"You have been planted together—with —Him, Jesus Christ, our Lord!"

This is sermon number 6 in a series that we're doing from Romans chapters 6, 7 and 8. I invite your attention once again to Romans chapter 5, verse 21. We'd like to share through verse 11, this morning, of chapter 6, beginning with verse 21 in Romans chapter 5. The reason we read **this** verse is it's **really** the **key** for the next three chapters, because in one way or another they are an **exposition** of what it means to be **under grace.** Paul says, *"...as sin **reigned**"*—as it did—*"as it **reigned** in death, grace also might reign through righteousness to eternal life through Jesus Christ our Lord."* [1] Well, *"What shall we say then?"*—question—*"Are we to continue **in** sin that grace may abound? **By no means!**"*—That's not the logical conclusion to **make.** Though you can understand why one **might** make that. *"How can we"*—strangely, he says here—*"How can we who **died to sin** still live in it? Don't you know that all of us who have been baptized into Christ Jesus were baptized into his **death?** We were **buried** therefore **with him** by baptism into **death,** so that as Christ was raised from the dead by the glory of the Father, we too might walk in newness of life. For if we have been **united with him** in a death **like his,** we shall certainly be **united** with him in a resurrection like his. We know that our old self"*—and Paul is not talking about, at this point, the resurrection of the physical **body.** He's talking about what it means to be in newness of **life.** *"We know that our old self **was** crucified with him so that the **sinful body** might be destroyed, and we might no longer be **enslaved to sin.** He who has **died** is"*—obviously—*"freed from sin. But if we have **died** with Christ, we believe that we shall also **live** with him. For we know that Christ being raised from the **dead** will never die again; death no longer has dominion over him. The death he died he **died to sin, once for all,** but the life he lives he lives to God. So also you must consider yourselves"*—understand this to be—*"**dead to sin** and alive to God in Christ Jesus."* [2]

Now we mentioned that there are **two key words** to understand Paul's great teaching in Romans. The first part of the epistle, the first few chapters, I would say that the key word **is—substitution—what Jesus Christ has done <u>for us</u> and <u>instead</u> of us.** You see over and over again the preposition "for." **Christ died <u>for</u> our sins. He was <u>raised</u> <u>for</u> our justification. Jesus Christ <u>instead of me</u>. He died <u>for</u> my sins. All of my sins were visited on Jesus Christ. He <u>bore</u> the wrath of God <u>instead of me</u> and because of that I am <u>not under law</u>. <u>All</u> the claims of God have been satisfied in Jesus Christ. I am totally and absolutely <u>under</u> grace.**

Now, that may, logically lead one to believe. If that's true, then what **stops sin?** If it **is** true that you cannot out sin grace because where sin abounds grace does much more **abound** and if you are not under law, which means **there is no claim** upon your life. You are free. Utterly free. That's what that means. If you're not under the law, there is **no claim.** All those claims have been **met and satisfied!** So, the question actually comes then: "Now wait a minute, why don't we sin that grace may abound?" Is there anything that **stops sin?**" Well, the Apostle Paul has brought us to this very, very, enlightening—beautiful—wonderful—doctrine of substitution. **Now** he will begin to emphasize the **next phase** of it. You would **think** that Paul might **say**—"Now then, it's important for you to start doing this or that"—and in a subtle way reintroduce the law.

He does **not. Rather,** Paul introduces the **next key word** to understand Romans and particularly chapters 6, 7 and 8. And that's the word "identification," **or** we might use the word "incorporation." Whatever word we choose to use, it's essentially expressing the same thing. Now **here** the key preposition is **"with."** What Jesus did <u>for</u> me—**instead of me** as a **substitute.** Now, we're going to meet the word, **again and again,** "<u>with</u>." You'll notice it says that we are **buried <u>with</u>** Him. We have been **united <u>with</u>** Him. Our old self was **crucified <u>with</u>** Him. You see this repeated, again and again.

"For if we have been united with him in a death like his, we shall certainly be united with him in a resurrection like his."
- Romans 6:5 RSV

And I would say that verse 5 is probably the most significant verse for our consideration. **"...<u>If</u> we have been <u>united—with—him</u>."** Notice that phrase. **"<u>United—with—him</u>"**—incorporated—identified—involved—participating. Actually *"united <u>with him</u> in a death like his, we certainly will be united with him in a resurrection like his."* [3] And so, here's the Doctrine of Identification **with** Jesus Christ. Now it can be very simply **stated.** It simply means **this: That when Jesus Christ acted, <u>we acted</u>. What He did, <u>we did</u>. When He died, <u>we died</u>. When He arose, <u>we arose</u>. When He ascended to the Father, <u>we ascended to the Father</u>.** Now, that's what that means. But the first time you hear it you know, you've got to say, "Quit your kidding!" You know, you hear something like that, and it sounds like **mythology.** It sounds like **legal fiction. But let's stop and see for a moment.** Upon what **basis** we could make a statement like **this,** that Jesus Christ acted **with us,** and **we with Him.** He's identified **with us,** and we are identified with Him. To what extent can we believe this Doctrine of **Incorporation?**

Well, let's begin, just at a very simple level. Does that truth operate for us in life now? It does, all the time. You see it particularly say, in a legal sense, in family life. **I'm legally** responsible for my family. Anything **they do, I do legally.** If my children get in trouble the police come and get **me.** They lock **me up.** Is that fair? I don't know. It's true anyway. (*Don chuckles*) That's true. **That's legally true!** We see it operating at all kinds of levels. You can even see that, for example, in our government. And we've illustrated that we have a **federal** type government. That's what this doctrine is talking about. We call it **"Federal Theology"**— that when Adam, the **first man** in the garden acted, **we acted. We were there—legally.** And when Jesus Christ the **last Adam** acted, **we acted— federally.**

See, we have a **president** and when he signed laws, **you're involved**—the United States people. This **body of people** are involved in **that** signature. He represents me. Now for ancient Israel they had little trouble with this because they believed strong in a corporate personality at work in a nation. **When that high priest went into the presence of God, <u>Israel</u> went in there. When King David spoke, he spoke <u>for the nation</u>**—for the people—<u>**one man acted as the entire nation**</u>. So, you see this happening just constantly and in various ways. We have corporations. To <u>in</u>corporate means that you become **one body.** You can have two or more people who <u>in</u>corporate. When they act, when that corporation acts, **they all act.** It's **one** person **acting.**

And so, there's no problem for us to understand this. That **God** who is the **King** and the **Judge** of the Universe, has His **courts,** has His **laws,** and that Jesus Christ **can federally and legally—act—for— us. And when Jesus Christ is the head of the new creation, when He died and when He rose again, <u>I was there</u>. Were you there when they crucified my Lord? Yes, you were <u>there</u>! Were you <u>there</u> when they raised Him from the dead? <u>Yes, you were THERE!</u> Jesus Christ was** coming up out of that grave <u>for</u> us and <u>with</u> us. We—were—with—Him—united with Him—legally.

Not only that, but it's a little bit deeper than that. You just can't have legal fiction. Behind all law is **generally** some **rational premise.** There's usually something taking its rise out of **natural law** that gives validity to any kind of other type **law.** You can see that the husband or the father of a family, he's really **tied into** that family. This is more than **law.** They're really a part of his **body.** That takes its **rise** out of a very **real** unity. And when President Nixon acts, he's acting for **a people,** a national people. So there is a connection. We belong to this society. This is more than just **legal. I believe that it's really racial. <u>Biologically</u> we are in Jesus Christ.** It happened.

Now I don't know where you make a distinction between parents and children. Like I was explaining my last trip home. I was **greatly impressed** by this trip. It made a **big** impression on me. I watched some of my uncles and my **dad,** and I realized why I do certain things **I do.** It's just in me. That's all. I'm in **them** and they're in me. I don't know how you separate my dad from **me.** I'm a product of his being. I don't know where you separate me from my **grandfather,** and I don't know how far back you **go. But the Bible says,** *"He has made us all of one blood."* [4] **That mankind is <u>really</u>, perhaps distantly related, but there's really just <u>one</u> humanity. There is a common humanity. There is in a sense <u>one</u> race, <u>one</u> blood. He's made us all of <u>one</u> blood,** Paul said on Mars Hill.

Now, the Bible uses the same illustration. Do you remember when the patriarch Abraham had won the great battle? He was coming back with the spoils of the war and out came a tremendous king, the king of Jerusalem. His name was Melchizedek. He was the king of righteousness. King of Jerusalem. He was also a priest of the **most high God.** And Abraham **gave** Melchizedek a part of these **spoils. He tithed.** He gave a tenth part of the spoils of war to Melchizedek. You know what the Bible says? **The Bible says that <u>all</u> the decedents of Abraham, the tribe of Levi, and the house of Aaron <u>paid tithe to Melchizedek</u>, which makes Melchizedek greater than Aaron. Now the point is this, that they were <u>really in his loins</u>, biologically and racially, they were <u>there</u>!**

Now let me ask you a question. If your grandmother and grandfather on both sides had died when they were 10 years old, where would you be? Would you be here? No, **you were there!** You were **in** them. Now you hadn't shown up yet **historically. But racially, biologically, you were resident in your grandparents. So, can you <u>see</u> that Jesus Christ is the Son of <u>Man</u>? That biologically, <u>really</u>, we are tied in with Jesus Christ. He acts for the human race.**

Now, it's also true, I think, psychologically. I think this has some very **real** qualities to it. Now I don't know that I understand **thoroughly** all of **this.** But let me explain to you that there is a **very reputable** psychiatric school founded by a Swiss doctor by the name of Carl Gustav Jung. And C.G. Jung said, that in his dealing with people and treating them for their emotional psychological problems, he said that he was discovering what he called a **collective unconscious.** That there were **remnants** of ancient humanity **present** in us. He said that **all mankind** has a kind of a **collective unconscious,** and that if you're going to treat any given individual, you **have** to understand these **racial overtones** to understand a man's dreams or his myths or his symbolism. ᴬ It was **locked in,** to what he called this **"collective unconscious"** of all humanity. And it's a **very reputable notion,** I might add. We are understanding that **sociologically <u>you</u> can't really separate people.** What happens anywhere in the universe is happening to **all of us. It's an amazing thought that we are locked in this thing together.**

But I hurry on to **remind you** that we are not only identified **with** Jesus Christ and **incorporated** with Him in His death and resurrection, but I tell you that the Holy Spirit of God who <u>dwells</u> in us makes that real. <u>We are indwelt by that common Holy Spirit.</u> <u>The Spirit that was in Jesus is in ME!</u> <u>And I tell you this is real!</u> <u>It's not mythological!</u> It's <u>not</u> mystical! It's not a figment of your imagination. This—is—a—<u>FACT</u>! And that's the important thing to <u>see</u>! It's not just something **we're hoping we'll be.** And we've got to get **this** straight because so many people want to strain for it to happen. In other words, they'd say, "I'm united with Him. Now that means I've got to struggle **real hard** and try to **feel** that way." **No, it's a fact.** You don't struggle to **make** it true. **It <u>is</u> true! I—<u>am</u>—<u>crucified</u>—<u>with Christ</u>.** It's true! It happened, legally **and really.** And that common Holy Spirit **makes** it so. Can you see how important this is? And that's why Paul says, **"Don't you know?"** Over and over in this chapter he's going to say, "Now, you've got to **know** certain things."

Does it make a difference what we **know?** A lot of people don't know this. Most people know that Jesus died **for** them. They know very little about this Doctrine of Identification and the Doctrine of Incorporation. And this is why, when you see **that,** then you'll understand that you can preach the—**free—full—pure—absolute grace of God.** And realize that it leads you nothing but to holiness because there's this other Doctrine of Incorporation, of Identification, and union **with** the Lord Jesus. **We are united with Him.**

Now, **I am** Don Pickerill. I'm not **struggling** to be Don Pickerill. I don't work at it. I don't wake up and say, "Oh, I wish I were Don Pickerill today." (*Congregation chuckles*) Now, if I told you that I was **Maurine** Pickerill, **that may be something else!** (*Don and congregation laugh*) **I'd have to work at that!** (*More laughter*) And, if I told you, I was Napoleon, you'd run for the nearest telephone (*more laughter*) in there and call out the folks.

See, it makes a difference, what **you are. I am crucified with Christ! I am <u>dead</u> to sin!** I am **freed** from sin. I must tell you more about that tonight. I think it will be probably, the most **important sermon** of this series, when I talk about **freedom from sin.** I trust you won't miss that sermon tonight.

Freedom <u>from</u> sin. So it's a <u>fact</u>! And **that** makes a difference. **Then** I am not trying to **make it so.** And this is what a lot of people **do.** They hear something like this and then **they're striving. They're struggling. "Oh, I've got do that. I've got to get united with Him." You <u>ARE</u> united with Him! It's true!** And it makes **such** a difference whether a thing **is** or not. This **is** a pencil I'm holding. It's **not trying** to be a pencil. If that could talk, it could say, **"I <u>am</u> a pencil." I <u>am</u> crucified with Christ.** I'm identified with Him. And I don't care what sense experience—I don't care what—**you—devils—conscience—or anyone else says—it is true! It has happened to me.**

"I am crucified with Christ: nevertheless I live; yet not I, but Christ liveth in me: and the life which I now live in the flesh I live by the faith of the Son of God, who loved me, and gave himself for me." - Galatians 2:20 KJV

"I am crucified with Christ; nevertheless I live; yet"—no—*"not I."* Paul had to **define** himself—*"not I,"*—there's an "I" here that lives and another "I" that doesn't—*"yet not I, but Christ lives in me: and the life which I now live in the flesh,"*—this earthly life right now—*"I'm living by the faith of the Son of God who <u>loved me</u> and gave Himself <u>for</u> me."* [5] This is not even a mystical relationship. It's not something that happens **mystically,** beyond sense experience. **It is a fact.** It is a truism. It is a reality. We are identified with Jesus.

Now, the Apostle uses a very wonderful illustration in verse 5, when he **says** that, *"we have been <u>united</u> <u>with</u> him."* Translated in the Revised Version—*"united with him."* [3] I think the King James says, *"we have been **planted** together."*—or something—doesn't it? Does somebody have a King James here? *(A faint voice is heard from the congregation-then Don continues)* Planted, yeah, *"we have been **planted** together."* [6] It's an illustration from horticulture or from **grafting**. It means we have been **grafted**. Like two plants, we have been **joined** together. It could be like the thought of two seeds that were planted at the same time and went together, and they just grew up together. Or it could be like an **in**-grafting. Like here's a beautiful plant or something or a tree, and it has a little **slit** that's put in that tree, and it actually is put down inside the **bark**. I think Brother Charlie is good at this with fig trees. Am I correct? I've seen your fig trees. They're **beautiful** over there. And as I remember don't you actually split the bark someway and take another little sapling and put in there? Now **is there a difference** really then? Aren't they together? Aren't they one tree? They become the branch of that tree. It's united with it. What **happens** to that branch **happens** to the tree. And what happens to the tree happens to the branch. We have been **united <u>with</u> Him. Joined with Jesus Christ. <u>Planted</u> together in the likeness of His death.**

Do we have to struggle then to kill or be crucified? You know that's one way you cannot kill yourself. You cannot commit suicide by crucifixion. You might take poison. You might stab yourself. You might jump off of a bridge. Have you tried to crucify yourself lately? **You can't do it! You need somebody else to crucify you, you see, and all through the Bible we use this illustration of <u>crucifixion</u>.** And I think it's almost as though God wanted us to see that what happened to Jesus Christ— **that** form of death—is what **happens to us. I am crucified with Him.** I can't do that to myself. And so **I don't try** to be crucified, **I am.** I don't try to **be** justified. **I am justified.** All that Jesus Christ has done **for** me is a **fact!** It's true. He took **all** my sins away. When Jesus died for me, He satisfied all the claims of the law against me. But also, it's just as true that when **He died—I—died.**

Now, what's the purpose for all this? The **purpose** is what we mentioned in our last series. That we might walk **now** in newness of life. When Paul, envisions the resurrection here, he's talking about a **physical literal bodily resurrection** when Jesus Christ comes **back.** But in the interim, he's talking about something that can go on between what he calls the **"old man"**—the **"old self"**— and this inferred **"new <u>self</u>."** *"We know that our **old self**"*—the old way of doing things—that old level of life—*"was crucified **with Him** so that the sinful body might be destroyed, and we might no longer be **enslaved to sin."** [7]*

Now we'll need our series **tonight** to explain **fully** in what sense we are freed from sin. **But I tell you church, this is one of the most important significant parts of the gospel. What Jesus Christ has done <u>for</u> me and what has happened <u>with</u> Him. He was <u>there</u>, and I was there.** When Jesus went up Calvary's road, **I went up Calvary's road. My old self—my flesh—my carnal life—my old way of doing things— my old way of thinking, it went along <u>with</u> Him. It was there, and thank God, I am <u>dead</u> to sin.** You'll notice it doesn't say that "sin is dead to me." Again, we'll talk about that further. **I am dead to sin. I am dead. I am no longer <u>answerable</u> to that. I am <u>freed</u> from that.** And so, I can **now** walk in newness of life by the power of Jesus Christ's resurrection.

I tell you this is **real.** This is something that can **happen.** There is a part of you, your old self, your old man, that can be crucified. That can die. It's possible for you to live in newness of life. **You will <u>not</u> get it by struggling. You will <u>not</u> get it by mysticism. You <u>will get it</u> by simple faith <u>knowing</u> that this is a truth. You will get it by <u>knowing</u> the truth.** And when the truth of that dawns upon your mind and understanding—

you—are—**free**. Then conscience, man, nor devil has any claim upon your life anymore. Those powers, you're dead to them.

We all remember the awful tragedy of the start of this country when men actually possessed and held **slaves**. The Civil War was fought, and Lincoln issued the Emancipation Proclamation. That meant at that **moment** every man possessed by another man was **free**. Now **unfortunately** there were some very evil **men** who didn't want that **news** to be **known** and in various pockets of the country they **still** tried to keep their slaves by **intimidating them**. Some slaves did not get that **information** and they went on living under their **serfdom**—under their **thralldom**—and under their **slavery**—simply because they didn't know it was **true! But it was true. It was the law of the land and there were Union forces to back it up. There was a dynamic power to make it <u>true</u>.** Unfortunately, there were also some who over many years of habit had a servile mentality and they were willing to go on **being** slaves **even** when they were **freed.**

I think something is often true like **that** in the Christian life. We have **so long** been **habituated** with some of these forces. We have so often **failed** and **struggled** that we sometime **despair** and go on believing that we are **still enslaved** by these **powers**. Now we'll see there are very real **objective powers** that must be broken. **But thank God, that the death of Jesus Christ has unleashed the <u>power</u> and by the resurrection of Jesus Christ there is that <u>gift</u> of the Holy Spirit that comes and gives you a <u>whole new way</u> of thinking. You can have a <u>whole new mind</u>. You can understand your <u>freedom</u> and you can enter into a life that is free from this <u>bondage</u> and this awful servitude. You can have a conscience that's lifted above the <u>law</u>, and you can begin to walk in <u>newness</u> of life. <u>Thank God, the grace of God, when it reigns</u>, leads us to <u>newness of life</u> through what Jesus has done <u>for us</u>, and what we have done <u>with Him</u>.** This wonderful Doctrine of Identification.

We'll have an occasion to allude to **this** in the series I'm sure, from time to time, but we're praying that the Holy Spirit will teach us. That He will make it **clear** to our **understanding.** To our **hearts.** Not that He'll give you some great spiritual **experience.** It's **not important** for you to experience anything. **It's what Jesus experienced that** <u>counts</u>. **It's** <u>His</u> **death. And if you'll keep your eyes on** <u>that</u>**, then you'll be set free. But if** <u>you're</u> **trying to do it,** <u>mystically</u> **identify with it,** <u>you're off base</u>**. And that's what** <u>most</u> **people are trying to do, is get identified with Him when it** <u>is</u> **a fact.**

I <u>AM</u> **crucified with Christ.** <u>It's true</u>**! I** <u>died</u> **to sin,** so obviously I'm not going to live in it any longer. Well **thank God,** for this beautiful, wonderful doctrine. And those of you who struggle to make it **so,** we're going to pray that the Spirit is going to make it perfectly clear how it's done. It's going to be by **grace through faith,** just like anything else. **Not** by your struggling. **Not** by your trying. You have been **planted together—**<u>with</u>**—Him,** Jesus Christ our Lord.

SERMON 6 ENDNOTES:

A Boeree, C. George. (date unknown). *Carl Jung 1875 - 1961.* Retrieved from https://webspace.ship.edu/cgboer/jung.html

SERMON 6 SCRIPTURE REFERENCES:

1 Romans 5:21 RSV

So that, as sin reigned in death, grace also might reign through righteousness to eternal life through Jesus Christ our Lord.

2 Romans 6:1-11 RSV

1 What shall we say then? Are we to continue in sin that grace may abound? 2 By no means! How can we who died to sin still live in it? 3 Do you not know that all of us who have been baptized into Christ Jesus were baptized into his death? 4 We were buried

therefore with him by baptism into death, so that as Christ was raised from the dead by the glory of the Father, we too might walk in newness of life. 5 For if we have been united with him in a death like his, we shall certainly be united with him in a resurrection like his. 6 We know that our old self was crucified with him so that the sinful body might be destroyed, and we might no longer be enslaved to sin. 7 For he who has died is freed from sin. 8 But if we have died with Christ, we believe that we shall also live with him. 9 For we know that Christ being raised from the dead will never die again; death no longer has dominion over him. 10 The death he died he died to sin, once for all, but the life he lives he lives to God. 11 So you also must consider yourselves dead to sin and alive to God in Christ Jesus.

[3] Romans 6:5 RSV

For if we have been united with him in a death like his, we shall certainly be united with him in a resurrection like his.

[4] Acts 17:26 KJV

And hath made of one blood all nations of men for to dwell on all the face of the earth, and hath determined the times before appointed, and the bounds of their habitation.

[5] Galatians 2:20 KJV

I am crucified with Christ: nevertheless I live; yet not I, but Christ liveth in me: and the life which I now live in the flesh I live by the faith of the Son of God, who loved me, and gave himself for me.

[6] Romans 6:5 KJV

For if we have been planted together in the likeness of his death, we shall be also in the likeness of his resurrection.

[7] Romans 6:6

We know that our old self was crucified with him so that the sinful body might be destroyed, and we might no longer be enslaved to sin.

SERMON 7

FREEDOM FROM SIN

*"We can walk freed—from—sin—but alive
—to God through Jesus Christ our Lord!"*

Romans 6, beginning with verse 1, *"What shall we say then? Are we to continue in sin that grace may abound? By no means! How can we who **died** to sin still live in it? Do you not know that all of us have been baptized into Christ Jesus we were baptized into his death? We were **buried** therefore with him by baptism into **death,** so that as Christ was raised **from the dead** by the **glory** of the Father, we too might walk in **newness of life.** If we have been united with him in a death like his, we shall certainly be united with him in a **resurrection** like his. We know that our **old self** was **crucified** <u>**with him**</u> so that the sinful body might be destroyed, and we might no longer be **enslaved** to sin. For he who has **died is** <u>**freed**</u> **from sin.***

"For he who has died is freed from sin."
- Romans 6:7 RSV

*But if we have died with Christ, we believe that we shall also **live** with him. For we know that Christ being raised from the **dead** will **never die again;** death no longer has dominion over him. The death he died he died to sin, **once"** — **"once for all,** but the life he lives he lives to God. So you* *also must consider **yourselves _dead_ to sin** and alive to God in Christ Jesus. Let not sin therefore **reign** in your mortal bodies, to make you obey their passions. Do not yield your members to sin as instruments of wickedness, but **yield yourselves to God** as men who have been brought from death to life, and **your members** to God as instruments of righteousness. For sin will have **no dominion** over you, since you are not under law **but** under grace."* [1]

Now, I believe that this section should be **titled** as follows, **"Freedom from Sin."** I think the key is **verse 7,** where the Apostle says, *"he who has **died is freed from sin.**"* [2]

I suppose that **all** of us, in one way or another, realize how serious is our individual and our collective attempt to deal with what we call **evil.** In some way or another, I think most of life is organized to cope with good and bad, right and wrong. We're trying to **handle, whatever** you want to call it, this thing in our nature that leaves us with guilt and leaves us in a state of **bondage.** The Bible calls it **sin.** Now it's very obvious what it includes. Over and over the Bible associates the manifestations with sin with various things. Whatever definition you may attach to it, we **recognize it** for what it **is.** I was impressed to note that there are at least six things closely identified with the subject of sin and it's these things that we want to **cope** with some way to diffuse if possible.

Sin for example is connected with what the Bible calls **blasphemy.** Matthew 12:31 describes *"sin and blasphemy."* [3] Now, blasphemy **basically** means to speak **evil.** It has to do with insolence, to insult, evil speaking, the type of things that comes out of our lives, the whole idea of the lack of **reverence** and all the things that have to do with **speech.**

Sin is very clearly identified with **deception and deceit.** Hebrews 3:13 says, *"Don't be **hardened** to the **deceitfulness** of sin."* [4] This has to do with **lying,** with **dishonesty—** **deception—cheating**—things we do in secret and all that. It has to do with **deception.**

Sin is also identified with **desire—lust.** James 1:15, *"When **lust** is conceived, it brings forth **sin**."* [5] Now, this word translated **"lust"** really means a reaching **after** satisfaction or **pleasure.** It's wanting what is not **ours,** or **uncontrolled passion.**

Sin is also identified with **lawlessness.** 1 John 3:4 says, *"**Sin is lawlessness**."* [6] And that basically means doing what's **wrong—breaking rules**—of being **rebellious,** primarily.

Sin is also clearly associated with **wrongdoing.** 1 John 5:17, it says, *"All wrongdoing is **sin**."* [7] Here's what we mean by being **bad**—by being **evil**—by being **unjust**—and all these things are manifestations of and associated with sin.

Number 6, sin is identified with **partiality.** James 2:9, *"If you show partiality, **you commit sin**."* [8] Now, that means being full of **prejudice— bigotry—clannishness—narrow-minded**—being born out of our own little **"world"** as it were—not able to understand the truth.

But **primarily sin, this evil, comes out of what we call the "self-life."** Now that's a little bit difficult for us to see at times because we know that there are various levels of **"self"** within us which we want to talk about in just a **moment.** But if you'll just add the word **"ish"** to that word **"self"** then you get the implication. **Sin is "self—ish."** It's putting the **"self"** at the **center** and putting it in a position where it **will not submit.** As Paul defines the flesh in Romans chapter 8, verse 7, he says, *"**The mind that is set on**"*—what he calls— *"**the flesh**," "is hostile to God;"*—it has this **enmity**—bad will. And he says, *"**It does not submit**."* Now, that's the word, **it does not "submit."** He goes on to **add**—*"to God's law."* [9] But by submission, he's getting at the heart of **sin.** Sin is a "self" which **will not submit—"self" is on the throne—it's full of pride—it will not yield—it will not be open—it will not trust—it will not give—** that's "**self**." And it doesn't necessarily mean that it's any different from a person who's humble. Somebody was saying in our Bible study Thursday night that, "There's the pride of the worm." Well, some people are **like that.** They've just got the pride of the **worm,** you know. And that's still **self,** believe me. It doesn't make much difference whether you educate it or sophisticate it, it's still there.

And that leads us to the various ways that men cope with the **flesh, sin, the sin nature or evil.** Now there are two popular ways which are **false ways.** I'd like to look at those and then we are going to look at the **Biblical way** and we're going to see what the Bible solutions are to have **freedom from sin—to be <u>free</u> from sin. What a gospel! What a hope. What a possibility. But many people get off track because they start on a false road and the most popular method is by a self-reformation.** We try to **improve the "self".** Now, I would say that's the leading notion. That's **instinctively** what your mind tells you to do—is that if you're going to change your nature—your life—you ought to **get better.** And so, you have the **reformation idea** that you ought to **reform** or **get better.** Now, you see the **problem** with this, is that it is a **vast misreading** of the nature of sin. It's born out of a legalistic understanding of sin which **makes sin a series of moral missteps that you can overcome by the power of your <u>will</u>. But let me tell you that <u>self-improvement</u> is not the Biblical solution to overcoming and being freed from <u>sin</u>. <u>As a matter of fact, you can't make this self any better! Now that's an amazing statement, but the Bible is emphatic that the self is unredeemable!</u>**

Now, we've talked about this on earlier occasions but there are many Christian people who are **deluded** at this point. They often, for example, quote 2 Corinthians 5:17, that says, *"If any man be in Christ, he's a new creature; old things are passed away, all things will become new."* [10] And they imagine that their "self" life, their "flesh" life, has been **regenerated.** That's not what 2 Corinthians 5:17 is talking about. It says if any man is in Christ, he is a part of the new creation. It's a **new creation** life. It is not a regeneration—or a transformation—or a redemption of your "self-life." Your sin nature is <u>unredeemable</u>! It can<u>not</u> and will <u>not</u> be changed! And if you have been deluded by the doctrine of self-reformation or self-improvement, you're on the wrong track. Someone said it's like a woman trying to scrub a dirt floor. It just gets **muddier.** You can't redeem it.

Now we've talked about this on other occasions, but I remind you again that there is a part of you—your "self-life"—your "flesh"—what the Bible calls the *sarx* ᴬ or the "flesh"—**is unredeemable. It can—not— be—changed! It can only—sin! That's all!** You cannot change **that.** And if you'll get that clear in your mind, you'll see then that this **cannot be by self-improvement,** or the doctrine of **moral reformation. That is NOT Biblical teaching.** That is **carnal knowledge.** This has what Paul calls a certain "appearance of wisdom." Paul refers to this type of thing in Colossians 2:23, he says this has an—*"appearance of **wisdom**"*—such as—*"rigor of devotion and self-abasement and severity to the body"*—as you're trying to improve. But he says, *"they are of <u>no value</u> in checking the indulgence of the flesh."* [11]

And so, you must know that you **don't improve** the self. The self is **not improved.** It is **unredeemable.** It is not **changed.** It is **unchangeable.** And so, when we realize that we have a sinful nature, living in **dying bodies,** but **redeemable,** as we talked about on other occasions, then we'll see that you are **not** going to improve your life or be freed from sin by self-improvement and by **moral reformation.** That is **not** the way it's done.

The second false way and also a very popular way—and it may surprise you to hear me say this—but it is also **not** the way to be freed from sin. **Most** people **try** to fight it. They try what we might call the technique of **"resistance."** They think, you see, it they can just somehow **cope** with sin, and usually it's born out of **self-effort.** Now this is not the notion of **self-improvement** but it's the thought of **self-effort. That somehow, I've got it in me somewhere. I know I can cope with this and I'm going to <u>try</u> harder. Now I know I failed that time, but I'll vow again and I'm going to try again. And so, this doctrine is the doctrine of resistance to sin.** Now, that has one **valid** part to it, as we'll see. But let me tell you that if your "self" is trying to resist sin, **it's a losing battle.**

This is for two reasons. First of all, we must understand further and carefully about the nature of **sin. Sin is not just simply a series of moral missteps that you keep doing over and over again. Sin is an objective <u>power</u> that <u>enslaves you</u> and <u>is stronger than your will</u>! Now, if you could redeem your "self" by your <u>will</u>, you would not have needed a Savior. But so many people are <u>duped</u> at this point. They think they can <u>try</u> harder,** and I call them Avis Christians. [B] They're **trying harder** by **self-effort. That's a losing battle. It cannot be done by resistance to sin. Sin is greater than you are,** and this chapter talks about our being **slaves** to sin. You look at it very carefully in Romans chapter 6 and you'll see that it's talking about a serfdom—a thralldom—where we're absolutely **slaves to sin.** I tell you sin is a **very real power.** That's why sin ought to be spelled with a capital "S." **It is a very real thing.** It's very closely tied into **death** in the Bible, and **death** is an **objective power.** You could no more master **sin,** any more than you can master **death.** Now you just try to keep from dying. Just try. Brother, you may exercise. You may jog. You may improve your diet, and you may take all kinds of drugs, and go to all kinds of doctors, but brother **you're going to die.** Now you may stave it off for a few weeks, or hopefully if you keep healthy, for a few years. But there is an **objective power called death** that's going to **claim you!**

Now, Jesus Christ is redeeming us in **stages.** The **<u>last</u> enemy that will be destroyed is <u>death</u>, but thank God, Jesus Christ has come into <u>this life</u> and torn down the <u>dominion</u> of the power of sin.** So, it's possible for us at the level of the Spirit to be—**freed—from—sin.** But you cannot do this by self-effort, and more people are deluded at that point. They **struggle** and they **try** by **resisting sin** and it generally only leads them into frustration and despair—and they wonder what's **wrong** with them. Well, the problem is your will is in bondage. It's in bondage to an objective power called sin. It's just not some little bad things you **do. It's a terrible power that enslaves humanity** from which **they— must—be delivered. This takes a** <u>deliverance</u>**.** This is why the Apostle talks, I think, about a **deliverance doctrine.**

 "But thanks be to God, that, whereas ye were servants of sin, ye became obedient from the heart to that form of teaching whereunto ye were delivered;" - Romans 6:17 ASV

He says in verse 17 of chapter 6, *"thanks be to God, that you who were once **slaves** of sin have become obedient from the heart"*—the Revised Version says—*"that standard of teaching to which you were committed."* [12]—or the Authorized Version (ASV) says, *"that form of teaching whereby **you were delivered**."* [13] So, here we've got this **deliverance doctrine,** where we were once **slaves** of sin.

We've got to see that there are two false starts. Number one, it is not self-improvement. We are **not** talking about the doctrine of **reformation. And I can guarantee you that the best that man has to offer, whether it be education, or psychology, or whatever it may be; does <u>not</u> have the answers to the problem of <u>sin</u>.**

As a matter of fact, Henry Link of Harvard, whose done a great deal in psychological testing—he says, *"There **is** no correlation between education and character."* He says, *"on the contrary, it may very well be that the more educated a person is the more their character has the tendency* to *deteriorate, because they become **prideful**."* [C] That's **Henry Link.** So, here's an **amazing insight** that just moral reformation is not the answer. And I'm exposed to professional people **constantly,** and I see all of this going on, and I can tell you there are **no** solutions to the power of sin except the blood of Jesus Christ and His marvelous redeeming force. Thank God for what Jesus can do. And, by the way, having said that, I know you **know** that I am not taking an anti-educational standpoint. I believe God would have us to educate ourselves to the fullest. I don't believe in this anti-life notion at all, but I believe that ought to be harmonizing discipline to the Spirit and to the great gospel of our Lord Jesus Christ. He wants to educate our **minds,** but I tell you that salvation is **not** by education. Salvation is by the dynamic of the **Spirit.**

So that leads us to the Biblical solution. If it's not by reformation, and if it's not even by **resistance** or by self-effort, **then how is this done?** Well, the answer is so **shocking** that you **can't believe it.** The Bible says **it's by** a resurrection. The **Bible says** it's by a **death. That you do it by dying! But now you see, how can this <u>be</u>?** So, here's **sin,** and it presses its claim upon you. Here's this **sin nature** and it's coming close to your **heart** and wants to grip your **life.** Now normally, we generally think now, "I'll **try** harder. I'll try to resist **this.**" Do you know what the Bible says to do? The Bible says to commit suicide. *(Don chuckles)* Roll over. Don't play dead but be **dead.** You are **dead.** The solution is that we are incorporated into the death and the resurrection of the Lord Jesus Christ.

Now, let's see if we can make this clear because this may be ever so many words, unless the Lord Jesus will reveal it to us by His Spirit. Now first of all, we've got to understand the lesson of the **crucifixion** and that of **death.** Now Paul's leading statement is verse 7, *"He who has died is freed from sin."* [2] He used the illustration of a dead man. Now if you were **dead,** literally physically dead, could anything claim you? If we kicked you, would you bark back? If we pinched you, would you say anything? **No, you're dead!** And we've used the illustration that if you owed somebody a sum of money, could they collect? Let's suppose you ran a red light, and the policeman took in after you, but it scared you so much you had a heart attack. Could he give you a ticket? (*Congregation laughs*) **He might, but would you go to court?** (*More laughter*) <u>No, you're dead! Can you see that? That these powers have no control over a DEAD man</u>! So that's Paul's great illustration.

Now secondly, he says, in verse 10 *"that <u>Christ</u> died to sin, once for all."* [14] **That the Lord Jesus Christ is <u>beyond</u> sin. He is <u>beyond</u> law. He is <u>beyond</u> wrath. He is beyond sin and Jesus at this moment is beyond <u>death</u>! And then he says, to make the story complete, *"that— we—have—been—baptized—into—his—death"* [15]—meaning that Jesus Christ has incorporated us—has identified with us—in His death. Now Jesus of course, is talking about this level within us, this level of the "self" which the Bible calls the "flesh."**

You need to understand the difference between the flesh and the spirit. Now, they are **not** primarily anything within us. It is true that the Bible does include, at times, the flesh as being the **body** but you are **not** to think that the "flesh," in and of itself, is the **human body.** The human body basically is neutral. It is true however that the sin principle lays hold upon the body as the natural ally because the body is **dying.** The body has **death** at work in it. **It has not yet been redeemed. It is redeemable but your flesh is <u>not</u> redeemable.** So, when we talk about the **flesh,** we are not talking necessarily about **our body** nor are you talking about anything **in** you. I don't think the same is true with **your spirit.** When the Bible talks about the **spirit** neither is it talking about some **"thing"** necessarily within us, a metaphysical "thing." **It is talking about two <u>powers</u>. Two energies. Two life levels that can control <u>all of you</u>! You can be <u>totally in the spirit</u>, or you can be totally, as it were, in the flesh.**

I was impressed the way one of Hal Lindsey's books [D] put it, and somebody loaned me that little book. I think it was Ray down here. I thought it was a very good comment. You remember the four things I told you, perhaps the other day about sin? I was impressed to see how it's practically repeated here. Here's what he had to say about the **flesh** and it's worth passing on.

Number one, he said, "It is a basic **nature** or a **principle** which operates within us from the time we are born. This nature is **rebellion** against God"—as I read Romans chapter 8—"It is **self-centered**—it **wants** its own **way**." Now, that's that attitude—that **disposition**—that **energy**—that **power**—that wants to operate in your life and of which all these other evil things are born.

Secondly, he says, and properly so, "It is an inseparable part of our material body. **It can not be eradicated.**" Now if you'll hold to that, you're on the right track. **Sin can not be eradicated—"until we receive our transformed resurrected bodies."** That's why you can't **fight it.** The fight doctrine is a wrong doctrine.

Third, "Though it cannot be eradicated, **its power to operate in the life of the Christian can be neutralized by our being united with Jesus Christ in His death to sin. The flesh has no right to reign in the Christian's life any longer, and its power is broken in our lives when we count this as being true**"—when we understand this great truth. So, we're talking about a **death** to the "**old** self"—the **old** life—this **old disposition**—this **old energy**—that wants to reach out and claim you. **Now let me tell you that it's always there. Be careful to notice that it says, "we are dead to sin." It does not say that your sin nature is dead. Now that's where many Christians have gotten off. They thought that they somehow got better and better, and that their flesh was regenerated. And again, I tell you that is not true. Your flesh is there constantly, day and night. At any given moment you can lapse under** the power of that flesh, and you will <u>automatically</u> sin, because the sin is enmity with God, and it cannot submit to the law of God.

So, the Christian way, is you <u>don't walk in it</u>. You don't fall <u>prey</u> to the power or the dominion of that because the redemptive death of Jesus Christ has obtained a judgment against it. And when that power wants to claim you, you can look at that thing and say, "I'm a dead man. You can't touch me. I'm not answerable to you. You have no control over me because Jesus Christ has set me free." And you can walk in the power of that Spirit. But you see that flesh can also claim you. It's there to claim you at any given moment. And that's why a lot of people say, "Well, these Christians, they do as bad of things as the world. Of course they do! We're in the flesh. We're just like anybody else. We do just as miserable things—just—as—miserable—if we walk in the power of that.

And so, the first truth, is to **know,** that Jesus Christ has rendered us **dead**, as it were. We have gone through the processes of His death and then also into the aspect of His resurrection. Now you know what I think it really means to be dead. It means, of course, what Jesus Christ has done for us on the cross. But from **our** viewpoint do you know what it really means to be dead? It **means** that you must **know** that you **absolutely** and in no possible way can face sin on your own. **You must <u>know</u> beyond a shadow of a doubt that the Holy Spirit of God—must—do—this—for—you!** That means that you're dead. But as long as you're alive, as long as you think there's something within me, some good within me, then you're going to keep trying harder. I'm going to try harder. But the <u>key</u> to it is to roll over and die. That is to admit "I can't do it!" To come to what the Bible calls an end of yourself.

Now you remember that **very graphic** illustration of circumcision in the Bible. **Why <u>did</u> God circumcise the male reproductive organ? Because it's the center of his life. His ability to produce life. He was**

dead. He had to be cut off and that was a tremendous <u>sign</u> that man in his nature could not reproduce himself. But we think we can do it. And God says, "Cut it off!" And that's our problem. We won't lay over **and die**. We somehow think, "No, wait a minute, I can do it," and we try, and we try. And God says, "Okay, just keep trying; until you stop, I can't release my Spirit to you." You see, the Holy Spirit can only be **released** in us when <u>you quit trying,</u> because you're going to get some of the benefits from it. **If it's by works** then you're going to get some of the glory for it. **But I tell you God won't share His glory with <u>anybody</u>. And that's why God has to do all the work. This is why it's a <u>supernatural life</u>!**

God has to circumcise our hearts and gives us, as it were, a heart transplant. We talked about that the other day, you remember? You've got to have a heart transplant. You've got a bad heart. **You've** got a heart that's got to be taken out. There has to be a **new** heart that comes in and as long as you'll walk in the power of that **new** life then, you see, you'll be able to walk in newness of life. Otherwise, you cannot, and you will not.

And so, the Biblical solution is by **resurrection.** It's by **realizing** that we have been incorporated into the death and the resurrection of our Lord Jesus Christ. Now, we know that it's possible for these two energies to be operating within us—two life levels. The Bible calls it the **spirit** and **flesh.** And the question is which one of them is going to operate in you?

You know, a person might knock on the door. By the way, we can see that there is a clever little device today called transactional analysis, where it says the person can be in one of three ego states at any given moment. You can be in what's called a parent ego state. You can be in an adult ego state, or you can be in a child ego state. Let's suppose now you've been hurt. You're like a rebellious child, an angry child. Or let's suppose you're like an angry critical parent or something. Now somebody comes to the door. Who goes to the door? Your parent may go to the door within you. Your adult may go to the door, or you may go calm and cool and collective you see.

Well, life is like that. Life is **constantly** knocking on my door. Which is going to go answer? Will it be my "flesh" or will it be my "spirit?" Now this may seem very juvenile to you, but I tell you I literally have to do this. **I literally** will picture Jesus on the cross and when something that wants to come to the door where I might be "in my flesh"—or I would be in any of these things we've talked about—hostile—enmity—not willing to submit—I want my "self-life"—I see Jesus, **literally,** hanging on the cross. The Holy Spirit fixed a picture in my mind years ago and I can see him there and I say, "Jesus, You died to this and I died with You." And I'm telling you folks this **works.** I don't know whether it's what happens, but I can literally feel stuff draining right out of me. **It literally drains right out of me,** because Jesus Christ has taken the **power** of that from me.

Now, I would like to say that the Bible teaches **we are freed from sin. It does <u>not</u> teach that we are sin<u>less</u>. Please, get the difference. To be freed from sin is not the same thing as sinlessness.** I do not believe in the doctrine of Wesleyan perfection—as it is sometimes taught—that sin is eradicated from us, and we are sinless. I do not find that in the New Testament.

I do believe; however, it is possible to be **freed from sin.** That means that its power can be **broken** so that the **Spirit** can go to the door as it were and **answer** when **life** comes to knock at the door of my heart. I can answer it in the **power** of the Holy Spirit. Now, that sin is always there to claim me in one way or another but thank God the **power** of the Spirit can keep me freed from sin.

We talked about our prisoners of war that we brought out of prison camps. What for? We put them right back in the military. We took them

out of a prisoner of war camp to put them right back in the army. And that's what God does. **Now,** we can come to the doctrine of **resistance** against sin—or **coping** with sin—**fighting** sin, **but if you're doing it that side of death and resurrection, it's a losing battle. It's—still—done— out—of your—self-life.** It is **then** you can look sin in the face and say, "You have **no** answer over me. I'm sorry, I'm a dead man. You cannot control my life anymore."

I believe it's possible to walk in newness of life but, number one, we've got to come to an end of ourselves. And number two; we've got to trust **absolutely—always—completely—and entirely—**the Lord Jesus Christ and the gift of His Holy Spirit. If at **any** given moment, any second, you start to trust your self-life, it's **then** you're **right again** under the power of sin. You're in the flesh **right again.** Sin will claim you. But, if Jesus by His **mighty** Holy Spirit, will walk in us and live in us, **we can be—freed—from—sin.**

Thank God this can happen instantaneously. Once you understand it, it can open up a whole new life for you. I do want to say this; however, by word of caution, I do not want this message to be misunderstood. I believe even with this great truth that I'm teaching you; we still must **grow in grace and in knowledge of our Lord Jesus Christ.** There still is room for maturity and for growth and for **realizing** that these truths somehow come home to our heart in various ways. Some people have heard this doctrine and then they get discouraged. They say, "You know it didn't work for me." What they've got to understand is that **often** this **is a process** as God is revealing to us our **corruption**—our **flesh life**— and our **weakness**—our impotence. And I know periodically, it has to be taught to me again and again. We go on growing even with this marvelous doctrine of what Jesus has done for us through His cross and resurrection.

Well folks, I tell you, this is good news. It is **possible** for you to be freed from **sin. Jesus the Savior has broken it. Now, I don't know what has a hold of your life, but I'm glad to say that Jesus Christ can break every <u>power</u>. This is a supernatural life; it's not making your old character better. It's not trying to get good education. It's a—whole— new— supernatural—life. It's a heart transplant. Brother you can be a different person. Then you have to give the glory only to God,** and every step you take and every breath you breathe you know that as long as that new heart is beating Jesus is **doing it** and you know you've got to live there. Otherwise, if you fall back into your self-life, it's all over. It's right back into the mud again.

Thank God it's possible to walk in that newness of life. And some of you that have been so discouraged and you've looked within yourself to improve yourself or with self-effort—I've got some news for you. The Holy Spirit of God can come and do it instantaneously in your life and bring you right up into the level of the Spirit.

Number one, you've got to quit trying. You've got to die. Go ahead. Roll over and die. Quit. You can't do it anyway. You've tried all. You've read all these books and you've tried all this self-improvement. You're taking classes here or there and you're in counseling groups and so on. **Wonderful!** Keep that up but realize that Jesus Christ does it by His Spirit. So, it's really suicide or let's call it homicide. We're crucified with Christ. The Holy Spirit puts us to death. Here it is and all those energies of the flesh that have dominated you and destroyed you and made you such a miserable person that you are. You can walk free of that in the Spirit of God.

You want a new heart? *(Don repeats)* You want a new heart? I tell you I do. I'm not a very nice person. I'm **flesh** just like the rest of you are and I've seen the best of it. I've traveled in the highest of circles, spiritually. I know hundreds of ministers, supervisors, deans of Life

Bible College. They don't impress me. *(Congregation laughs – most likely because the Dean of Students was in the service)* They're flesh. They're flesh—flesh.

So, you see it's available to everybody. That's why it's a **gift.** That's why Jesus gets all the **glory** because it's a supernatural life that He gives by His Holy Spirit. It's called, "walking in the Spirit." Oh, I want that. I want that newness of life. May Jesus teach all of us this Doctrine of Identification and see how we can **walk freed—from—sin—but alive— to God through Jesus Christ our Lord.**

SERMON 7 ENDNOTES:

A *sarx,* pronounced: *sarx,* meaning: the flesh, Strong's Greek Dictionary #4561

B Avis Christians is a reference to the Avis Car Rental company that had the tag line: "We Try Harder" as part of their advertising.

C Link, Henry C. (1937). *The Return To Religion.* (pp.58,67,103), New York, New York: The Macmillan

D Lindsey, Hal & Carlson, Carole C. (1972). *Satan Is Alive and Well on Planet Earth.* (pp.68-69), Grand Rapids: Zondervan Pub. House

SERMON 7 SCRIPTURE REFERENCES:

[1] Romans 6:1-14 (RSV)

1 What shall we say then? Are we to continue in sin that grace may abound? 2 By no means! How can we who died to sin still live in it? 3 Do you not know that all of us who have been baptized into Christ Jesus were baptized into his death? 4 We were buried therefore with him by baptism into death, so that as Christ was raised from the dead by the glory of the Father, we too might walk in newness of life. 5 For if we have been united with him in a death like his, we shall certainly be united with him in a resurrection like his. 6 We know that our old self was crucified with him so that the sinful body might be destroyed, and we might no longer be enslaved to sin. 7 For he who has died is freed from sin. 8 But if we have died with Christ, we believe that we shall also live with him. 9 For we know that Christ being raised from the dead will never die again; death no longer has dominion over him. 10 The death he died he died to sin, once for all, but the life he lives he lives to God. 11 So you also must consider yourselves dead to sin and alive to God in Christ Jesus. 12 Let not sin therefore reign in your mortal bodies, to make you obey their passions. 13 Do not yield your members to sin as instruments of wickedness, but yield yourselves to God as men who have been brought from death to life, and your members to God as instruments of righteousness. 14 For sin will have no dominion over you, since you are not under law but under grace.

[2] Romans 6:7 (RSV)

For he who has died is freed from sin.

[3] Matthew 12:31 (RSV)

Therefore I tell you, every sin and blasphemy will be forgiven men, but the blasphemy against the Spirit will not be forgiven.

[4] Hebrews 3:13 (RSV)

But exhort one another every day, as long as it is called "today," that none of you may be hardened by the deceitfulness of sin.

[5] James 1:15 (KJV)

Then when lust hath conceived, it bringeth forth sin: and sin, when it is finished, bringeth forth death.

[6] 1 John 3:4 (RSV)

Every one who commits sin is guilty of lawlessness; sin is lawlessness.

[7] 1 John 5:17 (RSV)

All wrongdoing is sin, but there is sin which is not mortal.

[8] James 2:9 (RSV)

But if you show partiality, you commit sin, and are convicted by the law as transgressors.

[9] Romans 8:7 (RSV)

For the mind that is set on the flesh is hostile to God; it does not submit to God's law, indeed it cannot.

[10] 2 Corinthians 5:17 (KJV)

Therefore if any man be in Christ, he is a new creature: old things are passed away; behold, all things are become new.

[11] Colossians 2:23 (RSV)

These have indeed an appearance of wisdom in promoting rigor of devotion and self-abasement and severity to the body, but they are of no value in checking the indulgence of the flesh.

[12] Romans 6:17 (RSV)

But thanks be to God, that you who were once slaves of sin have become obedient from the heart to the standard of teaching to which you were committed.

[13] Romans 6:17 (ASV)

But thanks be to God, that, whereas ye were servants of sin, ye became obedient from the heart to that form of teaching whereunto ye were delivered.

[14] Romans 6:10 (RSV)

The death he died he died to sin, once for all, but the life he lives he lives to God.

[15] Romans 6:3 (RSV)

Do you not know that all of us who have been baptized into Christ Jesus were baptized into his death?

SERMON 8

HOW TO YIELD TO GOD – PART 1

*"We can walk in what the Bible calls 'newness of life,'
not the 'old self,' but this 'new life!'"*

This is the eighth sermon in a series that we are bringing from Romans chapters 6, 7 and 8, and I invite your attention one more time to the first fourteen verses of Romans chapter 6. We'll look at that beautiful—powerful—profound—precious—passage one more time. Now, for those of you who are visiting this morning, and this is your first in the series, we're learning what it means to be **under grace,** because these three chapters are an exposition of what it means to be **under grace and not under <u>law</u>.**

What happens when **grace abounds?** When grace is **all** you know? That grace might **reign** like a **king** in your life and be the **dominant passion** of your life force? Grace might reign to eternal life. What if the question comes up if we are under **grace** and everything is provided and **supplied,** we're not under law which means there **is no claim** upon us, then what are the consequences? What happens? And logically, you would **think** that a person would just continue in evil or perhaps in sin, they're only under grace.

So, Paul addressed himself to that as he says, *"What shall we say then? Are we to continue in* **sin***"*—doing wrong and so on—*"that grace may* **abound?***"*—of course not—*"By no means! How can we who* **died** *to* *sin still live in it? Do you not know that all of us who have been baptized into Christ Jesus were baptized into his* **death?** *We were buried therefore* **with him** *by baptism into* **death,** *so that as Christ was raised from the dead by the glory of the Father, we too might walk in* **newness** *of life. For if we have been united with him in a* **death** *like his, we shall* **certainly** *be united with him in a resurrection like* **his.** *We know that our old self was* **crucified with him** *so that the* **sinful body** *might be"*—rendered inoperative—*"destroyed,"*—or made ineffective—*"so that we might no longer be* **enslaved** *to sin. For he who has* **died** *is freed from sin. But if we have* **died** *with Christ, we believe that we shall also* **live with him.** *We know that Christ being raised from the dead will never die again; death no longer has dominion over him.* **The death he died he died to sin, once for all,"**—notice that important concept—*"but the life he lives he"*—also—*"lives to God. So you must* **consider yourselves** *dead to sin and alive to God in Christ Jesus. Don't let sin* **reign** *in your mortal bodies, to make you obey their passions. Don't* **yield** *your members* **to sin** *as instruments of wickedness,* **but yield yourselves to God as men who have been brought from death to life,"**—that's another very important concept—**"and** *your members to God* **as instruments of righteousness. For sin will have** <u>**no**</u> <u>**dominion**</u> **over you,"**—Why?—*"since you are not under* **law** *but under grace."* [1] Now you can see these are some **very profound ideas.** Somebody was saying today, "That's heavy duty." (*Don chuckles*) Heavy duty. But we're praying that we'll have a proper understanding of all this and that will become very clear to us.

Now we've established many truths but there is one thing that we must consider before we leave this section and that is, **what do** <u>**we**</u> **do?** What's **our** part in this? If we're under grace and there's nothing for us to do, no claim upon us, **is** there any role that we have? What is our response? And you'll notice that there are three things that were enjoined upon us, and I'd like to underscore those for this to become a reality in our lives.

"Do you not know that all of us who have been baptized into Christ Jesus were baptized into his death?" - Romans 6:3 RSV

First of all, you must **"know."** Romans 6:3 *"Do you not <u>know</u>?"* [2] Now so many things depend upon knowledge. Understanding. If a person is **badly** informed, or misinformed, or has no information, can he act? Will he know what to do? Well, no. That's true in all of life. If a person doesn't know how to drive a car, can he drive a car? Let's suppose a person didn't even **know** that an automobile existed—had ever been invented—would he ever think about driving one? Why, no! He'd think of walking or riding horses, I suppose. You've got to **know.** It's very simple. The first thing is **knowledge.** Does it make any difference what we believe? **It makes <u>all</u> the <u>difference</u> in this world!** Your **philosophy**— your **lifestyle**—your **theology**—your **religion**—your **faith**—**what <u>you</u> believe** is going to determine **your conduct and your life and the kind of man that you are.** You've got to **know** many basic things. And so, Paul through this chapter is saying, "Now I want to inform you. **Don't— you—know**—certain things as being true?"

Now, only very **briefly** will I touch on this point this morning, because the first seven sermons have been a form of **knowledge.** I've been talking about all the **knowledge,** the various things that we could **know.** But let me just very briefly for the purposes of our lesson this morning, see what we ought to know. You need to **know** that there can be two levels of life that can flow out of you potentially. There can be an **"old self"** and a **"new self."** The Bible calls it **"flesh"** and **"spirit."** That's the Bible terminology. Now, I just mean the "good you" and the "bad you." You can draw your life from two sources of **energies.** You can **live out** what the Bible calls the **"flesh"**—that can dominate you and control you—it can be your **master**—it can be your **lord.**

Now, I don't need to dwell on that. The Bible will tell you in detail what that is in Romans and Galatians. But I was reading the Amplified Version only this morning about Romans 8:6, and here's the way it translated essentially what this "flesh" is. *"The flesh is **death**, a **death** that comprises all the **miseries** arising from sin."*[3] That's what it is. If you want to know what the "flesh" is, **it's all the <u>miseries</u>—all the <u>condemnation</u>—all the <u>guilt</u>—all the <u>frustration</u>—all the <u>bondage</u>—all the hang ups—all of this thing we call the "flesh."**

Now, you can **live at that level,** and most of us do. We live out of the energies of our **"old self."** Or you can live at the level what the Bible calls the Spirit. And the Amplified translates Romans 8:6, *"But the Spirit is life and [soul] peace."*[3] Now, I like that. I don't know what "soul" peace is, but I like the translation. It just sounds good when I said it. I read the words and I thought, "Boy, that sounds good to have some "soul peace" (*Congregation chuckles*)—soul food." (*more chuckles*) Have some "soul peace." (*Don and congregation chuckle again*)

You need to know that you can have two levels of life flowing out of you. **You need to <u>know</u> that the flesh does not necessarily have to dominate you. It does not have to have <u>control</u>.** And the **reason** for that is you can **know** that you have been **involved with Jesus Christ in His death.** Now, that's the basic knowledge that you need to know.

Now we've said that there are two basic truths in Romans, and with reference to what Jesus Christ has done. The first is the Doctrine of Substitution—**What Jesus Christ—has—done—<u>for</u>—you. When Jesus died on the cross, what was happening? God was laying the sins of the world upon Him. Jesus died—for—our—sins—and the sins of the whole world.** The sins of the world are not being **imputed** to them. Now they don't know all that. Unfortunately, they don't know the good news and if they reject the reconciliation and will not accept that atonement, they must **bear** the penalty and guilt of their own sin. **But what good news—that all the sins past, present and future were meted on Jesus**

Christ! That's good news! That's gospel! You don't have to live under condemnation. You can have a **conscience** that's accepted in God's sight. That's what we preach—the grace of God.

But secondly, you need to **know,** that something goes on **subjectively.** Now, Jesus died **for you,** but what's going on, this whole **seething mass** of the old man, and the flesh and the spirit? How are you going to handle your life really and practically? Now, you need to **know something** about the Doctrine of **Identification** or **Incorporation.** That we are <u>involved</u> **with Jesus in His death,** and it has reference to what the Bible calls the "old self." Now, we need to make it very **clear,** as we have done earlier, that your flesh does not **die,** but you die. **You're dead** and the flesh no longer has authority over you. Is it still there? **Oh, yes!** A lot of people are **mistakenly** informed that when they're converted their flesh is transformed. **Your flesh is irredeemable!** Nothing happens to your flesh when you get converted. It goes right on brother, and it wants to live right there in the power of it. The only thing you can do is **crucify it or be dead to it.** This is the scriptural teaching. And so many people get off on this, and they're constantly frustrated and confused, and they don't know how to walk in victory. They do not have this knowledge or this understanding. And so, you need to know these basic truths.

 "So you also must consider yourselves dead to sin and alive to God in Christ Jesus." - Romans 6:11 RSV

But the Apostle goes on to say a second thing, and that's in Romans chapter 6, verse 11, *"You must also* **consider** *yourselves* **dead to sin** *and* **alive** *to God in Christ Jesus."* [4] Now, this is the second thing and in the King James Version, it is translated **reckon.** *"You must* **reckon** *yourselves dead to sin."* [5] The Revised Version says, *"You must* **consider** *yourselves dead to sin."* [4]

Now, I must get a tiny bit technical with you today, because it's **very** important. What I'm about to tell, you in my opinion, has such a fine element that it **demands** your utmost attention—because I know in my own understanding there was a problem along this line and I have taught this to others and they have been confused as well—because many people **think** that **by reckoning** you must **produce** this kind of death. That somehow you must, by your own mental, emotional, striving so identify with Jesus and **psych yourself out** almost until you **feel** this thing is true. Well, let me just say this, that reckoning does not produce this **death.** You **do not produce** this death that we're talking about.

I want to exegete or talk about this word, if I may this morning. I want to talk to you about this word translated "reckoning" or "considering." Some of you are taking Greek in our church and you'll appreciate a little lesson, won't you. This is the Greek word, *logizomai.* ^ We hear our word *logos, theology* and all these words come out of that. *Logos.* Now, *logizomai* has **three implications** to it. Three shades of meaning and they all play a part in "reckoning" or "considering."

Now the **first** and the Greek Lexicons say that *logizomai* **means:** Number one, it is a **calculation,** or an **evaluation,** or an **estimate.** Now this has a little bit of an **advance** on just **knowing** a thing. When you **calculate it**—you **reason** it through—you **get an understanding** on it—and you **base it** upon some **facts.** Now, we were talking about the piece of property that we need to buy, and are buying hopefully, if the congregation approves it. But we were asked to make an **offer** for this piece of property by our board of directors. So, we submitted an offer, and the man said on the phone, he said, "I'll have to calculate about that. I'll have to do a little reckoning." And so, he **reckoned,** and he didn't take the offer. (*Don and congregation chuckles*) So, he **reckoned** that he had paid so much for the property. He had **improved** the property so much and he has to **relocate his business.** He **reckoned** and he **calculated** and says, "I don't want to take your offer." (*Don chuckling*) So, **we** did a little **reckoning,** (*Don continues to chuckle*) and we're coming back with a **counteroffer** (*Don chuckles again*).

Alright, what is reckoning then? It is **simply** a **realization** of the **fact** of what you've got. As a matter of fact, this word "*logizomai,*" is a term out of **bookkeeping.** You have to keep **books.** It's a **mathematical term,** based upon some **facts.** Now you can't reckon anything more than is there. **You can't reckon that you're dead, if you're <u>not dead</u>. But reckoning is a realization based upon a calculation,** and that means an understanding of what Jesus has **done.** This same word, for example, is used in the **wages** that is paid to a man. Romans 4:4 where Paul says, "*to one who works*"—a workman, an employee—"*his wages are not reckoned*"—*logizomai,* calculated or estimated—"*as a **gift** but as <u>his due</u>.*" [6] If you've gone and worked, your boss has that coming to you, that's all. If you work for five dollars an hour, and you work forty hours, I reckon you've got two hundred dollars coming. That's **based** upon a fact, you see. So, I want you to see how important this is that **reckoning** or **calculating** is based upon a truth that is true. You're not trying to **imagine** that it's there. The death of Jesus is a <u>**fact**</u>. And what I'm telling you is also a **fact.**

Now, soon I'm going to talk with you more and I'd like the congregation to know about this little book. This is a very interesting man. He has had a profound effect on the entire world, internationally. He is a Chinese man, Watchman Nee is his name. He fell into prison when the Communist took over, and recently Watchman Nee passed away. But he was a **very, very** profound thinker. He has written a book called, <u>The Normal Christian Life</u>, which has to do with some of the things I've been telling you; and particularly, from Romans chapters 6, 7 and 8.

Watchmen Nee describes what took place and how it **changed** from just knowing a thing to reckoning. And it's such a beautiful illustration that it will clench what I'm trying to tell you this morning. He says, "<u>For years after my conversion I had been taught to **reckon. I reckoned** from 1920 until 1927. The more I **reckoned** that I was dead to sin, the more **alive** I clearly was. I simply could not believe myself **dead** and I could not **produce the death.**" You see this could be just ever so many words I'm saying to some of you. You're not able to reckon it at all. It means nothing to you. "Whenever I sought help from others I was told to read Romans 6:11. "...*reckon yourselves dead indeed unto sin*," [5] but he said, "I fully appreciated the teaching that I **must reckon,** but I **could not make out why nothing resulted from it.** I have to confess that for **months I was troubled.** I remember one morning -- that morning was a **real** morning and one I can never forget—I was upstairs sitting at my desk reading the Word"—the Scriptures—"and praying, and I said, `Lord, open my eyes!' **And then in a flash I saw it. I saw my oneness with Christ.** I saw that **I was** in Him, and that when **He** died **I died.** I saw that the question of my **death** was a matter of the **past** and not of the future," —or the present, it was a **matter of fact**—"The whole thing had dawned upon me. I was carried away with such joy at this great discovery that I jumped from my chair and cried, `**Praise the Lord, I am dead!**' I ran downstairs and met one of the brothers helping in the kitchen and I laid hold of him. `**Brother', I said, `do you know that I have died?**' I must admit he looked puzzled. `What do you mean?' he said, so I went on: `Do you not know that Christ has died? Do you not know that **I died** with Him? Do you not know that my death is no less truly a **fact** than His?' Oh it was so real to me! I **longed** to go through the streets of Shanghai shouting the news of my discovery."—I'm dead—"From that day to this I have **never** for one moment doubted the finality of that word '**I—have—been—crucified—with Christ.**'" [B] Now that's reckoning!

So reckoning is not a form of **make-believe,** and you can't psych your subconscious out. I'm experienced enough to **know** that what the subconscious believes you **will be** and you just can't mythologically **think** that this is true. It has to be reckoned upon **fact! And that's where the Holy Spirit, I think, enables us to see this Doctrine of Identification and then it becomes real.** You're reckoned, not that you're trying to produce it, but by this marvelous revelation—**it's real—it's real—it's real!**

Now number two, *logizomai*, also means, and I'm quoting from the lexicon, *to think about a thing, to consider it, or to ponder it, to let you mind dwell on it.* Now, that's another little shade of meaning. That has the thought of meditation—or pondering—of devotionally and emotionally identifying with a thing.

Now, I know two things. I know number one, that what you think about and believe will determine your life. I know also, that where your treasure is, there will your heart be also. That is, the **extent** that you consider a thing—the more you're thinking about a thing you're going to become that. So, I know it's important not only to **know this** but to give it some meditation. I have repeated on other occasions what I do, and I'll say it again because at least it's been helpful for me.

I have known these facts from scripture, and I came into an understanding of this oneness too, and what a help that's been to me. But there are times when I just <u>very naively</u> just picture Jesus on the cross. Now, years ago, the Holy Spirit seemed to **give me** a kind of a **vision** or a picture. I could see it. I made it up of course but I think it's real. Instantly I can get it. It's just so programmed into my subconscious that I can just see it at once. And I am seeing it right now as I talk to you. I can just see Jesus right there. I see Him on the cross. It's a picture I have in my mind. Now, I'm conjuring it. I'm just thinking about it. I'm considering, I'm meditating and that's *logizomai.* That's reckoning, considering. And folks, this works for **me.**

Alright, let's suppose that I'm offended. I'm hurt. I'm angry. I'm **whatever.** Anything of the old self life. Impatient, **you name it,** anything that's contrary to the Spirit of life or the fruit of the Spirit—something that wants to rob you of living in the Spirit. Do you know what I find? I just **do that.** It will work every time if I will stop and *logizomai*. If I will ponder, meditate from it and if I'll say, "Lord, I can see You there." And, I will say—I will reckon—I say, "Lord I <u>know</u> **that this is identified with You, this has no longer dominion over me.**" And I tell you **it works—every—single—time—without—fail.** Now, I'm not **trying** to conjure this up. I'm not **trying** to strain at it. I'm just *logizomai*, I'm just reckoning. I'm considering. I'm meditating.

Thirdly, the third shade of meaning for this Greek word is *to believe, to be the opinion of, or to be persuaded.* In other words, to let it **sway** you. Now, it seems to me that you **really** have three things in that word. When you have a <u>calculation</u>, and a <u>meditation</u> or a pondering and then when you have a <u>persuasion</u>, you're talking about the **whole** of one's personality. You're talking about your mental apparatus where you know intellectually—bookkeeping—arithmetic—you've figured it out—and you know a thing is true. Will it hold you up? If a thing is true mathematically by reckoning or calculation, **it's true.** Figures are about the only thing that will hold up anymore. Mathematics is based upon good scientific fact. **Then,** if you will meditate upon it, and be persuaded by it and that would be, I think, our emotional life, our volitional life. **In other words, it gets all of us.**

Now, here's what I'm trying to say. It's **all** there **objectively,** the death and the resurrection of Jesus. But when I also respond with my **all, not** that I'm **making** it true, I'm submitting to it and those **two** come together and you get the proper chemical action and the results. Jesus' dynamic death and His effective power and my whole hearted total response to that. **That** gives me this glorious liberty that we're talking about of the children of God. Now, it's amazing, you have to have the two chemicals though. **It's a fact!** Jesus' death is for every man's sin. But if a man will not accept that death, he must **bear** the wrath for his own condemnation.

The same is true with identification. The **fact** is **there,** but you have to **respond** to it with the totality of your personality. **Give** yourself to it. Not now that you're, all of a sudden, coming back under **law** and on your **own effort.** See that's what happens so often that people try to reckon and they're doing it with their own energies. And **that** is **utter devastation** and destruction. **It—will—not— work.**

Thank God for this truth, **because** I simply want to live life as it was meant to be lived. I want to live what the Bible calls "in the Spirit." I want the **good** me to come out. I want to have love—and joy—and peace—and longsuffering—and gentleness—and goodness—and meekness—and faithfulness—self-control. I want to have those things and the only way I know how, are along the lines that I'm telling you—by the **dynamic** that comes out of God through His Son, the Lord Jesus Christ. So, this is our part, and I tell you I want it with **all** of my heart and soul.

Here it is. Well, number one: Do you not know? Do you know that truth? And will you **reckon**—*logizomai*? Will you act upon it as true? Will you meditate upon it and conjure about it and consider it? It's yours. And we can **walk** in what the Bible calls **"newness of life,"** not the "old self," but this **"new life."** It's available to anybody and to everybody, in this congregation. To the whole world!

SERMON 8 ENDNOTES:

A   *logizomai,* means: (1) calculation or evaluation or estimate; (2) to think about, consider, ponder, dwell on; or (3) to believe, be of the opinion of, or be persuaded. New Testament Greek Lexicon. [exegete and taught by Pastor Don Pickerill in this sermon]

B   Nee, Watchman. (April 4, 1938). *The Normal Christian Life.* (pp.24-25). Retrieved from https://tochrist.org/Doc/Books/Watchman%20 Nee/The%20Normal%20Christian%20Life.pdf

SERMON 8 SCRIPTURE REFERENCES:

[1] Romans 6:1-14 (RSV)

1 What shall we say then? Are we to continue in sin that grace may abound? 2 By no means! How can we who died to sin still live in it? 3 Do you not know that all of us who have been baptized into Christ Jesus were baptized into his death? 4 We were buried therefore with him by baptism into death, so that as Christ was raised from the dead by the glory of the Father, we too might walk in newness of life. 5 For if we have been united with him in a death like his, we shall certainly be united with him in a resurrection like his. 6 We know that our old self was crucified with him so that the sinful body might be destroyed, and we might no longer be enslaved to sin. 7 For he who has died is freed from sin. 8 But if we have died with Christ, we believe that we shall also live with him. 9 For we know that Christ being raised from the dead will never die again; death no longer has dominion over him. 10 The death he died he died to sin, once for all, but the life he lives he lives to God. 11 So you also must consider yourselves dead to sin and alive to God in Christ Jesus. 12 Let not sin therefore reign in your mortal bodies, to make you obey their passions. 13 Do not yield your members to sin as instruments of wickedness, but yield yourselves to God as men who have been brought from death to life, and your members to God as instruments of righteousness. 14 For sin will have no dominion over you, since you are not under law but under grace.

[2] Romans 6:3 (RSV)

Do you not know that all of us who have been baptized into Christ Jesus were baptized into his death?

---

[3] Romans 8:6 (AMPC)

Now the mind of the flesh [which is sense and reason without the Holy Spirit] is death [death that comprises all the miseries arising from sin, both here and hereafter]. But the mind of the [Holy] Spirit is life and [soul] peace [both now and forever].

[4] Romans 6:11 (RSV)

So you also must consider yourselves dead to sin and alive to God in Christ Jesus.

[5] Romans 6:11 (KJV)

Likewise reckon ye also yourselves to be dead indeed unto sin, but alive unto God through Jesus Christ our Lord.

[6] Romans 4:4 (RSV)

Now to one who works, his wages are not reckoned as a gift but as his due.

SERMON 9

NEWNESS OF LIFE

"I tell you that flesh—has—no—
authority—over—you!"

How To Yield To God – Part 2

I invite your attention tonight to Romans chapter 6. And we're going to concentrate on verses 12, 13 and 14, which is the third element of the thing that we must **do.** Now, you'll recall, we said there are three things **suggested** that we **must do,** or our part, the **human** part in the grace of God.

Number one, we said, "We must **know.**" Paul said, *"Don't you know."* [1] So, we talked about the importance of **understanding** and **knowledge.** Then we went on to exegete **carefully** the word **consider** or to **reckon,** in chapter 6, verse 11, *"You must consider [2] or reckon [3] yourselves dead to sin and alive to God in Christ Jesus."*

"Let not sin therefore reign in your mortal bodies,
to make you obey their passions." - Romans 6:12 RSV

Now, we're coming to the **third thing** that is enjoined upon us and that is translated by the word **yield.** Paul writes in Romans 6, verse 12, *"Let not **sin** therefore **reign"**—*like a king, you see, because **grace now**

reigns. So don't let **sin reign** in your mortal bodies,—*"to make you obey their passions."* Because if they're **reigning,** if they're in lordship, then you're a slave and you must obey and you will. **If sin is reigning** you have no option, if sin is in **power.** And of course, I remind us all that sin is a greater power than **we are** outside redemption. *"Do not yield your members to sin as instruments"*—as **tools** for sin to use. Don't let sin employ **your members** anymore—your hands, your eyes, or your mind, or whatever. Don't let sin become your master to use these instruments for—*"wickedness, **but** yield yourselves to God **as** men who have been brought from death to life, **and** yield your members to God **as** instruments of righteousness. For sin is not going to have dominion over you, since you are not under law but under grace."* [4] Tonight, I want to talk to you about the third phase of that, and that is the call for us to **yield** or the subject of **consecration. How does one consecrate** his life to God?

I suppose if there were **any one problem** that has come to me in the spiritual realm, over the years in the ministry that I've enjoyed, **is this**—something like this: I **really** want to serve Christ. I **really** would like to be a victor. I **really** would like to be an **overcomer.** I would like to have all this **abundance** that you and others talk about, but somehow it doesn't work for me. **And I've done this**—I've gone to an altar, **and I really consecrate.** As a matter of fact, there was a period in my life when I would be down at the altar **every** Sunday night, or something like this. A decision was made, and I would always know that I would consecrate, but I would go back, and it was the same old thing, and I just despaired. And I **tried** to consecrate and **tried** to consecrate—and I don't know how you people **do it.** So, I would say, that that's been one of the **leading complaints** that has been given to me in a spiritual sense.

Now, I think sometimes, those of us who preach the gospel are party to this. I think sometimes we frankly misinform people. I think sometimes we do not **clearly** see what the scripture teaches and, in our anxiety, to bring people to Christ and deepen people in the Lord, we sometimes have a way of keeping **them** off-balance too—and urging them to **constantly** be making decisions—and **constantly** to be consecrating—and so we **leave them** with a notion that they're never quite **yielded**, you see. And every church service is a kind of a **new** dedication to see whether or not they're **saved.** Now, I have **really** heard people say, and particularly young people in summer camping programs that they get **saved** like every Sunday night, or they get **saved** at least every **summer.** They come back to summer camp, and they keep getting saved year after year. And so, we know that something is **wrong and faulty** with our presentation.

And then too you know, we'll run across scriptures like this where Paul says in 1 Corinthians, *"I die daily."* [5] And so, we get the notion that every day we must kind of some way **die.** And so, we're always struggling to **die,** but we always find ourselves **alive,** and we never quite **get dead.** Well, I would like to remind you, that that's probably one of the most misquoted verses in the Bible. When Paul says, *"I die daily,"* [5] he means that **physically** he was about to **perish** at any given moment. His life was periled. He was in jeopardy. He was at Ephesus and was under constant attack from people who were trying to **kill him.** And so, he means, I die daily that my life is in danger by enemies every day. I'm exposed to a physical assault. That's what he means. It has **no reference** to what we imagine I'm trying to **die daily,** and you know we just keep letting a little blood out and hoping one of these days we're going to **die.**

I want us to look very carefully at what it means to be consecrated to God and how we yield this third phase. I want us again to go back and see what we do **not** do, and often where we **make mistakes.** And then let's see what we **do** according to this passage of scripture.

First of all, let me remind you, **you do not and you cannot consecrate your flesh to God. You cannot—bring—your—flesh—into subjection. Many people, and I was even of this opinion when I was** trying to overcome my sin nature by fighting against it and hoping that by great efforts and I went through long seasons of <u>fasting</u> in my own background trying to <u>overcome</u> my flesh as it were. And I was just thinking if I could get another <u>hold</u> on it. If I could just <u>strangle</u> this thing out. And I would try to <u>wrestle</u> with this, and I'd <u>try</u> to bring it into subjection. But I <u>did not</u> understand Romans chapter 8, verse 7, that says, *"<u>the flesh does NOT submit to God's law, indeed it canNOT.</u>"* [6]

Now that's pure and simple. The <u>flesh cannot</u> submit to God's law, indeed it cannot. It is <u>futile</u> to consecrate your flesh. Your flesh will not be subject. So let me tell you, you are <u>not</u> basically trying to yield your self-life. It is <u>so bad</u>, that it is all you <u>can do is be dead to it</u> or to <u>crucify</u> it as it were. You can't <u>yield it</u>. You can't subdue it. It's always there. And if at any <u>moment</u> you are <u>subject</u> to it, <u>then you are subject to sin.</u>

A lot of people imagine that they are not <u>converted</u> because they have this experience. After they're Christians, low and behold, they run into their flesh life, and they begin to imagine if they are even <u>Christians</u> because they <u>will</u> to do many <u>things</u> and they thought that through regeneration they would no longer have those desires. But you must know that we are <u>not trying to consecrate our flesh life</u>. You cannot do it because all you can do is <u>kill it</u>. You can't consecrate it. You have to be dead to it according to Paul's thinking.

I'm even going to go one step further and it's very closely allied to what I was saying. Neither do you by great will power, summons up enough **will** to master this by self-effort. Now I've stressed this before and I won't tarry on it, but simply to underscore it one more time; Anything—**anything**, that throws it back on your self-life is doomed to fail. **Any <u>system that makes you a subtle self-savior</u> is doomed to fail!** **If it's not <u>totally</u> by God's power and <u>totally</u> by God's grace, you will <u>never make it</u>.** And this is what **happens.** We get a little **twist** in there thinking now that I must by self-effort conjure up enough **will.**

The Apostle in Colossians says that *"that has an **appearance** of wisdom."* [7] He refers to this in Colossians. That **looks** like wisdom. It has an **appearance** of it. But Paul turns around and calls it *"**will** worship"* [8] which means that it's a bonding the **will** to a place of **deity,** and that our **will** is not our **Savior.** Jesus Christ is our Savior and not even your own **will.** And that's why Paul will say in Romans 7:18, *"I can **will** what is right, but I cannot do it."* [9] And so if you're looking to your human **will,** then you're on the **wrong track** and that's what many people, I find, come to do. They come to an altar **hoping** that they can **yield** their flesh life to God and that He will make it **holy,** you see, and He will regenerate their flesh life. But this is not what happens, because regeneration does not involve a re-making of our self-life. Holiness is **not** an eradication of evil. As we're going to see, holiness is **living in the power of the new man.** And so, we've got to understand what we're out to do here. What we're yielding to God and what we are not.

Now then, let's see what the clear-cut teaching of scripture is in **yielding.** The Apostle says, that when you yield, you—*"yield yourselves to God __as__"*—**notice** the teaching—**notice** the scriptures carefully—*"__as__ men—who—have—been—brought—from—death—to life."* [10] So your yielding must begin from the point of death on! Now so many times we're trying to get dead, but the yielding begins at the point of death! You can only yield the NEW MAN! That's the only man that can yield to God! That's where the consecration goes on, and that's all God wants consecrated to Him. He wants the rest of it on the cross. He doesn't want to make over your old flesh. It's under judgment! This entire eon. This whole world is under the sentence of a cross! And that means Don Pickerill in and of his historical self and **you** too. The only thing you can do is **nail** it to a cross. You cannot repair it. **The only thing you can consecrate to God is the new life, the new man.** That's what God wants. That's the thing that we yield to Him.

So now notice carefully, you **yield** "<u>*as men*</u> *who have been brought from death to life.*" [10] And so if we can see **this,** then it changes the whole picture. Then we're standing on the side of **resurrection,** as it were, and we're making our lives **available** to God. And then it's not a struggle. It's no self-effort. Then I'm not trying to put anything down. **I'm not trying to do anything!** Because all I'm doing is **giving God** my new man.

> *"Do not yield your members to sin as instruments of wickedness, but yield yourselves to God as men who have been brought from death to life, and your members to God as instruments of righteousness." - Romans 6:13 RSV*

I want to look at this word that is translated **yield.** It's a Greek word which literally means to "be **beside** someone," [A] **or** it could be translated—or at least the implication is—you are "to put yourself at someone's **disposal.**" [A] That's what you are doing. You are making yourselves **available** when you are yielding. That does not mean **straining** or **self-effort.** It's does not mean that you're trying to overcome **sin.** It simply means that you are presenting the new man to God. You are presenting "*your members <u>**as** instruments **of** righteousness</u>.*" [10] Now notice the **difference. They are there <u>as</u> instruments of righteousness.** The old man has none of them. You are presenting them **<u>as</u> instruments <u>of</u> righteousness.**

Now the Old Testament is so very, very valuable to us, because it so often will give us visual sermons. Illustrated sermons of the theological truth of the New Testament. If you want to understand the atonement, if you want to understand what Jesus did both by contrast and by parallel, go back, for example, and look at the Tabernacle. Any teacher can build a model of it and just show little children, and it makes God's redemptive plan **so easy.** But when you talk about the cross, and sanctification, redemption, identification, now that gets to be kind of hard. But the Old

Testament **abounds** in about any illustration you want. **Thank God for our Old Testament** that so **beautifully** illustrates this truth.

The Bible **anticipates** this whole work that we're talking about, and in the book of Exodus chapter 29, we see how men were consecrated to God particularly through their priesthood and what is known as the "Ram of Consecration" or the "Ram of Ordination." God ordained people. He consecrated them. He accepted them and He did it by a ram called the "Ram of Consecration." Now this is found in Exodus chapter 29, verse 19, and it's **amazing** how the Lord has made this clear to us.

Exodus 29:19: Now He says, Moses is writing, *"You shall take the other ram;"*—there were two rams to get the whole picture, but this is the Ram of Consecration. *"You shall take the other **ram**; Aaron and his sons shall lay their hands upon the head of the ram,"*—now notice that, it's important—**they shall lay their hands on this ram** and touch him— *"then you shall **kill** the ram, you shall take part of its blood and put it upon the tip of the right ear of Aaron"*—touch the lobe of his right ear—*"and upon the tips of the right ears of his sons, and upon the **thumbs** of their right hands"*—and believe it or not—*"on the great toe*—on the big toe— of their **right foot**. Then you are to sprinkle the rest of the blood against the altar round about."*—because this represents God, this altar, and the atonement before Him and the consecration before Him. *"Then you shall take part of the blood that is upon the altar, and the anointing oil, and then you shall sprinkle it upon Aaron and his garments,"*—upon his priestly garments—*"upon his sons and his sons' garments with him; **and his garments shall be holy,** "* Notice what makes a man holy. **Then—he— shall—be—holy**—and his **sons**—and everything he wears—all about him will be **holy**. Now *"You shall take the **fat** of the ram"*—it goes on to describe all the various parts of it here you'll take. I won't read that in verse 22—furthermore, you're to take some bread—*"take a **loaf of bread**, take a **cake of bread** with oil, and take **a wafer,** out of the basket* *of unleavened bread that is before the Lord;"*—and **now watch**—you shall take the **fat of this ram—you shall take this bread—and Aaron and his sons are standing there with empty open hands—***"and you shall take this and put all this in the hands of Aaron and the hands of his sons,"*—and **they** shall take them—*"and wave them,"* "back and forth before the Lord—*"Then you shall take this out of their hands, and burn them on the altar in addition to the burnt offering, as a pleasing odor before the Lord"*—that is going up before the Lord and is acceptable to Him—*"it is an offering by fire to the Lord."* [11]

Now if you'll look at that beautiful story, you'll see that we have all the parts that we've been preaching about **lately**. First of all, you **have** this beautiful illustration of identification. Remember that we are identified with Jesus? **When He died, we died.** Now, what did the priests do? They went out, and they placed their hands on the head of that ram. **Why? Because they're identified with him—they touched that ram—what happened to that ram is now happening to them. They're identified with it, in God's mind, legally and really. They're tied in with this ram. So, there's the Doctrine of Identification or Incorporation. They are identified with that ram.**

Secondly, you have this beautiful Doctrine of Substitution—the ram and his blood—what is happening for them. Now **notice** that the **blood of the ram** is going to be placed on all parts of their bodies. First of all, it touches their right ear. Now, your **ear** is the place of **hearing**. It represents your **mind.** It represents your **understanding**—what goes in your **ear**—the things that you **hear**—the voice that calls to you and how you answer that. The blood was applied to their right ear, **meaning** that their **mind**—their **heart** was to belong to God—it was to be **holy** and **consecrated** and **yielded** for God's service. Then it touched the thumb of their right hand, meaning everything that they did. Everything their hand touched. The hand represents man and his activity. All that they did belonged to God and should have been yielded to the Lord. Then they touched their right toe and that meant everywhere they **walked**—their **activity**—their going—their conversation as the Bible talks about—or their walk—their manner of life. So, their ear, their hand and their foot—in other words their **total personality.** You had the blood of substitution that belonged here **for God.**

But here's the beautiful part—because they stood there—and guess what? Their **hands** were **empty.** Did they do anything? No, they didn't do anything because all they did was, they had **empty hands.** Now here's a delightful little insight, and we have some who are studying Hebrew in our church, so you Hebrew students get ready. Do you know what the Old Testament term for consecrate is? In the Old Testament, do you know what it means to consecrate? Well, the Hebrew word is *"malé yad."* [B] The word *"yad"* is "your hands," and *"malé,"* means "fill"—"fill the hands." Anybody who is consecrated to God simply has their **hands filled.** The blood meant that their old life was dead, because all they could do is present their **hands,** as men brought back from life. **And God filled their hands with the fat of the ram and with the bread that He supplied. I tell you there isn't anything you <u>do</u>, because all you've got is <u>empty hands</u> that you present to God like a new man! You let your instruments be made <u>available</u> to Him. So, all you've got to do, so to speak, is wave it before the Lord in thanksgiving and rejoicing. With those empty hands you just wave it in thanksgiving to Him.** This is a wonderful thing when you **know** that **you** belong to Jesus and your instruments, your body and all that is of His doing, and He is the Lord of it. You are to present yourself **as** instruments of righteousness—not to **become** instruments of righteousness—but because you **are,** you make them available.

I can remember hearing someone say, "You know, I don't really belong to myself. My hands are not my hands to use, they're Jesus' hands, they're His to use." I'll never forget the little talk I had with Sharon's grandmother, sister Heidner, all of you know her very well—and she is a very godly, Spirit filled woman. I wanted her to do something, and I had asked her if she would be involved in something. And she paused for some time, she thought a little while and she said, "I'll pray about it and see what the Lord tells me to do." Well now, if had been **me,** I'd have just blurted out "**Yea! I'll do it!**" You know, "**Sure, whatever!**" *(Don chuckles)* But not sister Heidner, **no** she thought for a long time, and she says, "I'll pray about it and see what the Lord wants me to do." So, I talked with her about that. And she says, "You know, **I know** that my life truly belongs to God." And whatever happens she wants to make sure that her **members** are being used for God and His glory. Do you get the principle? That's the idea.

So, I want us to see that **yielding** is not an attempt to overcome your flesh life. Because all you can do is put blood on it and have done with it, as were. It has to be crucified. You can't subject your flesh to God. But you **can** realize that you've gone through a **death** experience, **and** that there is a new life that's available to you—and **that** you can **present** to God.

Now, **why** has the Lord done all of this? **Why** has He made it this way? Because look folks, it makes a **big difference** who gets the glory. **And we so are given to wanting to boast within ourselves.** The self-life, you can always spot it, because it always wants adulation and praise. It wants to in effect to be worshiped. It wants to be **God.** And you can **especially** spot your flesh life when it's **left out**—or when it's ignored— or when it's crossed. You let somebody do that to you, and you'll tell whether your self-life is out or **not.** To the degree that you get **hurt** that's the degree that you are **not dead.** Can you hurt a dead man? No, you can kick him pretty hard. He won't say anything. *(Don chuckles)* But when we **realize** this **then** we see that all we can do, is present the **new man** that is brought up by Christ's resurrection, as it were, and with **empty hands** He comes to fill them. And so, we let our hands, that is our life, be filled with God's gifts. All we do then is just **wave** them before the Lord and we go on walking in newness of life.

Well, here I am Lord. I'm like a son of Aaron. I'm glad I've touched the ordination ram. I'm glad that it was Jesus Christ's consecration on the death and not mine. All I do is touch His head. I reach out and identify with Him. **He** goes to the cross. I'm glad that He takes that redemptive blood and puts on the vital spots of my life. What I **think,** what I **do,** where I **go,** and He puts **death** to it, as it were. But then I'm also glad that I can stand forth with empty hands, and I can be consecrated—**not by will power**—but by *"malé yad"* [B] —by having my "hands filled" with the <u>fat</u> of the ram—and the wonderful bread and cakes—and all the other that is put right in my hands. And so, **life** has just been a constant rejoicing as I wave these before the Lord.

Church, I tell you this, that **that power is available <u>to</u> us.** And if we'll understand clearly the teaching of scripture, **that—works—for—us.** Now you'll go through the battle constantly—will it be the flesh or the spirit? **But I tell you that flesh—has—no—authority—over—you! Sin shall not have dominion over you. And you can tell that "to go," because you've got the ordination ram.** All you do is stand there with empty hands and present them to God, and you are consecrated to Him. And you are holy. **Now, it's up to <u>Him</u>** what He puts in your hands and what you do. **A lot of us** want to reach down and pick up some dirt and pick up some rocks and throw at people and so on. No, we've got our empty hands.

What does **He** put in your hands? What does **He** want to do? Well, here I am Lord, and I want to yield myself and my members **as** instruments of righteousness that they already are. We'll give the glory to Jesus!

SERMON 9 ENDNOTES:

A *paristemi,* means: to yield, be beside someone or to put yourself at someone's disposal. New Testament Greek Lexicon. [exegete and taught by Don Pickerill in this sermon]

B *male' yad, male'* means: to fill; *yad* means: hands; *male' yad* means: has their hands filled, Old Testament Hebrew Lexicon. [exegete and taught by Don Pickerill in this sermon]

SERMON 9 SCRIPTURE REFERENCES:

[1] Romans 6:3 (RSV)

Do you not know that all of us who have been baptized into Christ Jesus were baptized into his death?

[2] Romans 6:11 (RSV)

So you also must consider yourselves dead to sin and alive to God in Christ Jesus.

[3] Romans 6:11 (KJV)

Likewise reckon ye also yourselves to be dead indeed unto sin, but alive unto God through Jesus Christ our Lord.

[4] Romans 6:12-14 (RSV)

12 Let not sin therefore reign in your mortal bodies, to make you obey their passions. 13 Do not yield your members to sin as instruments of wickedness, but yield yourselves to God as men who have been brought from death to life, and your members to God as instruments of righteousness. 14 For sin will have no dominion over you, since you are not under law but under grace.

[5] 1 Corinthians 15:31 (KJV)

I protest by your rejoicing which I have in Christ Jesus our Lord, I die daily.

[6] Romans 8:7 (RSV)

For the mind that is set on the flesh is hostile to God; it does not submit to God's law, indeed it cannot;

[7] Colossians 2:23 (RSV)

These have indeed an appearance of wisdom in promoting rigor of devotion and self-abasement and severity to the body, but they are of no value in checking the indulgence of the flesh.

[8] Colossians 2:23 (KJV)

Which things have indeed a shew of wisdom in will worship, and humility, and neglecting of the body: not in any honour to the satisfying of the flesh.

[9] Romans 7:18 (RSV)

For I know that nothing good dwells within me, that is, in my flesh. I can will what is right, but I cannot do it.

[10] Romans 6:13 (RSV)

Do not yield your members to sin as instruments of wickedness, but yield yourselves to God as men who have been brought from death to life, and your members to God as instruments of righteousness.

[11] Exodus 29:19-25 (RSV)

19 "You shall take the other ram; and Aaron and his sons shall lay their hands upon the head of the ram, 20 and you shall kill the ram, and take part of its blood and put it upon the tip of the right ear of Aaron and upon the tips of the right ears of his sons, and upon the thumbs of their right hands, and upon the great toes of their right feet, and throw the rest of the blood against the altar round about. 21 Then you shall take part of the blood that is on the altar, and of the anointing oil, and sprinkle it upon Aaron and his garments, and upon his sons and his sons' garments with him; and he and his garments shall be holy, and his sons and his sons' garments with him. 22 "You shall also take the fat of the ram, and the fat tail, and the fat that covers the entrails, and the appendage of the liver, and the two kidneys with the fat that is on them, and the right thigh (for it is a ram of ordination), 23 and one loaf of bread, and one cake of bread with oil, and one wafer, out of the basket of unleavened bread that is before the Lord; 24 and you shall put all these in the hands of Aaron and in the hands of his sons, and wave them for a wave offering before the Lord. 25 Then you shall take them from their hands, and burn them on the altar in addition to the burnt offering, as a pleasing odor before the Lord; it is an offering by fire to the Lord.

SERMON 10

GRACE AS A SOLUTION TO SPECIFIC SINS

*"I'm only going to trust God. And I believe
that He restores our soul!"*

I wonder what has most impressed you about this series of sermons on Romans. We're looking at Romans chapters 6, 7 and 8 at length and in detail. There have been a number of personal remarks shared with me. A number have said that they have been impressed by certain various truths that had been precious or even perhaps new to them. But I wonder what's happening or what the Lord's showing you? I think we have learned a lot of things, but the most **significant truth** of these three chapters, as suggested in the closing verse of chapter 5, is that **grace reigns through righteousness to eternal life.** I think we're learning more and more that it **has to be** necessarily by the grace of God. The **only life** that pleases God has to be of His own product, and that's grace. The only thing that gives us real soul peace is the message of the grace of God when properly understood.

I know we've all learned, and we are learning that we are in and of ourselves, our historical selves; we are **slaves** of sin. We sin even when we **will** not to sin. If left to our own energies, if we are **under the law,** if left to ourselves, we are absolute slaves of sin. I think we are learning, and I think we understand that our **self-life, our flesh,** to use the Biblical term—Paul's terminology—**is unredeemable.** Regeneration—

conversion—does not change it. The only thing that can be done is **crucify it.** You cannot make it better.

We've looked at the folly of self-improvement and self-effort. We're talking about walking in **newness** of life—a life that takes place **beyond** the cross. We present ourselves **as men who have been brought from death to life.** We notice what it really means to **consecrate ourselves**— to **yield** to God. And so many people are misled on that because they're trying to **yield** or consecrate their flesh life to God. It will **not** be subject to the law of God. It **cannot.** It's at enmity with God and that's a false start. But we do make a presentation of this new man to God. We yield to Him. We give God our members.

We're all learning to walk **free** from sin. Notice that free from sin is not **sin<u>less</u>ness.** Again, that's an important point. When the Bible talks about you being **freed from sin,** it doesn't mean you're **sin<u>less</u>.** It's another emphasis altogether. To be freed from your sins, means to be separated from them so you can **cope** with them. The Apostle is giving us a **very, very,** deep and profound insight.

"Let not sin therefore reign in your mortal bodies, to make you obey their passions. Do not yield your members to sin as instruments of wickedness, but yield yourselves to God as men who have been brought from death to life, and your members to God as instruments of righteousness. For sin will have no dominion over you, since you are not under law but under grace." - *Romans 6:12-14 RSV*

I want to **underscore** one more time this great passage in Romans 6:12-14, and I want you to see how specific Paul is and how he shows that the grace of God **is** the solution to specific sins, or member sins, mortal body sins. He says in Romans 6:12, *"Let not sin therefore **reign**"*—don't let it be your lord or your master. Don't let it lord it over you. Don't let it—"*reign*"—he says—"*in your **mortal** bodies.*" Now notice how concrete that is. We saw, you'll remember, that we have an **unredeemable** part called the **flesh,** but we also have **redeemable** but **unredeemed** bodies. And that our bodies become the agent of sin. That this **impulse,** this **drive,** must come up through your **members** either your **mind** or your **body.** And your body which is **corrupt** and **dying** becomes the agent of **sin,** you see. It's a natural ally because it is subject to death and is not **yet** redeemed. Romans chapter 8 makes that very clear. So, "*don't let sin **reign** in your mortal bodies to make you obey their passions*" [1]—their **drives**—those **forces**—those **lusts.**

"*Do not yield your members*"—now here we get specific. We're talking about specific sins now. "*Do not yield your **members** to sin as instruments*"—tools—weapons—it could be a military term like it's a warfare. Like, don't let sin capture it and use it as a weapon, or an instrument"—a tool—"*of **wickedness,** **but** yield yourselves to God*"—and **notice** this **very** important point—"***as men who have been brought back from death to life*"** [1] You can't yield anything this side of the cross. Impossible. All you can do is crucify it. You can only **yield** anything **beyond** the cross. That is this newness of life. It's the new man. God is not interested in the flesh or the old life and **everything in this age is under the sentence of a <u>cross</u>!** That's **very** important for us to see. **Everything** in this eon. **Everything** in this age.

We pointed that out by the dedication of the priests. When the priest came to God by the Ram of Ordination or the Ram of Consecration, they were touched in three parts of their body after the ram had been **killed.** The substitutionary ram was applied to their **right ear,** their **right thumb,** and their **right toe.** What they **heard,** what they **did,** and where they **went**—all their whole personality—their whole life attitudes— actions—activities, and so on. So, the consecration then came at that point and only after that point. Then you remember they **stood with**

empty hands, and we saw the Hebrew word *malé yad,* ᴬ means to "fill the hands." God must fill our hands. And He only fills the hands of the **new** man, as it were. That's what He wants yielded to Him. He doesn't want anything else. It has to be under the judgment of a cross. So, **yield** yourself to God *"as men who have been brought from death to life."* [1] Now, that makes **all** the difference in the world. Now you know what you're trying to consecrate. So many people come down and beat on the altar. I remember one young boy he was just **screaming** and holding out. I said, "What are you trying to do?" He said, "Give myself to God." (*Don chuckles*) I said, "Wait a minute." (*Don continues to chuckle*) So we talked a little bit. And so, it's very important for us to see how we make this **yielding,** this consecration.

"*...and your members*"—now we're getting **specific**—"*your members to God as instruments of righteousness.*" Now that's grace. Now here's **why,** and the impact, how you can **do** this. This is the **way** to have victory over the **specifics**—member sins—mortal body sins— "*for sin will have no dominion over you, since you are not under law but under grace.*" [1] So the **solution to sin** is to be **totally under grace,** when properly understood, and not to be under law.

Now again, I want to fortify and explain how that works to the best of my ability. And today, I would like to be an illustrated sermon to you, if I may, because I think I've been going through something where I'm **thankful** that I'm in the grace of God and understand it. These last two weeks have been very difficult weeks for me physically and personally. It started when I went to Texas. (*Congregation chuckles*) **Precious Texas folk, they received me wonderfully, so it's not the fault of Texas.** (*Don laughing*) I want you to know that. But that must have been a much more difficult week than I was prepared for and physically, and when I came home, I had the flu. So, then I just absolutely physically could not quite get going again and have not been able to **since.**

Sometimes when your **physical frame** is **weak** something happens to your spirit. You get **dis-spirited,** you get **depressed,** you get **overwhelmed,** and things look much bigger than they are. Now in those moments it is very easy for us—now I had a moment of temptation or weakness—to do things that we normally would **not.** For example, if you were an alcoholic, you'd probably go out and get drunk, I suppose. So, here's an opportunity, you see, for the battle between what we call the flesh and the spirit. But I tell you I am **thankful** that **I know** the **grace of God.** Now, I have **not done well.** I've done very little praying. I felt about as spiritual as a **toad.** *(Congregation chuckles)* Alright, now what is the thing I am not going to do?

Number one, I am **not going to let <u>sin</u> do its damage by bringing a form of <u>death</u> or <u>guilt</u> to me.** Let me explain that. You see, you must know that **sin** is a part of a chain or package. You can never separate the following things—**law—sin—guilt—and death.** Now, guilt is a form of death. *"The **wages** of sin is **death.**"* [2] And when the Bible talks about **death,** particularly in Romans 6, 7 and 8, it means **both physical death, the separation of the spirit from the body,** that's death. The wages of sin will be death. But **you** can also have your **spirit** separated from your body **now** in **terms** of the emotional and the personal **upheavals.** Where that your spirit is **disquieted,** where that you lose your **spirit.** Anytime you are **under guilt**—anytime you are under <u>condemnation</u>—anytime you have that uneasy feeling and get <u>down</u> on yourself—that is always a <u>devastating</u> thing and that's the consequences of sin. You can't really separate sin from that. That's a package—<u>unless</u>—<u>the grace of God can come in to FREE you from that guilt</u> and let you stand back and see that appropriately.

Normally, I would feel **guilty.** But I don't. **I'm <u>not</u> going to let sin have that advantage over me. Because I <u>know</u> that I'm in the grace of God, and I'm not going to go into that type of a death like existence. I know where I stand in the <u>grace of God</u>.** All my sense experience will tell me to be guilty. All my sense experience would be to identify with that, but I refuse to do it. **Because—I—know—I'm—under—the grace of God. I'm <u>free</u> from that. I tell you it's a <u>wonderful</u> thing to be under no <u>condemnation</u>—to <u>know</u> that you are under the grace of God and that you are <u>not</u> under law.**

So, the **first thing** that the grace of God does—**it frees you from <u>guilt</u>! That's very, very important.** We know that guilt is the **most devastating** thing that can happen to the human personality. It absolutely robs you of your **spirit.** It puts you in **a lethal, deadly, death-like existence.** And so, the grace of God separates you from your sins **by its guilt.** Sin does not reach you because you are dead to its guilt. Do you see that? I tell you that's quite a nice experience. So, it couldn't be better. I'm having a great time. Are you worried about me? *(Congregation chuckles)* Don't be. All of us go through these types of things. Am I going to interdict **guilt** and **compound that? <u>I am not</u>!** I am under the grace of God. I'm okay. I don't care what you say. *(Congregation laughs)* I'm okay. God knows I'm okay. Am I making it? **Why sure, I'm victorious! But if that <u>guilt</u> and that <u>condemnation</u> were to <u>seize</u> upon me—no telling what I would do.** I'd want all kinds of relief from that. So, I'm **not** going to compound the problem by internalizing **guilt.** Do you see? The first thing that must happen is you must be freed from the consequence of sin, and that is **guilt.** That's the way we are freed from these specific **member** sins.

Now secondly, we're also talking about these **powers** that operate within us and as we have noted, to be under the law means to be under a position where you feel a **claim** upon you— that **claim coming upon you.** And by **self-effort** you must rise to meet that claim. Now, my self-life, under normal conditions, would think, "Hey wait a minute, I better start doing something." And so, I would set all the wheels into motion, and I would begin all kinds of scheming and planning and activity as to what I'm going to do. Am I doing that? No, I'm not. Why? I don't trust Don Pickerill. **The minute I get into self-activity, at that moment I am under the <u>flesh</u> and under the power of <u>sin</u>. I <u>know</u> the grace of God teaches me that I must <u>totally</u>, <u>absolutely</u> and <u>utterly</u> trust someone else to do the work.** There's **no** question about it.

Now, why is this so? Because if I'm striving—if I'm under a spirit of <u>works</u>, <u>then</u> the spirit of grace is frustrated and the Holy Spirit is not released to release my spirit. Therefore, grace lets me know that I must <u>totally</u>, <u>utterly</u>, <u>completely</u> trust someone else. Because, all I can do is die. And, if I'm going to have any new life, it's got to be that heart transplant that beats. And if I walk, if I do anything in **newness of life**, it has to be by the release of the Spirit. And so that leads us to the power **over** sin by the great work of the Holy Spirit. So, this is the second way it works. Not only relieving us from the guilt and separating us from it, **but by the power and the dynamic of the Holy Spirit** to come in and take over our lives for us.

Paul has a very strong statement about this in his letter to the Galatians. And in some way the **best** commentary that I know on this truth is Galatians the fifth chapter. It's a beautiful chapter, and I would like to just briefly look at it with you.

 "For freedom Christ has set us free; stand fast therefore, and do not submit again to a yoke of slavery."
- Galatians 5:1 RSV

Paul begins in Galatians chapter 5, verse 1 by telling us what the goal is. And he says, *"For **freedom** Christ has set us free; **stand fast therefore**, and don't submit again to a yoke of **slavery**."* [3] **Now,** that's the goal, is this marvelous freedom. Am I going to get hung up in **guilt** and **self-effort** anymore? I'm not. No, because I know the grace of God and I know this marvelous call of freedom.

Now he's going to **very carefully** underscore the problems of mixing law and grace. "*A little leaven leavens the whole lump*," [4] he says, and I want you to very carefully look at this. "*I, Paul, say to you that if you receive circumcision*,"—which was the symbolism of the law—**"Christ will be of <u>no</u> advantage to you."** [5] Why? Because you're trusting something else other than Jesus Christ. And does that make a **difference?** It makes all the difference in the world what your **boast** is or what you're **trusting.** The sooner we come to an end of ourselves, and know we have no power to produce, the better.

"*I testify again to every man who receives circumcision, **he is bound to keep the whole law.***" Then you've fallen under the whole system. And I tell you it's either **all law** or **no law whatever. Don't you dare mix these.** "*You are **severed from Christ,** you who would be justified by the law.*" [6] That's very strong terminology. That's why I say this is **deadly serious.** I think some of you have wondered why we're getting so excited about law and grace. **I tell you this is <u>deadly</u> serious! And some of us who've gone around in the energies of our self-life for years don't even know it. We're just doing our religion. I tell you that's lethal! There's no newness of life in us whatever.** And by the way, that can be very sophisticated, I might add. I'm not talking about doing all kinds of **naughty, dirty things.** I'm talking about just your self-life, your pride, the energies of your self-life—all your sensitivity.

We'll take a look at the fifteen works of the flesh in a moment. You'll see that **eight** of them have to do with very acceptable things, normally. You are **severed** from Christ. "*You've fallen away from grace. For through **the Spirit**,*"—now notice it's **by the Spirit**—"*by faith, we wait for the **hope of righteousness.** For in Christ Jesus neither circumcision nor uncircumcision is of any avail*,"—doesn't do anything—"***but—faith— working—through—love. You were running well.*" What happened?— "*who hindered you from obeying the **truth?** This persuasion is not from him who called you.*" I tell you God's not teaching you that doctrine. The

Holy Spirit is not revealing it to you. *"A little leaven leavens the whole lump."* [6] **You let just** a little bit of self, a little bit of legalism, a little bit of false information come in, and I tell you it can throw you off entirely.

That's why it's so <u>very</u> important that you hear the <u>pure preaching</u> of the gospel, and the grace of <u>God</u>. And like Paul, *"<u>let any man be accursed</u>,"* [7] <u>who teaches something else</u>! Oh, that the Holy Spirit would **reveal** this to us very clearly. We're talking about the matters between **death and life.** Between Jesus getting all the glory and our pride intruding and the self-life being sustained. A little leaven, **just one gram of works, one gram of law** will begin to upset this entire thing. It leavens the whole lump.

"I have confidence in the Lord,"—now, that's a real key. If you have confidence in the Lord, do you have to do your manipulation? No, you don't. See, you'd have to go through all your scheming—and all your planning—and you think all this out in your mind—I'm going to say this—and he's going say that—and I'm going to do this and all that. You don't have to do that. It's nice by the way to just be spontaneous. *"I have confidence in the Lord,"* you don't have to help the **Lord out.** We start laying our hands on people. We try to help the Lord out. *"I have confidence in the Lord that you will take no other view than mine; and he who is troubling you will bear His judgment, whoever he is."* [8] —this teaching in the church.

Now the Apostle is going to explain that the preaching of the cross, the **full** preaching of the cross, brings about sometimes this opposition from those who would **unsettle** people. *"Brethren, if I still preach circumcision, why am I still persecuted? In that case the stumbling block of the cross has been removed."* You see the stumbling block to the cross? **Is that you're a wipe out.** You can't do anything. You see? Now, what did that do to your pride? It just totally takes it away, and that's a stumbling block. Don't we like to get our licks in there and make our brownie points? Yes, we do. *"I wish those who unsettle you,"* and here's the opposite by the way. The grace of God will lead you to **peace.** Legalism and this self-striving—you can feel it even in a congregation, when people they get that striving among themselves. They get like emotional cannibals as Paul says in verse 15. *"I wish those who unsettle you would"*—cut themselves off—*"mutilate themselves!"* In other words, I wish they'd just cut themselves away. *"For you were called to freedom, brethren; only don't use your **freedom** as an opportunity for the flesh,"*—do we continue in sin that grace may abound? Of course **not, "but** through love be servants of one another."*—and that's a motto of our church. We put it on our advertisements—<u>Serving One Another Through Love</u>. *"The whole law is fulfilled in one word, 'You shall love your neighbor as yourself.' But if you **bite and devour** one another"*—which legalism always does—it's a **manipulating,** cannibalistic type of thing out of your **own need** where you begin to do this type of program—*"you bite and devour one another take heed"*—you don't wind up being a bunch of bones—*"you're consumed by one another."* [9]

"But I say,"—now, here it is—*"walk by the Spirit, and do not gratify the desires of the flesh."*—It has to be by the **Spirit.**—*"For the desires of the flesh they're against the Spirit"*—**right or wrong,** these **drives** of my flesh, they're **against the Spirit—as I, in myself,** would want to do those things—except the Holy Spirit is my **only hope.** *"...but the desires of the Spirit"*—**thank God**—*"are against the flesh; these are opposed to each other, to **prevent** you from **doing what you <u>would</u>.**"* [10] Now, what I would to do, would be to be **guilty** and in weak moments to **sin**—to become **irascible**—to become **peevish**—to become **anxiety laden**—or whatever it may be. But you see the Holy Spirit comes along to prevent me from doing what I **would, from doing my own thing.** Do I need the Holy Spirit? **It's my only hope.**

And now, Paul will make it very clear what these works of the flesh are. He says, *"Now the works of the flesh they are very plain:"*—you don't

have to **guess** what **they** are. The New English Bible describes them as—
"fornication, impurity, indecency, idolatry, sorcery, quarrels, contentious temper, envy, fits of rage, selfish ambitions, dissensions, party intrigues, jealousies;"—notice over **half** of them have to do with your attitude. Don't present your **members**—that includes the faculties of your **mind**—your disposition as well— *"drinking bouts, and orgies. I warned you before, that those who do these things are not going to inherit the kingdom of God."* [11] —we're not going to enter into that kingdom. That way of life will not be there if we walk in the flesh. *"But the fruit of the Spirit is"*—and can you name them? Look how **real** they are. And they're the fruit of the Spirit. These aren't **magical.** These aren't **mystical.** These are **moral.** These are **personal.** These are **real,** and here they are— *"the fruit of the Spirit is love"*—love appears four times in this chapter— *"love, joy, peace, patience."* Would I have patience normally? No, I wouldn't. If you were to cross me, I might like to snap at you. When you get low, when you're discouraged, when you're physically not well you might get that way. You lose your patience. *"...kindness, goodness, faithfulness"*—dependability, stewardship— *"gentleness, and self-control; now against such"*—against such men or against such thing, we don't know what to make of this last phrase— *"there is no law."* [12] —meaning that law doesn't have reference to this. In **no way** can law get involved in this, because this is the fruit of the **Spirit.** This is this **newness of life** that we are talking about.

All of us are caught up in our **struggle.** Sin wants to reign through our **mortal bodies**, and it wants to seize your **members.** Now, I don't know what members in your body it wants to seize. Have you ever looked at the sins of the tongue? They're amazing. But I do know that we need blood applied to our right ear, our right thumb, and our big toe. That all of our personality, all of our members need to be yielded to God.

Now, I cannot do that. So, I am making myself available to the Lord. **Am I going to let <u>guilt</u> come in and rob me of my peace?** No, I'm under grace. **Am I going to feverishly start <u>doing</u> something in** a moment of weakness? I'm not! I'm only going to trust God. And I believe that He **restores our soul.** That that **marvelous grace of God** comes along and **keeps** us from sin.

You know, it's wonderful to know what Jesus Christ can do, and to rest in His grace. **I thank God for the good news of the grace of God that I can be—freed—from—sin, its guilt and its power, by the marvelous work of the Lord Jesus Christ.**

SERMON 10 ENDNOTES:

A *malé yad, male'* means: to fill; *yad* means: hands; *male' yad* means: has their hands filled, Old Testament Hebrew Lexicon. [exegete and taught by Don Pickerill in this sermon]

SERMON 10 SCRIPTURE REFERENCES:

[1] Romans 6:12-14 (RSV)

12 Let not sin therefore reign in your mortal bodies, to make you obey their passions. 13 Do not yield your members to sin as instruments of wickedness, but yield yourselves to God as men who have been brought from death to life, and your members to God as instruments of righteousness. 14 For sin will have no dominion over you, since you are not under law but under grace.

[2] Romans 6:23 (RSV)

For the wages of sin is death, but the free gift of God is eternal life in Christ Jesus our Lord.

[3] Galatians 5:1 (RSV)

For freedom Christ has set us free; stand fast therefore, and do not submit again to a yoke of slavery.

[4] Galatians 5:9 (RSV)

A little leaven leavens the whole lump.

[5] Galatians 5:2 (RSV)

Now I, Paul, say to you that if you receive circumcision, Christ will be of no advantage to you.

[6] Galatians 5:3-9 (RSV)

3 I testify again to every man who receives circumcision that he is bound to keep the whole law. 4 You are severed from Christ, you who would be justified by the law; you have fallen away from grace. 5 For through the Spirit, by faith, we wait for the hope of righteousness. 6 For in Christ Jesus neither circumcision nor uncircumcision is of any avail, but faith working through love. 7 You were running well; who hindered you from obeying the truth? 8 This persuasion is not from him who calls you. 9 A little leaven leavens the whole lump.

[7] Galatians 1:8-9 (RSV)

8 But even if we, or an angel from heaven, should preach to you a gospel contrary to that which we preached to you, let him be accursed. 9 As we have said before, so now I say again, If any one is preaching to you a gospel contrary to that which you received, let him be accursed.

[8] Galatians 5:10 (RSV)

I have confidence in the Lord that you will take no other view than mine; and he who is troubling you will bear his judgment, whoever he is.

[9] Galatians 5:11-15 (RSV)

11 But if I, brethren, still preach circumcision, why am I still persecuted? In that case the stumbling block of the cross has been removed. 12 I wish those who unsettle you would mutilate themselves! 13 For you were called to freedom, brethren; only do not use your freedom as an opportunity for the flesh, but through love be servants of one another. 14 For the whole law is fulfilled in one word, "You shall love your neighbor as yourself." 15 But if you bite and devour one another take heed that you are not consumed by one another.

[10] Galatians 5:16-17 (RSV)

16 But I say, walk by the Spirit, and do not gratify the desires of the flesh. 17 For the desires of the flesh are against the Spirit, and the desires of the Spirit are against the flesh; for these are opposed to each other, to prevent you from doing what you would.

[11] Galatians 5:19-21 (The New English Bible online)

19 Anyone can see the kind of behaviour that belongs to the lower nature: fornication, impurity, and indecency; 20 idolatry and sorcery; quarrels, a contentious temper, envy, fits of rage, selfish ambitions, dissensions, party intrigues, 21 and jealousies; drinking bouts, orgies, and the like. I warn you, as I warned you before, that those who behave in such ways will never inherit the kingdom of God.

[12] Galatians 5:22-23 (RSV)

22 But the fruit of the Spirit is love, joy, peace, patience, kindness, goodness, faithfulness, 23 gentleness, self-control; against such there is no law.

SERMON 11

THE DELIVERANCE DOCTRINE

"We must—yield—to—obedience!
Grace requires that of us!"

The scripture reading today is from Romans chapter 6 beginning with verse 15 to the end of the chapter. The Apostle **begins** by asking this question—*"What then? Are we to **sin** because we are **not under law** but under grace? By no means! Do you **not** know that if you yield yourselves to any one as obedient **slaves,** you are **slaves** of the one whom you obey, either of **sin,** which leads to death, **or** of **obedience,** which leads to righteousness? But thanks be to God, that you who were **once** slaves of sin have become **obedient from the heart** to that **standard of teaching** to which you were committed, and, having been **set free** from **sin,** have become **slaves of righteousness.** Now I am speaking in human terms,"*—I'm using a human illustration—*"because of your natural limitations. For just as you once yielded your members to impurity and to greater and **greater** iniquity, so now **yield** your members to righteousness **for** sanctification. When you were **slaves of sin,** you were **free"**—so to speak—*"in regard to righteousness. But then what **return** did you get from the **things** of which you are **now** ashamed? The **end** of those things is **death."**—that's the return you get—*"But **now** that you have been **set free from sin** and have become slaves of God, the **return"**—the **payoff, the wages**—*"is sanctification and* *its **end**,"*—the end product is—*"eternal life. For the **wages of sin is death,** but the free gift of God is eternal life in Christ Jesus our Lord."* [1]

We've been studying together Romans chapters 6, 7 and 8. And you'll remember that these three chapters are **basically** an explanation of what it means to be **under grace.** Aren't you glad that grace is the king? **The Reign of Grace!** That's what we're talking about. As chapter 5, verse 21 says, *"...sin reigned **in death,** but **grace** reigns **through righteousness** to eternal life through Christ our Lord."* [2] I don't know anything more important than to know what it means to be under **grace.** We're seeing the implications of this in this great sixth chapter of Romans. And we're praying that the Lord will increase our understanding more and more and help us, by the way, to **experience** it **as well,** because we want to have this translated in our **lives,** not merely to **understand it.**

You know, I was awakened today with this phrase in my heart, "We are **not** under grace, **because** we are free from **sin.** But we are **free** from **sin,** because we are **under grace.**" I want to say that one more time. That's worth noting. "We are **not** under grace, **because** we are free from **sin.**" I think we often think that if we could become **sinless,** then all of a sudden, we'd be **under grace** and be **acceptable.** But it's just the reverse of that. "We are **free** from sin, **because** we are **under grace.**"

We didn't **stop** being a **sinner,** when we stopped **sinning**! To make my point, we stopped being a sinner when Jesus Christ died on the **cross.** You know, in such a **subtle way** we tend to put **sin** and **unrighteousness** upon ourselves and if **that's** the ground for living, then I tell you we're hopeless. We're going to be **entangled, enmeshed,** and **mixed up** the rest of our lives. It's **wonderful** to know that the **grace of God** cancels out **all guilt** and the **power of sin.** So, we're either under law or under grace. They simply won't **mix.** And if we are **under grace,** it's such a thrilling freedom that it can hardly be described. It means we **are not under condemnation or guilt.** There—is—no—condemnation to those who are in Christ.

Now, if we are only under grace, what's to keep us from **sinning?** Now that's the big question. If it's **true,** as Paul says, *"Where sin **abounds,** grace does much **more abound."** ³* By the way, do you know that doctrine? I can only get a percentage of people to **believe** that. **Where sin abounds, grace does much more abound.** That's **exactly** what the Apostle **says** in Romans chapter 5, verse 20. It's amazing how few people can **understand that** and grasp the implications of it. But what do you think took care of **your sins?** Did you do **anything** to stop them? It's only the **grace of God** that abounds all the more, and that's true, by the way, **past, present and future.** Some people have such a job believing the **straight forward gospel.** We **stumble** over the grace of God. How we **love** to be Galatian Christians, because we want to have something left over of our self-life as it comes out on the other **side,** so to speak. We can do nothing to establish our worth before **God.** It's either **by grace,** or it's by **nothing.** So, the Apostle says, *"Where **sin abounds,** grace does much more abound."* ³ What a **wonderful** doctrine.

Now then, having said **that** isn't the **conclusion** of all this: "I can just go right on **sinning?"** Well, the Apostle is going to work out **the relationship** between **grace and sin.** If we are not under law, if there's no claim upon us, no threats for wrongdoing, if we are only under **grace** and only **acceptable,** then what keeps us from **sin?** The sixth chapter of Romans is an attempt to work out that **relationship** between **sin and grace.** The Apostle is going to give two basic reasons why it does **not** follow: "That **we** go on and sin because we're under **grace."**

 "What shall we say then? Are we to continue in sin that grace may abound?" - Romans 6:1 RSV

He asks two very pertinent questions which divide this chapter to look at it in terms of an outline. The first question is in verse 1, *"Are we to continue in **sin** that grace may **abound?"* ⁴ Since he **has** said that *"Where*

sin increased, grace abounds all the more." [5] So does it **follow then** that we continue in **sin?** The answer of course is **no!** The **first** reason, and it's rather **shocking** to most people, is because strangely enough—we are **freed**—from sin. Because of our identification with the Lord Jesus Christ, **we—became—dead—to sin.** Now, we have seen that in Romans chapter 6, verses 1 to 14. The Apostle closes this discussion, and this point he's making by **stating** in verse 14, *"Sin will have no dominion **over** you, since you are **not under law** but under **grace.**"* [6]

Now, he poses the **second** question similar to the first one, *"Are we to sin because we are not under law but under grace?"* [7] Alright, if we are not **under law,**—if there's no **claim** upon us—no **condemnation**—but we're under **grace**—are **we** to go on **sinning?** Again, of course, the answer is **no!** The Apostle is going to give us the **second** reason why it **does not** follow that we are under grace and that that leads to a **looseness** and a **flaunting** of grace. On the **contrary,** it leads to a **true liberty** and **not** to a **carnal license.** He gives us the **reason** in the form of an **illustration,** and you can **see** that he really wants to make it **very clear.** He notes in verse 19 that he is, *"speaking in **human terms,"*** or what we would say, "he's using an illustration." He says, *"because of our natural limitations,"* [8] so that we can **thoroughly** understand. Sometimes it **is** difficult. I think **all of us** struggle with words like **law** and **grace.** What do they **mean?** Are they just **words?** We often don't understand the reality that's behind them and I'm praying that the Holy Spirit will **really** help our **hearts.**

He **uses** the illustration from **a slave.** He simply tells the story of a slave. In the first century a large part of the Roman Empire **was** in **slavery,** by the way. I understand that at least every other person, 50% of the population, was a **slave** at one time or another. Many times, people were even **born** into slavery if you can imagine. Their **parents** were slaves, and they were slaves too. They were **born** slaves. Slaves, of course, had no **rights.** They were like **cattle.** Like pieces of **property** or **furniture** to be sold **at will.** If they did **wrong,** they were under the **constant threat** of their master. Their master could demand what **he wanted.** If they did not perform, they could be liable even to death. So, **great** threats were upon people who were **slaves.** It was just a **miserable life.** Like a form of **death.** That's the only word you can use for it. As a matter of fact, the only way **most** people got out of slavery was **by death.** It was the **only** way they got out. If a slave **died, literally died,** then you see he would be **freed** from his **old master.**

Well, the only way **we** can get out of the mastery of sin is by **death,** and of course, by the death of our Lord Jesus Christ on the **cross.** Also, slaves at times could be **purchased.** If some master wanted to transfer a slave, they had quite a ritual to do this. So, they could **exchange** masters by means of **purchase.** Paul tells us in verse 16 about this **slave principle.** Then he goes on to describe the two masters; what it **means** to go from one master to another. And **finally,** in verse 19 to the end of the chapter, he tells us what the **wages** are of each of these **masters.** What it means to **serve** one as over against the other, "*the **power** of sin*" or the "***power of righteousness.***" That is the **flesh** or the **spirit.**

Now, let's take a look, first of all, at the **slave principle.** It's described in verse 16, "*Do you **not know** that if **you** yield yourselves to **any one**"—* **anything—any principle—any power—**"*as obedient slaves*"—if you **give yourselves** over to anything—"*you are **slaves** of the **one** to whom you **obey,**" [9] —* you're in its **power. You obey it. You yield to it. You're <u>under</u> it.**

Now, on the **one** hand, you **might** "*yield to **sin** which leads to **death,**"* or you might "*yield to **obedience** which leads to **righteousness.**"* [9] So the **slave** principle is very **clear.** It's **very obvious** that if you are **under** something you're **dominated** by it. It's going to be the **driving passion of your life.** You'll be **subjected** to it, to that **course** or that **thing.**

The Apostle, of course, is very **knowledgeable** about **human nature** and he knows that a man can never be **morally** or **personally** neutral. We're going to be motivated by some force, I can tell you that. **We simply** cannot be morally neutral. It's impossible. We're like hungry vacuums that are **constantly** taking in something. We were made to be **under** something—to be **submitted** to something—to **yield** to something. We will be **motivated** and **dominated,** in this case, either by **sin** or by **righteousness.** We can see that in life in a practical way. It shows up in **all** forms of life.

The second part of this **slave way** is given in verse 19, *"as you once yielded your members to impurity to **greater** and **greater** iniquity, so now yield your members to **righteousness for** sanctification."* [8] For this is the process that brings us to **greater and greater wholeness.** If we give ourselves over to some **power,** that power wants to control us **more** and **more.** That's the point the Apostle is making. We can see that in very dramatic ways. Take **drugs** for example. If someone gives himself over to drugs, they go into a greater and a greater **bondage.** If we give ourselves over to a certain **sin** or a certain **thing,** it tends to possess us **more and more.** We become **more and more** under its **bondage.** That's why the great psychologist, William James, said, "We have to make our **habits** work **for us."** [A] Some people have **bad habits,** and these habits work **against** them. They're **dominated** by them and more and more they're **subject** to these **powers** and **forces** in their life.

To follow up the story of the slave and the master, the freedom is in the **choice, not** so much in the **power,** because once we give ourselves over to a **power,** we are **dominated** by that, and our **life** will be **controlled** and **manipulated** by **these forces** to a greater and greater **bondage.** That's a very simple principle, I think, to understand. The Apostle is saying in effect, "Now look, this is the way **life** is. We're going to **yield** to something and the **consequences** of that yielding are going to be **momentous."**

It's very interesting how he describes the **wages.** "What do you **get?"** he asked. He makes a contrast and a parallel, and he points out **three different contrasting factors.** For example, in verse 19 he says, *"as you **once yielded** your members to **impurity"** [8]* —so **sin** leads to impurity. That's the **wages** that it pays. On the other hand, the opposite of that would be **purity** or what **we** call **sanctification.** The old word **sanctification,** which we understand very little, I think, in modern times, has a thought of it of **purity.** It's a **wholeness** or a **wholesomeness** really, so that our life becomes **intact;** whereas before, we **yielded** to **corruption** and **shame** and **wound up** with that. You know sin always does **that.** It leads to **greater and greater** impurity, but *"righteousness leads to sanctification."* [8] So the first contrast is **impurity versus purity**—or **impurity versus holiness**—impurity versus wholeness and sanctification.

Now, the **next contrast** is in verse 20, *"When you were **slaves of sin,** you were **free** in regard to **righteousness."** [10]* So it's a contrast between **shame** versus **righteousness.** When you were slaves of sin you were **free**—basically with reference to **goodness**—or **godliness**—or **righteousness. And** what was the **return?** What was your **paycheck?** What did you **get back?** What return did you get from the thing of which you are now ashamed? Many people **live in** shame, and of course, and are **not ashamed,** because they've not been **awakened to righteousness.** But with their new understanding, having been **awakened** by the Spirit of Christ, they would even be **ashamed** to describe what they **did** with their life. All their **dishonesty** and all the many things that goes on. But—*"the end of those things"*—the paycheck—*"is **death.**"* [11] But he says, *"now that you have been **set free** from sin"*—in verse 22—*"and have become **slaves of God,** the **return** you get"*—the **payoff**—the **paycheck**—*"is **sanctification** and the end is eternal life."* [12] So the contrast is **shame versus acquittal.** That is, **condemnation or guilt.** That's an **awful** state to be in, to feel shame. It makes us feel like we don't want to wake up in the morning. We don't like to look **life** in the eye. We feel **shifty eyed.** We don't **like** to look God in the face. We don't feel His **approval** and His **blessing.** We go around with that uncomfortable **uneasy feeling,** because if we found out what we **really** are, we would **never** be **acquitted.**

But under the new master, Jesus Christ, we get acquittal. We get **righteousness,** and **righteousness** means that we are in the **right.** We have a **right** relationship with God. We have a **right** to live, and we **feel** that way. We **experience** it.

The third parallel is in verse 23, *"the* **wages** *of sin is death, but the free gift of God is eternal life in Christ Jesus our Lord."* [13] The **comparison** is really between **death** and **life.** Those are the only **adequate** words that describe the **difference** between them. We're talking about **ultimate** death and **ultimate** life in a **physical** and an absolute sense. **Real death and real resurrection.** But we're also talking about the **quality** of life that could only be described as a **form of death.** Are there **some** people who would rather be dead than alive? **Many** of them, because **life** has a death like **quality.** It's lost its **meaning.** There is no **life.** It's just an **existence.** A very **bland,** often **meaningless, frustrating** type of existence, where a person feels in **bondage** to forces beyond his control. We feel **guilt** and **shame** and go through life wondering is there any **meaning**—any **liberty**—any **freedom?** Well, that's basically what it means to be on **your own**—to be under the **law**—and to be in a **self-life. But thank God** the grace of God comes along and **cuts** through all of that—and puts us under a new master.

"But thanks be to God, that you who were once slaves of sin have become obedient from the heart to the standard of teaching to which you were committed, and, having been set free from sin, have become slaves of righteousness." - Romans 6:17-18 RSV

So, the Apostle begins to tell us about the **two masters.** In verse 17 and 18,—*"thanks be to God, that you who were* ***once slaves of sin*** *have* become *obedient from the heart* to *that standard of teaching to which you have been* **committed** *and, having* **been set free from sin,** *you have become* **slaves of righteousness.**" [14] That's a very **beautiful** and important verse. I'm particularly interested in verse 17 which says, "...*you who have from the* **heart** *become* **obedient** *to that* **standard of teaching** *to which you were* **committed.**" [14] There are three items in that verse for us to look at.

First of all, let's see that it's **something** to which we have been **committed.** It is not something committed **to us.** That's a very important insight. So many times, we're trying to get a **hold** of **something.** You know, we're hoping to get **a hold** on **grace.** We're hoping that **maybe** something will come along and **deliver us. But this says that we are delivered to it.** Paul of course is carrying on his **analogy** of the **slave.** The word **deliver** here or **commit** is really the word, **betray.** It means to **give over.** You remember the word is used when Jesus was betrayed by Judas. Judas **gave Jesus over to the soldiers.** [15] And once Jesus was **given over to them,** He fell into their **power.** And eventually of course, He was in the hands of **Pilate.**

Now the marvelous truth is this; God has **delivered us** over to Jesus Christ and His **doctrine.** God by His Spirit has taken us **from** sin— **redeemed** us by the death of Jesus Christ—from the former master— and has **delivered us** over to righteousness. It isn't something **we** have to hold on to. I've got good news! I am not **trying** to be good. I gave that up a long time ago. First of all, I am **no good.** If someone doesn't deliver me over to goodness, I am lost. Maybe **you** found the energies to be good, but **I haven't.** It takes the **power** of the Lord Jesus Christ, by His **redemptive blood,** to **cut through** all the shackles of **death,** and **sin**— and to **hand** me over to **righteousness.**

So, we have been **delivered.** That's why this is a deliverance **doctrine**—a true deliverance doctrine. As a matter of fact, the American Standard Version says, translating, "this is the **doctrine** that delivered you." [16] Do you want to be delivered? This is the **doctrine that delivered you.** It's a **deliverance** teaching. Notice, he says that,—*"It's a standard of teaching to which you were delivered."* [16] That standard of teaching, by the way, is a Greek word (*didache* [B]) which has the idea of a **type** or a **mold. It's a mold.** We are **molded** by the **truth.** We're being **fashioned** and **shaped** by the grace of God. That's a beautiful thing, by the way. That's the way Jesus does it. He **molds** us and **fashions** us. He doesn't have to whip us into line like the **law.** He's not like the old master. He just doesn't work that way. He's a gentle wonderful **teacher,** and He has a gentle wonderful **touch.** It comes by His **marvelous** doctrine of grace. It's that **standard of teaching** [17] which we know is the grace of God.

I want to underscore this point. There is **no way** for us to come into full liberty and to be set free from the **power of sin,** except by the grace of God. There **is** no other way. And if we don't get anything else from this passage of scripture with **this truth—it's the grace of God alone that can do it.** Now, we might get some **external righteousness.** Can we keep people in check by force? Yes, we can do that. What **must** we do though? We have to hire a police force. We have to put **guns** on their sides. We have to put them in black and white cars roaming up and down the street just **hoping** to keep people in check. Does **God** want it that way? Of course not, that's no way. That's why the law will make **nothing perfect.** Can the law change the heart? **Not one heart! Not one tiny <u>bit</u> of the heart can be change by the law.**

That leads us now to the third element. Why don't we **abandon** ourselves to sin, if we are under grace? The answer: Because **God** has touched our hearts. The grace of **God** brings the God of grace. *"From the heart"*—he says,—*"you have become obedient"* [17] —**obedient from the heart.** In other words, we have met Jesus Christ. The reason we don't go on to **sin** is because we have met the **Savior**—we've met the **Master** and what a gracious glorious person He is. **I've fallen in love with Him.** I don't want to hurt Jesus. I want to do what's **right.** That's the thing that keeps me from sin. It's the **only thing** that will keep us from **sin.** It's something that happens to our **heart.** We have been **regenerated** by the power of God. That's where the **power is** that keeps us from **sin.**

I know a lot of people don't **understand this.** They think they have to **help** the Lord out. They have to **manipulate**—they have to **scold**—they have to **lecture**—they have to **use the law**—they have to **constantly** do it. But that makes nothing perfect, as a matter of fact, it really only drives people farther **from us.** It's only the grace of God that can transform the human heart. It's wonderful to see how that happens.

I've had many people tell me how this works in their life. I know a person recently was telling me they had a chance to make **a lot of money** in a **shady deal** and **nobody** would've known about it. But this person said, "You know I knew Jesus was there, and I said, 'Jesus I don't want to do anything wrong before you.' So, I just put it all back." That's what the **Spirit** does, and that's the way it **must be** in **living** before God. **It—must—be—from—the heart.** Everything else is just **sham** and **hypocrisy.**

So, the grace of God **alone** can lead us into **true** holiness. Who can run around **watching** others all the time? Who **wants** to do that? That's why it **has to be from the heart!** You can see how **practical** this is. How it ought to work in **families** and with **husbands and wives.** You know husbands and wives love the same marriage vows? What if they had to send detectives around **following** each other to see what they were up to? Would that be a marriage? Of course not. What if parents had to be constantly checking up on their children? Opening their mail—listening on the other line of the telephone. Well, if something is not happening in our children's hearts, all that is going to do them absolutely no good. The minute they're out of the door they'll do what they **want to do.** So, if **we think** we can do these things, we're just **sadly mistaken** on our own. It has to be done **from the heart,** and that's the **marvelous** grace of God.

Notice that he says that *"We **yield** to **obedience**."* That's a very important truth. We don't even basically yield to the Master. We don't even **yield** to righteousness. We **yield** to **obedience** which leads to righteousness. Notice that phrase—*"**You yield to obedience which leads to righteousness!**"* [8] Now, let's see how that works out. There's nobody in this congregation that doesn't feel a **claim** upon his life. **Nobody.** We were **born** with a sense of **claim.** We're made that way. Now, we feel this **tug.** And as we feel this **tug,** this inner claim, we **yield** to that in obedience. Like we like to say, "It is victory through surrender." Am I **struggling** after righteousness? Am I trying to be good? No, I'm not! **I am yielding to obedience, and obedience leads to righteousness.**

The battle is to yield to obedience, and **then** I fall into the hands of my Master. **He alone,** of course, can make me **good.** *"He alone can lead me in paths of righteousness for his namesake."* [18] I can't do that. The only thing **I can do** is become a **slave** to Jesus Christ and to yield to **obedience.** That makes all the difference. And you can see it; say in family life, if we just **submit.** If we can **give up** our **rebellion** or **resistance.** If somebody is just **submissive,** you know, everything is alright then you can begin to get somewhere. So, we **yield to obedience.** That's what scripture says and then the **Master** takes over from **there.** And **that's** the difference.

Let me tell you, there's nothing **more** important in a **practical** and a **theological way,** than for us to simply know what it means to be *"saved by grace through faith and that not of ourselves it is the gift of God, not of works lest any man should boast."* [19] The most important thing is to understand the grace of God. **Why?** Because that's the thing that leads us **away** from ourselves and **unto Jesus Christ.** That's what makes us give up our **struggle** and keeps us from our **hypocrisy.** And if we have any kind of **self-struggle,** we are left to our own, and **we** are going to be subject to the bondage of sin. It's that simple.

The **only hope** is that we'll **meet** a new Master, and that new Master will say, "I'll take this miserable slave. That person in bondage.

I'll take this one that everybody else has rejected and I'll put them over into this new sphere. I'll give them **acceptance,** and I'll lead them into **righteousness** for my namesake."

Do **we** continue in sin that grace may abound? Of course not! And the reason **is, Jesus—Christ—has become—our—Lord!** Do I need the **law?** Do I need your **help?** No, I don't. Jesus Christ is **my Lord.** He's very sufficient, thank you. **He alone** can touch my heart. **He alone** can get at my motivations and put me in the grace of God. Its **amazing** grace, and how sweet the sound.

Now, we **must—yield—to—obedience!** Grace **requires** that of us. That's what we do, and then we **fall** into the hands of Jesus Christ who is our **new Master.** And so, when Paul asks the question in verse 15, *"Are we to **sin** because we are **not** under law but under grace?"* [7] The answer is **no,** because we have met **Jesus Christ face to face,** by His marvelous grace. **May God** teach it to our hearts, as our prayer, in **His** Name.

SERMON 11 ENDNOTES:

[A] James, William. (1895). *The Letters of Williams James,* chapter: *Habit.* (pp.130). Retrieved from https://plato.stanford.edu/entries/james/

[B] *didache,* means: instruction (the act or the matter):--doctrine, hath been taught. New Testament Greek Lexicon. Which has the idea of a type or a mold. It's a mold. We are molded by the truth. We're being fashioned and shaped by the grace of God. [exegete and taught by Don Pickerill in this sermon]

SERMON 11 SCRIPTURE REFERENCES:

[1] Romans 6:15-23 (RSV)

15 What then? Are we to sin because we are not under law but under grace? By no means! 16 Do you not know that if you yield yourselves to any one as obedient slaves, you are slaves of the one whom you obey, either of sin, which leads to death, or of obedience, which leads to righteousness? 17 But thanks be to God, that you who were once slaves of sin have become obedient from the heart to the standard of teaching to which you were committed, 18 and, having been set free from sin, have become slaves of righteousness. 19 I am speaking in human terms, because of your natural limitations. For just as you once yielded your members to impurity and to greater and greater iniquity, so now yield your members to righteousness for sanctification. 20 When you were slaves of sin, you were free in regard to righteousness. 21 But then what return did you get from the things of which you are now ashamed? The end of those things is death. 22 But now that you have been set free from sin and have become slaves of God, the return you get is sanctification and its end, eternal life. 23 For the wages of sin is death, but the free gift of God is eternal life in Christ Jesus our Lord.

[2] Romans 5:21 (RSV)

So that, as sin reigned in death, grace also might reign through righteousness to eternal life through Jesus Christ our Lord.

[3] Romans 5:20 (KJV)

Moreover the law entered, that the offence might abound. But where sin abounded, grace did much more abound:

[4] Romans 6:1 (RSV)

What shall we say then? Are we to continue in sin that grace may abound?

[5] Romans 5:20 (RSV)

Law came in, to increase the trespass; but where sin increased, grace abounded all the more,

[6] Romans 6:14 (RSV)

For sin will have no dominion over you, since you are not under law but under grace.

[7] Romans 6:15 (RSV)

What then? Are we to sin because we are not under law but under grace? By no means!

[8] Romans 6:19 (RSV)

I am speaking in human terms, because of your natural limitations. For just as you once yielded your members to impurity and to greater and greater iniquity, so now yield your members to righteousness for sanctification.

[9] Romans 6:16 (RSV)

Do you not know that if you yield yourselves to any one as obedient slaves, you are slaves of the one whom you obey, either of sin, which leads to death, or of obedience, which leads to righteousness?

[10] Romans 6:20 (RSV)

When you were slaves of sin, you were free in regard to righteousness.

[11] Romans 6:21 (RSV)

But then what return did you get from the things of which you are now ashamed? The end of those things is death.

[12] Romans 6:22 (RSV)

But now that you have been set free from sin and have become slaves of God, the return you get is sanctification and its end, eternal life.

[13] Romans 6:23 (RSV)

For the wages of sin is death, but the free gift of God is eternal life in Christ Jesus our Lord.

[14] Romans 6:17-18 (RSV)

17 But thanks be to God, that you who were once slaves of sin have become obedient from the heart to the standard of teaching to which you were committed 18 and, having been set free from sin, have become slaves of righteousness.

[15] Matthew 26:45-46 (RSV)

45 Then he came to the disciples and said to them, "Are you still sleeping and taking your rest? Behold, the hour is at hand, and the Son of man is betrayed into the hands of sinners. 46 Rise, let us be going; see, my betrayer is at hand."

[16] Romans 6:17 (ASV)

But thanks be to God, that, whereas ye were servants of sin, ye became obedient from the heart to that form of teaching whereunto ye were delivered;

[17] Romans 6:17 (RSV)

But thanks be to God, that you who were once slaves of sin have become obedient from the heart to the standard of teaching to which you were committed,

[18] Psalm 23:3 (RSV)

He restores my soul. He leads me in paths of righteousness for his name's sake.

[19] Ephesians 2:8-9 (KJV)

8 For by grace are ye saved through faith; and that not of yourselves: it is the gift of God: 9 Not of works, lest any man should boast.

SERMON 12

THE SPIRIT WITH WHICH WE SERVE

"I don't serve under the old written code,
but I serve in the new life of the Spirit!"

I'd like to read Romans chapter 7, verses 1 to 6, with special emphasis on **verse 6.** I'd like us to underscore that particularly. There are two major things for us to look for. First of all, notice the **doctrine,** the doctrinal statement or the truth that we are **free from the law.** Watch how clearly that will be stated. Then number two, let's notice the **practical part of this** and notice how we're to **serve** or how to **live.**

Romans chapter 7, the first six verses: *"Do you not know, brethren—for I am speaking to those who **know** the law—that the law is **binding** on a person only during his life? **Thus**"*—using an illustration now—*"a married woman is **bound** by law to her husband as long as he **lives; but if** her husband **dies** she is **discharged** from the law concerning her husband. Accordingly, she will be called an **adulteress** if she lives with another man **while** her husband is **alive.** But if her husband dies she is **free** from that law, and if she marries **another man** she is **not** an adulteress.* So, let's apply that illustration now—*"Likewise, my brethren, you have **died to the law** through the body of Christ, so that you may belong to another, to him who has been **raised from the dead** in order that we may **bear fruit** for God. While we were living in the **flesh,** our **sinful passions, aroused** by the law, were at work in our members to bear fruit for death. But **now** we are* *discharged from the law, **dead** to that which held us **captive**"*—and here's why, here's the practical part—*"so that **we should serve not under the old written code but in the new life of the Spirit.**"* [1]

Well, let's call this sermon, <u>The Spirit With Which We Serve</u>. I'd like us to see, first of all, how we should **not** serve, and then let's see how we **should** serve in this new life of the Spirit. Now, the word **serving,** of course, means **basically** how we **live,** the way we **do** things, how we go about our activities, our **attitude** toward God and toward **others.** And if we **serve** in the spirit of the **law,** we're in trouble. Now, Paul points out two things that are **wrong** with **serving** under this **old written code**— *"that we serve <u>not</u> under the **old written code.**"* [2]

"But now we are discharged from the law, dead to that which held us captive, so that we serve not under the old written code but in the new life of the Spirit." - Romans 7:6 RSV

Now, the first thing that's wrong with it—**it's old!** Now of course, not **everything** that's **old** is **bad.** Some things that are **old** get **better.** But **in contrast** it means that we are facing something that lacks life. It's **boring.** It's **lifeless,** in other words. **It's worn out by time and use.** In the scriptures this same word translated **old** is used of old clothing. It's become thread bare. It's shiny. It doesn't cover you adequately. **It's old! It can<u>not</u> add to the renewal of man.** And that's what we need, is something that **renews** us and gives us **life.** And the law can't do that because it's **old**—it **lacks** the capacity for **renewal** and for change.

The second thing about this is it's **written.** It is a **written code. Literally,** it means it's a **letter** or it's a **thing written.** Any time you have something that's **written,** a code or a **written code,** you have two problems. First of all, it's a **code** and by a code we simply mean **rules.** How do you **like** living by **rules** especially, **external** rules, a set of **rules** that are handed down to you? We just don't like it. You can't run, say your **family,** your **personal relationships,** by a set of **rules.** You **cannot** live life at a **high, personal, loving level** with a **code. With rules.** We simply **can't** do that. **We** only yield to grace. We do not **yield** to **codes.** Now, if we want to have an external **discipline** of the inner life of the Spirit, that's another **matter.** But if you're talking about a **written** set of **rules** and regulations, free human people don't respond well to that. **We—only—yield—to grace!**

And then secondly, when a thing is **written,** it's always external to us. And anything that's external to us has no power to get inside us. It has absolutely no **power!** That was what was wrong with the Law of Moses. It's a very **good law** but it was written on tables of **stone.** And there it is with this wonderful moral standard, but it has **no power** to get inside my heart and to **energize** me. It cannot be **written** on my **inner life.** So, anytime you have an **old written code,** you can be **certain** that it's not the best way to **serve.**

Now, if you're living under an old written **code,** you've got a couple of problems here. I like to call this, by the way for sake of memory, the **DT's** of the law. Have you ever heard about the **DT's?** When a fellow is given over to the power of alcoholism or drugs, he gets what we call the **DT's.** Well, the DT's of the law are first of all the **"Demand"** and then second the **"Threat."**

The **law is binding** it says on a person. "*A married woman is **bound** to the law.*"[3] So, to be under the law means that we are under the **constant** sense of **duty** and **claim.** And that's an awful thing to live your life with a **demand.** If you're under the law, you feel that **demand** upon you and that's a **very** uncomfortable feeling.

Now, the second thing is the **threat** of the law. The DT. Notice Paul says in chapter 7, verse 3, "*...she will be called an **adulteress**"* [4] —that is under the law she will be **threatened.** So, under the law you have the idea of condemnation or punishment—you have the **threats** of the law. And the law is full of all kinds of solemn **warnings** and **threats** against **death.**

I'd like us to note, by the way, the **practical ways** that we can spot ourselves, when we serve under the **old written code.** You know, some people **really** don't know when they're under the law—the spirit of the law. **They really don't!** So, here's the way you can spot it. You can **always** tell when you're **serving** under the old written code this way: Number one, **when you tend to overly stress life as a duty.** When you feel that life is an obligation and when you have this **attitude** about yourself and others you can be **sure** that you're **under the law.** In other words, you stress **duty** beyond personal relationships.

And then **secondly,** you can always spot it when **things must be right.** Notice I said, they **"must—be—right!"** I think that's a very important thing. Now we all want things done right. We're not talking about **minimizing right** or **goodness.** But it's so **easy** for a person **under the law** with a **conscience down under the law** to be more concerned about the **"right"** than about **people.** You know, Jesus had to fight with this thing, all of His ministry. He fought **that attitude,** I think, above everything else; because the Pharisees were so **"right."** They **made man for the Sabbath,** but Jesus came along and **shattered** all this false thinking and that by the way, **infuriated** others. [5]

I have a little **statement** that's very meaningful to me: "That Christians do not do **things right,** but they do **right things.**" Now, that's not original with me. It's a little statement out of **management,** that "**Good managers** do not do things **right,** but they do **right things.**"

That's the difference between Christianity and **religion,** or that's the difference between law and grace.

So, things **must—be—right!** I might add, by the way, they must be right or **else.** It must be **right,** or it deserves our **anger.** We get **upset** if it's not **right.** We **drive** people out of the **church.** We **drive** children out of our **homes,** but it's **going to be <u>right</u>.** Well, that's the way you can **spot** a conscious, bound under the law, when somebody is under the **old—written—code.** It **must** be **right,** and it **must** be right or—**else!** It's **important** when we get to the point where we're not **fussy perfectionists,** and we learn that our **relationship** with God is <u>far</u> **more important** than our **blamelessness** before Him.

Let's see how we are to serve. That's what we're really after. And here's this beautiful, beautiful phrase about to **drill** itself in our hearts and minds. *"…we do **not** serve under the **old written code** <u>but</u> in the new life of the Spirit."* [2] I just **love** to say that phrase: *"We—serve—in the—new—life— of the—Spirit!"*

Now, here also we have two ideas. First of all, is this **newness,** the **new** life of the Spirit. There's something **exciting** about that isn't there? Fresh and **spontaneous!** You know the excitement ought not go out of our Christian life. **In** the Holy Spirit and **by** the resurrection of Jesus there's a kind of a creative **newness** about the work of God in us. We **serve** with that spiritual **excitement** as the Holy Spirit keeps it **new** and **alive** and **fresh.** Then it says it's, *"in the new life of the Spirit!"* And, of course, that means the **Holy Spirit.** But we need to be practical here and see what we mean by *"the new life of the Spirit."* [2]

You know the Spirit is also a very practical **concept,** because the Spirit is **always** talking about the kind of **life** that the Holy Spirit **brings,** or that is, a **life level.** And the most **important** concept of the **life of the Spirit <u>is</u> freedom.** You serve with an **exciting freedom.** We serve—in this—new—wonderful—freedom—in the Holy Spirit.

You know, the more you go up in life, the **higher** you go up in life, the chain of life, the freer it becomes? Take for example the mineral kingdom. There's a certain amount of **life** there, but you have the **static** quality of life. Then you come on up to **plants**. The plant kingdom. Here you have a little more **bending** and **freedom** as it were. When you get up to the animal world all that much more **freedom**. By the time you reach **man** however, you have a being who is **made** for freedom and can never be **happy** and satisfied **without** freedom. But when you reach the level of the **Spirit, there's** where you reap absolute and **perfect <u>freedom</u>.** The Holy Spirit has that **beautiful, wonderful <u>freedom</u>.** And so, **we** serve *"in the—new—life—of—the Spirit."* [2]

Now, how can we be free from the law? How can we **know** and be **certain** that we are **not** under the law? How can we be free? Well, it's important for us to see—**that we—are—not— under—the law.** Paul says three things about this, and he really uses kind of word pictures, or illustrations.

The first might be from the **employment agency.** He says a couple of times here that we are **discharged** from the law. Notice verse 2, he says that this wife—*"is **discharged** from the law concerning **her husband.**"* [3] And he says down here in verse 6, *"But **now** we are **discharged** from the law."* [2] In ancient times, if a Greek man was **unemployed** this word applied to **him.** He was not **working.** He wasn't **operating.** The word here is *argos.* [A] We get our word **energy** from that word or **erg.** It means a thing that works. But here it is **not** working. This Greek word, and it's a tiny bit technical, but it's worth passing along. The Greek word is *katargeo.* [B] You add a prepositional prefix to that word—"working" or "not working," and it's an **intensification.** It **means** it is **utterly** powerless—**empty—abrogated—canceled—brought to an end— destroyed—<u>annihilated</u>.** We are **not under the law.** We are **discharged** from the law. We are **free** from it. Utterly free. The law is **not working.** It is unemployed.

And the second word is **free.** We are **free** from the law. This is a figure of speech taken from the realm of **slavery.** In ancient times the slaves were the **property** of their **masters.** They were like **captives.** They were **subject** to them, in **submission** to **their masters.** But we are **free** from the law like a **slave** who has been **redeemed** from an old master. We are set free. We are **free men.** And **then** if that isn't **enough,** Paul uses a word from the funeral. He says, *"We're **dead** to the law."* We are **discharged** from the law, <u>dead</u> **to that which held us captive.** That's a very strong term. We're **dead** to it. It doesn't **exist** for us anymore. By the way, notice Paul says that we are **dead** <u>through</u> the <u>body of Christ</u>. That's a very interesting phrase. He says in verse 4, *"You are **dead to the** law <u>through</u> the body of Christ, so that you may **belong** to another, to him who has been **raised** from the dead in order that we may bear **fruit** from God."* [6]

You see the Apostle Paul won't let us get very far away from the work of the Lord Jesus Christ. He wants us to see how **important** it is to keep close to Jesus Christ in being delivered from the law, because we are **dead** to the law <u>through</u> the body of Christ. And that means that the **death** of Jesus Christ **ended** the law for us.

 "Likewise, my brethren, you have died to the law through the body of Christ, so that you may belong to another, to him who has been raised from the dead in order that we may bear fruit for God." - Romans 7:4 RSV

I tell you, that's a wonderful thing to know. How **wonderful to know** that we have **full emancipation** from the law. I don't think we'll every grasp this **glorious freedom** that comes to us until we know that we are **not** under this claim, **not** under this law. We are **free** by the Lord Jesus Christ.

In one of his books the **famous writer,** Watchman Nee, has a kind of a **daring** statement. But I think I'd like to use it here in a summary and concluding fashion. Watchman Nee has this to say, What does it mean in everyday life to be delivered from the law? Well, at the risk of a little over statement, I reply, **it means that, from henceforth, I am going to do nothing whatever for God. I am never again going to try to please Him.**" C

Now, don't misunderstand that. You've **got** to grasp the **spirit** and the **intent** of this in light of this message. But translated, this is what that means—"You know I'm going to enjoy life. I'm going to be perfectly relaxed. I'm not going to be a **fussy perfectionist, all** hung up on doing **right,** and that's all I know and understand. But **I'm** going to know that I have been **raised from the dead** and that I can have fruit for God. I can **live** my life, **married** as it were, to the Spirit of God, to our **risen Lord Jesus Christ.** Jesus Christ has **ended** that kind of a life for me. **I don't serve under the <u>old written code</u>, but I serve in the <u>new</u> life of the Spirit."** Hallelujah! That's a **wonderful** way to live. May Jesus Christ teach it to us by His Spirit and by His Word.

SERMON 12 ENDNOTES:

A *argos,* means: inactive, i.e. unemployed; (by implication) lazy, useless:--barren, idle, slow. Strong's Greek Dictionary #692

B *katargeo,* means: it is utterly powerless, empty, abrogated, canceled, brought to an end, destroyed, annihilated. Strong's Greek Dictionary #2722. [exegete and taught by Don Pickerill in this sermon]

C Nee, Watchman. (April 4, 1938). *The Normal Christian Life.*(pp.67).

SERMON 12 SCRIPTURE REFERENCES:

[1] Romans 7:1-6 (RSV)

1 Do you not know, brethren—for I am speaking to those who know the law—that the law is binding on a person only during his life? 2 Thus a married woman is bound by law to her husband as long as he lives; but if her husband dies she is discharged from the law concerning the husband. 3 Accordingly, she will be called an adulteress if she lives with another man while her husband is alive. But if her husband dies she is free from that law, and if she marries another man she is not an adulteress. 4 Likewise, my brethren, you have died to the law through the body of Christ, so that you may belong to another, to him who has been raised from the dead in order that we may bear fruit for God. 5 While we were living in the flesh, our sinful passions, aroused by the law, were at work in our members to bear fruit for death. 6 But now we are discharged from the law, dead to that which held us captive, so that we serve not under the old written code but in the new life of the Spirit.

[2] Romans 7:6 (RSV)

But now we are discharged from the law, dead to that which held us captive, so that we serve not under the old written code but in the new life of the Spirit.

[3] Romans 7:2 (RSV)

Thus a married woman is bound by law to her husband as long as he lives; but if her husband dies she is discharged from the law concerning the husband.

[4] Romans 7:3 (RSV)

Accordingly, she will be called an adulteress if she lives with another man while her husband is alive. But if her husband dies she is free from that law, and if she marries another man she is not an adulteress.

[5] Mark 2:27 (RSV)

And he said to them, "The sabbath was made for man, not man for the sabbath;

[6] Romans 7:4 (RSV)

Likewise, my brethren, you have died to the law through the body of Christ, so that you may belong to another, to him who has been raised from the dead in order that we may bear fruit for God.

WHY WE MUST BE FREE FROM THE LAW – PART 1

"We are not—under law—we are—under—grace.
Do you believe it?"

This is sermon number 13 in a series on Romans chapters 6, 7 and 8. We're learning what it means to be **under grace** and **not** under law. *"You are **not under law but under grace.**"* [1] That's the great truth of Romans chapters 6, 7 and 8. I would like to **point out** that the most singly important thing in **life** is the **state** of your **spirit,** the **state** of your **soul,** your **mind,** your **attitude** or whatever you want to call it. Your **soul.** Is it **quiet?** Is it **happy?** Is it **restful?** If so, you have life. And we say over and over again, the most important thing in life **is life.** Not just an **existence,** but a **quality** that comes to **life.**

The Apostle says in Romans 5:21, *"...that grace might reign through righteousness to eternal life."* [2] So we want **grace to reign to life.** We're all trying to find **life. But** unfortunately, many times we try to do **that** by what is known as **law.** We are **under the law.** We have a **conscience under the law.** We are **bound by the law.** We don't know what it means to be **under grace.** So, we're seeing in Romans chapters 6, 7 and 8 what it means to be freed from the **powers that bind** and that bring us into captivity.

Now little would we **know** that one would have to be **freed from law.** We would not know that connection, in my mind most of us would not. We would know that we ought to be freed from **death.** We would know that we ought to be freed from **corruption,** and from **evil.** But who would have associated **law** with those? **Law, sin and death, the terrible triad.**

So, the Apostle Paul in Romans chapter 7 is telling us, number one, that we are **freed from the law.** He uses an illustration in the first six verses of a married woman who is **bound** to her husband **by** the law, and if she lives with another, she would be an **adulteress.** [3] That illustration tells us a simple **fact** that we <u>are</u> discharged, <u>free</u> from the **law.** Now, that's such a **mind shattering statement.** But it's true,—*"You are not under law, but under grace,"* [1] and may the Holy Spirit help us to understand the simple **truth** of that.

Now, the Apostle goes on in the **rest** of the chapter, beginning with verse 7 **through** verse 25, to tell us <u>why</u> **we must be free from the law.** After making the illustration of the married woman and saying that by the body of the Lord Jesus Christ we are **dead** to the law, then he will explain to us **why it is necessary to be free from the law.**

Now, **why?** Why are we making such a **fuss** of the point? Now really, Paul gives two main reasons. In verses 7 through 13 he will **explain** to us why we must be free from the law because of **what it <u>does</u>.** What the law <u>can</u> do. And then, in verses 14 through 25, he will tell us why we must be freed from the law because of what it **can<u>not</u> do.** So, this chapter is both a negative and a positive lesson telling us what the **law <u>does</u>** and what it **can<u>not</u> do.** Why it is weak and why it is an ineffective system.

Today we're going to look at this **great** reason, **why we must be free from the law.** I might add that this is going to have to take two parts, I know. And in tonight's sermon we're going into the most **significant profound** part of Romans, that's verses 14 through 25.

I would suggest that we get this entire passage before us, however.

I'd like to read please beginning with verse 7. Romans chapter 7, verse 7—*"What then shall we say? That the law is **sin?** By no means!"* Don't let that even come into your **minds.** *"__Yet__, if it had __not__ been for the law, I should not have known sin."* For example—*"I should not have known what it is to **covet** if the law had said, 'You—shall—not—covet.' But—sin, finding an **opportunity**"*—an **occasion**—getting a **toehold**—a base of operation—*"finding an **opportunity** __in the commandment__, __IT WROUGHT IN ME ALL KINDS OF COVETOUSNESS__. Apart from the __law__—sin—lies—dead."*—so to speak. Some of these would no doubt be in parentheses today if Paul were writing it, he'd use the word **dead,** no doubt you see, in parentheses. *"Now **I was once alive** apart from the law, but when the **commandment __came__**"*—when that moral awaking came and the commandment reached me—the awful understanding of **holiness**— *"when the **commandment came, sin revived and I __died;__"***—a death-like existence under condemnation and guilt—*"**the very commandment which promised life it proved to be __death__ to me. For sin, finding an opportunity in the __commandment__, it deceived me"***—**thinking that I could do that** and low and behold it brought me to **death** and not to life—*"and by it, it just **killed me.**"* It left me under the curse and under condemnation and worthy of death. *"**So the law** it's **holy** and the **commandment is holy** and very just and good."* [4]

"Did that which is good, then, bring death to me? By no means! It was sin, working death in me through what is good, in order that sin might be shown to be sin, and through the commandment might become sinful beyond measure." - Romans 7:13 RSV

(Don continues reading here at verse 13) *"Did that which is **good**, then, bring **death** to me?"* In other words, was it the law itself? **No.** No

now don't draw that conclusion. *"By no means!"* There's nothing wrong with the law per se. ***"It was <u>sin</u>, working <u>death in me</u> through what's good,"***—sin will take any good thing and use it wrong and sin took the law—*"so in order that sin might be **shown** to be sin, and **through the commandment** might become **sinful beyond** measure."* Exceeding sinful. *"We know that the law is"*—all you can say is—*"is **spiritual;**"*—it's from the **Spirit** and it's **holy**, it's **good. But** the problem is—*"**I'm carnal,"***—I'm a human being.** More about that tonight. ***"I'm <u>sold</u> under sin."* I'm deluded!** *"I don't understand my own actions."* I'm **puzzled**, I'm **frustrated.** *"I do <u>not</u> do what I <u>want</u>, I do the very thing that I **hate**."* Now notice I **hate** it. I don't **love** it, but I **do it.** I **hate** it but I **do it!** *"Now if I do what I do not want, then **I** agree that the law is good."* Still nothing wrong with the law. *"So then,"*—in a way you would say this, don't take Paul absolutely here, he corrects himself and he's only in an **intensive deep way** showing all the issues of this—*"it is no longer <u>I</u> that do it, but sin that dwells within me."* Not that I'm **not** responsible. **I am.** But I see that I'm **captive** here. Sin's power is **so great** that only **God** can break it. *"It's no longer I that do it, but sin that dwells **within me.** I know that **nothing good dwells within <u>me</u>,"***—Nothing!**—*"that is, in my flesh. I can <u>will</u> what is right, but I can't do it."* I can **will** it. I want to do it. I can understand it, but I can't do it—a gap between my insights and my instincts. *"I do **not** do the good I want, but the evil I do not want is **what I <u>do</u>**. Now if I do what I don't **want**, it's no longer"*—in a **sense**—*"I that do it, but sin that **dwells** within me."* [5]

    (Don continues reading here at verse 21) *"So I find this **law**"*—this **habit**—this **tendency**—this **power**—*"that when I want to do right,"*—I **habitually** find that—*"evil lies close at hand."* It's very close. *"Now I delight in the law of God, in **my inmost self**, but **I see** in my members another"*—**power**—*"another **law**"*—another authority—*"it's at **war** with the law of my mind"*—**my insight**, my rational self—*"and it makes me **captive**

*to the **law of sin which dwells in my <u>members</u>**.*" My bodily members. *"**Wretched man that I am!**"* Miserable. *"Who will deliver me from this **body**, this body of **death**? **Thanks be to God through Jesus Christ our Lord!** So then, I of myself, I serve the law of God with my **mind**,*"—with my rational—my better self—my inmost man—*"but with my **flesh** I serve the law of sin."* [6] We perhaps, should go on and read the first verses of Romans 8 just to let you know that that figures very much into what we have to say as we start this insight on <u>Why We Must be Free from the Law</u>, today.

Now once again, I want to clarify just some basic issues, and again I want to say in a practical way what we're talking about when we refer to the **law**. What do we mean now in a practical way? What's this all **about?** Well, let me say this, that to be under the law in a practical way means: **You—must—be—right—in order—to live! You have no right to exist! You have no place in the Son** unless you're **right**—unless you're in the right. **For you to be <u>accepted</u> with <u>yourself</u>, and with <u>others</u> and with God; you have to be <u>right</u>!** Now that's **law,** pure and simple. That's what it means to be under the law. **Everything is based on <u>right</u>. You have to be right to be accepted. <u>Acceptance</u> is based upon performance, and if you're not right you are unacceptable. Now, we call that the righteousness of the law.**

That has **another** part to it. Not only that thought, "You must be right to be acceptable—to live—to exist". But also, in addition to that, "You must **become right** by your own works—by your effort." We call that the principle of **works!**

Those two things essentially make up what we call, **the law.** Now, I don't know whether you know it or not, or have thought it through; but most people live that way. Most people treat themselves that way. They think **God** is that way. They relate to **others** that way. Most of us are constantly going through a testing. "Am I acceptable with that person?"

"Do they really like me?" Many people tell me to meet anybody is a chore just to **face them**—be in their presence. They're wondering, "Am I acceptable?" **That's the way they live! It's what <u>motivates them</u>! And furthermore, they will relate to other people that way. They're always checking to see if they're in the <u>right</u>. They don't know anything at all about the righteousness of <u>faith</u>, because all they know is the righteousness by the law.** Many people, by the way, of this persuasion, believe that Jesus Christ gives us the power to **keep** the law in order to be **righteous**. <u>They don't know there's another whole way! That the chief thing in life is NOT being in the right</u>! The most important thing in this world is **not being good**. Did you know that? **That's not what life is all about. It's all about a relationship.** It's called **faith**—and it's called **love**—and it's called **hope**. Israel had fifteen hundred years of the law. The revealed will of God. This marvelous code. But what did they do? They—<u>missed</u>—the—whole—point! **An entire nation of people** for one thousand, five hundred years, and they **still** haven't seen it.

Paul writes later in Romans chapter 9, *"**The Gentiles who did <u>not</u> pursue righteousness, <u>they've obtained it</u>,"**—**they didn't even go after it, and they're righteous**! "...that is, the righteousness through faith; but Israel who pursued the righteousness which is based on <u>law</u> did not succeed in fulfilling the law. <u>Why</u>? Because they did not pursue it through <u>faith</u>, but as it were based on works."* [7] *(Don continues reading here at Romans 10, verse 1) "Brethren, my heart's desire is that they might be saved. But I'm going to bear witness about these people. They have a zeal for God, but it is not **enlightened**."* Have you ever met anybody like that? They are **very** religious people, but they are not **enlightened**. They **live** under the **law**. They have a **conscience** under the **law**. That's all they **know** on **those** terms. *"Being <u>ignorant</u> of the righteousness that comes from <u>God</u> and seeking to establish their <u>own</u>, they don't submit to God's righteousness. Christ is the <u>end</u> of the law that everyone who has faith may be <u>justified</u>!"* [8]

(Don continues reading here at Romans 10:5) **Now, "Moses writes,"—and here's the spirit of the law. This is the way most people live—***"the man who <u>practices</u> the righteousness which is based on the law, he'll live by it."* **That's it. You have to do it to be accepted.** You must be **right,** and you must be **right or <u>else</u>.** That's the spirit of the **law.** *"But the righteousness **based on faith** says, don't say in your heart,"*—**what are we going to have to do? Is something to be done?** *"Don't say in your heart, 'Who's going to ascend into heaven?' (that is to bring Christ down)"*—we've got to have something **happen** here or—we've got to have something **deep** happen—we've got to do something **profound.** *" 'Who's going to descend into the abyss?' (that is, to bring Christ up from the dead).* **What does it say? The word is <u>near</u> you, it's on your <u>lips</u> and it's in your <u>heart</u>** *(and that's, this word of **faith** which we **preach**); if you confess with your lips that Jesus is Lord and believe—in—your—heart—that God— raised him from the dead, you'll be saved."* Hear it? *"For man <u>believes</u>* **with his heart and so is <u>JUSTIFIED</u>,"**—**just by <u>faith</u>!** You can <u>never</u> be <u>GOOD</u> <u>ENOUGH</u> to be <u>justified</u>, <u>NEVER</u>! **You have to be <u>absolutely</u> <u>PERFECT</u>.** Are any of you absolutely perfect? No, every one of you has sinned in thought, word, and deed every day. **Our only <u>hope</u> is another system <u>altogether</u>. It <u>cannot</u> be the righteousness based upon the <u>law</u>.** We've got to be <u>freed</u> from that system and the whole concept of legalism. It is <u>fundamentally wrong</u>! *"The scripture says, "No one who* **believes** *in him will be put to **shame**."* [9] Everything else will make you feel **shame,** and guilt, and wrath, and condemnation.

"The scripture says, 'No one who believes in him will be put to shame.'" - Romans 10:11 RSV

The Apostle has made a number of things about the law in Romans chapter 7 and let me briefly summarize them. I have written out in a mechanical way what he said and there are **ten key statements** about the law. And I just repeat them:

1. We have **died** to the law through the body of Christ. Verse 4

2. The law **arouses** sinful passions and leaves us in the condition of **death.** Verse 5

3. The law in and of itself is **not** sinful or **bad.** Verse 7

4. The law reveals **sin.** Verse 7

5. Apart from the law, sin lies **dead.** (That is "unawakened.") Verse 8

6. The law is **holy, just and good.** Verse 12

7. The law is **spiritual.** Verse 14

8. The law is **good** and men who long to do good **know** that it's good. Verse 16

9. Rational men love the law with their **better** or their deepest self. Verse 22

10. The law is **powerless** to **help** a person do what is right. It can **promise** life, **but it can** only **bring you death.** Verse 10 and Chapter 8, Verse 3

Now, if you'll **summarize** all that, there are **three major statements** being said about the law in this chapter. First of all, **the law is good.** We must remember that. The law is **good!** There's nothing wrong with the law. What's wrong with **standards?** What's wrong with **holiness?** What's wrong with **right?** What's wrong with telling people about it? **Nothing!** We're not talking about that in and of itself. Please remember that. So, to be **under the law** and the **spirit of the law** is not necessarily the same as just talking about **standards** and doing **right** and holiness. We're concerned about that. So, the law is **good.** Let's remember **that.**

Number two; but because of **sin** and the **connection,** the way **sin** uses **law,** it takes a **good thing** and makes it **bad.** What **could** produce life if you kept it, **winds up bringing you death.** That's why you've got to be **freed from the law.**

And then **finally,** third, **there—is—no—inherit—power—in the law.** It can only be a lesson of a **negative kind.** The law will **always be a destructive** rather than a **creative force** in our lives.

We're going to look this morning at the **three things** that the law **can** do. The three things that the law **does.** Tonight, we'll go on to look at the things that the law **cannot** do. And, by the way, I do regard that sermon tonight as the most **important** of all that I'm going to preach in this entire series. I hope **nobody** will miss that sermon, Romans 7:14 to 25. It's **vastly** important that you hear that sermon in my opinion.

Now, why must we be freed from the law and this whole concept? Why must we be delivered from legalism? Well, for these reasons: Number one, **the law can** and **does** show up sin—because the law is a **code. It makes it very clear what's right and wrong.** Would you **know** everything that was **right** and **wrong** if it were **not—for—a—code?** The law **shows up sin,** verse 7, **"I—had—not—known—sin, except— by—the law."** For example, *"I wouldn't have known, say it was wrong to covet if the law hadn't said 'You—shall—not—covet.'"* [10] I might have thought that these desires were wholly normal. Are there happy pagans? Of course there are! Happy savages? **Sure!** The law hasn't come to them. They don't have an awakened moral sense. Their whole conscience, as it were, is not **aroused.** They've not been **awakened** to this **awesome holiness.** And so, unless the law comes along, it won't necessarily show you up as a sinner.

I have a very **human** illustration. I don't know that it's a **good one.** We live up in La Crescenta and we **used** to go up La Crescenta Avenue, a little **two-lane** highway. I used to drive up and down there 50-55 miles an hour on that little two-lane highway. *(Don chuckles)* But then **traffic** began to **build up** and they made it four lanes and they put up a signal—a zone— speed limit 35, I think it is. *(Don chuckles)* Am I correct or not? And I got a **ticket** there one day. A policeman was there with radar, you know, and I got a ticket. *(Don continues chuckling)* **Alright! The law went up boy!** And it let me know that it was **wrong** to go through that **speed zone,** you see. *(One last chuckle)*

Alright, when you have that sense of morality that comes to your heart—when you're <u>awakened</u> and all of a sudden you start knowing the difference between right and wrong, it <u>shows</u> you that. You read that commandment and there's no question in your mind what's right and wrong anymore. The law can do that. It does a very good job of that. And, in a sense we **need** that by the way.

But secondly, and this is the **key** thing, and this is the **heart** of it, **this is—why—you—must—be—free—from the law!** Because, **strangely enough,** the **law** in connection with **sin, stirs up sin.** You not only have this **code,** but you **also** have **the law** working in such a way that it *"wrought in me,"* Paul says, *"all kinds of covetousness. Apart from the law sin lies <u>dead</u>."* [11] But he explains here that it **works death** in me, that the law has a way of **stirring—up—sin.**

Now, **how** does that work? It's very **simple. Anytime** you have a **prohibition** laid upon **any** human person, they **always** want to do **the opposite.** Did you hear that? If somebody says to you, **"<u>You can't!</u>"** Do you know what you'll say? **"I will."** *(Congregation murmurs)* That's human nature. **That's <u>sin</u> in human nature. And so, you let the <u>claim</u> of the law**—you let somebody start putting <u>pressure</u> on you—you let somebody start getting you in a legalistic <u>bind</u>—and human nature will <u>always</u> get this rebellious quality to it. It will <u>stir—up</u>—your nature. Your <u>instincts</u>, all of a sudden come <u>alive!</u> That's why this is always and always will be an inadequate system. Because it <u>fails</u>

to take into account the **sinful** part of **human nature.** You husbands know when your wife starts giving you advice on how to drive the car you know what you'll do. You either speed up and drive reckless or you won't say a word. *(Don and congregation chuckles)* **It's in human nature!**

Alright furthermore, when **that** happens it **always** gets tied up with **guilt. Now then,** if a person is **confronted** with this **code** and then is **alive** to this **claim, now comes along this feeling of uneasiness and guilt. Now I'm not at peace, and I've got to someway handle that dispirit in my soul. And so, what will I do? My guilt will lead me to all kinds of sin. It will make me angry. It will make me defensive. It will make me want to hide. It will make me want to do further sin to appease that guilt. It does—all—kinds—of—THINGS! And so, it's a very simple thing that when you lay that claim—when the law comes to human nature—it begins to stir up all kinds of problems.**

And I've mentioned about LIFE Bible College *(now Life Pacific University)* and the only reason I do that, by the way, is because they're the **cream** of the "Christian crop." And if anybody was going to do it by law, LIFE Bible College students would have done it long ago. Do they like the rules, when you lay on rules? I know what happens, none of them **fool me!**

Now why did we ever think this would work any differently? We get deceived! It's a deception! Sin comes along and deceives us. Same is true with parents. We think we can run our families by law. We wind up just getting disillusioned rebellious children. **We're deceived! The principle of legalism is wrong from the core.**

And then thirdly, **it slays the sinner.** Paul says, *"It kills me."* [12] Now by that he means: Then I come under the **curse** of the law. I get under the sense of **condemnation.** Then I have a sense of **death** in me. In that sense, **it kills me,** you see. I feel **guilty** and **miserable** and **uncomfortable and know** that I'm worthy of **death.**

And so, the law in all three aspects: As a **code**—as a **claim**—and as a **curse**. They're all wrong. So, all it can do—**ALL the law can do**— now listen—**this is ALLLLL it can <u>do</u>**—**that's it, period!** It can **show up sin**. It can **stir up sin** and **does stir up sin**. And it—**can—slay—you**. And that's **ALL**! That's why you can't be under the <u>law</u>. If you're under the law you're <u>UNDONE</u>! There is—<u>only</u>—one—possible—way! And that's to be freed from this entire <u>principle</u>. To live under a totally new kind of concept and that is <u>grace</u>.

Now, let me again make this as practical as I can. **If you—are— relating—to yourself—or any other <u>self</u>—including <u>God</u>—on the basis of <u>right</u>—then you—are <u>wrong</u>!** That's worth writing down. I memorized it. *If you—are relating—to yourself—or <u>anybody</u> else—on the basis of <u>right</u>—you—are <u>wrong</u>!* **Because the law has to do with RIGHT! You must be RIGHT—<u>or</u> ELSE! See the problem folks, is we're <u>all</u> WRONG. <u>Every</u>—<u>single</u>—<u>one of us</u>! And even in the very <u>best</u> we do, we still count ourselves as unworthy servants.** Again, more about that tonight. Don't miss that sermon. This is a "lulu," I'm telling you! *(Congregation chuckles and murmurs)*

Most—people—live—at that—<u>basis</u>! They can't live with themselves because they don't feel <u>right</u>. Of <u>course</u> you <u>can't</u>! But that's to be under the <u>law</u> and to have a conscience under the <u>law</u>. You're free from all of that. Say, did you know something? You're <u>okay</u>! You're <u>acceptable</u>! You are <u>made</u> <u>acceptable</u> by the imputation of the righteousness of the Lord Jesus Christ! <u>What do you think Jesus died for</u>? <u>All of your sins</u>! <u>Do you have to atone for them</u>? <u>No</u>! They were all taken care of! You're made acceptable in the beloved.

I tell you, I'm alright and don't you <u>dare</u> tell me any different. Now I can take some **chiding** and **exhortation** but you better do it in the spirit of **grace**. I tell you what'll come out of me. Just don't try it! *(Congregation chuckles)* I'm not going to do that too much with you either, *(Don and congregation chuckles)* because I know **you** and you're no different than **I am.** *(Don and congregation continue to chuckle)*

Folks, we've got to **see** that there's another whole **system** that's totally different from the **righteousness of the law.** So many people are **caught up** in that, that they actually let **that** come between them and other people and the Lord Jesus Christ. That's why that **has** to be **removed.** That has to be a **direct confrontation with God** through the Holy Spirit.

And I'm going to say further, that if you are by the same token constantly **appealing** to people or using **force,** then you're still with a conscience, bound under the law. You think that's going to work. No way. No way could it change the human heart. It can **only be changed** by the **marvelous, wonderful,** grace of God.

Thank God that Jesus Christ has come **into** this whole scene. And as Romans chapter 8 goes on to say, *"There is **no** condemnation to those who are **in** Christ Jesus."* [13] **It didn't say, "Who keeps the law!" Nobody can do that! It has to be another whole basis!** And he says that Jesus Christ has come, through His incarnation, and has done all this **marvelous, wonderful work** that we call, "In the Spirit," which we'll have to explain further.

But let me tell you, it is **absolutely essential** that you be freed from the law. Because if you're trusting anything but the grace of God and anything else but faith, you're trusting the wrong thing. You'll either wind up totally frustrated and miserable and wretched—or you'll wind up a religious Pharisee, which is a **self-righteous, rigid** kind of a soul. And it's **amazing** how **hateful** Christians can be. **I've met them.** They can just **spew out liquid fire everywhere they go. They're griped and upset, and their spirit is critical, and they go around with a harsh mean spirit. What's WRONG with those people? They've got a conscience under the law.** They don't know the grace of God.

I could tell you **hundreds** of illustrations of this. Just last night in one of our couple's groups, a dear, dear friend has been **so critical** and **mean** and **harsh** with his wife and his little baby, and he couldn't understand that. But he says all of a sudden, "You know, I must be learning the grace of God." He said, **"It's transforming my life!"**

I'm not talking about something just on the pages of the Bible. I'm talking about a <u>life</u>—a <u>doctrine</u>—a <u>truth</u> that—sets—you—free— into the glorious liberty of the children of God. And this ought to work in <u>our lives</u>—in our <u>marriages</u>—in our <u>families</u>—and in our <u>relationships</u> with <u>one another</u>. It—ought—to be—that way.

You've <u>got </u>to be free from the law to enter into life. Just start running your marriage and your family by law, let me know how far you get. **You'll utterly make a <u>horrible mess</u> of everything.** And the **same is true** with your relationship with God. You think **God** wants it that way? **No, He doesn't!** He wants it on another basis altogether where you just **love Him** for His marvelous grace that comes to you through the Lord Jesus Christ.

We are **not**—under law—we are—**under**—**grace.** Do you believe it? Do you **dare** believe it? Some of you have looked daggers at me the past thirteen sermons. I don't know whether you know whether you ought to believe this or not. (Don chuckles) Please believe that's the gospel. That's the good news of the grace of God in Jesus Christ our Lord.

SERMON 13 ENDNOTES:

None

SERMON 13 SCRIPTURE REFERENCES:

[1] Romans 6:14 (RSV)

For sin will have no dominion over you, since you are not under law but under grace.

[2] Romans 5:21 (RSV)

so that, as sin reigned in death, grace also might reign through righteousness to eternal life through Jesus Christ our Lord.

[3] Romans 7:1-6 (RSV)

1 Do you not know, brethren—for I am speaking to those who know the law—that the law is binding on a person only during his life? 2 Thus a married woman is bound by law to her husband as long as he lives; but if her husband dies she is discharged from the law concerning the husband. 3 Accordingly, she will be called an adulteress if she lives with another man while her husband is alive. But if her husband dies she is free from that law, and if she marries another man she is not an adulteress. 4 Likewise, my brethren, you have died to the law through the body of Christ, so that you may belong to another, to him who has been raised from the dead in order that we may bear fruit for God. 5 While we were living in the flesh, our sinful passions, aroused by the law, were at work in our members to bear fruit for death. 6 But now we are discharged from the law, dead to that which held us captive, so that we serve not under the old written code but in the new life of the Spirit.

[4] Romans 7:7-12 (RSV)

7 What then shall we say? That the law is sin? By no means! Yet, if it had not been for the law, I should not have known sin. I should not have known what it is to covet if the law had not said, "You shall not covet." 8 But sin, finding an opportunity in the commandment, wrought in me all kinds of covetousness. Apart from the law sin lies dead. 9 I was once alive apart from the law, but when the commandment came, sin revived and I died; 10 the very commandment which promised life proved to be death to me. 11 For sin, finding opportunity in the commandment, deceived me and by it killed me. 12 So the law is holy, and the commandment is holy and just and good.

⁵ Romans 7:13-20 (RSV)

13 Did that which is good, then, bring death to me? By no means! It was sin, working death in me through what is good, in order that sin might be shown to be sin, and through the commandment might become sinful beyond measure. 14 We know that the law is spiritual; but I am carnal, sold under sin. 15 I do not understand my own actions. For I do not do what I want, but I do the very thing I hate. 16 Now if I do what I do not want, I agree that the law is good. 17 So then it is no longer I that do it, but sin which dwells within me. 18 For I know that nothing good dwells within me, that is, in my flesh. I can will what is right, but I cannot do it. 19 For I do not do the good I want, but the evil I do not want is what I do. 20 Now if I do what I do not want, it is no longer I that do it, but sin which dwells within me.

⁶ Romans 7:21-25 (RSV)

21 So I find it to be a law that when I want to do right, evil lies close at hand. 22 For I delight in the law of God, in my inmost self, 23 but I see in my members another law at war with the law of my mind and making me captive to the law of sin which dwells in my members. 24 Wretched man that I am! Who will deliver me from this body of death? 25 Thanks be to God through Jesus Christ our Lord! So then, I of myself serve the law of God with my mind, but with my flesh I serve the law of sin.

[7] Romans 9:30-32 (RSV)

30 What shall we say, then? That Gentiles who did not pursue righteousness have attained it, that is, righteousness through faith; 31 but that Israel who pursued the righteousness which is based on law did not succeed in fulfilling that law. 32 Why? Because they did not pursue it through faith, but as if it were based on works. They have stumbled over the stumbling stone,

[8] Romans 10:1-4 (RSV)

10 Brethren, my heart's desire and prayer to God for them is that they may be saved. 2 I bear them witness that they have a zeal for God, but it is not enlightened. 3 For, being ignorant of the righteousness that comes from God, and seeking to establish their own, they did not submit to God's righteousness. 4 For Christ is the end of the law, that every one who has faith may be justified.

[9] Romans 10:5-11 (RSV)

5 Moses writes that the man who practices the righteousness which is based on the law shall live by it. 6 But the righteousness based on faith says, Do not say in your heart, "Who will ascend into heaven?" (that is, to bring Christ down) 7 or "Who will descend into the abyss?" (that is, to bring Christ up from the dead). 8 But what does it say? The word is near you, on your lips and in your heart (that is, the word of faith which we preach); 9 because, if you confess with your lips that Jesus is Lord and believe in your heart that God raised him from the dead, you will be saved. 10 For man believes with his heart and so is justified, and he confesses with his lips and so is saved. 11 The scripture says, "No one who believes in him will be put to shame."

[10] Romans 7:7 (RSV)

What then shall we say? That the law is sin? By no means! Yet, if it had not been for the law, I should not have known sin. I should not have known what it is to covet if the law had not said, "You shall not covet."

[11] Romans 7:8 (RSV)

But sin, finding opportunity in the commandment, wrought in me all kinds of covetousness. Apart from the law sin lies dead.

[12] Romans 7:11 (RSV)

For sin, finding opportunity in the commandment, deceived me and by it killed me.

[13] Romans 8:1 (RSV)

There is therefore now no condemnation for those who are in Christ Jesus.

SERMON 14

WHY WE MUST BE FREE FROM THE LAW – PART 2

"Unless Jesus Christ breaks in and frees us from the law, we'll be carnal—we'll be captive —and we'll be corrupt!"

Today we've come to one of the most **profound, difficult,** and **controversial** parts of Romans. The passage that has exercised, I think, the **greatest** of minds in the church history, and has provoked, I might add, considerable differences of opinion. We're starting with Romans chapter 7, verse 14, and we'd like to go to the end of the chapter.

I'd like to remind you of the basic outline of this chapter. Paul is telling us in Romans chapter 7, **why** we must be **free** from the law. By his illustration the first 6 verses, based upon a **married** woman—he tells us that we are **dead** to the law and **discharged** from its **claims** by the **body** and the **death** of the Lord Jesus Christ. The purpose of all this is **enunciated** in verse 6. *"That we should serve"*—that is we should **live**—we should **relate**—*"not under the old written code but in the new life of the Spirit."* [1] Then the rest of the chapter, beginning with verse 7, tells us <u>why</u> **it is necessary** to be **under** grace and **not** under the law.

You'll remember that in an earlier sermon we indicated that in verses 7 to 11 the three things that the law <u>can</u> do and why we **must** be delivered from the law. But now beginning with verse 14, we'll notice what the **law can<u>not</u> do.** And **that's** why we must be freed from the law for what it **can<u>not</u> do.** Its lack of power.

I believe if there were any **key** that explains Romans chapter 7, verse 14 to 25, is the words in Romans chapter 8, verse 3. Now, this is a kind of a **conclusion** and should be read in **connection** with Romans chapter 7. As Paul goes on to say, beginning with Romans chapter 8, verse 1, *"There is therefore **now no condemnation** for those who are in Christ Jesus. For the law of the Spirit of life in Christ Jesus has set me free from the law of sin and **death**. For God has done what the law, weakened by the flesh, could **not** do: sending his own Son in the **likeness** of sinful flesh and **for sin**, he **condemned—sin—in the flesh.**"* [2]

Now notice that *"God has done what the **law**, weakened by the flesh, could **not** do."* That's what I want you to notice in Romans chapter 8, verse 3—*"what the **law—could—not—do.**"* So, we're about to read what the **law cannot do.**

"For God has done what the law, weakened by the flesh, could not do: sending his own Son in the likeness of sinful flesh and for sin, he condemned sin in the flesh" - Romans 8:3 RSV

Let's notice this passage in Romans chapter 7 together, shall we, beginning with verse 14. *"We know that the law is spiritual; but I am carnal, sold under sin. I do not understand my own actions. I do not do what I want. I do the very thing I hate. Now if I do what I do not want, I agree that the **law** is good. So then it's no longer I that do it, but **sin** which dwells within me. For I know that **nothing good** dwells within **me, that is, in my flesh.** I can **will** what is right, but I cannot do it. I do not do the good I want, but the evil I do not __want__ **is what I do.** Now **if** I do what I do not **want,** it is no longer"*—in a sense—*"I that do it, but **sin** which dwells within me. So I find it to be a law"*—a habit—*"that when I want to do right,* *evil lies close at hand. For **I delight** in the law of God, in my **inmost self,** but I see in my members another law at work with the law of my mind and making me **captive**"*—notice that—*"to the law of sin which dwells in my members. **Wretched man** that I am! Who will **deliver** me from this body of death? Thanks be to God through Jesus Christ our Lord! **So then**"*—and watch the conclusion—*"**I of myself** serve the law of God with **my mind, but** with my flesh I serve the law of sin."* [3]

Now there are various theories as to the meaning of this passage. And I'm going to speak a little softly because I **do** reverence other people's opinion. However, I do want to share my understanding of it, and I think it's **vastly** important that we think **correctly** about this particular passage. It's the most **significant passage** describing man's spiritual psychological being in the New Testament.

First of all, when Paul uses the pronoun "**I**" to whom is he referring? Does he mean **just** himself? Is this a personal testimony as he lays bare his heart and gives us a spiritual autobiography? Is it just a public confession? Well, **I doubt that.** I'm not questioning the fact that **Paul had** this **experience.** He's no armchair theologian. This is coming out of the **depths** of his own soul. His own inner **life** is rant apart and he's **struggling** to conform to the law of God. So, this is **born out** of the depths of his **own soul.** I **can't imagine** however, that in this great treatise of Romans that the Apostle Paul has just stopped, to give us say, a kind of a personal testimony. It doesn't fit Romans because Romans is a **grand** theological treatise. It's telling us about the spiritual journey of **every** man. I believe that Paul is using, what we might call a rhetorical "**I**". The Apostle does this in other of his letters. He uses an "**I**" when he's **identifying** with his **reader** and **describing** the state of all **man.** And here he means the "**I**" of **every man.**

This is the **struggle** of the **human** soul. It's a struggle of **my** own inner soul and of **your** own inner soul. This is a **journey** that **we all**

take no doubt to varying degrees. I know that **some** experience this in various ways. I'm prepared to admit that some are not exposed to the **full** lethal powers of this like others. You know God really **deals** with us differently. But I think the Apostle is showing the **great potential**— the **intense** **implications** of what it means for **a man** to be **under the law.** That's the way I understand Romans 7. The implications of what it means for a man to be under the law.

Another important question: Is Paul talking in this passage about a **non**-**Christian** or is he talking about a **Christian?** Is he talking about an **unenlightened** Christian? Well, in **my** opinion this is not the **best** way to approach this chapter. **I think** he's showing rather, the different ways that a **man** can be **related to the law of God** and how anybody is going to **handle** the moral **claim** upon their **life.** So, in this sense, **I find three phases** to this chapter.

And here, I really can't keep out my own personal testimony because I've gone through **three spiritual phases** with **reference** to the **law,** and I very readily find them in this great passage. Well, Paul, **first** of all, describes what he is **"apart" from the law. Then** he describes what it means to be **"under" the law.** And **finally,** he'll tell us what it means to be **"free" from the law.** We might remember those things—**apart** from the law, **under** the law, and **free** from the law. I don't believe he's **basically** talking about a **believer** or an **unbeliever**—or an **enlightened** or **unregenerate person.**

Let's look at these three levels. The first one is described in verse 9. Paul says, Romans 7:9, *"I was **alive**—once—**apart**—from the law."* [4] There **was a time** when Paul was—he used the word *"alive"*—and we should put that in quotation marks all **along** here—*"he was 'alive' apart from the law."* So let this be **Phase Number One**—somebody who is *"alive."* The word **"alive"** of course means they're not especially **troubled**—they have an **un-awakened conscience**—they're in a **phase** best described as, *"apart—from the law."* We might call this the **innocence** stage—the **non-moral** stage—the **blissful** stage—the **untutored** stage—since the law is likened to a tutor. Here's someone that's **untutored.** They're not **subject** to the law, **as it were,** they're **"alive"** but **"apart"** from the law. I'd like to call this stage and this man, **"The Deceived Man."** He's **deceived** because he doesn't know the **awesome moral claims of <u>God</u>.** He's un-awakened to it.

 "I was once alive apart from the law, but when the commandment came, sin revived and I died." - Romans 7:9 RSV

This may be true say, of a **physical child.** Children are **generally, not** awakened by great moral claims. They can feel, of course, **shame** and of course you can project tremendous **guilt** into children. But it's also **possible** for a child to be **relatively uncluttered, morally.** As a matter of fact, the Bible calls children, those who do not **distinguish** between right and wrong. We speak, for example, about the age of accountability. So, a **child** is **"alive,"** so to speak, **"apart"** from the law. He's not intensely worried about the **inner stresses** and **claims** of his personality. He's not **striving morally** with his own strength to do good. He's not **thinking** about all that. He's just **alive!** That's the only word that really describes this person.

Now, that could also be said of say, a happy pagan. Are some savages happy? Yes, I suppose so. Many **adult** people are **even** like that. They go through life, and they're not greatly **bothered.** What's all this **business** about **sin?** What's this **fuss** about **being saved** and about **guilt?** It doesn't really **bother** them much. They're **alive** apart from the law. The law has not made its **strong claim** and by the Spirit of God done its **work** in their lives.

That was partly true of me. For twenty-one years, I think I got by **fairly well.** I had an uneasy, vague sense, that **something** was **wrong.** And in my **better moments,** in my **quiet times,** I would reflect a little bit, but I wasn't terribly upset by the whole thing. I was "alive" apart from the law. As a matter of fact, it wasn't until after I was **converted to Jesus** that I **began** to understand some of these moral **claims,** and **some** of the **depths** of my own inner **being.**

It may be that the Apostle Paul was also talking about his pre-Damascus Road experience when he said that he was **"alive"** apart from the law—for he **delighted** in the law of God as he understood it. He saw it as a means of salvation. It wasn't particularly threatening to him. He had a **conscience** void of **offense,** as he testifies.

So, it's **possible** to conclude that in **Phase One,** people are **not troubled.** That is **not** <u>deeply,</u> greatly **troubled,** <u>but</u>—they <u>are</u>—deceived. They don't **know the depths** of their own nature and sin. They don't **understand** their own **depravity.** They don't **know** how <u>holy **God**</u> **is.** They don't know how **awesome** His just claim is upon their lives. And so, it's a **false life.** It's an **inauthentic life.** It's a <u>deceived life.</u> So, let's call this **"The Deceived Man."** He is **"alive,"** but he's **"alive" apart** from the law.

You see, the law is **necessary** to do its **work** in getting man out of this **naïve—deceived—false stage.** Therefore, the Apostle is describing what **happens** when the **commandment comes.** He says, *"I was alive apart from the law once, **but** when the **commandment came,"** * [4] —he means when I was **awakened** to the **full** implications of the **law.** That awesome **"just" claim** that came upon my life, when I began to see God's holy standards—when I <u>discerned</u> truly, **right from wrong.** Now he's beginning to describe what happens when a man is **awakened,** and **I believe that's** the story of a **believer, a Christian.**

The Apostle says in verse 14, "*We know that the **law** is spiritual; but I am **carnal**. I am **sold** under sin. I don't understand my own **actions**.*" So here's a man who's **bewildered**. He's a man who's, well, **defeated**. "*I do not do what I want,*" he says. "*I do the **very—thing—I—hate**.*" Now, **notice** that this man does **not—love—his—sin**. He hates it! But he **does** the very thing **he hates**. "*Now if I do what I do not **want**, I agree that the law is good.*" The claim of the law is good. I believe I **ought** to do right. "*So it's no longer **I** that do it, but **sin** that dwells within me. **I know** that **nothing good** dwells in **me**, that is, within my flesh. I can **will** what is right. **I—cannot—do—it**. For I do not do the good that I want, but the evil I do not **want** is what I do.*" And I **hate it** all the time. "*Now, if I do what I do not **want**,*"—it's in the sense—"*no longer **I***"—I think you have to really put **this** in quotation marks too—"*it's no longer,*" '*I*'—quote—"*that do it*"—but **some** kind of a **power** in me—"*it's **sin** that dwells within me.*" So, we're learning here that **sin's power** is so great that **God alone** can break its grip in our life. "*It's no longer '**I**' that do it, but **sin** that dwells in me.*" [5]

(*Don continues reading here at Romans 7:21*) So I **find** this law"— this **habit**—this **power**—this **authority**—this **practice**—"*that when I want to do right, **evil—lies—close—at hand**. I **delight** in the law of God, in my inmost self,*"—I **approve** of it—**I want to do it**—"*but I find in my members **another law**"*—another **power**—another **authority**—"*at **war** within the law of my **mind**. It makes me **captive** to the law of sin that dwells in my members. **Wretched man that I am!**"* [6] Now, that's **Phase Number Two**, in relationship to the law. Here's the **miserable** man. Here's the man who's **defeated** and **wretched**. Let's call him the man who is **awakened,** but he's **still** in an **ignorant stage**. He's a man who is **defeated** and **under** the law.

Now, **notice** this man. There are basically two things about him and there are two things that he knows. First of all, this man **knows** that he **really—wants—to do—good**. Quote—"*I **delight** in the law in my in-*

most self." [7] **He doesn't want to do evil. Is that the commentary on an unregenerate man?** Well, not necessarily. Here's somebody **who—really—wants—to please—God! He's not divided about right and wrong. He hates wrong.** That's very clear. Some read this and think that He **loves** the **wrong,** and He also loves the **right** and so He's **divided.** But that's not the case of this man. This man **wants** to do what is **right.** But here's his **big problemHe is unable to do**—what he **knows**—is right. As Paul says, "*I **do not do** the good that I want.*" [8] This man **fails** with **unfailing regularity!** He's a failure. He wants to do good but he's **never** quite able to do **all the good** or all the right that he wants.

So, consequently **he knows** that he's **carnal.** That's the only word you can use for this man. Verse 14 calls him as "*carnal.*" [9] Now let's define this word. It's a very **important** word. Probably the best interpretation of this word would be something like this—**"I am flesh and blood."** Or as we would say today, "I'm a human **being. The law** is spiritual but I'm a **human.**" That's what he's really saying. He's saying that "I'm **weak.**" And that's the **problem. The law** is **good, but I'm weak!** And it doesn't give me any power. I'm a **human being** with **all** that that implies. Meaning that I'm here with an **unredeemable** power in my personality, called the flesh, and I'm **living** in a **redeemable,** but **unredeemed** body. I'm living in a **body** that's weakened, **constantly** subject to all **kinds** of things. **In living my life in this** physical **body, I'm carnal. I'm physical. I am flesh—and—blood.**

And the **next thing** he knows is he's **captive!** He **cannot** within himself **gain** the victory. He's having a **clash** between his **instincts** and his **insights.** There's a **struggle** between his **inner desires** as a Christian and the **deeply ingrained habits** that have been **programmed** into his **nervous system** in which he can **hardly avoid doing.** Now, is there **anyone here** that does **not** have a clash between his instincts and his insights? *(Congregation is very quiet)* Well, I thought so. Here is a man at **battle** with his **passions** and his **conscience.** What he **knows** is **far better** than what he **does. Again,** is there anybody here **able to do all the right** that he **knows** to do? *(Congregation continues to be very quiet)* I didn't think so. Are we talking about a **believer** or an **unbeliever** in what we've just read? Well, all I can tell you is that it **perfectly** describes **my entire** Christian life.

I've been a Christian for **well over** 20 years and I'm **exactly** like what we have just read. In and of myself—**in me**—I have **number one: Always** wanted to do right since I became a Christian. I've always <u>yearned</u> to do what I understood to be **right** before the Lord Jesus Christ. But **number two:** I have **failed with unfailing regularity.** You didn't know that I was that way, did you? Well, I'm **carnal! I'm weak! I'm limited! I am made of flesh and blood.** I have **all <u>kinds</u> of problems** within myself. **I always wanted to do better than I've done.** My **instincts never** matched my **insights. I understand a whole lot better than I'm performing.**

Also, I've got some <u>gossip</u> for you. You want to hear some gossip? I've been **intimately** associated with the **finest** of the Christian world. I have **personally** known <u>**thousands**</u> of clergymen, and I can tell you not a **single one** of them **differ** from your pastor. And I've pastored this church long enough to say that **none of you** differ whatever.

Can you see that when we are <u>**under the law,**</u> it does its work and lets us know what we **really are?** I **never** am changed from that. **Regeneration** didn't change **me.** I've not been changed **at all.** So, what's going to **happen** to this man who **says,** *"Oh wretched <u>man</u> that I am. Who's going to **deliver me** from the **body** of this **death?"** [10]* And of course the Apostle answers in those beautiful, victorious words, *"Thanks be to God through Jesus Christ our Lord! So then, I of myself"*—in my inmost man—*"I serve the law of God with my mind"*—with my rational self—with my <u>insights</u>—*"But with my <u>flesh</u> I go right on serving the law of <u>sin</u>."* [11]

So, it's **important** that we learn not to walk in the **flesh** you see, but in the Spirit. Well, **what's the difference then with this shout of victory?** What **happened** to the Apostle Paul? Did he **change?** No. Some people say that you go from Romans chapter 7 to Romans chapter 8. I'm not **quite** sure what that means. I'm not **exactly** certain what they're talking about when they say that. I don't believe that any **inner** change has come to this man whatever, but there are some **very** important **differences.** And **what is** the difference in this man?

Well, number one, this man is **not miserable!** He's not **changed.** He still has all those characteristics we've read about, but he's not miserable! He's not **defeated!** He's got the **victory!** Now, that's a different **experience** altogether, whether you're **defeated** or **delivered** by **victory.** And I've got news for you; I have been **this man** also, for over 20 years. I **haven't** been **miserable** all that time. I've been shouting the **victory** during my Christian life. I am **joyous** in the Lord. I am **not** miserable. Am I **changed? No,** but I <u>know</u> something. I have an **understanding.** Now, **this man under the law** was **bewildered.** He says, "I don't **understand** myself. I don't **know** what I'm doing. I don't **understand** my own actions." But, you see, **I** <u>know</u> **what I'm doing.** I've been **enlightened.** I'm able to conclude as the Apostle does in verse 25—"*I* **know** *that of myself I* **serve** *the law of God with my* **mind,** *but with my* **flesh** *I go on serving the law of sin.*" [11] I don't **trust** myself anymore. I gave that up a **long time ago. I quit trying** to be **holy.** I quit **trying** to be **righteous.** So, the **difference** is what the Apostle calls **"being—**<u>in</u> **the Spirit."**

Now that's going to take considerable time to develop what we mean by "being in the flesh" and "being in the Spirit." But let me briefly tell you that when we're talking about "being in the flesh and the Spirit," we are **not primarily** talking about **two components** in our personality. We're **not** talking about our **visible** and **invisible parts.** When we talk about the **flesh** and the **Spirit,** we're talking about **two creations**—two different **realities** that we can **experience.**

I want to just briefly say this: When the Lord Jesus Christ arose from the dead, where did He go? Well, according to the New Testament, He went **into** the presence of God, and He **entered into** the new creation. He **went into** the **new creation.** That's where He is now. What's going to happen when we are all resurrected from the dead? We're going into the **new creation.** <u>All</u> of this creation is going to be **changed.** So, to "be in the Spirit" **refers** to the **power** of this new creation.

Now, that new creation has some **great** wonderful **powers** and the flesh, and the Spirit are talking about these two **powers**—a **destructive power** versus a **delivering power.** One that brings **death** and one that brings **life.** These **two creations**—these **two powers** can give two kinds of **experiences.** One puts you under the law and all of this **old creation.** The **other** puts you in the **Spirit** and in the **new creation** and **gives you and gives us a <u>victory</u>!**

I'm <u>still</u> living my life out in this physical body. I **still** have the flesh. I'm **still utterly** unable to keep the law. I **cannot** be good, **but I'm not miserable.** I'm not under **condemnation,** and I'm experiencing something **happening** to me that's giving me peace and freedom from myself. That's the **only** hope for me and **I think** for anyone else. **We have to find the powers** of the new creation being **mediated** back to us so that we can have a **different kind** of an **experience**—a **different kind** of an **understanding** as it enters into our **knowledge** and our **mind.**

I'd like you to know, by the way, that a person **who is—in** that **new creation**—a person who is **justified**—and don't forget justification has reference to the creation to come—we call it an eschatological, that is a **prophetic** term, because it's the sentence of the **last** judgment of God. It has already been **handed down.** His sentence **came down** to us in this **old** creation and God has said to me in this kind of a condition, "You are justified." I—have a— righteousness—that does—not come out of the law. It does not come out of my flesh—out of <u>my</u> life—it only comes from **Jesus Christ,** and **that** puts me at peace. It's a **great peace** to know that I'm not under the **law,** that I have a **righteousness** which is not of my own. You know we can be **free** from the law. **Not changed**—still having the **same** essential struggle but with **no condemnation** and finding it **possible** to live in the powers of the new creation.

Thank God that something is <u>happening</u> to us! This gives us the capacity to be **honest. I'm carnal**—**I'm captive**—but I'm experiencing something else also. **It's something that's <u>happening</u> to me.** This is the **freedom** from the **law** and its **claim,** and it lets me say, *"Thanks—be unto God—through Jesus Christ the Lord!"* [11]

"Thanks be to God through Jesus Christ our Lord! So then, I of myself serve the law of God with my mind, but with my flesh I serve the law of sin." - Romans 7:25 RSV

I'd like to say that the full **benefits** of this are **yet future.** In Romans chapter 6, we are **free** from sin, yet we **fight sin.** Romans 7, we are **free** from the law, **yet** we're not able to do all that we'd like to do. Romans chapter 8, we are **free** from **death,** and yet our **bodies** are not yet **redeemed.**

The delivering **power** of the new creation is going to **break** someday with <u>**all**</u> of its fullness into this old creation. This old creation will be **completely changed.** My **body** is dying now because of sin but my **spirit** is alive because of righteousness. I—have—the—victory. I **shout** the victory! Jesus Christ delivers me. I don't **dwell** on the old self. I'm not ashamed to admit it. The Apostle opens his heart and says, **"This is the way it is."**

This is a **vital step** in the law, and I hope that the law will bring **all** of us **quickly** to this point so that we can use the language of Galatians chapter 2, verse 20, *"I am crucified with Christ; nevertheless **I live; yet not I,** but Christ lives in me, and the life which I now live in the flesh I **live** by the faith of the Son of God, who loved me and gave himself for me."* [12]

We don't even know who does it anymore. It's hard to distinguish what part **we** have, and **Jesus** has. We **just** know it's His life. **Thank God we can be—free—from the law.** The law can't make us **good.** It doesn't have the **power.** Unless Jesus Christ breaks in and **frees** us from the law, we'll be **carnal**—we'll be **captive**—and we'll be **corrupt. But thank God for the victory! There is no condemnation to those who are in Christ Jesus!** I am **in Him!** And what the law could not do, in that it was **weak** through the flesh, Jesus Christ has done. He has **come**—He has entered into my experience—and by the **power** of the Holy Spirit He continues to give **me** the victory and help me to live **free—from—the—law.** Though in and of myself, I would be **under the law,** or I would be just like a happy pagan in **ignorance**—in a **blissful ignorance**—alive but **apart** from the law. **God,** help us to see **exactly** what the truth is—and yet to **shout** the victory in our Lord Jesus Christ.

SERMON 14 ENDNOTES:

None

SERMON 14 SCRIPTURE REFERENCES:

[1] Romans 7:6 (RSV)

But now we are discharged from the law, dead to that which held us captive, so that we serve not under the old written code but in the new life of the Spirit.

[2] Romans 8:1-3 (RSV)

1 There is therefore now no condemnation for those who are in Christ Jesus. 2 For the law of the Spirit of life in Christ Jesus has set me free from the law of sin and death. 3 For God has done what the law, weakened by the flesh, could not do: sending his own Son in the likeness of sinful flesh and for sin, he condemned sin in the flesh,

[3] Romans 7:14-25 (RSV)

14 We know that the law is spiritual; but I am carnal, sold under sin. 15 I do not understand my own actions. For I do not do what I want, but I do the very thing I hate. 16 Now if I do what I do not want, I agree that the law is good. 17 So then it is no longer I that do it, but sin which dwells within me. 18 For I know that nothing good dwells within me, that is, in my flesh. I can will what is right, but I cannot do it. 19 For I do not do the good I want, but the evil I do not want is what I do. 20 Now if I do what I do not want, it is no longer I that do it, but sin which dwells within me. 21 So I find it to be a law that when I want to do right, evil lies close at hand. 22 For I delight in the law of God, in my inmost self, 23 but I see in my members another law at war with the law of my mind and making me captive to the law of sin which dwells in my members. 24 Wretched man that I am! Who will deliver me from this body of death? 25 Thanks be to God through Jesus Christ our Lord! So then, I of myself serve the law of God with my mind, but with my flesh I serve the law of sin.

[4] Romans 7:9 (RSV)

I was once alive apart from the law, but when the commandment came, sin revived and I died;

[5] Romans 7:14-20 (RSV)

14 We know that the law is spiritual; but I am carnal, sold under sin. 15 I do not understand my own actions. For I do not do what I want, but I do the very thing I hate. 16 Now if I do what I do not want, I agree that the law is good. 17 So then it is no longer I that do it, but sin which dwells within me. 18 For I know that nothing good dwells within me, that is, in my flesh. I can will what is right, but I cannot do it. 19 For I do not do the good I want, but the evil I do not want is what I do. 20 Now if I do what I do not want, it is no longer I that do it, but sin which dwells within me.

[6] Romans 7:21-24 (RSV)

21 So I find it to be a law that when I want to do right, evil lies close at hand. 22 For I delight in the law of God, in my inmost self, 23 but I see in my members another law at war with the law of my mind and making me captive to the law of sin which dwells in my members. 24 Wretched man that I am! Who will deliver me from this body of death?

[7] Romans 7:22 (RSV)

For I delight in the law of God, in my inmost self,

[8] Romans 7:19 (RSV)

For I do not do the good I want, but the evil I do not want is what I do.

[9] Romans 7:14 (RSV)

We know that the law is spiritual; but I am carnal, sold under sin.

[10] Romans 7:24 (RSV)

Wretched man that I am! Who will deliver me from this body of death?

[11] Romans 7:25 (RSV)

Thanks be to God through Jesus Christ our Lord! So then, I of myself serve the law of God with my mind, but with my flesh I serve the law of sin.

[12] Galatians 2:20 (KJV)

I am crucified with Christ: nevertheless I live; yet not I, but Christ liveth in me: and the life which I now live in the flesh I live by the faith of the Son of God, who loved me, and gave himself for me.

SERMON 15

THE DOCTRINE OF THE TWO CREATIONS

"The Spirit of Christ can dwell in you, and it's going to raise your body and all your miserable emotions some day from the grave, and they're all going to be changed!"

If the book of Romans were a gold ring, the 8th chapter of Romans would be the pearl in the setting. The most precious and beautiful part of Romans is perhaps the 8th chapter.

Now we have observed that the book of Romans is a description of the gospel of the grace of God. And Romans chapters 6, 7 and 8 are describing to us what it means to be **under the <u>Reign</u> of Grace.** Now it's nice to have **grace,** but it's wonderful to have the **<u>Reign</u> of Grace.** We're talking about the **abundance** of grace. Romans chapter 5 speaks of the "*abundance of grace and the free gift of righteousness.*" [1] And when **grace reigns** then we reign in **life.** So, everything is about life, and the grace of God is to cause us to reign **in life.** It's wonderful to know that you are **under** grace and nothing **but** grace. And not only grace, but the **abundance** of grace. It's the only thing that can set the human heart properly free. It's nice to know about this **maximum love. Not just love, much more love!** You'll find that in Romans chapter 5 which is simply what grace is all about.

If God **loved you** while you were **weak,** and while you were a **sinner,** and while you were an **enemy,** much **more** is He going to love you while you're in a state of reconciliation. It's amazing how many

Christians stumble over their post-baptismal sins. They're Galatian Christians. They start in grace but now, quote, "it's up to **you.**" That's **heresy**! And so, it's **wonderful** to **know** that you are **constantly** under the **maximum love of God. Nothing** can separate you from the love of God. **Nothing!** I'm just about ready to read it in Romans the 8th chapter. When you **know maximum love,** you're beginning to understand the grace of God, and how important it is that we have that.

You see, there are many destructive **powers** that want to keep us from **life.** According to Romans there are four lethal powers. They are **wrath—sin—law—and death.** According to the first five chapters of Romans the grace of God frees us from **wrath—all condemnation.** There **is** no **condemnation.** You are **not under wrath.** You're under grace. You're in a **state of justification.** Romans chapter 6 discusses the subject of **freedom from sin** by the grace of God. Romans chapter 7 tells us we are **not under law.** And now, Romans chapter 8 is about to tell us what it means to be free from the powers of **death.**

Now in order to understand this chapter and what we're about to introduce with emphasis on "walking in the Spirit," we must know how **broad** this subject is. And just a surface reading of the 8th chapter will demonstrate to us, that if we're going to walk in the Spirit, we must have a very broad **understanding,** because the Apostle Paul is going to talk to us **about** the "eternal purposes of God," and he's going to introduce the "*Doctrine of the Two Creations.*" That's what we're going to be talking about this morning.

Basically, there are two powers that work within us to bring us to death. There is a power at work **within us,** a power of death—it's called— **"the flesh."** Now the solution to that as we will see is walking—in—the Spirit, but that can be ever so many words to people. We often don't know what that **means,** and we **must** understand what that **means.** Secondly, there is a power working **outside me.** The Bible calls it **"the world."** Now that's going to also figure into Romans chapter 8, and we're going to see how that we can live during **this—present—time.** One important key to understanding Romans 8 is the phrase in verse 18—*"I reckon that the sufferings of—this—present—time."* [2] We must understand **that** terminology right there, "this—present—time."

"I consider that the sufferings of this present time are not worth comparing with the glory that is to be revealed to us."
- Romans 8:18 RSV

Now, according to the scriptures, there are two great **decisive** events in world history. That is the **first coming** of Jesus Christ and the **second coming** of Jesus Christ. During **this age,** after the first coming of the Lord Jesus Christ, we are living in the age of **the fulfillment of the promise. But we are anticipating the consummation of the promise when Jesus Christ comes back the second time to regenerate <u>all</u> of creation and establish the new heavens and a new earth. <u>But</u> we are <u>now</u> living—in—this—present—time.**

Now, Romans the 8th chapter, is about to tell us how that by the **Reign of Grace** we are going to become **super conquerors—in—this— present—time.** If you'd like to write that down, it's worth noting. That's what ought to be over Romans chapter 8—**<u>How the Reign of Grace Makes Me a Super Conqueror in This Present Time!</u>** That's what Romans chapter 8 is trying to describe for us.

Now, we'll see what we have and what we do not have. We know, for example, we are **under no condemnation—none whatsoever.** Now many people **are,** unfortunately, because they think they're under the law, but you are **under <u>no</u> condemnation** in any way shape or form. You're absolutely free. **Nobody** can lay anything to the charge of **God's**

elect, because it's **God** who's done the justifying. Furthermore, our spirits are **alive.** We'll see what that means as we come to it. And also, we are **super conquerors—more than conquerors.** That may sound like strange doctrine to you, but this is what we are. We are super conquerors through grace.

Now, we do **not** have; however, **redeemed bodies.** Our bodies are **dead. They—are—dying!** They are **dead** because of **sin.** And furthermore, we are living in a **world**—an **unredeemed world**—in **this** creation that has all kinds of stressful things that make us **suffer,** and also **tempt** us to draw us away from God and walking in the Spirit. So, we're out to see what it **really means,** now, to be a super conqueror, and how we can walk—in the—Spirit.

Let's read this great chapter. In my mind it's one of the most **precious documents** that ever came from human hands. It's, of course, by the inspiration of the Holy Spirit. We believe that!

Romans chapter 8 verse 1, *"There is therefore now **no** condemnation"*—none—*"for those who are—in—Christ—Jesus."* Remember that phrase. *"For the **law** of the Spirit of life in Christ Jesus has set me <u>free</u> from the **law of sin and death.** For God has done what the law, weakened by the flesh, could **not** do: sending his own Son in the likeness of sinful flesh and **for sin, he <u>condemned</u> sin in the flesh,** in order that the just requirement of the law might be fulfilled **in us,** who walk **not** according to the flesh but according to the Spirit. Those who live according to the **flesh** they set their <u>minds</u> on the **things of the flesh,** but those who live according to the **Spirit** they set their <u>minds</u> on the **things of the Spirit.** Now to set the mind on the **flesh"*—the only word you can say for it is *"death,"*—that's the only word that qualifies. It's a <u>**lethal—deadly—**</u> **bondage—that corrupts.** <u>**Death!**</u> *"...but to set the mind on the Spirit is life <u>and</u> peace."*—soul peace. *"Now the **mind** that is set on the **flesh** is hostile to God; it does **not** submit to God's law, indeed it **can<u>not</u>.**"* So many people are trying to consecrate their flesh—down to an altar—**beating** their **fist** on an altar. You can't consecrate your flesh. It's unredeemable. All you can do is crucify it and get out of it. Don't walk in it. *"It does not submit to God's law, **indeed it ca<u>nnot</u>;** those who are in the **flesh cannot please God.** [3]*

"There is therefore now no condemnation for those who are in Christ Jesus." - Romans 8:1 RSV

*"**But** you are not **in** the flesh, but in the Spirit, **if** the Spirit of God really dwells in you. Any one who does not have the Spirit of Christ does not belong to him. But if **Christ** is in you, **although your bodies are dead"**—* death is claiming them, they're dead, they're dying—*"because of sin, your* **spirits—are alive—because of—righteousness.** *If the Spirit of him who raised Jesus from the dead dwells in you,"*—guess what?—*"he who raised Christ Jesus from the dead **will give <u>life</u> to your mortal bodies"**—*they **are** redeemable, your flesh is not, but your body is—*"also through his Spirit which **dwells in <u>you</u>."** [4]*

*(Don continues reading here at Romans 8:12) "So then, brethren, we are debtors, **not** to the flesh, to live according to the flesh—if you live according to the flesh you'll die, **but if by the Spirit you put to death the deeds of the body you will <u>live</u>.** All who are led by the Spirit of God are sons of God."* And now we're about to start this very heady doctrine that moves us into the eternal plan of God and the two creations. *"You did* **not** *receive the spirit of slavery to fall back into* **fear. You have received the spirit of sonship. When we cry, 'Abba! Father!' it's the Spirit Himself bearing witness"** with us—*"with **our spirit** that we are children of God, and if"* we are *"**children, then"** we are **"heirs."** Heirs—inheritance here—we are, *"**heirs of God, fellow heirs with Christ,** provided we **suffer** with him in order that we might also be glorified with him." [5]*

"*Now, I consider,*" I reckon, "*that the sufferings of—this—present—time*"—remember that phrase. It's a **most important key** to understand what we're starting to say this morning. **TPT: This—Present—Time.** I give the young people some little abbreviations so it will lodge in their mind. **TPT** is one of them. This Present Time and **ROG: the Reign of Grace.** "*...this present time is **not worthy comparing with the glory** that is to be revealed **to us.** For creation*"—the **creation!**—"*waits with eager longing for the revealing of the sons of God; creation was subjected to futility.*" That brings us to the Doctrine of Emptiness—what I want to talk to you about **tonight.** The second part of this, **knowledge in the Doctrine of Emptiness. It's a <u>most</u> important truth.** Creation was subject to—**"emptiness"** and man with it. "*...futility, not of its own will but by the will of him who subjected it in **hope**; because creation itself will be set free from the **bondage**,*"—"*it's **bondage** to decay and will obtain the glorious liberty of the children of God.*"—Oh! That's the goal of it all! This **glorious liberty! Not just liberty! <u>Glorious</u> liberty!** "*We know that the whole creation has been **groaning in travail** together until now; not only the creation, but we ourselves, who have the first fruits of the Spirit, we groan inwardly as we wait for adoption as sons,*"—that is the resurrection and—"*the redemption of our **bodies.**" Now we'll spell out the whole connection between the flesh and the body in this series of sermons. "*In this hope—<u>we</u>—<u>are</u>—<u>saved</u>. Now hope that is seen is*"—that's—"*not hope. For who hopes for what he sees?*" If you are seeing something and you've got it, you're not hoping for it you've **got it.** "*But if we **hope** for what we do **not** see, then we wait for it with **patience.**" [6] That's this new creation we're going to talk about.

(Don continues reading here at Romans 8:26) "*Likewise the Spirit*"—it also—"*helps us in our **weakness;**"—not only to counter the flesh but to live out our life in this world—"*we do not know how to **pray as we <u>ought</u>, but the <u>Spirit himself</u> intercedes for us with <u>sighs</u> too deep for words. He*

who searches the hearts of men, he knows what is the mind of the Spirit, because the Spirit intercedes for the saints according to the will of God." [7]

"We know that in everything—God—works—for—good—with those who love him." Can anything bad happen to you? Of course not, it's working for good. *"...who are called according to his purpose. For those whom he **foreknew** he also **predestined** to be conformed to the image of his Son, in order that he might be just the **first-born** among **many** brethren."* That includes you and me. *"And those whom **he predestined** he also **called;"**—*that's the phase we're in right now—*"and those whom he called he also **justified; and those whom he justified he also <u>glorified</u>."*** [8]—put in the past tense because it's a completed passage.

(Don continues reading here at Romans 8:31) **"Now, what are you going to say to all this? Well, if <u>God</u> is for you, who can be against you? He who did—not—spare—his—own—Son—but gave him up for us all, will he not also give us all things with him?"** Of course, if He gave you the very best, won't He give you the least? **"Who shall bring <u>any</u> charge"**—any kind—*"against God's elect?"* They're His pets. They're special. They're elect. *"It is <u>God</u> who justifies; so who is going to condemn?"* Now, this enemy would like to condemn you. Your own **conscience** would like to condemn you. But if God does not condemn you, what does all the rest make any **difference?** You can stay down in that bondage all you want. Let God be true and every man a liar. *"It is <u>God</u> who justified; and who's going to condemn us? It's Christ Jesus, who died, yes, who was raised from the dead, who is at the right hand of God, who indeed he intercedes for us? Who shall separate us from the love of Christ?"*—the <u>maximum</u> love? Can anything separate you from the **maximum love** of God? **Never!** How about *"tribulation?"* **No?** *"Distress?"* Ever been distressed? **No?** How about *"persecution?"* How about *"famine?"* Maybe you went a little hungry. Maybe you don't have enough clothes. Not enough money, could that do it? How about some

"peril?"—perilous thing? How about the *"sword?"* What if you even **died? Would that be it?** No, you'd just go right into His presence and see Him face to face. *"As it is written,"* in the Psalms, *" 'For thy sake we are killed all the day long; we're regarded as sheep to be slaughtered.' "* [9]

(Don completes reading Romans chapter 8 here with verses 37-39) *"NO—IN—ALL—THESE—THINGS"—WE ARE—SUPER—CONQUERORS!* *"...we are—MORE—THAN— CONQUERORS—THROUGH HIM WHO LOVED US. I am SURE—that neither death, nor life, nor angels, nor principalities, nor things present, nor things to come."* Are you afraid about the future? Things to come? *"...nor powers, nor height, nor depth, nor ANYTHING ELSE in all creation, will be able to separate us from the love of God in Christ Jesus our Lord."* [10]

So, this **great** chapter is introducing these **marvelous themes** that show us how we can be **super conquerors** through the **Reign of Grace.** That's what that's trying to tell us. To cope with the **powers** at work within us called **"the flesh,"** and to cope with the **powers** external to us—**called—"the world."**

If we're going to learn to walk in the Spirit, which is the **main exhortation** of Romans 6 through 8, and all of these doctrines that we've been preaching are leading us up to this conclusion: That we might have a life **"in the Spirit!"** But now what does that mean? That can be just ever so many words. We often do not **know.** And as we will see in detail, it is absolutely imperative that you have **knowledge** to walk in the Spirit. I will point that out very clearly tonight when we talk about **knowledge** in the Doctrine of Emptiness.

But the first thing that you must understand to "walk in the Spirit" is the Doctrine of The Two Creations. This is where it begins, and this is what we must grasp. Now, according to the Bible, God has **two** creations, not one, but two. Everybody knows about the first creation. You can read about that in the first chapter of the Bible, page one, it starts about the **first** creation. So, God created the universe, and He made **Adam** as its representative head. He put Adam as the **head** of that creation and put him in **dominion.**

But the Bible also talks about **another creation.** You'll read about that in the **last chapter,** the **last pages** of the Bible, the last chapter actually. God also put an **Adam,** called the "**last Adam,**" at the head of that **new creation.** His name happens to be Jesus Christ.

Now, you're going to go into that new creation fully, **when** you have a resurrected **body. <u>BUT WAIT!</u> GOD—RAISED—JESUS—FROM THE DEAD—2000 YEARS AGO AND PUT HIM IN THE NEW CREATION! And so, the new creation does <u>not</u> begin in the last pages of our Bible. The new creation began—when God—raised—Jesus Christ—from the dead! And that's where He is right now! He's in that new creation as the last Adam.** You can read about that in Romans chapter 5, and 1 Corinthians chapter 15.

Now we've come to this great doctrine of what it means to be "**<u>in</u> Christ.**" "*There is no condemnation to them who are <u>in</u>—Christ.*"[11] That's the key to the New Testament theology, to be **<u>in</u> Christ.** Now to be in Jesus Christ means that **positionality** you're standing before God and anyone else that counts as **identical to that of Jesus Christ! You are as righteous right now as Jesus Christ is. You have the same identical standing as He <u>does</u>.** Experimentally, you have the **possibility** of quote, "**walking—in—the Spirit!**" We're talking about of course the powers of the **new creation.**

Now let me explain this to you. In order to understand what it means to walk in the flesh or the Spirit, you must know that the first creation has two phases. There are two parts or two phases to the first creation. That is simply creation **before the fall** and creation **after the fall;** P1 and P2, Phase 1 and Phase 2 of the **first** creation.

So, when God created man, basically in Genesis chapter 1 and 2, you can read these statements: God created man, quote *"in the image and the likeness of God."* [12] And God looked at that, man and creation, and said, *"This is—very—good."* [13] He didn't say this was innocent. This has **positive righteousness.** This man is in a right relationship with me. This is **positive goodness.** He's in my image, and he is—**very**—good. But everyone knows that Phase 2 came in. And you can read this, of course, all through scripture, how that, man **fell.** He fell into what the Bible calls **sin.**

Now, **sin** is basically, in its simplest form and definition—sin is simply **disobedience.** That's what sin is. God created man in this positive state of righteousness, in His image, but He gave him a commandment—**a very direct commandment**—the law of God or the commandment of God—and says, *"The day you eat of the wrong tree here you will die."* [14] **So, Adam sinned. He went into disobedience and he lost—righteousness. He lost his positive goodness. Now, disobedience means he is not in a "right standing" or a "right relationship" with God. He's wrong with God! He's not right with God!**

And so there must come this restoration. There must come this re-creation—this regeneration. Our Bible is the story of how God, in love, reaches out to restore that image and likeness of man and to bring him back into a state called, righteousness. Into a right relationship with Him! And that brings us to this **great, tremendous book of Romans** that is telling us about how God is restoring that image and that likeness in us.

According to our New Testament, man basically lost three things. God is renewing, or restoring—regenerating—three things and these three things must be there for us to **walk—in the— Spirit.** They are all three named in Ephesians chapter 4, verses 23 and 24. I'd like to read that passage for you. And again, I mention it's imperative to know this to understand what you're doing when you walk in the Spirit. Ephesians 4:23 and 24, *"...be renewed"*—restored, regenerated, a new creation—*"be renewed"*— number one— *"in the spirit of your **minds.**"* It begins by a restoration of your **mind.** And again, I'll need an entire sermon to explain that to you in connection with the Doctrine of Emptiness. We'll talk about that tonight. *"Be renewed in the **spirit of your minds. And put on the new nature.**"* Put on the **new creation.** *"Put on the **new nature, created**"*—notice—*"**after the likeness of God.**"* That's what we want—*"the likeness and the image of God **in true righteousness and holiness.**"* [15]

There are many other scriptures that support this. Colossians picks it up similarly. Colossians chapter 3, verses 9 and 10 says, *"Don't lie to one another, seeing that you have put off the **old nature** with its practices and have put on the **new nature,** which is **being renewed—in— knowledge.**"* Please notice that. *"**It is being renewed—in—knowledge.**"* [16] Grace isn't something that floats around here in space that you magically bump into. Grace—comes—through knowledge! You grow in grace—and—knowledge! *"Grace and truth came by the Lord Jesus Christ."* [17] You cannot separate them.

So, the life in the Spirit, this new man, *"is being renewed **in knowledge** after the image of the creator."* [16] And this is why I say and I'm not trying to make any kind of a contest, but I've met people for years that have had all kinds of experiences, but they're still legalistic at heart. They've not got **knowledge.**

We bore witness to a man last night who had been, unfortunately, a Christian 35 years, and had **never** heard of the grace of God. He didn't know what it was **all about.** No wonders he was in such awful trouble. He didn't know about the **abundance of grace,** and the **Reign of Grace.** What a thrilling doctrine. You're *"being renewed **in knowledge** after the image of the creator."* [16]

That's why the Catechism, by the way, puts it this way: The Shorter Catechism asks the question, "How did God create man?" And it answers, "God created man, male and female, after His own **image in knowledge, righteousness, and holiness with dominion over the creatures.**" ᴬ And so, God is restoring His image and likeness—we see what that fall meant. Now we're in Phase 2 of creation. We're living our life out **in this old creation,** you see. **But God through Jesus Christ by the powers of the <u>new age</u>—<u>by the powers of the resurrection are restoring to us through KNOWLEDGE that glorious image and likeness.</u> He is imputing His righteousness TO ME!** He is restoring that marvelous thing whereby I can walk pleasing to God.

But listen church; there is <u>nothing</u> in this first creation. There is <u>nothing</u> in this age that has life or righteousness in it. It is under the wrath of the <u>cross</u>. God took all of this old creation in the likeness of sinful flesh, and God—gave—His—judgment against this world—by putting Jesus Christ to death on a cross. That's what the holiness of God regards of all this creation. And there are many people trying to draw their life from <u>this </u>creation. They're trying to improve their flesh. Self-improvement! I tell you it's <u>impossible!</u> It's under <u>DEATH</u>!

You can't walk in the flesh and set your mind after this world, and after the things of this world, and be a super conqueror. No wonders many people don't get anywhere. They don't know how to live. Friends, you've got to draw your life from the new age. This whole age is dying! Thanks be unto God, Jesus Christ came up out of that tomb—Jesus Christ went into the new creation, and by the Holy Spirit, He breathes the powers of that back into my old dying body, as it were, and lets me walk in the Spirit so that I become a super conqueror. Oh, I tell you, I'm not under condemnation.

I—don't—have—all of these frustrations. Do I suffer? Am I tempted by the world? Of course! I'm living my life out in the two creations. The old and the new! My body just hasn't caught up with what I've got down inside yet. I'm waiting for the redemption of my body. I am living now by **hope.** My salvation is primarily future. But don't you know the powers of that new creation have been breathed back into this old dying creation. And God looked down at me and said, "Hello son. Hello son. You're **justified** by the **death** of the **Lord Jesus Christ.**" And I'm just free as a bird! I've got glorious liberty.

You could find all kinds of things wrong with me. I could live with you a day or two and find **more,** by the way! *(Don chuckles)* You're no better than I am! *(Don chuckles some more)* **Oh, but thanks be unto God, the Reign of Grace! This marvelous, maximum love,** that **nothing** can separate me from that love. It lets me enter into the powers of the new creation.

Thanks be unto God for this truth. It is being renewed in **knowledge.** And folks, every time **that doctrine** and **that Bible** is preached, not just by your pastor, you ought to be there to intake that truth. That's why I don't **ding** at you to come to church. **You've got—to—hear—truth! It only comes by the truth! It's the intake of truth! The new man is renewed in <u>knowledge</u>! And oh, how I'm praying God is going to get our heads on straight, and everybody's going to understand a simple gospel of the grace of God! That's the way you walk in the Spirit.**

 "And you will know the truth, and the truth will make you free."- John 8:32 RSV

And that's not feeling woozy or feeling spiritual or anything. That comes—through—your—mind. You've got to have your <u>mind</u> renewed. *"Don't be conformed to this world. Be transformed by the <u>renewal—of your—mind</u>."* [18] And Paul says, *"I serve God with my*

mind." [19] That's the way it goes by this **truth,** this intake of the grace of God that transforms and changes our lives.

Well folks, it's available for us. *"The truth—sets—you—free."* [20] See it's not your **trying.** It's you're getting the truth. Once that truth lodges in your heart **then** you can walk in the Spirit. All that **struggling;** all that **striving,** all that **lashing and straining and twisting and whipping,** it's all gone! Now, it's that **marvelous** walk in the Spirit. That means you're participating in the powers of the new creation. Oh, hallelujah!

It's <u>available</u> in this old dying body and this old trying creation! It's available by the power of the Holy Spirit! But I want to tell you something. Please make this clear. You see your emotions and your sentiments, your feelings; **they** are part of your body's structure, and people run hot and cold. They feel this or that. **Don't—trust—your feelings.** We're talking about our **minds.** We're talking about the **mind** and **knowledge.** We're talking about the spirit of our **mind.** It has to be renewed and if you'll let that intake come of the **truth,** and act on the **basis of that truth, because that won't change**. Jesus Christ has risen from the dead, and He stands in the new creation to breathe back His Spirit to you. The Spirit of Christ can dwell in you and it's going to raise your body and all your miserable emotions some day from the grave, and they're all going be changed. So don't live at that basis, you see, don't live at that basis, but respond what is, to the truth.

SERMON 15 ENDNOTES:

[A] The Shorter Catechism by The Orthodox Presbyterian Church. (2020). *Question 10.* Retrieved from https://www.opc.org/sc.html

SERMON 15 SCRIPTURE REFERENCES:

[1] Romans 5:17 (RSV)

If, because of one man's trespass, death reigned through that one man, much more will those who receive the abundance of grace and the free gift of righteousness reign in life through the one man Jesus Christ.

[2] Romans 8:18 (KJV)

For I reckon that the sufferings of this present time are not worthy to be compared with the glory which shall be revealed in us.

[3] Romans 8:1-8 (RSV)

1 There is therefore now no condemnation for those who are in Christ Jesus. 2 For the law of the Spirit of life in Christ Jesus has set me free from the law of sin and death. 3 For God has done what the law, weakened by the flesh, could not do: sending his own Son in the likeness of sinful flesh and for sin, he condemned sin in the flesh, 4 in order that the just requirement of the law might be fulfilled in us, who walk not according to the flesh but according to the Spirit. 5 For those who live according to the flesh set their minds on the things of the flesh, but those who live according to the Spirit set their minds on the things of the Spirit. 6 To set the mind on the flesh is death, but to set the mind on the Spirit is life and peace. 7 For the mind that is set on the flesh is hostile to God; it does not submit to God's law, indeed it cannot; 8 and those who are in the flesh cannot please God.

[4] Romans 8:9-11 (RSV)

9 But you are not in the flesh, you are in the Spirit, if in fact the Spirit of God dwells in you. Any one who does not have the Spirit of Christ does not belong to him. 10 But if Christ is in you, although your bodies are dead because of sin, your spirits are alive because of righteousness. 11 If the Spirit of him who raised Jesus from the dead dwells in you, he who raised Christ Jesus from the dead will give life to your mortal bodies also through his Spirit which dwells in you.

5 Romans 8:12-17 (RSV)

12 So then, brethren, we are debtors, not to the flesh, to live according to the flesh— 13 for if you live according to the flesh you will die, but if by the Spirit you put to death the deeds of the body you will live. 14 For all who are led by the Spirit of God are sons of God. 15 For you did not receive the spirit of slavery to fall back into fear, but you have received the spirit of sonship. When we cry, "Abba! Father!" 16 it is the Spirit himself bearing witness with our spirit that we are children of God, 17 and if children, then heirs, heirs of God and fellow heirs with Christ, provided we suffer with him in order that we may also be glorified with him.

6 Romans 8:18-25 (RSV)

18 I consider that the sufferings of this present time are not worth comparing with the glory that is to be revealed to us. 19 For the creation waits with eager longing for the revealing of the sons of God; 20 for the creation was subjected to futility, not of its own will but by the will of him who subjected it in hope; 21 because the creation itself will be set free from its bondage to decay and obtain the glorious liberty of the children of God. 22 We know that the whole creation has been groaning in travail together until now; 23 and not only the creation, but we ourselves, who have the first fruits of the Spirit, groan inwardly as we wait for adoption as sons, the redemption of our bodies. 24 For in this hope we were saved. Now hope that is seen is not hope. For who hopes for what he sees? 25 But if we hope for what we do not see, we wait for it with patience.

[7] Romans 8: 26-27 (RSV)

26 Likewise the Spirit helps us in our weakness; for we do not know how to pray as we ought, but the Spirit himself intercedes for us with sighs too deep for words. 27 And he who searches the hearts of men knows what is the mind of the Spirit, because the Spirit intercedes for the saints according to the will of God.

[8] Romans 8:28-30 (RSV)

28 We know that in everything God works for good with those who love him, who are called according to his purpose. 29 For those whom he foreknew he also predestined to be conformed to the image of his Son, in order that he might be the first-born among many brethren. 30 And those whom he predestined he also called; and those whom he called he also justified; and those whom he justified he also glorified.

[9] Romans 8:31-36 (RSV)

31 What then shall we say to this? If God is for us, who is against us? 32 He who did not spare his own Son but gave him up for us all, will he not also give us all things with him? 33 Who shall bring any charge against God's elect? It is God who justifies; 34 who is to condemn? Is it Christ Jesus, who died, yes, who was raised from the dead, who is at the right hand of God, who indeed intercedes for us? 35 Who shall separate us from the love of Christ? Shall tribulation, or distress, or persecution, or famine, or nakedness, or peril, or sword? 36 As it is written, "For thy sake we are being killed all the day long; we are regarded as sheep to be slaughtered."

[10] Romans 8:37-39 (RSV)

37 No, in all these things we are more than conquerors through him who loved us. 38 For I am sure that neither death, nor life, nor angels, nor principalities, nor things present, nor things to come, nor powers, 39 nor height, nor depth, nor anything else in all creation, will be able to separate us from the love of God in Christ Jesus our Lord.

[11] Romans 8:1 (RSV)

There is therefore now no condemnation for those who are in Christ Jesus.

[12] Genesis 1:26-27 (RSV)

26 Then God said, "Let us make man in our image, after our likeness; and let them have dominion over the fish of the sea, and over the birds of the air, and over the cattle, and over all the earth, and over every creeping thing that creeps upon the earth." 27 So God created man in his own image, in the image of God he created him; male and female he created them.

[13] Genesis 1:31 (RSV)

And God saw everything that he had made, and behold, it was very good. And there was evening and there was morning, a sixth day.

[14] Genesis 2:15-17 (RSV)

15 The Lord God took the man and put him in the garden of Eden to till it and keep it. 16 And the Lord God commanded the man, saying, "You may freely eat of every tree of the garden; 17 but of the tree of the knowledge of good and evil you shall not eat, for in the day that you eat of it you shall die."

[15] Ephesians 4:23-24 (RSV)

23 and be renewed in the spirit of your minds, 24 and put on the new nature, created after the likeness of God in true righteousness and holiness.

[16] Colossians 3:9-10 (RSV)

9 Do not lie to one another, seeing that you have put off the old nature with its practices 10 and have put on the new nature, which is being renewed in knowledge after the image of its creator.

[17] John 1:17 (RSV)

For the law was given through Moses; grace and truth came through Jesus Christ.

[18] Romans 12:2 (RSV)

Do not be conformed to this world but be transformed by the renewal of your mind, that you may prove what is the will of God, what is good and acceptable and perfect.

[19] Romans 7:25 (RSV)

Thanks be to God through Jesus Christ our Lord! So then, I of myself serve the law of God with my mind, but with my flesh I serve the law of sin.

[20] John 8:32 (RSV)

and you will know the truth, and the truth will make you free."

SERMON 16

THE DOCTRINE OF EMPTINESS

"Walking in the Spirit depends upon your knowing the Doctrine of Emptiness—the futility of the first creation—subjected to absolute futility!"

Now we're trying to learn what it means to walk in the Spirit. And we have reached one of the most significant truths in the Christian life and in Paul's letter to the Romans and Galatians, particularly. "What does it mean to walk in the Spirit?" and "How does one walk in the Spirit?" We're looking at that and I'd like to share the 8th chapter of Romans which exemplifies this doctrine and gives us some of the clues for walking in the Spirit.

Romans chapter 8, let's begin reading with verse 1, and we'll go clear down to verse 25. *"There is therefore **now** no condemnation for those who are in Christ Jesus. For the law of the Spirit of life in Christ Jesus has **set me free**"*—isn't that beautiful? —*"...**has set me free** from the **law** of sin and death. For **God has done** what the **law,** weakened by the **flesh,** could **not** do: sending his own Son in the likeness of sinful flesh and for sin, he **condemned** sin in the flesh, **in order that** the just requirement of the law might be fulfilled in us,"*—now notice—*"who walk **not according to the flesh but according to the Spirit.** For those who live according to the **flesh** set their **minds** on the **things** of the flesh,"*—notice the reference to the **mind**—*"set their **minds** on the things of the flesh, but those who live according to the Spirit—**set—their—minds**—on the things of the Spirit."*

We call that an **SOS** mind. **A mind—Set—On—the—Spirit. A mind**—set—on the—Spirit. *"Now to set the mind on the flesh is **death**, but to **set the mind** on the Spirit, the consequences are **life** and **peace**. For the mind that is set on the flesh is **hostile** to God; it does **not submit**"*—that's a way you can detect it—*"it does not submit to God's law, **indeed it cannot;** and those who are **in** the flesh cannot **please God.**"* [1]

*"**But** you are not in the flesh, but in the Spirit, if the Spirit of God"*—really—*"**dwells—in you.** Anyone who does not have the Spirit of Christ does not belong to him. But if Christ is in you, although your **bodies are dead,**"*—or dying—our bodies are dying—death is at work in them—*"because of sin, your **spirits** are alive because of righteousness. Now if the Spirit of him who raised Jesus from the dead **dwells** in you, he who raised Christ Jesus from the dead will give **life** to your mortal bodies also through his Spirit which dwells in you."* [2]

"But if Christ is in you, although your bodies are dead because of sin, your spirits are alive because of righteousness."
- Romans 8:10 RSV

*"So then, brethren, we were debtors, not to the flesh, to live according to the flesh—for if you live according to the flesh you'll **die, but if by the Spirit** you put to death the deeds of the body you will live. For all who are **led** by the Spirit of God are **sons of God.** You did not receive the spirit of slavery"*—bondage and so on—*"to fall back into fear. You have received the spirit of sonship. When we cry, 'Abba! Father!' it's the Spirit himself bearing witness with our spirit."* In other words, if you can just say those words and mean them. If you can say "Father," "God is my Father," that's the Holy Spirit. You could not do that without the enablement of the Holy Spirit. *"...it's the Spirit bearing witness with our spirit that we are children of God, and if **children,** then we are **heirs,** heirs of God, fellow*

heirs with Christ, provided we suffer with him in order that we may also be glorified with him." ³

"I consider"—now I want you to watch this passage carefully—"I consider that the sufferings of **this present time** are not **worth** comparing with the **glory** that is to be revealed to us. **For creation**"—all creation— "**waits with eager longing for the revealing of the sons of God;** creation"— **all creation**—"was subjected to futility, not of its **own will** but by the will of him who **subjected it in hope;** because the creation itself will be set free from its **bondage** to **decay** and obtain the **glorious liberty of the children of God.** We know that the whole creation has been **groaning** in travail together until now; **not only the creation, but** we ourselves, who have the first fruits of the Spirit, **we groan inwardly** as we wait for adoption as sons,"—that is—"the redemption of our bodies." The resurrection of our bodies—"For in this **hope** we are saved. Now hope that is **seen** is **not hope.** For who **hopes** for what he **sees?** But if we hope for what we do **not** see, we wait for it with **patience.**" ⁴

So, we're trying to determine what are the factors involved in **"walking in the Spirit."** And we're going to look at the significance of Romans chapter 8, verse 20, which gives us Paul's commentary on **life** after the fall. As sin entered the world, we have a creation that has been subjected to **futility.** Romans 8:20, "creation was **subjected** to futility." ⁵ This Greek word that is translated "futility" means, and I quote, here are all the various meanings of that word, it means—vanity—unreality— purposelessness—ineffectiveness—instability—worthless—and empty. Now I particularly like that word, "empty." So, I want to talk about the **Doctrine of Emptiness** in connection with **knowledge.** We are calling this **knowledge** and the **Doctrine of Emptiness.**

Now, this word "futility," the Greek word is *mataiotes,* ᴬ represents the world of appearance as distinct from that of being. Appearance as distinct from that of being. In other words, we could say that the first creation after the fall, including **man** in that creation, has **non-being.** Creation—is—futile—empty—**non-being.** The world like the flesh is of the **appearance** of having value, fulfillment and reality. But actually, it's a **sham.** It's empty. For **without God** the world and creation is quote, "empty!" It is futile. And everyone knows what happens to an empty thing. Anything that's left **empty** soon runs to seed. You take an empty house, for example, it's always a target of vandals, right? And it soon becomes **corrupt** and is given over to all **kinds** of things. So, Paul is saying that **creation has been left to futility and must, as a result, suffer the pain and the corruption of this** *mataiotes,* or this futility or emptiness.

Paul is describing, of course, what it means for a person to **live** in this creation, and a person thinks they can draw their **life** from this creation, you see. They're going to be full of a lot of decay, and a lot of *"groaning in travail"* [6] he says.

Now we must see that **man** along with creation, including his **mind especially,** has been given to futility or emptiness. Along with all creation, **man himself** is subjected to futility. The wrath of God, which means "love taking itself seriously," that's what God's wrath is, "love taking itself seriously," **justly delivered man over to the awful consequences of his own sins.** Left to himself, without God, in his own emptiness, man then falls **prey to these powers of corruption,** and really, perversion. The devastating results of that are described for us in Romans the first chapter and I'd like you to see what **man is** when he is **"left to himself."** Take a look at Romans chapter 1 and you'll see the awful consequences as Paul, **three times** here, says that *"God—gave—man—up."* [7]

Look at verse 18. *"The wrath of God is revealed from heaven against all the ungodliness and wickedness of men who by their wickedness suppress the truth. What can be known about God is plain to them, because God has shown it to them. Ever since the creation of the world his invisible* nature, namely, his eternal power and deity, has been **clearly perceived** in the things that have been made. So they are without excuse; **although they knew God they did not honor him as God or give thanks to him,** but"—now notice—"**became futile**"—same word—"**futile in their** <u>thinking</u> **and their** <u>senseless minds</u> **were darkened. Claiming to be wise, they became fools.**" [8]

"Therefore," verse 24 says, "**God—gave—them—up**" [7] —and you'll see all the various things that happened because of this **giving up** to futility or to emptiness. Now that's the picture of the first creation, and as someone has said, "the **natural** without the **supernatural** soon becomes **unnatural.**" And you'll see all the **perversions** and all the **corruptions** that come into this world because of futility.

Now notice verse 21 says that "…*they became futile in their* **thinking** *and their* **senseless minds** *were darkened.*" [9] Biblical psychology, by the way, tends to equate what we call the "mind," with the "heart," and the "will." The Bible uses those terms in a popular way, just like we do. The mind, of course, is the **center** of our conscious life, and it's the controlling factor really, of our personality—our mind—our attitudes—our beliefs—our thinking. So, **man,** all of him really, body—soul—spirit—heart—**is**—given over or subjected to **emptiness.** So, a part of the first creation **after sin,** man in that creation is—**futile.** That is, his whole personality <u>**outside God,**</u> and **that's** what the Bible means by the **flesh!** Now we'll look at that in detail but if you're going to **walk** in the flesh or **walk** in the Spirit, you've got to know what you're talking about. And as we'll see the flesh is **not** the body. We're talking about <u>**all**</u> **of man—walking—in—the creation—that's been given over to futility** and drawing his life from that.

You'll notice, by the way, that Romans talks about a **"base mind"** and this depraved, social and twisted emotional behavior, stemming out of man's empty mind, is horribly described. "*They did not see fit to* acknowledge God, so God gave them up to a **base mind** and to improper conduct." [10] Then follows, a **long** list, of **over twenty** sociological evil things and all kinds of perversions and that dark list is a very, very, awful thing to read, if you'll go on to look at Romans chapter 1. [11]

This word translated **"base,"** by the way, means unqualified—worthless—**unfit for any good deed.** So Paul, is able to say in Romans chapter 1, *"I know that in me, that is, in my flesh,"*—in Saul of Tarsus taken alone—me and my historical self—**me as a part of creation outside redemption**— *"dwells—no—good—thing."* [12] **We—will—never walk in the Spirit until we know that truth.** The reason being— because we're wanting to draw our **life from somewhere.** We want to establish our life **in** this creation. We have got to see; however, the absolute **emptiness** of the first creation, and ourselves included, **or we will never turn from it and begin to walk in the Spirit. Because walking in the Spirit has reference to the new creation.**

You'll **notice** now that it **begins by—the mind—and knowledge.** This is why walking in the Spirit **starts** by a **renewal in knowledge. Knowledge** is the instrumental means whereby the human mind is **renewed** from its futility. Obviously, one cannot **live** under the **emptiness** of a **futile mind** and at the same time walk in the Spirit. Walking in the Spirit **requires a renewal in knowledge.** Paul states in Romans 7:25, *"... we serve God with our minds."* [13]

"And have put on the new nature, which is being renewed in knowledge after the image of its creator."
- Colossians 3:10 RSV

There are numerous passages in the Bible that talk about the role of knowledge and the renewal of the mind and let me read a few of them for you. Colossians 3:10 says, *"The new nature is being renewed in knowledge after the image of the creator.*" [14] Did you note that? "*The new nature is being renewed in* **knowledge** *after the image of the creator.*" Romans 12:2, a very famous verse, "*Do not be conformed to this world* **but be transformed by**"—can you finish it? *(The congregation quotes the rest of the verse with Don)*—"*the renewal of your mind.*" [15] 2 Peter, chapter 1, verse 3 indicates, "*His divine power has granted to us* **all things** *that pertain to life,* **through**—*the* **knowledge** *of him.*" [16] That divine life and power comes through **knowledge.**

Now I think the most thorough going statement on this is Ephesians chapter 4, verses 17 to 24. I'd like to read part of that please, with reference to our minds and the renewal in knowledge. Paul says in Ephesians 4:17, "*...you must no longer live as the Gentiles do,* **in the futility of their minds**"—same word—the **emptiness**—the **baseness**—the **senselessness**—the **purposelessness**—in the *mataiotes* [A] of their **minds**—"*they are* **darkened in their understanding** *and thus* **alienated** *from the life of* **God** *because of the* **ignorance** *that is in them, due to the hardness of their heart;* **You**—**did not**—**so learn Christ!**—*assuming that you've heard about him and were* **taught** *in him, as the truth is in Jesus. Put off your old nature which belongs to the former manner of life and is* **corrupt** *through deceitful lusts, and* **be renewed**"—notice how you're to do it—"*in the* **spirit** *of your minds,*"—be renewed, the renewal is coming **through knowledge** and by the spirit of your minds—"*and thus put on the new nature, created after the likeness of God in true righteousness and holiness.*" [17]

Now, we need to see though, what this kind of knowledge is. What kind of **knowledge** are we talking about that renews us? Let me say that knowledge is not mere academic or intellectual facts. Spiritual renewal does not depend solely upon what we call "IQ." Remember we said you cannot separate the **heart** and the **mind.** We can **academically** call a distinction between them. But **Biblical knowledge** is inseparable from the attitude of the heart, and one's moral life.

Paul prays in Ephesians 1:17 to 18, *"the eyes of your **hearts** will be enlightened."* [18] He speaks about being **renewed in the spirit of your mind,** and by the spirit of your mind he means that **attitude**—that **disposition**—that kind of an **understanding** that you have and not ever so many **facts** that you may or may not be able to quote. In other words, you don't have to be **super intellectual** to walk in the Spirit. That's the point I'm trying to make. Walking in the Spirit is not reserved for PhD's. Some of the most **simple people** that I know walk **beautifully in the Spirit.** Their minds have been renewed by the Spirit of the Lord Jesus.

So **Biblical knowledge** is really more akin to what we call **wisdom.** Wisdom is the ability to recognize reality, and to respond to truth in all of its forms. **Wisdom** understands the principles of life. It **grasps truth** when it **hears it.** So, we **might say** that **knowledge** is the ability to appreciate and receive the things of God. That's what knowledge is.

1 Corinthians 2:14 is a good commentary on the **moral** or **spiritual elements** that make it necessary for us to receive truth. *"The natural man,"* meaning the **unspiritual man,** *"receiveth not the things of the Spirit of God: they are **foolishness** unto him, neither can he **know them,"***—appreciate them—respond to them—**hear them**—he doesn't really **respond to them**—*"because they are **spiritually discerned."*** [19] — not necessarily thought out in an academic **classroom.** So, the point we are making is that you do not have to be super smart to walk in the Spirit. So, if **you're struggling** with a **bad memory** or whatever, we are **not excluding** you from walking in the **Spirit.**

Walking in the Spirit **springs out** of the **Spirit! That is the intention of your heart and your soul.** Your disposition if you please. Now, I might add by the way, I'm **not minimizing** the intellect. I think we need to love God with our **mind,** and we need to **study.** We need to give ourselves over **to that.** But, basically, walking in the Spirit is something that is done with what we call **the heart,** but it's a renewal in knowledge.

Now knowledge, of course, is always a means to an end. It should **never** turn in upon itself. Paul makes that point in 1 Corinthians chapter 8, verse 1. He says, *"Knowledge"*—taken by itself—*"puffs up,"*—but he adds—*"love—builds up."* [20] So we're not talking about a **knowledge** that centers on itself. Sometimes people who have a little bit of knowledge, by the way, become kind of self-centered, and anything they can even **ground themselves in** or establish their life in, **they will.** And so, if they can **glory in their degree,** or if they can **glory in this or that,** often they will. But that's just a part of the first creation, and in and of itself that's still **futile. That's not life!** That isn't walking in the Spirit.

The **end** of Biblical knowledge **is: The grace and the power of God.** We receive **knowledge** in order to receive **grace—transforming grace**—the **super grace** we've been talking about **and** the power of God. Remember 2 Peter chapter 3, verse 18 says, *"grow—in—grace—and—knowledge."* [21] John 1:17 notes, *"...grace—and truth—came by Jesus Christ."* [22] So you see, **grace,** and really the power of God, it is not some mysterious element that you bump into on a fine day. **Grace**—is **mediated**—to your **minds** through **knowledge. Grace,** like faith, comes by hearing the Word of God, and **hearing** comes by the **preaching of Christ.**

So, walking in the Spirit requires an intake of <u>truth</u>. And of course, since I'm your preacher that would give me every reason to tell you to be **faithful to hear the preaching of truth.** I think there needs to be a **constant intake** of Bible doctrine and knowledge. My **mind** is renewed that way. It's a renewal of my **mind.**

I'd like to draw a **conclusion** from this then, that **walking in the Spirit** is **not** primarily a **mystical** experience. Can you see this? You do **not get <u>lost</u>** in some other metaphysical world when you walk in the Spirit. Now I think a lot of people get confused here, because they think in order to be in the Spirit, they have to some way be kind of almost **ecstatic.** They have to kind of be **lost** in some other realm somewhere, as though there's a spirit realm beyond what we see and if I could just someway penetrate through there and think hard enough and **fast** or whatever, I'll **break through** to that other spiritual world. Now that's a false road.

As I have said, and I don't mean to be irreverent by this, you walk in the Spirit with your **eyes wide open.** Not with your eyes closed. It's something that is **imparted** through **knowledge** to us. The **emphasis** upon walking in the Spirit is **not upon experience.** It is not **primarily** upon an experience. So, it's not important whether you **feel** or **experience** anything necessarily. Because, you see, these **sentiments,** the **feelings** that we have, they're tied in often with our body and our psychological life. And our <u>body</u>—is <u>dead</u>! **Our body is <u>dying</u> and has <u>not</u> experienced redemption and <u>will</u> <u>not</u> until the second coming of Jesus!**

It's so easy to think that you're walking in the Spirit by a certain **kind** of a **mystical** or **holy feeling.** You cannot **trust** those holy feelings— whether you feel good or feel bad. You can't begin by looking at a **mystical** experience or some kind of a **sentiment** that you may be in. **Walking in the Spirit <u>begins</u> by a <u>renewal of our minds</u> where we start <u>thinking straightly</u>, and we start drawing our life from that <u>word</u>—that <u>truth</u> that's coming up from us out of the new creation. And <u>that's</u> going to do something very, very real to me in this life. I'm going to start living life at the right kind of a level. But if I think it's here in this first creation, I'm mistaken.** So many people are **constantly** running out here **hoping** that they're going to **find it.** "Maybe if I can just do this or acquire this or do this." Basically, they look to **themselves** and their own energies, **hoping** that by some **effort** or by **something** that they can **do,** they can **establish themselves** and all of a sudden start to walk in the Spirit. Walking in the Spirit comes out of the new creation. **It is—not— in—this—creation. It is—not—resident—in you.** And the sooner you learn that lesson and I learn that lesson, the better.

When we—turn—totally—from ourselves and from this first creation, and turn wholly to God and His Word, and the truth of the new creation, we're on our way to walking in the Spirit. So, walking in the Spirit depends upon your knowing the Doctrine of Emptiness— the futility of the first creation—subjected to absolute futility.

SERMON 16 ENDNOTES:

A *mataiotes,* means: vanity, unreality, purposelessness, ineffectiveness, instability, worthless, and empty." I particularly like that word, "empty." New Testament Greek Lexicon. [exegete and taught by Don Pickerill in this sermon]

SERMON 16 SCRIPTURE REFERENCES:

¹ Romans 8:1-8 (RSV)

1 There is therefore now no condemnation for those who are in Christ Jesus. 2 For the law of the Spirit of life in Christ Jesus has set me free from the law of sin and death. 3 For God has done what the law, weakened by the flesh, could not do: sending his own Son in the likeness of sinful flesh and for sin,[a] he condemned sin in the flesh, 4 in order that the just requirement of the law might be fulfilled in us, who walk not according to the flesh but according to the Spirit. 5 For those who live according to the flesh set their minds on the things of the flesh, but those who live according to the Spirit set their minds on the things of the Spirit. 6 To set the mind on the flesh is death, but to set the mind on the Spirit is life and peace. 7 For the mind that is set on the flesh is hostile to God; it does not submit to God's law, indeed it cannot; 8 and those who are in the flesh cannot please God.

² Romans 8:9-11 (RSV)

9 But you are not in the flesh, you are in the Spirit, if in fact the Spirit of God dwells in you. Any one who does not have the Spirit of

Christ does not belong to him. 10 But if Christ is in you, although your bodies are dead because of sin, your spirits are alive because of righteousness. 11 If the Spirit of him who raised Jesus from the dead dwells in you, he who raised Christ Jesus from the dead will give life to your mortal bodies also through his Spirit which dwells in you.

³ Romans 8:12-17 (RSV)

12 So then, brethren, we are debtors, not to the flesh, to live according to the flesh— 13 for if you live according to the flesh you will die, but if by the Spirit you put to death the deeds of the body you will live. 14 For all who are led by the Spirit of God are sons of God. 15 For you did not receive the spirit of slavery to fall back into fear, but you have received the spirit of sonship. When we cry, "Abba! Father!" 16 it is the Spirit himself bearing witness with our spirit that we are children of God, 17 and if children, then heirs, heirs of God and fellow heirs with Christ, provided we suffer with him in order that we may also be glorified with him.

⁴ Romans 8:18-25 (RSV)

18 I consider that the sufferings of this present time are not worth comparing with the glory that is to be revealed to us. 19 For the creation waits with eager longing for the revealing of the sons of God; 20 for the creation was subjected to futility, not of its own will but by the will of him who subjected it in hope; 21 because the creation itself will be set free from its bondage to decay and obtain the glorious liberty of the children of God. 22 We know that the whole creation has been groaning in travail together until now; 23 and not only the creation, but we ourselves, who have the first fruits of the Spirit, groan inwardly as we wait for adoption as sons, the redemption of our bodies. 24 For in this hope we were saved. Now hope that is seen is not hope. For who hopes for what he sees? 25

But if we hope for what we do not see, we wait for it with patience.

5 Romans 8:20 (RSV)

for the creation was subjected to futility, not of its own will but by the will of him who subjected it in hope;

6 Romans 8:22 (RSV)

We know that the whole creation has been groaning in travail together until now;

7 Romans 1:18-22 (RSV)

18 For the wrath of God is revealed from heaven against all ungodliness and wickedness of men who by their wickedness suppress the truth. 19 For what can be known about God is plain to them, because God has shown it to them. 20 Ever since the creation of the world his invisible nature, namely, his eternal power and deity, has been clearly perceived in the things that have been made. So they are without excuse; 21 for although they knew God they did not honor him as God or give thanks to him, but they became futile in their thinking and their senseless minds were darkened. 22 Claiming to be wise, they became fools,

8 Romans 1:24,26,28 (RSV)

24 Therefore God gave them up in the lusts of their hearts to impurity, to the dishonoring of their bodies among themselves, . . . 26 For this reason God gave them up to dishonorable passions. Their women exchanged natural relations for unnatural, . . . 28 And since they did not see fit to acknowledge God, God gave them up to a base mind and to improper conduct.

9 Romans 1:21 (RSV)

for although they knew God they did not honor him as God or give thanks to him, but they became futile in their thinking and their senseless minds were darkened.

[10] Romans 1:28 (RSV)

And since they did not see fit to acknowledge God, God gave them up to a base mind and to improper conduct.

[11] Romans 1:29-31 (RSV)

29 They were filled with all manner of wickedness, evil, covetousness, malice. Full of envy, murder, strife, deceit, malignity, they are gossips, 30 slanderers, haters of God, insolent, haughty, boastful, inventors of evil, disobedient to parents, 31 foolish, faithless, heartless, ruthless.

[12] Romans 7:18 (KJV)

For I know that in me (that is, in my flesh,) dwelleth no good thing: for to will is present with me; but how to perform that which is good I find not.

[13] Romans 7:25 (RSV)

Thanks be to God through Jesus Christ our Lord! So then, I of myself serve the law of God with my mind, but with my flesh I serve the law of sin.

[14] Colossians 3:10 (RSV)

and have put on the new nature, which is being renewed in knowledge after the image of its creator.

[15] Romans 12:2 (RSV)

Do not be conformed to this world but be transformed by the renewal of your mind, that you may prove what is the will of God, what is good and acceptable and perfect.

[16] 2 Peter 1:3 (RSV)

His divine power has granted to us all things that pertain to life and godliness, through the knowledge of him who called us to his own glory and excellence,

[17] Ephesians 4:17-24 (RSV)

17 Now this I affirm and testify in the Lord, that you must no longer live as the Gentiles do, in the futility of their minds; 18 they are darkened in their understanding, alienated from the life of God because of the ignorance that is in them, due to their hardness of heart; 19 they have become callous and have given themselves up to licentiousness, greedy to practice every kind of uncleanness. 20 You did not so learn Christ!— 21 assuming that you have heard about him and were taught in him, as the truth is in Jesus. 22 Put off your old nature which belongs to your former manner of life and is corrupt through deceitful lusts, 23 and be renewed in the spirit of your minds, 24 and put on the new nature, created after the likeness of God in true righteousness and holiness.

[18] Ephesians 1:17-18 (RSV)

17 that the God of our Lord Jesus Christ, the Father of glory, may give you a spirit of wisdom and of revelation in the knowledge of him, 18 having the eyes of your hearts enlightened, that you may know what is the hope to which he has called you, what are the riches of his glorious inheritance in the saints,

[19] 1 Corinthians 2:14 (KJV)

But the natural man receiveth not the things of the Spirit of God: for they are foolishness unto him: neither can he know them, because they are spiritually discerned.

[20] 1 Corinthians 8:1 (RSV)

Now concerning food offered to idols: we know that "all of us possess knowledge." "Knowledge" puffs up, but love builds up.

[21] 2 Peter 3:18 (RSV)

But grow in the grace and knowledge of our Lord and Savior Jesus Christ. To him be the glory both now and to the day of eternity. Amen.

[22] John 1:17 (RSV)

For the law was given through Moses; grace and truth came through Jesus Christ.

SERMON 17

WALKING IN THE FLESH

"It is impossible, in my opinion, to walk in the Spirit without a constant intake of Bible doctrine and the truth!"

We're doing a series of sermons taken from Romans chapters 6, 7 and 8. We have noticed that these three chapters are **explaining** to us what it means to be **"under grace."** That's the **major doctrine** of these three chapters. **You're not <u>under</u> law, but <u>under</u> grace.** We also observe that it's not only the word **"grace,"** but it's talking about the **"reign"** of grace. **Grace—might—reign!** We're talking about **"king"** grace—grace as **king.** We're talking about **"abundance" of grace.** Romans 5:17, *"Those who have received the **abundance of grace."** [1] That word means grace raised to the highest power, by the way. Or we probably would say **grace and nothing <u>but</u> grace** because that's what the <u>Reign</u> of Grace is. And any add mixture of faith and works, law and grace, old and new creation, flesh and spirit, it will **<u>always</u> be defective** and defeating. How important that we understand the teaching of scripture.

The reason we are under grace; however, is defined in that same passage that says, *"**sin shall not have dominion over you."** [2] We want to be **under grace** so that we can, quote, *"walk—in—the Spirit."* And so, for the last two or three sermons we are defining what it means to *"walk in the Spirit."* That would be the **major exhortation** of Romans chapter 8. The eighth chapter of Romans is telling us how the **Reign of**

Grace can make us **super conquerors during—this—present—time.** That's basically what this great chapter is and the first part of the chapter, roughly about the first 17 verses, are describing the differences between walking in the **flesh** and walking in the **Spirit.**

To **get at** this doctrine and show how profound and complex it is, we have to introduce the **Doctrine of the Two Creations** with special emphasis upon *"this—present—time,"* [3] Romans 8:18. We also spoke about the **Doctrine of Emptiness,** Romans 8:20, *"all creation"*—that is the **first creation**—*"has been subjected—to—futility,"* [4] —**emptiness** is the word and we need to **understand that,** or we will not **absolutely** turn to the **new** creation. We will always subtly try to walk in the flesh.

If we're going to know what it means to walk in the Spirit, we must in connection with that know what it means to be **"in the flesh."** We also need to see the connection between **flesh and the human body.** And so, this morning, we're going to look at that phase, and then tonight we'll see **directly** what it means to be—**walking in the Spirit.** We'll see the difference between being **in** the Spirit and **walking** in the Spirit. We'll see the **benefits** of being in the Spirit, and the three requisites for walking in the Spirit.

Let's one more time take a look at Romans chapter 8, and we'll read the scripture; particularly, up to about verse 13. Romans chapter 8 verse 1, *"There is therefore—now—no condemnation"*—there is none—*"no—condemnation for those who are in Christ Jesus."* Now here's why—*"For the law of the Spirit of life"*—probably meaning the Holy Spirit here—*"in Christ Jesus has set me free from the law of sin and death."* So, if I'm free from sin, I cannot be under condemnation. He has set me free from the law of sin and death.—*"For God has done what the law, weakened by the flesh, could not do: sending his own Son in the likeness of sinful flesh and for sin, he condemned sin in the flesh,"*—in Christ Jesus—*"in order that the just requirement of the law might be fulfilled in us, who walk not according to the flesh but according to the Spirit. Now those who live according to the flesh, they set their* __minds__ *on the things of the flesh, but those who live according to the Spirit"*—that would be walking in the Spirit—*"they set their minds on the things of the Spirit. To set the mind on the flesh"*—well the only word you can have for it is just *"death,"* that's the only word that qualifies is death—*"but to set the mind on the Spirit is* life and peace. *For the* mind *that is set on the flesh is* hostile *to God;"*—notice that hostility—*"it does* __not__ __submit__ *to God's law, indeed it cannot; for those who are* __in__ *the flesh—*__cannot__*—please—God." [5]*

(*Don continues reading here with Romans 8:9) "*__But__*—you are not— in the flesh, you are—*__in__*—the Spirit, if the Spirit of God"*—really—*"dwells in you. Anyone who doesn't have the Spirit of Christ doesn't belong to him.* But *now if Christ is in you,* although your bodies are dead*"—notice this—"because of sin,* your spirits are alive because of righteousness. If the Spirit of him who raised Jesus from the dead dwells in you, he who raised Christ Jesus from the dead will give* __life__ *to your* __mortal bodies__*— through his Spirit which—dwells—in you. So then, brethren, we are debtors, not to the flesh,"*—you don't have any obligations to that, no debt to that whatever—*"to* __live according__ *to the flesh—for if you live according to the flesh you will* __die__*, but* __if by the Spirit__ *you put to death the deeds of the body—you—will live." [6]*

So, our task this morning is to define **"flesh"** and see its relationship to the human body, and hopefully, that will enable us to understand **clearly** what it means to—**walk—in—the Spirit.** Anyone who's carefully looked at this **Bible** with reference to the word **"flesh,"** in its Hebrew and Greek terms, will know what a **bewildering** and a **variety of terms** confront you. I have been able to find **seven shades of meaning.** And just to show you how **careful one must be** in looking at the word "flesh," which is the Greek word, by the way, *sarx,* [A] —on the one hand, we are told that if we live or walk in the flesh, or if we're **in** the flesh, it will be **death.** On the other hand, we are told that **God was manifest in the flesh,** and Jesus Christ came among us—**in**—**the flesh.** Well, at once you can see that we have **different concepts** using the **same identical word.**

Here are the seven shades of meaning and this morning we are interested, primarily, in meaning number **seven:**

First of all, the flesh is **merely** the soft part of the body that covers the bone. Often it will be used that way. The **flesh** is the **soft** part of your **body.** We'll see how that **probably** became a symbol then to the **weakness** of human nature.

Then secondly, the flesh is also the **entire human body,** viewed as a substance. Your body, your entire body is called flesh. In that sense, Jesus Christ was born in the **flesh.** He was **man**—a very man. **He was a human being** with a body just like ours.

The Bible also uses the word "flesh" to mean every single human being, the entire human race. When the Bible says, *"all flesh is grass,"* [7] it means every human being—all human people.

Fourth, it's what we mean when we say **human nature.** Flesh is being a human person. A **human being** is just called flesh.

Number five; it is man with his physical limitation. When you call man flesh, Jesus said for example, *"the Spirit is willing but the flesh is weak,"* [8] He was talking about His sleepy disciples who couldn't stay awake because they were physical beings.

Number six, it often is used for the **external** or the **visible part** of human life, and that leads to the expression, "judging after the flesh." You judge according to what you **see externally. Now God does not judge according to the flesh. He judges according to the heart.** You can see, by the way, that that can be deceptive. Because a person's **external**

being, that which covers them, might be **deceptive.** It is soft. The flesh is soft, and the external part could be **deceptive.** Now that leads you then only a step away to **symbolically describing human nature** and its characteristics as being quote, "in the flesh."

And the seventh meaning, and the one that we're concerned about in Romans chapters 6, 7 and 8, "in the flesh," *is man—in—sin.* **Man in his unregenerate—sinful state—is—flesh**—or to create this little formula: **MAN + SIN = FLESH**

Now, can you see how that the Bible might use the same word, because that which is soft, the soft part of us, is the **weak part?** It easily decays. It easily falls away as it were and so when you're talking about human nature as being weak—innervated—not able to perform, then you're talking about **man as flesh.** And because man can be **deceptive** in his external covering, it's only a **step away** to talking about an **ethical evil.**

So, when we talk about the <u>flesh</u>, we are <u>not</u> talking in the sense of number seven—an ethical term—a moral term. We are not talking about a <u>metaphysical component</u>. You are <u>not</u> talking about a <u>thing</u> that you could find, say with a surgeon's knife or an x-ray machine. You could <u>not find</u> flesh and Spirit. They are <u>not</u> metaphysical terms. They are not <u>things</u>. Rather they are <u>powers</u>. Or to put it in another way— the <u>flesh</u> is talking about <u>man</u>—<u>all</u> of man—<u>all</u> of your personality— <u>living</u> a certain kind of <u>way</u>. And that way would be according to the old creation, we say. <u>Man</u> separated from <u>God</u>—human creation in its <u>emptiness</u>. <u>Man</u> left to himself—is—<u>flesh</u>! Now, he goes on having a life—he subsists—he has an existence, but the Bible calls it <u>flesh</u>. Meaning—man—in—sin.

When we talk about flesh or Spirit, we're talking about **two life levels—two <u>ways</u> in which you can <u>live</u>.** You can be living in the flesh— all of you, or you can be living in the Spirit—**all of you. It's a life level.** Or technically we call it a *modus vivendi.* [B] That means a **mode of life, a— way—of—living**. We're talking about an **attitude.** We're talking about a **lifestyle.** We're talking about the thing that **dominates you,** whether you are in the flesh or you are in the Spirit.

In a very **practical way** and in everyday terms, the flesh shows up in what we call one's "dispositional complex." Now everybody has a **disposition.** Your **disposition** is the **bent** of your personality. The way you **live**—it's your **attitude—your disposition.** Now we call it a dispositional **complex,** because it's complex—it has many factors. And basically, we break it down into one's mind—the way you think— your attitudes—your beliefs. And it's possible to have a **mind** that is egotistical—a mind that is **based**—a mind that is **corrupt**—that's a mind after the **flesh.** You also can have your **emotional life**—your sentiments, that can be **hostile and alienated from God—and perverted emotion.** That's a part of the dispositional complex. That's the way the flesh **shows up** in your everyday life. It also can show up in your **will,** by having a **rebellious—and an ineffectual—captive will.** The flesh shows up that way.

We're not talking about anything mysterious. When we say you're in the flesh, we're talking about the kind of person you are. We're talking about the life level that flows out of you. We're talking about what we feel when we meet you. Do we meet a mind that's corrupt and dark and egotistical? Do we meet emotions that are alienated and hostile and angry? Do we meet wills that are rebellious and captive? Or do we meet a dispositional complex that is "Christ-like," that is **like** the Lord Jesus Christ? That's what we mean by walking in the flesh or in the Spirit.

I would like to say, by the way, it's a very important thing to **know** that just because you are **religious** does not mean that you are out of the **flesh.** One of the **worst manifestations** of the flesh is—**"religious flesh."**

Religious flesh shows itself up primarily in **self-righteousness,** and **self-righteousness** is born out of your own need to establish **your worth and gives you a feeling of being <u>better</u> than someone else. And Christians have a very subtle way of <u>refining</u> their sin. They think that their sins are a little more <u>refined</u> than everybody else's; therefore, they're a little bit <u>better</u> than everybody else. I've got news for you—in and of yourself, your historical self, you <u>never</u> get any better. You increasingly get worse. There is <u>never</u> any ground for self-righteousness and the accompanying criticism and <u>haughtiness</u> that is born out of that with reference to other people. That's the self-righteous spirit.**

It also shows up in Christian circles in what we call **legalism.** Now we've developed that on other occasions, but I just have you bear that in mind. Man in his religion may be farthest from God, because he put a religious cloak over his **flesh,** and that's the worst kind. That's the one that Jesus could not penetrate. Jesus met all these **very** religious people who were living self-righteous **lives,** and they said, *"We see,"* therefore, Jesus said, *"Your sin remains,"* [9] because you're still caught up in **religious flesh.**

So, we're talking about a **dispositional complex** that is **very, very, practical.** We're not talking about something in some other metaphysical world. We're not talking about two different components within your personality. We're talking about—**how—you—live,** and I tell you that shows up. Whether a person is either living in **their self-life** or whether they're living **in** the Spirit—and that's our only hope, I might add.

It's very important that we understand the close connection between **flesh** and the **human body.** I'd like to go over that with you this morning. And you'll notice, in a mechanical way with me, what the Apostle teaches us about our **body.** There are ten statements made about the body in Romans 6, 7 and 8, and from that we're going to draw three major practical truths about the human body and the flesh. I'm only going to read the scriptures for you.

Ten Statements about the body in Romans 6, 7 and 8:

1. Chapter 6, verse 6, *"The old self"*—that's your flesh—the old way of life—the old *modus vivendi*—**"that was crucified"**—**"that the sinful body might be destroyed."** [10] The word destroyed means, rendered ineffectual, **not put into operation, not being used,** set aside.

2. Chapter 6, verse 12, **"Let not sin reign in your mortal bodies, to make you obey their passions,"** [11] —the passions of your bodies.

3. Chapter 6, verse 13, **"Yield your members"**—implied of your body—yield the members of your body—*"to God as instruments of righteousness."* [12]

4. Chapter 6, verse 19, *"As you once yielded your members"*—the members of your body—*"to impurity and* **greater and greater iniquity,** *so* **now** *yield your members to* **righteousness** *for sanctification."* [13]

5. Chapter 7, verse 23, **"The law of sin dwells in the members,"** [14] —**of my body.**

6. Chapter 7, verse 24, **"Who shall deliver me from this body of death?"** [15]

7. Chapter 8, verse 10, **"Christ is in you even though your bodies are dead because of sin."** [16]

8. Chapter 8, verse 11, **"He who raised Christ will give life to your mortal body."** [17]

9. Chapter 8, verse 13, **"If by the Spirit you put to death"**—render inoperative—*"the deeds of the body you will* **live.***"* [18]

10. Chapter 8, verse 23, *"We **groan** inwardly as we await the redemption,"* [19] —that is the resurrection of our bodies.

Now that list of scriptures will bear out the following <u>three major truths</u>. The most significant thing said about our bodies is this:

<u>Number one, it is **"mortal,"**</u> and the word mortal means **dead.** Your bodies—are—**dead.** Chapter 6, verse 12 and chapter 8, verse 10. They're ready for the mortician. *"Even though Christ is in you, your bodies—are—dead."* [16] Now it's <u>**very**</u> important for us to see that **redemption** is not reaching us basically at the physical level, during "TPT"—during—"This Present Time." You must live out your life in an **unredeemed—mortal—body.** Now fortunately, the Spirit that dwells in us <u>**will**</u> **redeem our bodies.** Our bodies are going to be redeemed, but in this age they are **not.**

And so, we have this formula—**your bodies—are—unredeemed—but redeemable.** God has designs on these bodies. As a matter of fact, those who study scripture carefully, you will see **that the Bible does not teach the immortality of the soul. That is <u>not</u> Christian doctrine.** That is pagan teaching. **The Bible teaches the <u>resurrection of the body</u>. That's an altogether different <u>concept</u>. These bodies are basically ethically neutral. Some people thought that "matter," this physical stuff, in and of itself was <u>sinful</u>. It is <u>not,</u>** in and of itself. But the bodies are—**dead.** They are mortal.

<u>Secondly, number two</u>, and I want you to listen carefully now at this point. It's a very, very sensitive point I'm about to make. <u>Our bodies are, quote, "sinful" unquote.</u> We have to identify sin with our bodies, because of its connection with the **flesh.** The Apostle says, *"the old self was crucified that the **sinful body** might be destroyed."* [10] He says, in 7:23, *"the law of sin dwells in the **members**"*—**of my <u>body</u>.** [14]

"But I see in my members another law at war with the law of my mind and making me captive to the law of sin which dwells in my members." - Romans 7:23 RSV

We have to conclude that our **bodies** are, quote, "sinful" unquote, when used in a **special sense. The body is not essentially sinful, but it is actually sinful. The body is not essentially sinful.** That is, the body is just made up of dirt. How many chemicals in the body? 93 or whatever? This is just **stuff,** that's all. But I'm living my **life** out in this **stuff!** So, we must not think that **matter** or **creation** is in and of itself **sinful.** The flesh is an **ethical concept,** you see. It's not a metaphysical term. But **my body** in practice, in **real living,** actually **becomes sinful. And the reason being, is because it is unredeemed, and it is constantly being assaulted by this unredeemable power!**

Now my body has its **natural drive.** The Bible calls it here, its **passions**—its **lusts**—its **needs.** In other words, I need **food** and I become a **glutton.** And I need **sleep** and I become **lazy.** And we are incomplete and in our sexual drives we become lustful. And so, you have these various **drives** or **energies** that come up from **within you. And because the flesh, this ethical thing or sin within you, wants to seize these unregenerate drives then the body for all practical purposes winds up to be, quote, "sinful."** In other words, question: "If you are not in your body would sin have a control over you?" **No!** It's coming up through your **body** as it were. If you could just get out of your **body,** you'd be in pretty **good shape. You cannot separate, really, flesh and the body. The body is not essentially sinful, but it is—actually sinful. It's called a sinful body!** So, we've got this **body,** as it were. So, our bodies are mortal. Our bodies are **dead.** Our bodies are, quote, unquote, **"sinful."**

But thanks be unto God, point number three, and this is the **beautiful truth** of Romans chapters 6, 7 and 8, our bodies **can be yielded** to God, and become members of the Lord Jesus Christ, and temples of the Holy Spirit. It is **possible** for the members of our body to be **controlled** by the **power** of the Holy Spirit. But if that's going to **happen,** you have **got to get—out of the flesh.** Your only possible solution, to do that, **is—to—walk—in—the Spirit.** But you see, if you are for a split-second in the flesh, that is dominated by this power, by this ethical force of sin, **instantly** the members of your body will be **used** as captive for the expression of sin. Your dispositional complex will be dominated **by the flesh.** And all of a sudden, **something will happen to your mind. Your feelings will go berserk and your "will" will go ineffective and will become rebellious,** and all of a sudden, we are at a very low level of defeat.

The <u>only</u> possible solution is for me to be, quote, "in the Spirit"— that is to—walk—in the Spirit. Now, what happens? If I am **walking in the Spirit,** now I have <u>neutralized</u> this neutral body, and <u>then I can consecrate it to God</u>. I can <u>yield</u> the members of my body to God to be used from Him, if they are <u>not dominated</u> by the power of the flesh. **My only solution then is to be in the Spirit. So, the culprit is not your** <u>body</u>. The culprit is the <u>flesh</u>, that ethical evil, that <u>dominating force</u> of sin that wants to <u>seize</u> the members of your body and <u>always will</u>. That's why you cannot consecrate your <u>body</u> through the power of the flesh.

See a lot of people come and want to **yield their bodies.** So, they come down and pound on the altar and so on, and what they're trying to do is get their **flesh consecrated. You cannot consecrate your** <u>flesh</u>! It's <u>unredeemable</u>! It is hostile to God! It <u>cannot</u> submit to God's law! There is a <u>thing in you</u>—there is a <u>power in you</u>—that you absolutely **cannot control.** It's greater than you are. Now, if we believe in self salvation, we wouldn't have wanted a Savior a long time ago. Why did Jesus come into the world? Why does the Holy Spirit have to dwell in us?

Because we've got to have outside help. My body will go on just being a captive slave to the **drive** of my flesh, unless somehow by the **power of the Holy Spirit,** I can put to death the deeds of my body. That's the only way I can do it.

Now, maybe you've found a **better** solution. Maybe you can run around the track and take cold showers and everything else, I don't know. But I think it's done by the **power of the Spirit.** By the power of the Spirit. And thereby, you can put to death the deeds of the body, and now **that** body can be—**yielded**—to God. I remind you however, *"You yield yourselves <u>as men</u>—who—have—been—brought back—from the dead."* [12]

You only yield from the cross on. You've got to understand what consecration is. If you're trying to yield anything this side in the old creation to God, forget about it. God doesn't want anything to do with it. All He wants to do is to **crucify it.** He wants to put it to **death!** He only wants that which is in the power of the new creation which we call, "in the Spirit." That's what God wants consecrated to Him. You've got to first of all come to a cross as it were, and everything in this **old creation** in this doctrine of emptiness is over.

I think it is very important for us to summarize this in a practical way, so we can see what we **can** and **cannot** expect. Now this is a very popular way to do it, and I would like to seize on that popular division. I think there are **three connections** that **we have** variously with **sin** or with the **flesh.** This is called the "Penalty," and the "Power," and the "Presence" of sin. The three P's. Would you remember **them?**

First of all, what do we have in this present age as we live our lives out, quote, "in the flesh" in this bodily existence? Number one, we are freed absolutely and completely from the **"Penalty" of sin.** I am living my life out in this body under the pressure of the flesh and sin—**but**—I am not—I am <u>not</u>—under the penalty of sin. *"There is therefore **now** **no** condemnation"* [20] —no condemnation. The word condemnation means, "a judgment against." **Grace means that God by a free decision is <u>for</u> <u>me</u> and not against me.** That's what grace is. **Grace is God's free choice to be <u>for</u> <u>me</u>,** and not against me. He is so **for me** that He **elects me.** I am **elect in Jesus Christ. I'm God's pet.** I'm His favorite. God likes me. God loves me! He loves me with **maximum love**—and that constantly. **Nothing can separate me from maximum <u>love</u>!** This is the great blessing of being **in grace.**

Oh, that we might see that important doctrine. **Because if there can come guilt and condemnation, just a tiny bit into your life, then you see you're thrown back upon yourself and you're caught up in this self-effort again, trying to establish your own worth.** Folks, you've got to die. Everything—all of you. **Don't try to refine your sins. <u>You can't</u> <u>do it</u>! You just break the law that much and you're under the whole condemnation of the law. So, if you're trusting the law, <u>you don't have</u> <u>any hope</u>! You got to trust another whole <u>system</u>, and the Bible calls it grace.**

There <u>is</u> no penalty for sin. <u>Where are my sins</u>? They were <u>visited</u> upon the <u>cross</u> of the Lord Jesus Christ and again I ask you this question, "<u>Was the death of Jesus sufficient for every sin that I ever have or ever will commit</u>?" Was <u>that</u> a <u>sufficient</u> sacrifice? Thank God, <u>it was</u>!

The death of Jesus has reconciled God. **The big question I tell you is <u>not sins</u>.** I want to repeat that. The sin question is over. So, if you're relating to yourself or anybody else on the basis of <u>right</u> or <u>wrong</u>, you haven't moved into the <u>new covenant</u> yet. That's not the <u>basis</u> anymore! It's not <u>law</u> anymore! We're only talking about our **faith** in the Lord Jesus Christ. **That's the big issue**—is our relationship to Him. Thank God that that holy one has become the lowly one. The accusing finger has become the helping hand. So, God's grace is **all** that He is free to do for me in Jesus Christ. His justice **is** satisfied. God is at rest. He has been propitiated. He is reconciled to me—**in—my—sins.**

Do you believe **that** doctrine? I trust the Holy Spirit will teach that to you. You see, the reason is, is we've got to get people from focusing on themselves. Anytime you're caught up in yourself, you're under the flesh. You're under the law. **So, if you're worried about yourself in any way, you've got to totally turn from yourself, or you never go into the Spirit.** So, we've **got** to have a doctrine that totally frees you from your self-life, or we'll **always** be then, ineffective.

Then we talk about the **"Power" of sin.** Now the power of sin **is** the way that the flesh would like to **dominate** me during this age. And as we'll see tonight, you can be **in** the Spirit, but not walking in the Spirit. In other words, it's possible to be a Christian and be **carnal.** It's possible to be living in the power of your **flesh,** and that your dispositional complex is **motivated by flesh,** and not by Jesus Christ.

The **big thing** is we want to be free from this **power—this force— this thing**—that wants to control our lives. This of course leads us to where we are **right now** is walking in the Spirit and you **do not— fulfill—the lust—of the—flesh**—if we walk in the Spirit by the power of the indwelling Christ. We want to live in victory.

Now, I want to caution you; however, we are **not free** from the **"Presence" of sin.** You have an unredeemed body, and that unredeemed body is a close ally with an **unredeemable evil,** called flesh. You are living in a world that is unredeemed, called **the world.** That's again an ethical term—meaning a **spirit**—an **attitude**—a **way**—and that's going to constantly **impinge upon you and tempt you. Something within you will answer to the world. You'll wish that it didn't, but it will. And so, it is a mistake to imagine that you'll be free from the presence of sin.**

It will be there constantly to dog your steps. The flesh will want to **constantly** dominate you.

And so, our **only hope** during this age is to **"walk—in—the Spirit."** I **begin** by saying that there is nothing within me—**nothing** within this old creation that I can bring to God, and I start using the language of wretchedness—one of the first requisites for "walking in the Spirit." **In me** dwells no good thing. I do not trust myself anymore. I have to **totally trust Jesus Christ** and the power of the indwelling Spirit. And **then** it's possible for those new creation powers to come in and let me start living a life that is **really real,** called **"love."** It is **then** that the righteousness of the law and it's just claims can start being fulfilled **in me. But oh,** how I want the Lord Jesus Christ to put me **"in** the Spirit." I don't trust myself. I have **bodily appetites,** and I have a **perverted drive in my mind,** my **emotions and will, that would utterly destroy me.** Now I can cloak it over and I can whitewash it, but inside are dead men's bones.

Thank God, there's a thing called the resurrection! *(Congregation saying amen)* **Jesus Christ came up out of this old creation. He's living at the right hand of the Father, and He has imparted that Spirit back to us and making it possible for us to live in the Spirit**—in the **power** of the new creation. **Thank God! Right in my mortal body. Jesus Christ can live—in—my—mortal body! My body** can become a temple of the Holy Spirit, and I can give it to God, and it can become instruments of **righteousness** for sanctification—for holiness and for wholeness.

Well, that's what I want. That's what I want. How many join me? "Pastor, I want to **walk in the Spirit.** That's where I want to be. *(Don rejoices)* I want that **life of Jesus Christ** to come into me and making me all that I ought to be. **Free me from myself!**" **Is that your cry? Free me from myself!** *"O wretched man that I am! Who shall deliver me from this body of death? I thank God through Jesus Christ, our Lord!"* [21]

I would like to add, by the way, this is baffling to some Christians. They say, "Why is it, that I receive Jesus and all of a sudden I'm under the old DC—the old Dispositional Complex?" You can go from the flesh to the Spirit within a split-second. You can be spiritual here one minute and step out that door and be in the flesh. See, those **powers** are wanting to constantly control you. That's what we want to do is be under the **dominance** of the Lord Jesus Christ and His Lordship.

"But grow in the grace and knowledge of our Lord and Savior Jesus Christ. To him be the glory both now and to the day of eternity. Amen." - 2 Peter 3:18 RSV

For those of you who may **not** have been here last Lord's Day evening, we talked about **Knowledge and the Doctrine of Emptiness.** And I want to tell you something as **faithfully** as I can as your pastor/ teacher. **You must <u>constantly</u>—<u>intake</u>—<u>the Word</u>. You <u>cannot</u>— walk—in the Spirit—without—<u>knowledge</u>. "You grow in grace <u>and</u>—<u>knowledge</u>."** [22] **"Grace—and <u>truth</u> comes through the Lord Jesus Christ."** [23]

It is <u>impossible</u> in my opinion to <u>walk in the Spirit</u> without a <u>constant</u> <u>intake</u> of Bible doctrine and the truth. That's why I <u>urge</u> you to <u>hear</u> these sermons. Not because I want to have you in this building. You <u>must</u> partake of that <u>manna</u> <u>regularly</u>. None of you can do it without the spirit of your minds being <u>renewed</u>. That's why you—<u>must</u>—<u>hear</u>—<u>this</u>—<u>truth</u>! It comes by knowledge and not by great mystical experiences. It comes by an intake of truth. When your mind is renewed and that <u>knowledge</u> comes in, it's <u>then</u> that you start to walk in the Spirit. There is a direct connection between <u>knowledge</u> and <u>walking in the Spirit</u>!

SERMON 17 ENDNOTES:

A *sarx*, means: the flesh, Strong's Greek Dictionary #4561

B *modus vivendi*, means: an arrangement or agreement allowing conflicting parties to coexist peacefully, either indefinitely or until a final settlement is reached or a way of living. Latin online definition from Oxford Languages.

SERMON 17 SCRIPTURE REFERENCES:

[1] Romans 5:17 (RSV)

If, because of one man's trespass, death reigned through that one man, much more will those who receive the abundance of grace and the free gift of righteousness reign in life through the one man Jesus Christ.

[2] Romans 6:14 (RSV)

For sin will have no dominion over you, since you are not under law but under grace.

[3] Romans 8:18 (RSV)

I consider that the sufferings of this present time are not worth comparing with the glory that is to be revealed to us.

[4] Romans 8:20 (RSV)

for the creation was subjected to futility, not of its own will but by the will of him who subjected it in hope;

[5] Romans 8:1-8 (RSV)

1 There is therefore now no condemnation for those who are in Christ Jesus. 2 For the law of the Spirit of life in Christ Jesus has set me free from the law of sin and death. 3 For God has done what the law, weakened by the flesh, could not do: sending his own Son in the likeness of sinful flesh and for sin, he condemned sin in the flesh, 4 in order that the just requirement of the law might be fulfilled in us, who walk not according to the flesh but according to the Spirit. 5 For those who live according to the flesh set their minds on the things of the flesh, but those who live according to the Spirit set their minds on the things of the Spirit. 6 To set the mind on the flesh is death, but to set the mind on the Spirit is life and peace. 7 For the mind that is set on the flesh is hostile to God; it does not submit to God's law, indeed it cannot; 8 and those who are in the flesh cannot please God.

[6] Romans 8:9-13 (RSV)

9 But you are not in the flesh, you are in the Spirit, if in fact the Spirit of God dwells in you. Any one who does not have the Spirit of Christ does not belong to him. 10 But if Christ is in you, although your bodies are dead because of sin, your spirits are alive because of righteousness. 11 If the Spirit of him who raised Jesus from the dead dwells in you, he who raised Christ Jesus from the dead will give life to your mortal bodies also through his Spirit which dwells in you. 12 So then, brethren, we are debtors, not to the flesh, to live according to the flesh— 13 for if you live according to the flesh you will die, but if by the Spirit you put to death the deeds of the body you will live.

[7] 1 Peter 1:24 (RSV)

for "All flesh is like grass and all its glory like the flower of grass. The grass withers, and the flower falls,

[8] Matthew 26:41 (RSV)

Watch and pray that you may not enter into temptation; the spirit indeed is willing, but the flesh is weak."

[9] John 9:41 (KJV)

Jesus said unto them, If ye were blind, ye should have no sin: but now ye say, We see; therefore your sin remaineth.

[10] Romans 6:6 (RSV)

We know that our old self was crucified with him so that the sinful body might be destroyed, and we might no longer be enslaved to sin.

[11] Romans 6:12 (RSV)

Let not sin therefore reign in your mortal bodies, to make you obey their passions.

[12] Romans 6:13 (RSV)

Do not yield your members to sin as instruments of wickedness, but yield yourselves to God as men who have been brought from death to life, and your members to God as instruments of righteousness.

[13] Romans 6:19 (RSV)

I am speaking in human terms, because of your natural limitations. For just as you once yielded your members to impurity and to greater and greater iniquity, so now yield your members to righteousness for sanctification.

[14] Romans 7:23 (RSV)

but I see in my members another law at war with the law of my mind and making me captive to the law of sin which dwells in my members.

[15] Romans 7:24 (RSV)

Wretched man that I am! Who will deliver me from this body of death?

[16] Romans 8:10 (RSV)

But if Christ is in you, although your bodies are dead because of sin, your spirits are alive because of righteousness.

[17] Romans 8:11 (RSV)

If the Spirit of him who raised Jesus from the dead dwells in you, he who raised Christ Jesus from the dead will give life to your mortal bodies also through his Spirit which dwells in you.

[18] Romans 8:13 (RSV)

for if you live according to the flesh you will die, but if by the Spirit you put to death the deeds of the body you will live.

[19] Romans 8:23 (RSV)

and not only the creation, but we ourselves, who have the first fruits of the Spirit, groan inwardly as we wait for adoption as sons, the redemption of our bodies.

[20] Romans 8:1 (RSV)

There is therefore now no condemnation for those who are in Christ Jesus.

[21] Romans 7:24-25 (RSV)

24 Wretched man that I am! Who will deliver me from this body of death? 25 Thanks be to God through Jesus Christ our Lord! So then, I of myself serve the law of God with my mind, but with my flesh I serve the law of sin.

[22] 2 Peter 3:18 (RSV)

But grow in the grace and knowledge of our Lord and Savior Jesus Christ. To him be the glory both now and to the day of eternity. Amen.

[23] John 1:14,17 (RSV)

14 And the Word became flesh and dwelt among us, full of grace and truth; we have beheld his glory, glory as of the only Son from the Father. . . 17 For the law was given through Moses; grace and truth came through Jesus Christ.

SERMON 18

WALKING IN THE SPIRIT

"You are not perfected ever by the flesh. It starts "in the Spirit" and it will end "in the Spirit!"

Tonight, we're going to talk about what it means to walk in the Spirit. Now we have come a **long** way, by way of introduction, to this particular sermon and I wish that all of you could have heard all these sermons that have been leading up to this particular one, because they are all **introductory** as to what it means to be walking in the Spirit.

We mentioned this morning, in a negative way, what the **flesh is** and its relationship to the **body.** And you'll remember we pointed out that in the Bible the words **flesh, and spirit** are **not** talking about **things.** That is, a metaphysical component. Something you could **see.** You couldn't find the flesh or the spirit with an x-ray machine, we said, or with a surgeon's knife. That's not what we're talking about.

The words flesh and spirit are **not metaphysical terms.** They are **moral terms. Or,** we said they're talking about **a kind of life—a life level**—the way you **live** in other words. That's whether you are in the flesh **or** in the spirit. A technical term for that would be one's *modus vivendi* and a *modus vivendi* means your **mode** or your **manner of living**—how you **live.** So, the flesh and the spirit are referring to your **"life level."** Now the word **"walk"**—to **"walk"** <u>in</u> the Spirit means how you **"go about"**— **"your gait."** You see. **Where** you're walking. **How you're living. Your**

lifestyle. So, you **walk,** talking, you're going about, your conversation or your manner of life. So, walking in the Spirit is referring to that.

There's a very close connection of course between walking in the Spirit and being in Christ. They are one and the selfsame thing. See, if you walk in the Spirit <u>like</u> **Jesus,** if you are <u>like</u> **Christ,** if you have a **Christ like life,** then that's being in the Spirit. So, to be <u>in</u> **Christ** is essentially the same thing as—walking—in—the Spirit. That means that Jesus is our **model.** So, if you walk **according <u>to</u> the Spirit** that means you **model** your life after the Spirit. Or Jesus is your **model.** You're walking "according to"—like—that—would—be, you see. And so, it's an important thing to see that we are **modeling** our lives **after** the Spirit.

Now the **source** of that life, the Spirit, is coming from the new creation. **It is—not—in—this—world.** It's not **in** this creation. It's not in the first creation. So, you can't **model** or **walk after this life, which is called the world and the flesh.** The flesh is that with this subjective in us. The world is that which is round about us and impinging upon us. So, if you're going to walk in the Spirit, you're really walking in the power of the Holy Spirit which is coming from the new creation. We are participating then in the **powers of the new creation.**

I want to summarize that one more time. To walk in the Spirit is talking about **a mode of living. A life level.** And Ephesians chapter 5, verse 9 says, *"it is found in all that is good and right and true."* [1] If you're walking in the Spirit, it is **found** in all that is **good** and **right** and **true, or** it is having a **Christ like Spirit.**

 *"But you are not in the flesh, you are in the Spirit, if in fact the Spirit of God dwells in you. Any one who does not have the Spirit of Christ does not belong to him."*
- Romans 8:9 RSV

The Bible makes that very clear, that *"If anyone does not have the Spirit of Christ, he's none of his."* [2] So, you are walking in the Spirit, when you have a **Christ like Spirit.** But you're walking in the flesh, when you have **your** spirit. When **you** show up, that's the flesh. When **Jesus shows up** in His life, that's the life in the Spirit.

Secondly, it is the same as being "in Christ." That's your position. Our positional life is—**in**—**Christ. Then** the source is a participation **in** the new creation, or it's the **life in the Holy Spirit.** So, all those things, you see, are essentially the same thing as what it means to walk in the Spirit.

Now it's important for us to distinguish between three things that Paul talks about in Romans chapter 8, and I'd like to begin reading tonight with verse 5, and we'll go through verse 9. Romans chapter 8, verses 5 through 9, and I want you to notice the three different terminologies that Paul uses with reference to our **life in the Spirit.** You'll see that we have three different relationships **with** the Spirit. *"Those who **live** according to the flesh set their **minds** on the things of the flesh, but those who live according to the **Spirit** set their **minds** on the things of the **Spirit.** Now to set the mind on the flesh—is death,"*—it's lethal—it's deadly—it's confusion—it's guilt—it's bondage—it's all kinds of things that only can be summarized by a word **"death."** Life is not worthwhile in other words. *"To set the mind on the flesh is **death,** but to **set the mind on the Spirit**—is life—and—peace. For the mind that is set on the flesh is **hostile** to God, it does **not submit** to God's law, indeed it **cannot,** and those who are in the flesh can**not**—please—God! But, you are not in the flesh, but in the Spirit if the Spirit of God really dwells in you. Any one who does **not** have the Spirit of Christ **does not—belong—to him."* [3]

There are three different phrases that are used with reference to our life in the Spirit, and you need to **distinguish** them. We need to see that being "in the Spirit" is not the selfsame thing as "walking in the

Spirit." Now the most **basic** relationship that we can have with the Spirit and the new creation is to be **in it.** Paul talks about being **"in the Spirit"** or, **"living in the Spirit."** Those are essentially the selfsame things and that is the basic position of all Christians, regardless of their moral condition. In other words, you cannot be a Christian, if you are not "in the Spirit." To be in the Spirit means to be a Christian. That does not mean that you are walking in the Spirit. In other words, "in the Spirit" is the sphere. Nowhere does Paul ever say that a Christian is in the flesh. Now, he says they may have a mind after the flesh, and they may be walking according to the flesh. But if you have received Jesus Christ as your Savior, you are "in the Spirit." That is yours by grace. You have positionally been placed in the new creation. If any man be in Christ, he's a part of the new creation, or he is "in the Spirit."

Now Paul makes that very clear in Romans 8:9, *"You are not in the flesh, but you are in the Spirit if the Spirit of God dwells in you."*—In other words, if you're Christian. *"Anyone who does not have the Spirit of Christ is none of his."* [2] So the line is drawn up between a person who is in the flesh and **in** the Spirit. There **is no** Christian who is in the flesh. Every Christian **regardless** of their moral condition is **"in the Spirit." Every Christian regardless of their moral condition is "in the Spirit."** That's your standing before God by way of imputation. The Holy Spirit **puts you there.** So that's our basic position, as it were, **in** the Lord Jesus Christ. In other words, it's the same thing as being "in Christ." And that's this beautiful thing, *"we received the spirit of adoption that puts us in the Spirit."* [4] So that is true of **every single believer. There are** no believers in Jesus Christ who are **not** "in the Spirit."

Now, however, you will notice that the Apostle goes to a second step though, and he says that we are to—set—our—mind—on the Spirit. If you are in the Spirit, Paul says, *"You are to set your mind on the Spirit."* [5] I'd like to call that an SOS mind. A mind SOS: Set—

On—the Spirit. Now we're talking about your inner attitude. There are some people who are Christians, but their <u>mind</u> is not set <u>after</u> the Spirit. <u>All</u> the way through the epistles and all the way through Romans, Paul is encouraging us to set our <u>mind</u> on the Spirit. That is to *"set our <u>affections</u> on the things which are above."* [6] We are to have <u>minds</u> that go <u>after</u> the Spirit.

This is the dividing line between what we call spiritual and carnal Christians. Are there such things? Oh, absolutely! There are many people who are not walking worthy of their calling. Now everybody here, if you are "in Christ" you're a son of God. You're a son. You may not be walking worthy of that sonship. And if you <u>are</u> a son you want to be <u>led</u> by the Spirit. There are some people who are sons, but they are not being <u>led</u> by the Spirit because they do not have a mentality or an <u>outlook</u> <u>after</u> the things of the Spirit. <u>This is the turning point then</u> <u>between "walking in the Spirit."</u> If you are "in" the Spirit that is your position—**and if your mind is set "after" the Spirit, <u>now</u>** you have the possibility of **"walking in the Spirit."**

The word "walk" basically means that you are showing up. That is the **outworking** of your **life in the Spirit.** We ought to be able to see it. If anybody is in the Spirit, we ought to **know that.** "Walking <u>in</u> the Spirit" shows that you **are** in the Spirit. Do you see what I'm trying to say? So, the **walk** would be the **physical outworking or the manifestation.**

"If we live by the Spirit, let us also walk by the Spirit."
- *Galatians 5:25 RSV*

This is why Paul makes statements like this. It is rather strange until you see the difference. Galatians 5:25, *"If we live by the Spirit, let us **walk** by the Spirit."* [7] He means if your <u>**life**</u> is **in the Spirit** <u>**then let it**</u>

show up! **Walk according to the Spirit. Let people know it.** Let it come out in our lives in a very direct and obvious visible manner. And so, we need to make a distinction between being in the Spirit and walking in the Spirit. And the **great exhortation** laid upon Christians is that their "**life** in the Spirit" will become a "**walk** in the Spirit." It will show up in their everyday life.

Now, can you see that this first great point is still a work of grace? You didn't **merit** or **earn** being in the Spirit. Jesus Christ **put** you there. By your faith in Jesus, you go into the new creation. **But now you have all these exhortations: "Set your mind on the Spirit." "Walk in the Spirit." "Set your affections on things above."** In other words, **now** begins this marvelous "**walk—in the Spirit.**" And here's a life. People can see it the way you walk. It shows up. By the way, I think you ought to be able to see it. I think it ought to show up on your face. I think **some way people ought to <u>know</u>** that you're in Christ, and that you're drawing **your life** from Him.

You ought to have a **different life level** that is **very discernible.** Can you tell whether a person has love or hate? **Of course you can!** Can you tell whether somebody is unforgiving or releases you through the Spirit? **Of course you can!** There's a **tremendous** difference. It makes **all** the difference in the world. And so, here's the exhortation now: <u>**Walk— in the Spirit. Let your lives be visible. Let your concourse through life be one that manifests the life of Jesus. Let that life of Jesus show up in your mortal body.**</u> That's what the Apostle is trying to tell us, by walking in the Spirit.

There are a number of benefits that come from this and there are **three very clear requisites.** I'm not sure whether we're going to get all this through tonight or not, but I want to talk at least about the **two major benefits** that come from walking in the Spirit. Let's start there and see how far we can go.

According to Romans the 8th chapter, there are two things that happen if you walk in the Spirit. The **first** is defined in verse 4. Romans chapter 8, verse 4. I'd like to go back to verse 3, *"God has done what the **law**, weakened by the flesh, could **not** do: sending his own Son in the likeness of sinful flesh and for sin, he condemned sin in the flesh,"*—What for?—*"in order that the **just requirement of the law might be <u>fulfilled in us,</u>** who **walk** not according to the flesh but according to the Spirit."* [8]

Now the first consequence. The first major benefit that comes from walking in the Spirit is this: <u>The just requirements of the law are satisfied.</u> <u>The just requirements of the law are **fulfilled,** for those of us who walk in the Spirit and not in the flesh.</u>

Now, we need to be very careful at this point, and I want you to listen with both ears at this. You see, we come into a marvelous freedom when we walk in the Spirit. **You're not under the law. There is no claim upon you, in other words. You are free from all pressures.** Now, a lot of you didn't know that did you? Because anytime you use the word law, you're talking about pressure. Have you ever put pressure on somebody? You've tried to use the law. That's all. **Anytime you use pressure you're using the law!**

Alright, so we have this marvelous freedom. Now, does that mean that being in grace makes us an outlaw? **On the <u>contrary</u>! The reason we're <u>not</u> under law and under grace, is that sin is not to have dominion over us—is that the just requirement of the law might be fulfilled in us. Now, having said that, we are not thereby, putting anybody back under the law. That is <u>not</u> Paul's way of reintroducing the system of the law again. That's not what he's after, whatever; because I want you to remember this: <u>The law always looks beyond itself to be fulfilled in something else. What was the law after? What fulfills the law? The law pointed toward the righteousness of faith! The law is being fulfilled in the righteousness of faith!</u>**

This is why Romans chapter 3, verse 21 and 22 explains, *"But now the righteousness of God has been manifested apart from the law, although the law and the prophets bear witness to it."* They __point__ to it! The law __pointed__ away from itself to __another righteousness__! __Always__, the law kept saying, "It's not here, it's __there__! Go after it!" The law bears witness to that righteousness of faith. That is—*"the righteousness of God through faith in Jesus Christ for **all—who—believe**."* [9] So the just requirement of the law is that a person goes to the righteousness of __faith__. That's what the law wanted you to have—is the __righteousness__ that comes from __faith__! Not the righteousness of the __law__. __The righteousness of the law makes nothing perfect__. It always points away to another righteousness, and __that's__ the righteousness of __faith__.

Now, what is the righteousness of faith? The __rightness of faith__ is that a person has turned __wholly to God__ and loves Him with all their heart, soul and mind. That's what the law wanted you to do—is bring you to loving obedience so that God had every bit of you! That's what the law was trying to get at all along.

That's why Paul explains in Galatians chapter 5, verse 13, *"You were called to freedom, brethren; only don't use your freedom as an opportunity for the flesh, **but** **through love** be servants of one another."* Now, notice this statement—*"**The whole law is fulfilled**"*—this is the way the just requirement of the law is fulfilled—*"The whole law is fulfilled in **one** word, 'You shall __love__ your neighbor —as—your—self.'"* [10]

"For you were called to freedom, brethren; only do not use your freedom as an opportunity for the flesh, but through love be servants of one another." - Galatians 5:13 RSV

And so, **the just requirement of the law is to bring you into a life of absolute devotion and love for God and love for one another.** That's why we've made the motto of our church, "Serving one another in love," because that's the consequences of walking in the Spirit and **that's** what fulfills the **law.** Love of course, is a many splendored thing and if you'll look at the fruit of the Spirit, if you'll look at the fourteen characteristics of love, you'll see what fulfills the just requirement of the law. And that's exactly what happens when you walk in the Spirit.

All of a sudden, you're beginning to take on these characteristics which you **cannot have under the law.** I don't care how hard you **try. Authentic *agape* love is not resident within you. God is love, and He has to shed abroad that love in our hearts by the Holy Ghost. And if you're going to enter into authentic *agape* love which the law pointed out and wanted at, you're only going to find that through faith in the Lord Jesus Christ,** and that comes by— walking—in—the Spirit.

All through the Bible, it makes it very clear what grace is trying to do. A beautiful passage, a corollary one, is in Titus chapter 2, verse 11, *"The grace of God has appeared for the salvation of all men, **training us** to renounce irreligion and worldly passions, and to live sober, uprightly, and godly lives **in—this—world.**"* T.P.T.: In This Present Time. In **this** world— in the old first creation— *"awaiting our blessed hope, the appearing of the glory of our great God and Savior Jesus Christ, who gave himself to redeem us from **all** iniquity, and to purify for himself a people of His own who are zealous of good works."* [11]

And so, the grace of God <u>teaches</u> us to deny ungodliness and worldly lust. It <u>trains</u> us, in other words. So, <u>one reason</u> we want to walk in the Spirit, frankly, is we just want to be <u>good</u>! <u>That's all</u>! We'd like to be <u>good</u>! Not within ourselves because it's not there. It's not in the flesh. I will <u>constantly</u> be selfish. I will <u>constantly</u> be a manipulator unless the grace of God comes along and does something marvelously

and supernatural in my life and puts me in the Spirit. And it is <u>then</u> that the <u>just requirement</u> of the law starts being fulfilled in me.

Now can you see that, without reintroducing the whole legal system? A lot of people think you've got to resort to the preaching of the **law** and everything to get that done. It's the **grace** of God that does it, and <u>only</u> the grace of God. And again, I make this clear. **You—must— be totally—delivered—from—your—self.** And as long as you're **concentrating** on yourself, **thinking** about yourself, **worried** about yourself, hung up in **guilt** and anything else **then you're going to be in the flesh. Anything that starts with the self will wind up in the flesh and that will <u>always</u> be failure, and bondage, and defeat, and guilt, and condemnation. You—must—get—totally—delivered—from— your—self!** Because the self-life. . . well, you just read about the works of the flesh, and I know what we do to try to hide it over. But I tell you inside are all those hostile **feelings,** are all those miserable **thoughts** where you **sin in thought word and deed,** and there **is no** true deliverance until you're set free from yourself.

It's **then** that the Holy Spirit comes in, helps us **walk** in the Spirit, **and now,** all of a sudden, some **genuine love** can start coming out of our lives. You can start serving one another in love. But it's amazing how most people are so hung up in themselves. They're **worried** about themselves. They **think** about themselves. They've got their sensitive egos. And they're **this** and they're **that** and they go through all of life. **It's just nothing but <u>self</u>! And the whole thing begins to <u>stink</u>! <u>It gets wretched</u>!**

Isn't it **marvelous** when that grace of God starts **delivering** you and accepts you, you see, with all this wretched self that you are makes you accepted in the beloved, gives you imputed righteousness not a righteousness of your own? You never really have any of that. But the grace of God comes along and by the power of Jesus Christ helps you start **really** taking on a life of love. And you love in a way that's not **from** you. **You don't have it, but you do it.** That's why a lot of people are beginning to see that they can become spectators in life. They do things they never thought possible. Before, somebody would have hurt them, and like Barbara said, "They would have had this **grudge.** They would have been bitter. They would have been hurt. They would have gone home and cried for a few days and all that. But all of a sudden, you'd just start living a supernatural life. That's really beautiful. That's the life that's coming from the Lord Jesus Christ. That's the way you fulfill the **just** requirement of the law—that righteousness that the law pointed at, and that's the righteousness of faith and only faith in the Lord Jesus Christ. You **never** go from faith to works ever. **Ever!** Those principles **are totally opposite!** Again, I repeat, **you cannot mix flesh and Spirit—faith and works—law and grace—new creation and old creation. They are—totally—different—concepts altogether.** That's why it is from *"faith—unto—faith."* [12]

Now a lot of people often say, "You know, now the Lord saved me, and He helps me and now it's up to me." **That is sheer Galatian Christianity. It is false doctrine. Don't you believe it! You are not starting in the Spirit and perfected by the flesh—ever!** Here, you see, is a common doctrine: I've got to live this Christian life and Jesus helps me a little bit. **Yea, that's what people think!** *(Don sarcastically speaks)* You know He helps a little bit. Kind of pats you on the back every now and then and, you know, maybe, throws a little grace occasionally down your way, hoped you might bump into it, you know.

This is not your life! Life in the Spirit is a different life. It's not in this old creation. It's totally Jesus Christ! It's totally a life in the Spirit, and it starts by the new birth. It starts by that **new nature** that comes in and **awakens** you to that. And oh, it's **wonderful** when you see how that can work. So, this is not **straining** and **striving** and **struggling. I**

tell you, it's important to know that a life in the Spirit takes out all the tasks and all the demands and all the burdens and all the threats. Life is no longer a task! Life is no longer a burden! It's no longer a demand and a threat! Its freedom and you're at rest!

And that's why the second thing of "walking in the Spirit" in chapter 8, verse 6 that says, *"if you set your mind on the Spirit it is life—and—peace."* [13] How about making that an L.P. album? Life—and—Peace. One translation says it is *"life—and—soul—peace."* [14] It means you're glad you're alive! All of a sudden, life makes sense, and life is worthwhile. You're beginning to enter into life at the level it was meant to be. Life in the Spirit is life as it was meant to be, and the consequences are soul peace. Why? Because you quit trying. Your Spirit is not disquieted. You are absolutely at peace. Because you're not doing anything. Jesus did it all. And all of a sudden, you see, you don't have to do anything. **Well, what am I in a sweat about? Why have I been working all this time for?** I don't know. It's not doing you any good. It's filthy rags. That's all. And **all** of a sudden, comes this thing called peace. It's a kind of an inner quietness. It's a kind of trust. It's a knowledge that all—is—well.

Now if you have peace, are you upsetting everybody roundabout you? No! Now, all of a sudden, you're not out **demanding** and **pressuring** and **legislating**. All of a sudden **you** have peace, and you have a way of having peaceful relationship with other people. Does that make a difference to the way you live in your family? Isn't it **strange** how we hear all this theology on Sunday, and don't realize that this is about life? **This is the way life works. This is the way you were meant to live. And it's a very, very, beautiful thing,** when you begin to have **life—and—peace.**

Now I don't know whether you noticed it or not, but when we talk about fulfilling the **law,** the first thing that comes from walking in the Spirit, that's that just requirement of the law, which is a life of love, which makes us well pleasing to God. And so, we really have a beautiful triangle here.

To walk in the Spirit means, first of all, that you walk well pleasing to God. If you are in the flesh, you **cannot please God.** But if you're in the Spirit—here's this life now that trusts Him and Him **alone**—and that's all God wants, by the way, is our absolute trust and faith in Him. Again, I remind you, God is **not** concerned so much about right or wrong. That's not what He's **primarily** concerned about. He's concerned about whether **you love Him,** and whether you trust Him **completely. It's your faith in Jesus.** And again, I remind you the opposite of sin in the Bible is **never virtue.** The **opposite** of sin is **always faith.** And so, when you have faith in the Lord Jesus, that is when you're utterly trusting Him, and having this loving obedience, it's **then** that you walk well pleasing to God. **And that's what the law wanted all the time!** That's why the law was given—to tell you what God expected but the righteousness of faith lets you fulfill that.

Secondly, if you're having this life of love, walking in the Spirit, then you're of maximum benefit to everybody roundabout you, because you've broken with basic selfishness. You don't **have** to think of self anymore. Now, you can just live for others. You're free, see? Sufficiently free to live for others.

And then the most beautiful part is the third part. Now you start having some peace. You start having life and peace. So, a walk in the Spirit makes us pleasing to God, brings us into a life of love with others— authentic *agape* love—not just a selfish love that does things hoping to get something back. That's always the best that we can do at the human level. And then it brings this kind of **soul peace** that we **all yearn for and long for.**

Now I wonder if some of you are thinking, "Oh how wonderful that will be. I wonder what I could do to get it." *(Don chuckles)* "Yes, I know I have **got** to try harder. **I have got to be better.** That's what I must do." That's what some of you are thinking. You didn't hear your pastor, did you? *(Don chuckles)*

First of all, we're going to let this **marvelous knowledge, this word of grace** come home to our lives. We're going to receive that message down deep in our souls. And then we're just going to come to Jesus, **just as we are,** and believe that. And you see, the most wonderful thing is, is that God can put you in the Spirit. And that's this life that you've always yearned for. For some **peace,** and to **do good,** to live well pleasing to Him. And that comes by this marvelous, marvelous, grace of God. But you see, **watch, watch, watch** that you do **not** reintroduce a legal system to get that done. Because **many** people will get **saved** by grace, and they get up this far, and then they constantly bring the old system over to try to perfect it. You are **not** perfected **ever** by the flesh. **It starts "in the Spirit" and it will end "in the Spirit."** It is always faith in our Lord Jesus Christ.

SERMON 18 ENDNOTES:

None

SERMON 18 SCRIPTURE REFERENCES:

[1] Ephesians 5:8-9 (RSV)

8 for once you were darkness, but now you are light in the Lord; walk as children of light 9 (for the fruit of light is found in all that is good and right and true),

[2] Romans 8:9 (KJV)

But ye are not in the flesh, but in the Spirit, if so be that the Spirit of God dwell in you. Now if any man have not the Spirit of Christ, he is none of his.

3 Romans 8:5-9 (RSV)

5 For those who live according to the flesh set their minds on the things of the flesh, but those who live according to the Spirit set their minds on the things of the Spirit. 6 To set the mind on the flesh is death, but to set the mind on the Spirit is life and peace. 7 For the mind that is set on the flesh is hostile to God; it does not submit to God's law, indeed it cannot; 8 and those who are in the flesh cannot please God. 9 But you are not in the flesh, you are in the Spirit, if in fact the Spirit of God dwells in you. Any one who does not have the Spirit of Christ does not belong to him.

4 Romans 8:15 (KJV)

For ye have not received the spirit of bondage again to fear; but ye have received the Spirit of adoption, whereby we cry, Abba, Father.

5 Romans 8:5 (RSV)

For those who live according to the flesh set their minds on the things of the flesh, but those who live according to the Spirit set their minds on the things of the Spirit.

6 Colossians 3:2 (KJV)

Set your affection on things above, not on things on the earth.

7 Galatians 5:25 (RSV)

If we live by the Spirit, let us also walk by the Spirit.

8 Romans 8:3-4 (RSV)

3 For God has done what the law, weakened by the flesh, could not do: sending his own Son in the likeness of sinful flesh and for sin, he condemned sin in the flesh, 4 in order that the just requirement of the law might be fulfilled in us, who walk not according to the flesh but according to the Spirit.

[9] Romans 3:21-22 (RSV)

21 But now the righteousness of God has been manifested apart from law, although the law and the prophets bear witness to it, 22 the righteousness of God through faith in Jesus Christ for all who believe. For there is no distinction;

[10] Galatians 5:13-14 (RSV)

13 For you were called to freedom, brethren; only do not use your freedom as an opportunity for the flesh, but through love be servants of one another. 14 For the whole law is fulfilled in one word, "You shall love your neighbor as yourself."

[11] Titus 2:11-12 (RSV)

11 For the grace of God has appeared for the salvation of all men, 12 training us to renounce irreligion and worldly passions, and to live sober, upright, and godly lives in this world,

[12] Romans 1:17 (ASV)

For therein is revealed a righteousness of God from faith unto faith: as it is written, But the righteous shall live by faith.

[13] Romans 8:6 (RSV)

To set the mind on the flesh is death, but to set the mind on the Spirit is life and peace.

[14] Romans 8:6 (AMPC)

Now the mind of the flesh [which is sense and reason without the Holy Spirit] is death [death that comprises all the miseries arising from sin, both here and hereafter]. But the mind of the [Holy] Spirit is life and [soul] peace [both now and forever].

SERMON 19

THREE REQUISITES FOR
WALKING IN THE SPIRIT

"You can walk down here like all the other earthlings
as it were, or you can come up to the life of the Spirit
and that's the knowledge of Jesus Christ in work
by His marvelous Holy Spirit!"

Romans chapter 8 basically tells us how we can be **super** conquerors—**more** than conquerors through Him that loved us. And so, we call this chapter, "How the Reign of Grace Makes Us Super Conquerors During **This** Present Time." That's a key phrase to Romans 8, **"this—present—time."** We've spent **some** time already talking about what it means to "walk in the Spirit." That's terminology that comes out of Romans chapter 8. And once again were going to look at these opening verses of the eighth chapter, and we will conclude this morning that phase of what it means to "walk in the Spirit." We're going to underscore the three requisites or the three **conditions** for "walking in the Spirit."

Romans chapter 8 please, *"There is therefore now **no** condemnation for those who are **in** Christ Jesus. For the **law** of the Spirit of life **in** Christ Jesus has set me **free** from the law of sin and death. **For God has done what the law weakened by the flesh, could not do:** sending his own Son in the **likeness** of sinful flesh and **for sin,** he **condemned sin in the flesh,** in order that the **just** requirement of the **law** might be fulfilled in us, who walk not according to the flesh but according to the **Spirit. For** those who live according to the flesh, they set their **minds** on the things of the flesh, **but** those who live according to the Spirit, they set their **minds** on the things of* the **Spirit**. *To set the mind on the flesh is **death**, but to set the mind on the Spirit is **life and peace**. The mind that is set on the flesh is hostile to God, **it does not submit to God's law, indeed, it <u>cannot</u>, and those who are in the flesh cannot please God**.*" [1]

So, if we're going to walk in the Spirit, we must know how—what the requisites are. We initially spent much time defining what it means to be in the flesh and in the Spirit. And just to summarize briefly, we saw that this is very **practical.** It is nothing mysterious. We're not talking about an invisible quality within us—something you can't see. We're not talking about something in a mystical experience by walking in the Spirit. We're talking about a very concrete, **practical walk,** which **means** to walk like Jesus. To be in the Spirit, primarily means to have a life of **loving obedience.** We saw the two benefits, the two consequences of walking in the Spirit. One is that the just requirement of the law might be fulfilled in us. And that **just requirement** of the law, the thing the law aimed at, was **loving obedience.** To serve one another **in love.** That's the **just requirement** of the law.

Also, we noticed that to live in the Spirit or to walk in the Spirit is **life—and—peace.** One translator calls it life and **soul peace.** That's some real peace—authentic peace—true peace. **But** the problem is, how do we do it? What's **required** to walk in the Spirit? I think it's fair to conclude that there are **three requisites.** They are clearly indicated for us in Romans chapters 6, 7 and 8. I'd like to introduce those to you this morning.

Now the first requisite is somewhat of a **negative one.** It's the basic truth found in Romans chapter 7, and it amounts to this: That if you're going to walk in the **Spirit,** you obviously cannot walk in the flesh. **Or,** to put it this way; before you will **really** walk in the Spirit, you must come to an **end** of yourself. **Or** I would like to make this little formula; you must **learn—the language—of wretchedness.** That's based upon Romans 7:24 and 25, *"**Wretched man that I am! Who's going to <u>deliver me</u>?***

Thanks be to God through Jesus Christ our Lord." [2] **The first requisite—** the first condition for **walking in the Spirit** is to **learn the language of wretchedness.** L.O.W. The Language Of Wretchedness.

"Wretched man that I am! Who will deliver me from this body of death? Thanks be to God through Jesus Christ our Lord! So then, I of myself serve the law of God with my mind, but with my flesh I serve the law of sin." - Romans 7:24-25 RSV

Now, I've said before, and I repeat again, I thought the Lord got a good deal when he got me. I did **not** come to Jesus Christ because I really needed a Savior. I came out of selfish, self-centered reasons, because I wanted some of my needs met. I knew there was an emptiness within me. There was a kind of a basic existential loneliness. I **knew** that there was an unsatisfied **sense**—a lack of purposelessness. And so, I came, trying to **find some of my needs met.** I did not think that I was really a **sinner,** to tell you the truth. I knew that I did some bad things and all that. I was a Christian for over **a year** before it even **dawned on me** that I was getting close to being wretched. Now, I put up a good front, and I would sing how happy I was and all that. But inside I was **miserable.** And when I was honest, I **knew** that I sinned in thought, word, and deed. **I knew that I was undone!**

I began to sense my total inability! And so, I began **striving** to do better, and I thought, "Well, my problem is I'm just not **trying** harder. That's all. If people would just shape up and buck up and try harder, they could make it." And so, I would **try** to be **loving** and **stop sinning** and so on. **And I found out I couldn't! All of a sudden, I came to an end of myself, and I said one day, "You know, I can't live this Christian life!** Why, I can't do this, not in terms of Scripture. I can't fulfill the just requirement of the law with His loving obedience."

So, I just almost **despaired.** I wondered if I was even a Christian. **And it was at <u>that</u> time that I began to understand that God was just <u>waiting</u> for me to come to an end of my <u>self</u>.** And so, the first thing that a person must experience: **You must <u>learn</u> the language of wretchedness.** You must say, in effect, **"In <u>me</u> dwells no good thing!"** **You will <u>not</u> walk in the Spirit until you know that in—your—flesh— is—no—good! Dwells <u>no</u> good thing!** Romans 7:18, *"I know that nothing good dwells within me, that is, in my flesh."* [3]

We've talked about the Doctrine of the Two Creations, and we saw that man is living out his life in this first creation but under the powers of **sin and <u>death</u>. We need to <u>see</u> that within this first creation it has been subjected to futility or the Doctrine of Emptiness and that is left to itself, devoid of the Spirit of God. It does not have the capabilities of fulfilling the law of God in a sense of loving obedience.** Now **you** have to **learn** that. I think you have to **learn** the Language Of Wretchedness. I think God by His Holy Spirit has to bring you to an end of yourself. In other words, you won't turn to a Savior until you know **you can't do it!** But as long as you have **one shred** of self-works or one hope that somehow some good can come out of you, you will resort **to that,** and you'll try to find your life **from** this life.

You'll be looking to this first creation to find your satisfaction. But the truth of Scripture is, this first creation has been subjected to emptiness or to futility, and there **is** no authentic life here. Until you discover that, you will not turn to the new creation or to the life in the Spirit. You will go on **hoping** that you'll find your life here. I tell you friend it's not here. The only thing that's here—**is sin—and—death.**

Those who are **in the flesh,** those who are in the part of the creation, they **cannot—please—God.** They **cannot** live that life of *agape* love— and **loving obedience**—and **loving service** to others and enter into life and peace. It's not here! But you have to **know** that! That's the **first** step!

To **walk in the Spirit,** is to realize you're not going to find your life **here** in this creation. Now that takes a **long** time to learn that. **The Language Of Wretchedness—wretched man that I am.** Do you know that yet? Have you **really** reached an end to yourself? Well, when you **do,** it is **then** that you'll start turning to another power, to another source, and **totally trusting** Jesus Christ and God's work for you. That's what we mean by being under law and grace. See you cannot mix these two. You cannot mix, law and grace, faith and works, flesh and Spirit, new creation and old creation. They just won't **mix!** You've got to say, "No," to this whole first creation, and realize that this entire creation is **under—a cross.**

There is therefore now no condemnation for those who are in Christ Jesus. For the law of the Spirit of life in Christ Jesus has set me free from the law of sin and death."
- Romans 8:1-2 RSV

And that leads me to the second point. <u>If someone is going to walk in the Spirit, you must **be—in—Christ.**</u> That's the **second requisite.** That's Paul's most significant term in the New Testament, is what it means to **be "in" Christ.** Now, basically that means two things. There are two elements that enter into being **"in" Christ.** You'll notice how we use that terminology here, *"There is therefore now **no** condemnation to those who are—**in**—Christ. The law of the Spirit of life **in Christ** has set me free from the law of sin and death."* [4]

There are two things, two elements of being in Christ. Number one, we must **know** what Jesus Christ has done **"for" us.** Number two, we must **experience** Christ's work **"in"** us. Now, those are two distinguishable things. We call it "positional truth" and "conditional truth." Your **position** and your **condition <u>or</u>** your **state** and your **standing.** An **external work.** An **internal work.** What Jesus did **for** you. You don't experience that. It happened **for you, but it puts you "<u>in</u> Christ."**

Now let me explain that the best I can. You see, the Lord Jesus Christ, according to Scripture, is what we call the **last Adam.** The Bible is built upon what we call **covenants** or **federal theology.** We have a **federal type government.** President Nixon is our **representative.** He acts **for us** and signs laws **for us.** So, according to the Scriptures, **Jesus Christ entered this first creation by His incarnation. God became flesh. What does that mean? It means that <u>God</u>, in the form of His Son, came <u>into</u> this first creation. He identified Himself with us—in the <u>likeness</u> of sinful flesh.**

Paul comes **very** close to identifying Jesus Christ with our sin. But He's **careful.** He says it's only *"in the **likeness** of sinful flesh."* [5] And what He means is that Jesus Christ became a **man. God became a man! God came into focus, but He came as the last Adam. He came as the representative head into this old creation.**

Now what happened when Jesus was a man? <u>God</u> sent him to a cross! <u>God</u> <u>condemned sin in the flesh</u>—on its own <u>grounds</u>—<u>in</u> Jesus Christ. He condemned it! That was a condemnation upon this entire first creation—<u>everything has been condemned</u>. <u>It's under a cross!</u> <u>It's under God's wrath! Everything in this life, including you and your historical self</u>. <u>You are under condemnation and wrath!</u>

I've used the illustration of our motel up there. I'll use it again. We own a piece of property in Eagle Rock. A building, but it's condemned by the city. It's under **condemnation.** What does that mean? It means you can't **live** in it. It is **not fit for human habitation.** There is no possibility of having **life** in that. Now, the building is still standing. It's supposed to come down, I think, this week or the next. It's coming down in a few days.

Now, that's the way it is with **this creation. Here is <u>life</u>, but it's under <u>condemnation</u>. It's been condemned by a judgment of God. This creation is not fit for human life. There is no <u>life</u> here. There is no life or peace. There's nothing but sin and death.** And death is going to claim every one of us. There's a **thing** in our nature called **sin.** So, as long as you're in this first creation, as long as you're in the flesh, you are **under condemnation.** But you see, **God—judged—the world—in—Jesus Christ—** *"in the likeness of sinful flesh."* [5]

God has obtained a <u>judgment</u> against the <u>powers</u> of this creation—the powers of sin and <u>death</u>. Now, they're still <u>around</u> but they're no longer <u>powers</u> for me, if I'm <u>in</u> Christ. Because you see, Jesus Christ not only entered this first creation in the <u>likeness</u> of sinful flesh, and was put to death, He was manifested in the flesh, but He was justified in the Spirit. Jesus Christ <u>arose</u> from the dead, and where did <u>He go</u>? He went into the presence of God. He went into the new creation according to Scripture. And thereby, He breathes the blessings of that new creation back into this old creation. And the <u>best</u> gift of that new creation is what we call the Holy Spirit.

So, when I **know** what Jesus Christ has done **for** me, **I know that the powers of this creation have no authority over me.** *"The law of the Spirit of life in Christ has set me free from the law"*—the power—the authority—*"of sin and death."* [6] Does sin want to claim **me? All the time!** But that is no longer a **power.** It doesn't control my life because that has been condemned or judged—**by—God—through the Lord Jesus Christ.**

But now I need something done **in** me, and that's what Christ does in me. This is also what we call being **"in Christ."** Eighteen times in this chapter (Romans 8), you'll find a reference to the Holy Spirit. The Spirit of God, called the Spirit of **life.** The Spirit of Christ. All these terms are talking about **God's Spirit.** And you see the most wonderful truth is this, is that Jesus Christ not only did something **for me,** but Jesus Christ makes an impartation of **His** life **by the Holy Spirit** and—**actually—dwells—in me.** As the Bibles says, *"You are **not** in the flesh, but in the Spirit, if the Spirit of God"*—really—*"dwells in you. Any one who does not* *have the Spirit of Christ is none of his."* [7] It's **possible** for Jesus Christ to **indwell you by His wonderful Holy Spirit.**

Now, what does that do? Well, in days ahead we'll **look at** the ministry of the Holy Spirit in Romans chapter 8. But let me just initially say there are three great things that the Spirit does—three ministries that He has. First of all, He has a **ministry of liberation. His primary job is to set you free.** Romans 8, calls it, *"the glorious **liberty** of the children of God."* [8] *"He **sets me _free_** from the law of sin and death."* [6]

Now, we're made for freedom. There's something within us that **yearns** to be **authentically free.** Not a false freedom as some call it, **but the ability to truly be free. Authentically free!** And I tell you, you can always spot the true work of the Holy Spirit, because *"where the Spirit of the Lord is, **there—is—liberty.**"* [9] And we're talking about **true liberty— soul liberty—liberty** that sets the **soul** free from all of its **bondages.** There are all kinds of **powers** that want to **come in** and to **control** the human life and to **squeeze the _life_ out of you. But the Holy Spirit has that liberating ministry that sets you free.** I tell you it's wonderful when you've **got it.** Brother, to breathe some free air. Just to be **glad** you're alive. Not to labor under **guilt** and that uneasy feeling. To know **who** you are—**whose** you are.

And that leads us to the second thing that the Holy Spirit does. The Holy Spirit **establishes your identity.** He has a **witness bearing task.** As the Bible says, *"Those who are led by the Spirit of God are the **sons** of God. You haven't received the spirit of **slavery** to fall back into **fear**. You've received the Spirit of **sonship**. When we cry, 'Abba! Father!' **it's the Spirit bearing witness with our spirit that _we are_ the children of God.**"* [10] And so it's the **great** work of the Holy Spirit to establish our identity.

I tell you it makes a **big** difference, if you know **really** who you **are. I mean in a deep existential sense, you know _way_ down deep, what kind of a being you are. You know what kind of a creature you are, and** you know God. Something has happened to your <u>identity</u>! The Holy Spirit bears <u>witness</u> with your spirit. He <u>establishes</u> your identity. And I tell you there are <u>millions</u> of people wandering around wondering who they are—just in <u>mass confusion</u>, trying to get an <u>identity</u>! It's <u>wonderful</u> when you <u>know who you are</u> brother! And Jesus Christ by His Holy Spirit establishes that identity. It's the <u>work</u> of the Spirit to bear <u>witness</u> with your spirit that you're a son of God.

I tell you, when you know who you are, in a <u>deep</u> sense, that solves most of your problems. All of a sudden, life falls into place. You're not a nobody anymore. You know who you are. It's a wonderful, wonderful thing. So, it's the **work** of the Holy Spirit to **establish** your identity and to bear witness.

<u>Thirdly, it's the work of the Holy Spirit to **provide** a sufficient enablement that helps you overcome all of our weakness.</u> As he says, *"The Spirit helps us in our weakness"*—and He does this particularly down deep of the subconscious level. *"**We don't know** how we should pray as we ought, but the **Spirit intercedes for us with sighs too deep for words.** He who searches the hearts, the depths of men. He knows what is the mind of the Spirit. He makes intercession for the saints according to the will of God."* [11]

It's the work of the Holy Spirit to do that work that you don't understand. Now most of us are mysterious beings. We don't even know what our **needs** are. We don't know how to function. Most of us don't. Most of us are in trouble in our <u>depths</u>. And if anything, the modern psychological movement has shown that man is in trouble in his <u>depths</u>. Way down deep in his subconscious <u>life</u> that motivates him, basically. Well, this is where the Spirit does His work, down in the <u>depths</u> of our being, *"with <u>sighs</u> too deep <u>for words</u>."* [11] That is below your conscious level. You don't even know what the problem is. But the Holy Spirit does that enabling work—way—down—deep—in our personality. And He intercedes for us according to the will of God.

The Holy Spirit has this great task. **Number one:** Liberation—setting you **truly** free. **Number two:** Establishing your **identity**—witness bearing. **Number three:** Giving you an enablement to His intercessory work that gives you strength amidst **all** of your weakness and helps you live in a **life** and in a **world** that can be **very,** **very, difficult.**

Can you have suffering? Can you have trials and tribulations? All kinds of them. Is it possible to be a super conqueror? **You've got to have some divine help or like the rest of us you'll be going down the tubes.** Unless, somehow that Holy Spirit comes along and lifts you up, as it were, into that new creation life and helps you to **live—in—Christ Jesus.** That's a wonderful position. No guilt. No condemnation. It's all been condemned in Christ Jesus. That's where I'm at. Do I live without guilt? **You know it!** I don't want the **slightest** bit of guilt or condemnation. And when I do, I run right to Jesus. I get it right cleared up. I want to feel **peace.** I want to be **free.** The Holy Spirit **does** that for me in Christ Jesus. The second requisite to walk in the Spirit is to be "in Christ." That includes the **new birth.** That includes being **born again.** That includes **receiving that Spirit** into your life. **That—must—happen**—or you **cannot** walk in the Spirit.

The third requisite is a practical one. This is one that comes close to all of our minds by way of an exhortation and that is this—and I made up a little formula—I've preached these sermons to our Junior High kids and so I know we talked about some difficult terms so we try to make it plain: You must have an SOS mind. A **mind**—Set—On the—Spirit.

 "For those who live according to the flesh set their minds on the things of the flesh, but those who live according to the Spirit set their minds on the things of the Spirit." - Romans 8:5 RSV

Now this is made clear in verses 5 and 6, "*Those who live according to the **Spirit**—set—their—**minds**—on the things of the Spirit. To set the **mind** on the flesh is **death,** but to set the **mind** on the Spirit is **life—and— peace.**" ¹² So, we walk in the Spirit by having an SOS mind. A—mind Set—On the—Spirit.

Now, we mentioned earlier in another message that there are three relationships that you have with the Spirit. You can be "**in** the Spirit," a "mind **set on the Spirit,**" and you can "**walk** in the Spirit." Those three terms are used here. Now every Christian is "in the Spirit." You **cannot** be a Christian and **not** be "in the Spirit," because that's the gift that comes to you through Jesus Christ. **But** not every Christian **sets their mind** on the Spirit. Are they Christians? **Yes, absolutely,** because they're going to heaven by imputed righteousness by the grace of God, not upon the basis of their own works. You are saved **by grace** through **faith.**

But you see, if you're going to **walk** in the Spirit, and that is **make visible**—let it begin to show up in your **life**—it begins by this intermediate step of having your **mind** "**set**" on the Spirit. So, until you have a mind—an outlook—an attitude—and thoughts **after** the Spirit— you won't **walk** in the Spirit. Your **gait**—the way you're going about—the way you walk—**it won't show up!** So, <u>our</u> job is to take our <u>life</u> in the **Spirit and make it a <u>walk</u> in the Spirit.**

Is there such a thing as a carnal Christian? Absolutely. They live just like the world. You couldn't tell the difference between a non-Christian. They live on the job. Work on the job. Nobody knows they're Christians. They **talk** like those people do. They **think** much like they do. They might show up for church **occasionally.** But as far as scripture is concerned—the things of **God**—the truth of **God**—is that the way they think? Are their affections set on those things? **No!** So, as a result there's **no productivity.** There is **no fruitfulness** and there is basically no **life** and **peace.** They do not <u>walk</u> in the Spirit, because their **mind is not set on things—that—are above.** And this is why the Apostle tells us what we must do over and over again. *"If you've been raised with Christ, seek those things that are <u>above</u>, where <u>Christ is</u>,"*—in the new creation—*"He's <u>seated</u> at the right hand of <u>God</u>. Set your <u>minds</u> on things that are above, <u>not</u> on things that are on earth. For you have <u>died</u> and your life is hid with Christ in God."* [13]

That's where our conversation really is. That's where our **life** really is, is in Jesus Christ. Now, I'm not talking about just doing gross immorality. I'm talking about just living in this present time just like the world does.

Now, basically there are three primary things that occupy our affections in our minds, and this is where we don't walk in the Spirit. This is where we start **walking** in the flesh. That has to do **primarily** with our **family**—our marriages. Secondly, with our **social life.** And thirdly with our **job**—our economic life. That's all we live for. Have you ever met people that just live for their families? They just live for education or their social world—**just** for this world. **Yes,** you see them all the time.

That's why Paul wrote in 1 Corinthians, chapter 7, and said, *"The time has grown very short; from now on, let those who have wives live as though they had **none**, and those who **mourn**"*—this morning in rejoicing we talk about social life, happened to us socially—*"those who mourn as though they were not mourning, and those who rejoice as though they didn't rejoice, and those that **buy** as though they didn't possess. Those who **deal** with the world as though they had no dealings with it. For the form of this world is passing away."* [14]

So, people are just quote, "Always busy." They just live at a temporal life. **They're not doing bad things, but they're <u>earthbound</u>. They live <u>only</u> in <u>this</u> creation—all their values—everything comes out of that— their attitude—their mind—their thinking, and so consequently they don't walk in the Spirit. Now they may be <u>fairly</u> good people, by the way. You're not to imagine that they're all a bunch of <u>crooks</u> and so on. But they're just <u>temporal</u>. <u>God is not in their life</u>! They are not**

overwhelmed by the Spirit! They don't know who they are, and they're not caught up in the things of God. They don't have a <u>mind</u> that's set on above, and I'm not talking about <u>mystical</u> experiences. I'm talking about they hunger and thirst after the truth. Righteousness lays hold of them and they <u>long</u> for the things of God. That's that <u>walk</u> in the Spirit!

I tell you it's a wonderful thing when you see that happening to a person's life. All of a sudden, their finances—their family—their fortunes—everything now belongs to God, and they know that. They don't have anything in this creation anymore. They know that this old world is passing away. It's been condemned brother, and they're not drawing their life from it.

Do you meet people who get earthbound? Oh, all the time! They've got one house and they want a bigger one. They've got this job and they want a better one. And they've got a Master's Degree, and they want a PhD. All this is fine, of course, I want one myself. *(Don chuckles)* But it has to be in the proper way. It's a matter of these priorities.

We <u>use</u> the world, but we do not <u>abuse</u> the world. We set our minds on the things of the Spirit. And that brings us to a fulfillment of the **law.** And that brings us to **life and peace.** So, it's a matter of sorting out your priorities—your outlook—the set of your mind—where your affections are—and what you're **basically seeking.**

These are the **three requisites** for walking in the Spirit. One more time:

You must **learn** the Language Of Wretchedness. You must **know** that in this life there **dwells no good thing.** In you dwells no good thing. Wretched man that I am. And the sooner you learn that the better. Then you will turn **from** this creation, from yourself, and you'll say, "I can only trust something outside myself and outside this creation. It will have to come from above, from God through Jesus Christ."

Obviously, you must be **in** Christ. That means to enjoy what has happened **for you** on the **cross of Christ,** and what happens **in you** by the **gift of the Holy Spirit.** As God by His Spirit indwells you, and begins to set you free, and begins to do that marvelous enabling work, that **frees** you from yourself. And that's your big problem, by the way, is to get free of yourself. Get out of your self-life and into the life of the Spirit.

And then thirdly, you must have a **mind** that is **set on the Spirit.** That seeks after those things and sets your affections on the **right** sources.

Well, that's the requisite. **And here it is,** the possibility now, of **life** and **peace.** Here's a possibility of **pleasing God**—of loving obedience. Here's a possibility of knowing **who you are** and understanding what life is all about. You can walk down here like all the other earthlings as it were, or you can **come up** to the **life of the Spirit** and that's the **knowledge** of Jesus Christ in work by His marvelous Holy Spirit.

I trust everyone here will be susceptible to that word of the gospel. If you want to walk in the Spirit, you must first be **in** Christ. That means you've got to come to an end of yourself and say, "I need help." You've got to know you're a sinner. You've got to know you have needs beyond yourself. Jesus Christ can do that. He can meet those needs by His Holy Spirit.

SERMON 19 ENDNOTES:

None.

SERMON 19 SCRIPTURE REFERENCES:

[1] Romans 8:1-8 (RSV)

1 There is therefore now no condemnation for those who are in Christ Jesus. 2 For the law of the Spirit of life in Christ Jesus has set me free from the law of sin and death. 3 For God has done what the law, weakened by the flesh, could not do: sending his own Son in the likeness of sinful flesh and for sin, he condemned sin in the flesh, 4 in order that the just requirement of the law might be fulfilled in us, who walk not according to the flesh but according to the Spirit. 5 For those who live according to the flesh set their minds on the things of the flesh, but those who live according to the Spirit set their minds on the things of the Spirit. 6 To set the mind on the flesh is death, but to set the mind on the Spirit is life and peace. 7 For the mind that is set on the flesh is hostile to God; it does not submit to God's law, indeed it cannot; 8 and those who are in the flesh cannot please God.

² Romans 7:24-25 (RSV)

24 Wretched man that I am! Who will deliver me from this body of death? 25 Thanks be to God through Jesus Christ our Lord! So then, I of myself serve the law of God with my mind, but with my flesh I serve the law of sin.

³ Romans 7:18 (RSV)

For I know that nothing good dwells within me, that is, in my flesh. I can will what is right, but I cannot do it.

⁴ Romans 8:1-2 (RSV)

1 There is therefore now no condemnation for those who are in Christ Jesus. 2 For the law of the Spirit of life in Christ Jesus has set me free from the law of sin and death.

⁵ Romans 8:3 (RSV)

For God has done what the law, weakened by the flesh, could not do: sending his own Son in the likeness of sinful flesh and for sin, he condemned sin in the flesh,

⁶ Romans 8:2 (RSV)

For the law of the Spirit of life in Christ Jesus has set me free from the law of sin and death.

[7] Romans 8:9 (RSV)

But you are not in the flesh, you are in the Spirit, if in fact the Spirit of God dwells in you. Any one who does not have the Spirit of Christ does not belong to him.

[8] Romans 8:21 RSV

because the creation itself will be set free from its bondage to decay and obtain the glorious liberty of the children of God.

[9] 2 Corinthians 3:17 (KJV)

Now the Lord is that Spirit: and where the Spirit of the Lord is, there is liberty.

[10] Romans 8:14-16 (RSV)

14 For all who are led by the Spirit of God are sons of God. 15 For you did not receive the spirit of slavery to fall back into fear, but you have received the spirit of sonship. When we cry, "Abba! Father!" 16 it is the Spirit himself bearing witness with our spirit that we are children of God,

[11] Romans 8:26-27 (RSV)

26 Likewise the Spirit helps us in our weakness; for we do not know how to pray as we ought, but the Spirit himself intercedes for us with sighs too deep for words. 27 And he who searches the hearts of men knows what is the mind of the Spirit, because the Spirit intercedes for the saints according to the will of God.

[12] Romans 8:5-6 (RSV)

5 For those who live according to the flesh set their minds on the things of the flesh, but those who live according to the Spirit set their minds on the things of the Spirit. 6 To set the mind on the flesh is death, but to set the mind on the Spirit is life and peace.

[13] Colossians 3:1-3 (RSV)

1 If then you have been raised with Christ, seek the things that are above, where Christ is, seated at the right hand of God. 2 Set your minds on things that are above, not on things that are on earth. 3 For you have died, and your life is hid with Christ in God.

[14] 1 Corinthians 7:29-31 (RSV)

29 I mean, brethren, the appointed time has grown very short; from now on, let those who have wives live as though they had none, 30 and those who mourn as though they were not mourning, and those who rejoice as though they were not rejoicing, and those who buy as though they had no goods, 31 and those who deal with the world as though they had no dealings with it. For the form of this world is passing away.

SERMON 20

THE MINISTRY OF EMANCIPATION

"Death is not going to make me righteous. It's the blood of Jesus that makes me righteous, and I have that right now. That's this glorious gospel of His marvelous grace!"

We're engaged in a rather lengthy series of sermons based upon Romans chapters 6, 7 and 8. This morning we come to look at the **marvelous** ministry of the Holy Spirit. We have discovered that Romans chapters 6, 7 and 8 are a **commentary** on what it means to be **under** grace, and **not under law.** The most significant theological truth of these three chapters is **that. You are not under law, you are—under—grace.**

Now, we've seen how marvelous this is, the reign of grace—this **abundance** of grace. Ephesians describes it over and over what it's like, and in my devotions, I was reading this morning that passage that thrilled my heart so. In the first chapter of Ephesians it says, *"Blessed be the God and Father of our Lord Jesus Christ, who **has** blessed us,"* past tense, *"**in Christ** with **every** spiritual blessing in heavenly places,"* where it **really** counts—in heavenly places—at the source—at headquarters, *"even as he chose us in him before the foundation of the world, that we should be holy and blameless before him. He **destined** us in his love,"* in His grace, *"**to be his sons** through Jesus Christ, according to the purpose of his will, to the praise of his <u>glorious grace</u>."* [1] **His <u>glorious</u> grace!**

God shows His glory in many ways. God's glory, by the way, is the sum total of what He **is.** If you would equal out all of His attributes, you would have the word **glory.** Now, God has especially manifested His **glory in creation.** You take a look at the world—the sun, the moon, the stars—this great vast universe—how you see God's power **in** creation.

But you see, you see His **grace** in the church, and that's what Ephesians is trying to tell us. *"Unto him be **glory** in the church."* [2] I just quoted from Ephesians chapter 3. *"So, to the praise of his **glorious grace,** which he **freely** bestowed on us in the Beloved. In him we have redemption through his blood, the **forgiveness** of our trespasses, according to the **riches** of his grace, which he **lavished** on us."* [3] So, here's **lavished grace— glorious grace.**

 "That in the coming ages he might show the immeasurable riches of his grace in kindness toward us in Christ Jesus. For by grace you have been saved through faith; and this is not your own doing, it is the gift of God." - Ephesians 2:7-8 RSV

And you remember that great passage in Ephesians 2, starting in verse 7, *"in the coming ages,"* throughout all eternity, *"he will **show** the **immeasurable** riches of his grace,"* the **immeasurable** riches of His grace, *"toward us in Christ Jesus. For by **grace** you have been **saved through faith;** and that's not your own doing, it's the **gift** of God—**not of works,** lest any man should boast."* [4] Unto Him be **glory** in the church. God shows His **love**—His nature—His power—His grace—through **you.** He can't show His love really, you see, so much in the universe though it's there, I do believe, but He shows His **grace in the church.** In people like we are. *"Those of us who were **dead** in trespasses and sins, have now been, made **alive** by his marvelous, wonderful grace."* [5]

Romans chapters 6, 7 and 8 tells us what it means to be **under grace.** And we have seen that grace is **not** something to be distinguished from God. Grace is just a word. We're talking about the **life** of God, the being of God, or the Spirit of God. That's why you can't separate the reign of grace from a life in the Spirit.

So, we said that the most significant theological truth was you are not under law, but under grace. The most practical exhortation, however, is that you are to **walk in the Spirit.** Now the Spirit of course, means the **Holy Spirit**—means **that life of God.** And again, I would like to clarify, you can never separate the Holy Spirit, or the life of God, the Spirit of God, from a quality of life, because **He's called the Spirit of Life.** *"The Spirit of Life in Christ has set me free from the law of sin and death."* [6] So we want to walk in the Spirit. That's why Paul in Romans 8, after giving the exhortation to **walk** in the Spirit, begins to tell us now, about the **ministry** of the Holy Spirit.

There are three basic spiritual needs for man. We have three primary needs. First of all, everybody here needs **salvation.** You need to be **set free.** You need **deliverance.** You need to be **rescued.** You need to be **emancipated.** You need **saved** in other words. **That's salvation**— being **set free**—ransomed—delivered—**liberated.** And so, in this great chapter we're going to look at the **emancipating** ministry of the Holy Spirit.

Secondly, everybody here needs a self-understanding. You need to know **who you are.** You need to have an **identity.** You need to take out **all** the confusion, **all** the ignorance about **who you are. You need to establish** your **identity** and that's what the Holy Spirit does. That's His great ministry in this chapter, the second thing He does. He has a ministry of establishing identity as He bears witness that we are God's son.** He brings us right into the spirit of adoption.

And thirdly, everybody here needs **strength.** Are you weak? Yes, you are. And this brings us to the **enabling** ministry of the Holy Spirit. It's all right here in this great eighth chapter of Romans.

"So then, brethren, we are debtors, not to the flesh, to live according to the flesh" - Romans 8:12 RSV

So, we're going to underscore just that first part this morning and that's the **emancipating** ministry of the Holy Spirit as He **liberates** God's people. Romans chapter 8, beginning please with verse 12, *"So then, brethren, we **were** debtors, not to the flesh, to live according to the flesh—for if you live according to the **flesh** you will **die,** but if by the **Spirit** you put to **death** the deeds of the body"*—see and walk in the spirit—*"you will **live.** For all who are **led**"*—governed, controlled, under the power of the Spirit—*"all who are **led** by the Spirit of God they are **sons** of God." [7]*

Paul is starting a progression of logical thoughts here. **"You— did—not—receive the spirit of slavery to fall back into fear."** I want you to notice that verse because we're going to underscore it this morning. *"You **did not** receive a spirit of slavery **to fall back into fear.** You have received the **spirit of sonship. When we cry, 'Abba! Father!' It's the Spirit himself bearing witness with our spirit that we are children of God,** and if you're children,"*—notice how it progresses—*"then you are **heirs, heirs of God."**—to the eternal inheritance—*"you are **fellow heirs"**—joint **heirs**—*"with Jesus Christ, provided we suffer with him in order that we may also be glorified with him. I consider that the sufferings of **this present time** they're not worthy to be compared with the **glory** that's to be revealed in us. Creation **waits** for the eager longing of the **revealing** of the sons of God; creation was subjected to **futility"**—emptiness, the Doctrine of Emptiness—**"not of its own will, but by the will of him who subjected it in <u>hope</u>; because creation itself will be <u>set free</u> from its bondage to decay and they will obtain the <u>glorious liberty of the children of God</u>." [8]*

We're talking about this **marvelous liberty.** This **emancipating** ministry of the Holy Spirit. Now, if you're going to live in **this** life, *"in this present time," [9]* according to verse 18, and become a **super conqueror,** according to verse 37, *"more—than—conquerors"* [10] —you've **got to have** something happening to your spirit.

Now, we've said again and again, the **real issue** of life will **always** be the **quality** and the **level** of your spirit, because life is from within-**out.** It's going to be the **attitude**—the **outlook**—the characteristics—the quality of your <u>soul</u>—that's going to determine whether you're going to be a super conqueror.

It is **possible** to have a **spirit of slavery.** Now, what is the spirit of slavery? Well, at least it's a couple of things. First of all, I think it's a **spirit** that I don't belong—I don't quite fit in—I am not at home. It's a feeling that I am not a part of things—I am unacceptable. At least I am not a member of God's family, and God is not my Father. It's a sense of unworthiness—a feeling of inadequacy—a feeling, you know, that I don't have a right to exist. I'm just like a slave. Now, that's a terrible feeling.

I wasn't an orphan; brother George here was an orphan. I don't know want it is to be like being an orphan, but my mother died when I was in the second grade, and I was farmed out to **live** with **a lot** of people. Some of them I felt at home with and some I did **not.** *(Don chuckles)* I remember the fourth grade, I stayed with a boy in Coffeyville, Kansas, and his **special ministry** was to let me know, I wasn't a part of **that family.** *(Don and congregation chuckle)* **So, I never did feel a part of that family. For about a year I lived there like a slave,** I'm telling you. By the way, I beat that kid up **good** before I left. *(Don and congregation laugh)*

But it's wonderful to <u>know</u>, that you've got a spirit of adoption—that you **belong**—that you're **at home.** To know you have **a right to exist.** Are there people who live like that? **Yes!** There are some people who feel they don't have a **right** to exist in the earth. But thanks be unto God, *"We have **not received** the spirit of **slavery** that makes us fall back into **fear,**"* [11] What would a slave fear more than anything else? Just basically one thing. **A slave** would be **afraid** that he had **not done right** and would be punished. **That would be his basic fear.** If you were a slave, **you would constantly be subject to the anxiety,** "Have I pleased the master? Am I being acceptable?" You must remember, that at times, and back in the first century, masters had almost power of life and death over their slave. If they displeased them, they could be killed! They could be **severely punished.** And so, **slaves** were always in terror. "Have I pleased the master? Am I acceptable?" And so, they would live with this **haunting fear** of being **punished.**

And so, the **glorious liberty** of the children of God through the grace of the Holy Spirit, is to let us know that we **no longer have—any—fear—of—punishment.** The Bible calls it: **No condemnation.** Do you remember how 1 John put it? 1 John chapter 4, verse 16, *"We know and believe the love that God has for us. God is love, and he who abides in God abides in love. In this is love perfected with us, that we may have confidence in the day of judgment, because as he is"*—as Christ is—*"so are we in this world"*—right now. As He is right now, so are we right now. "There is no fear in love, perfect love casts out fear. For fear has to do with punishment, he who fears is not perfected in love."* [12]

We're not talking about **our** love. I used to think that if I were just perfected in love, if I could be more loving, then I wouldn't have fear. But then I realized I'm talking about **God's perfect love.** To be perfected in love is to know how **perfectly God loves you.** And if you know how **perfectly** God **loves** you, then you have no fear of **punishment** because they're directly opposite things. Perfect love—an understanding of God's love—His nature—His grace, sets you utterly free! That's this **glorious liberty of the children of God, where you have not received the spirit of slavery to fall back into fear.**

Do we have fear of being punished? No! No! Because we're not under law! We're under grace! There is no punishment. Because, you see, there really is no sin. **There is no law, so therefore, there cannot be sin. Therefore, there cannot be punishment.** You say, "Pastor, you're getting carried away there, aren't you?" **Absolutely not! I'm preaching you the simple gospel! I'm telling you <u>exactly</u> what Jesus Christ has done.**

It's <u>amazing</u> how many people think they ought to feel just a little bit <u>miserable</u>. "Now wait a minute, I can't be perfectly free. *(Don is speaking sarcastically)* I can't <u>really</u> enjoy all that Jesus did on the cross. I've got to feel just <u>a little</u> miserable. Just give me a little grain of condemnation. Let me be a cross stealer. Let me do <u>some</u> penance. Let me do something." <u>Oh no, you don't!</u> God says no. I've done it <u>all</u> in the Lord Jesus Christ. And that's what the Holy Spirit does. That's His **emancipating ministry** that sets us free. *"The law of the Spirit of life in Christ Jesus has—set—me—free."* [6]

"There is therefore now no condemnation for those who are in Christ Jesus." - Romans 8:1 RSV

"There <u>is</u> no condemnation to them who are <u>in</u> Christ Jesus." [13] **I don't want even a <u>tiny bit</u> of condemnation. I want to have an open-faced—an unveiled relationship with God. I want to be <u>very</u> bold. I don't want to live life "shifty-eyed" with my tail between my legs for one second. I want to enjoy <u>all</u> that Jesus Christ has done for me. We're talking about the marvelous <u>liberty</u> that the Holy Spirit can give you through Jesus Christ our Lord.**

The best commentary on this passage, I think, is 2 Corinthians chapter 3. Now, the Apostle contrasts the two covenants: Law and grace—the two dispensations. And here he's telling us what has come to us through Jesus Christ and what it has done for the Apostle Paul and the great liberty that he has through the Holy Spirit. Listen to this marvelous passage. 2 Corinthians chapter 3, verse 4, *"Such is the **confidence** that we have through Christ toward God."* [14] **Confidence—boldness—openness—free speech**—this is tied into the word, by the way, of a flowing. The root word here is something that **flows**—unhindered—unblocked—unimpeded. You can speak freely. You feel open. You feel free. You're confident. You're very bold. *"Such is the **confidence** that we have through Christ toward God."* [14]

Now, wait a minute, *"**Not** that we are sufficient of ourselves."* Do you **ever** have that confidence or sufficiency in yourself? **No!** No. *"To claim anything that's from **ourselves**; no our **sufficiency is from God,**"*—and His grace has been **lavished** upon us. This **billionaire** grace—this unsearchable **riches** of His grace—**millionaire** grace—**billionaire** grace. *"Our sufficiency is from God,"*—who has **qualified us.** He has qualified us—*"as ministers of a **new covenant, not in a written code but in the Spirit; for the written code kills.**"* And anybody who has a conscience bound under the law has to go under that deathlike existence. They have to feel a little uneasy some way or another. They've got to have a little **death** in them, you know. *"**But the Spirit gives life.**"* [15]

*"Now if the dispensation of **death,** carved in letters on stone, came with such **splendor** that the Israelites could not look at **Moses' face** because of its **brightness,** fading as this was, will not the dispensation of the **Spirit** be attended with **greater splendor?** If there **was** splendor in the dispensation of **condemnation,** the dispensation of **righteousness** must **far exceed** it in splendor. Indeed, in this case, what once **had splendor** has come to have **no splendor at all,** because of the splendor that **surpasses it.** For if what faded away came with splendor, **what is permanent** must have **much more splendor.**"* [16]

*"Since we have such a hope, we are **very bold,**"*—very confident— **very** bold—not just bold—we are VERY bold—*"not like **Moses,** who put a veil over his face so that the Israelites might not see the **end** of the fading splendor."* How quickly the splendor was fading. *"But their minds were hardened;"*—Israel's minds were—*"to this day; when they read the old covenant, the same veil remains unlifted, because only through Christ is it taken away. Yes, to this day, whenever Moses is read **a veil** lies over*

*their minds; but when a man turns to the Lord, **that veil is removed. And the Lord is the Spirit, and where the Spirit of the Lord is, there—is—freedom. And we all, with an unveiled face,***"—how about that—*"with an unveiled face,"*—we are—*"beholding **the glory of the Lord,"**—the grace and the power—all the holiness of God—we're looking right at it with an unveiled face. *"We are **being** changed into his likeness from one degree of glory to another; and this comes from the **Lord—who—is— the—Spirit.**"* [17]

Now, that story is taken from the way Moses received the law for Israel. He went up on top of Mount Sinai. And while he was there, in the presence of God, some of God's glory began to shine on his face. And Moses had such an effulgence, such a brightness in his face, that when he came **down** to talk to Israel, it blinded them. It hurt their eyes. So, Moses put a **veil** over his **face,** and this represented two things.

It represented, of course, how **glorious** was the giving of the law. Is this law a good thing? I tell you; it was **so glorious** it made Moses' face shine. But listen, if the giving of **the law** made Moses' face light up, **how much greater is the—grace—and truth—that came by Jesus Christ? Why it's so glorious that you can't even see the first covenant. You can't even look at it. It's just like the sun coming up in the daytime. It just hides the moon and the stars. They're still up there, but they just fade out because the sun is so great. I tell you the grace and the love of God is so glorious; it shines so brilliantly that it just fades away all of these other things. What Jesus Christ has done has absolutely eclipsed anything else. Here is His marvelous, wonderful grace.**

That veil also showed the hardness of their hearts. But isn't it wonderful that God by the Spirit causes us to come to Jesus Christ? And guess what? When we come to Jesus Christ, we can come with an **unveiled face.** Completely accepted—**very bold—very open.** And that **glorious grace** is just coming to us with an **unveiled face.** Do you have anything to hide? **Nothing.** Your sins are covered. Your sins are gone!

They have been put away. It is possible to **live** with an **absolutely— perfect—conscience.** Did you know the Bible teaches that? You can live with a **perfect conscience.** I'm using Bible language. And we'll see how it's possible to be **absolutely free. <u>Absolutely free!</u> <u>GLORIOUSLY</u> free! The <u>glorious</u> liberty of the children of God** because the Spirit of life has—set—me—free. Not a false freedom, but a **true** freedom.

2 Peter says, *"They promise freedom, but they themselves are **slaves** of corruption; for whatever overcomes a man, to that he is enslaved."* [18] And so we're talking about a freedom, that is a freedom **indeed.** I would say now that the **leading practical point** to Romans 6 through 8, is that **we** might come into freedom. That we might be **set free.** That's what this is all about. Galatians 5:13 says, *"You have been **called—to liberty."*** [19] That's what you have been **called to.** And you remember what the Lord Jesus said, *"if the Son sets you free"*—you will be—**really—free.** *"You will be—free—indeed."* [20]

I tell you it's a wonderful thing **not** to have a spirit of fear. No fear whatever. "Brother Don, aren't you afraid of getting punished by God?" **No! Not at all!** "Oh now, wait a minute! That's going to make you kind of 'gracey,' won't it? Aren't you going to start living kind of loose?" **<u>ABSOLUTELY NOT!</u> Because God by the Spirit has a <u>hold</u> of my heart. And that's the <u>only</u> message that can bring you into true authentic holiness. That's the <u>ONLY</u> message that will do it. It's <u>grace</u> that teaches you to deny ungodliness. Grace sets your heart sufficiently free from yourself that you can begin to love authentically. Now,** you can begin to love God and others whereas before you are **so bound up** in your condemnation.

Let me tell you something. You find anybody who's living in <u>sin,</u> and I'll tell you somebody who's <u>not</u> living in <u>grace</u>. If you live in the grace of <u>God</u>, you're going to come into this marvelous freedom that sets you free from your <u>sins</u> and sets you free from <u>yourself</u>. And it

begins by knowing—that you—do—not—have a spirit of slavery that makes you fall back into fear.

The thing of it is, you see, you can't do anything **wrong.** You can't be **punished.** That's such a glorious, glorious doctrine and it's so free that some people can't believe it. I've had people tell me, "You know I'm just afraid to believe the grace of God." *(Don starts speaking very passionately)* We're talking about the being of God. Unto Him be the glory in the church! Oh, how He wants to reveal what He is to you!

I implore you to let the Holy Spirit bring the **fullness** of His ministry of liberation to you, the **glorious liberty** of the children of God. *"You have **not** received a **spirit of slavery** to fall back into fear."* *(Don starts speaking very gently)* *"You have received the Spirit of sonship that makes you say Father"*—my Father—*"Abba! Father!"* [21] That's the Spirit that rings in our hearts this morning. Glorious freedom, wonderful freedom, through Jesus Christ our Lord.

(Don continues speaking gently) You know it's nice to be at home. It's nice to be comfortable. It's nice to take your shoes off and know that you're in your Father's family. You belong to Him. And to relax. To be at peace. Is that possible? That's exactly why Jesus Christ came. That's what the Holy Spirit does for us. To walk in the Spirit is—life—and—peace—in Jesus Christ our Lord. I commend it to you. It makes me love Him. The Emancipating Ministry of the Holy Spirit. That's what we have through Jesus Christ our Lord.

I wouldn't live another second of my life without the **true freedom** that can come to you through Jesus Christ. This is **available** to you. It could only happen at the level of your spirit. God can give you a spirit of **adoption** that lets you **know—you—are—as—He is—in—this— world.** I'm as Jesus Christ is right now. **I'm never going to be any more righteous than I am right now.** *(Don starts speaking very passionately)* Death is not going to make me righteous. It's the **blood** of Jesus that makes me righteous, and I have that right **now**. That's this glorious gospel of His marvelous grace. **As He is, so are we—in—this—world.** Perfect love casts out **all** fear. "Do you have one speck of fear?" **Not one speck!** I **know** whom I have believeth. I have no fear of punishment. **No** condemnation.

I don't know where the level of your spirit is, but I urge you in Jesus' name to receive that message, and to let the Holy Spirit of God **set—your—spirit free.** Don't go one more **second** without that **glorious freedom,** that **glorious liberty** of the children of God. **Don't** fall back into a **slave spirit** that makes you fear, but in Jesus' name receive that message this morning.

SERMON 20 ENDNOTES:

None.

SERMON 20 SCRIPTURE REFERENCES:

[1] Ephesians 1:3-6 (RSV)

> *3 Blessed be the God and Father of our Lord Jesus Christ, who has blessed us in Christ with every spiritual blessing in the heavenly places, 4 even as he chose us in him before the foundation of the world, that we should be holy and blameless before him. 5 He destined us in love to be his sons through Jesus Christ, according to the purpose of his will, 6 to the praise of his glorious grace which he freely bestowed on us in the Beloved.*

[2] Ephesians 3:21 (KJV)

> *Unto him be glory in the church by Christ Jesus throughout all ages, world without end. Amen.*

[3] Ephesians 1:6-8 (RSV)

> *6 to the praise of his glorious grace which he freely bestowed on us in the Beloved. 7 In him we have redemption through his blood, the*

forgiveness of our trespasses, according to the riches of his grace 8 which he lavished upon us.

[4] Ephesians 2:7-9 (RSV)

7 that in the coming ages he might show the immeasurable riches of his grace in kindness toward us in Christ Jesus. 8 For by grace you have been saved through faith; and this is not your own doing, it is the gift of God— 9 not because of works, lest any man should boast.

[5] Ephesians 2:5 (RSV)

even when we were dead through our trespasses, made us alive together with Christ (by grace you have been saved),

[6] Romans 8:2 (RSV)

For the law of the Spirit of life in Christ Jesus has set me free from the law of sin and death.

[7] Romans 8:12-14 (RSV)

12 So then, brethren, we are debtors, not to the flesh, to live according to the flesh— 13 for if you live according to the flesh you will die, but if by the Spirit you put to death the deeds of the body you will live. 14 For all who are led by the Spirit of God are sons of God.

[8] Romans 8:15-21 (RSV)

15 For you did not receive the spirit of slavery to fall back into fear, but you have received the spirit of sonship. When we cry, "Abba! Father!" 16 it is the Spirit himself bearing witness with our spirit that we are children of God, 17 and if children, then heirs, heirs of God and fellow heirs with Christ, provided we suffer with him in order that we may also be glorified with him. 18 I consider that the sufferings of this present time are not worth comparing with the glory that is to be revealed to us. 19 For the creation waits with eager longing for the revealing of the sons of God; 20 for the creation was subjected to futility, not of its own will but by the will of him who subjected it in hope; 21 because the creation itself will be set free from its bondage to decay and obtain the glorious liberty of the children of God.

[9] Romans 8:18 (RSV)

I consider that the sufferings of this present time are not worth comparing with the glory that is to be revealed to us.

[10] Romans 8:37 (RSV)

No, in all these things we are more than conquerors through him who loved us.

[11] Romans 8:15 (RSV)

For you did not receive the spirit of slavery to fall back into fear, but you have received the spirit of sonship. When we cry, "Abba! Father!"

[12] 1 John 4:16-18 (RSV)

16 So we know and believe the love God has for us. God is love, and he who abides in love abides in God, and God abides in him. 17 In this is love perfected with us, that we may have confidence for the day of judgment, because as he is so are we in this world. 18 There is no fear in love, but perfect love casts out fear. For fear has to do with punishment, and he who fears is not perfected in love.

[13] Romans 8:1 (RSV)

There is therefore now no condemnation for those who are in Christ Jesus.

[14] 2 Corinthians 3:4 (RSV)

Such is the confidence that we have through Christ toward God.

[15] 2 Corinthians 3:5-6 (RSV)

5 Not that we are competent of ourselves to claim anything as coming from us; our competence is from God, 6 who has made us competent to be ministers of a new covenant, not in a written code but in the Spirit; for the written code kills, but the Spirit gives life.

[16] 2 Corinthians 3:7-11 (RSV)

7 Now if the dispensation of death, carved in letters on stone, came with such splendor that the Israelites could not look at Moses' face because of its brightness, fading as this was, 8 will not the dispensation of the Spirit be attended with greater splendor? 9 For if there was splendor in the dispensation of condemnation, the dispensation of righteousness must far exceed it in splendor. 10 Indeed, in this case, what once had splendor has come to have no splendor at all, because of the splendor that surpasses it. 11 For if what faded away came with splendor, what is permanent must have much more splendor.

[17] 2 Corinthians 3:12-18 (RSV)

12 Since we have such a hope, we are very bold, 13 not like Moses, who put a veil over his face so that the Israelites might not see the end of the fading splendor. 14 But their minds were hardened; for to this day, when they read the old covenant, that same veil remains unlifted, because only through Christ is it taken away. 15 Yes, to this day whenever Moses is read a veil lies over their minds; 16 but when a man turns to the Lord the veil is removed. 17 Now the Lord is the Spirit, and where the Spirit of the Lord is, there is freedom. 18 And we all, with unveiled face, beholding the glory of the Lord, are being changed into his likeness from one degree of glory to another; for this comes from the Lord who is the Spirit.

[18] 2 Peter 2:19 (RSV)

They promise them freedom, but they themselves are slaves of corruption; for whatever overcomes a man, to that he is enslaved.

[19] Galatians 5:13 (KJV)

For, brethren, ye have been called unto liberty; only use not liberty for an occasion to the flesh, but by love serve one another.

[20] John 8:36 (RSV)

So if the Son makes you free, you will be free indeed.

[21] Romans 8:15 (RSV)

For you did not receive the spirit of slavery to fall back into fear, but you have received the spirit of sonship. When we cry, "Abba! Father!"

SERMON 21

ESTABLISHING IDENTITY

"I belong to the King. I have that same Spirit that indwelt Jesus in my spirit. This is a great and awesome truth. We have received—the Spirit—of sonship!"

I invite your attention once again to Romans chapter 8. We are sharing together from one of the most profound parts of the Bible and that's Paul's comments in Romans chapters 6, 7 and 8, as he discourses on the meaning of being **under** grace. The main theological truth are the words, *"you are __not under law__, but you are **under grace.**"* [1] Now, he explains that we are not only **under** grace, but we have a **super abundance** of grace. It is the **abundance** of grace. He says that **grace might __reign__.** And the purpose of this is that we might enter into **life. We reign unto life.**

We've reached chapter 8, verse 15, this morning and I'd like to share two verses please, Romans 8, verses 15 and 16. *"You did not receive the spirit of slavery to fall back into **fear**, but you have **received** the **spirit of sonship.**"* I want you to underscore that phrase—The spirit of **adoption** or the **spirit of sonship.** *"Now, when we cry, 'Abba! Father!' it is the **Spirit** himself"*—notice that—*"**the Spirit himself** bearing witness with **our spirit** that we are **children of God.**"* [2]

We've indicated that the Holy Spirit has a threefold ministry in Romans chapter 8. And this, in turn, answers to three of our basic needs. Man needs, first of all, **salvation.** He needs to be **saved.** And by that we mean he **needs to be delivered.** He needs to be **set free.** He needs to be **emancipated.** There's something **wrong** with all of us. And the chief culprit is called **the flesh.** That's that ethical **drag** in our nature. That thing at **work** in our **being** that keeps us out of **life** and away from **freedom.**

 "For the law of the Spirit of life in Christ Jesus has set me free from the law of sin and death." - Romans 8:2 RSV

The first work of the Holy Spirit **is to—set—us—free!** That's salvation. Romans chapter 8, verse 2 says, *"The law of the Spirit of life in Christ has set me free."* [3] And you'll notice our text says, ***You did not receive the spirit of slavery.*** You have not received the spirit of **bondage;** rather, *"You have received **a spirit of sonship."** * [2] —as though the two were in comparison and contrast. So, that leads us to the **great understanding** of the emancipating ministry of the Holy Spirit. That's all through this great chapter as we learn to **walk in the Spirit.**

Now I think, after all these sessions together, these sermons, we know that all of us have a nature which is unredeemable. It's unregenerate—cannot be changed—your flesh—you can only crucify it and **not walk in it.** And we've learned to use the language of wretchedness—*"O wretched man that I am!"* [4] That brings us to an **end** of ourselves, and then opens the door for us to **walk** in the Spirit—that supernatural life in the freedom of the Spirit of God. **That's the work of the Holy Spirit,** however. **He** helps you to come to an end of yourself, and He helps you to **walk** in the Spirit.

Secondly, we all need **enlightenment.** We need **self-understanding.** We need **self-identity.** And that's the **second great work** of the Holy Spirit, is to **establish** our **identity** or to **enlighten** us. We need to **know**

who we are. We're the kind of beings that we cannot survive without **meaning.** Being rational creatures that we are, we must have **self-understanding.** A person told me on the front steps of the church the other day says, "You know, it's just a **good thing** to know who you are." And if you were to ask some of us, I guess, who we were, we'd have to say my name is Legion. We don't know who we are. But how **significant** when you have that **deep inner identity**—that **self-awareness**—that **self-consciousness** of who you are. It's very, very, important. You know the world basically is heavy with religion. You travel around the world, and you'll **soon** find that the world is **God intoxicated.** But for many people it doesn't do much by way of an emancipation or **enlightenment.** It's almost a **burden.** You almost wish you could **free them** from their religion.

Now what's the big difference between the teachings of the Lord Jesus Christ, the gospel, Christianity, and the world's religions? By the way, what's the big difference between Christianity and Judaism? **One** primary difference. **Not so much the existence of <u>God</u>**—The fact that **God <u>is</u>.** The **crucial difference** is that <u>God</u> **is our <u>Father</u>! It's a spirit of <u>adoption</u>. It's a spirit of <u>sonship</u>. There's a <u>world</u> of difference— darkness and light between God, and God as Father. And the Lord Jesus Christ <u>came</u> to teach us primarily that God is our <u>Father</u>, and to give us an accompanying Spirit that identifies with that truth.** And that's what we're reading about this morning. **That's the deepest existential need of the human heart is to know that God <u>is</u>, and that God is my <u>Father</u>. I tell you when that's <u>resolved</u>, the pieces fall into place into the human mind and spirit. You can sort it out vocationally and professionally, educationally and socially. But unless—you've— got—that—deep—fundamental—spiritual—thing—straightened— out, you're in confusion. You're always wondering who you are and** where you're going. Thank God, Jesus Christ by the Holy Spirit can give us an identification!

The Lord Jesus means everything to us. For most people, we start by knowing Jesus as our Savior. What Jesus Christ has done **for me**— Christ **for me**—Christ **instead** of me—what Jesus did on the cross. That's a very, very, deep truth.

It's another thing to **know** that I'm **identified with** Jesus—Jesus **with** me. This Doctrine of Identification where Jesus becomes my ethical model—I become **like** Jesus. **But it's still a deeper <u>thing</u> when you understand the work that Jesus does <u>in</u> you. When Jesus <u>actually gives you</u> His own self-consciousness. When that same Spirit that indwelt the Lord Jesus Christ comes in you and causes you to say, "Abba! Father!"** Now that means, in one sense, that you're willing to lose your search for identity and take on the identity that Jesus Christ gives us. That <u>His</u> self-consciousness becomes <u>your</u> self-consciousness—for me to live is Christ! You don't know how to distinguish yourself from that of Jesus, because you've taken on His identity!

I'd like to remind you that that was <u>won</u>! Jesus' self-identity was <u>won</u> at great expense, temptation, and suffering. From the beginning of His ministry to the end, Jesus' self-identity was at stake. The devil began by saying, "_If you're the son of God, perform all these miracles._" And on the cross, they said, "_If you're the son of God._" It was a question about His identity. Who was He? And all the way through the gospels you'll find that cropping up, particularly in John's gospel.

John's gospel is a great **key** for understanding the spirit of adoption and the identity of the Lord Jesus. Because if it's the **Spirit** of that <u>**Son**</u> that comes in our hearts, crying, Abba! Father! We need to see how He **won** the self-identity and His own self-understanding.

I would say that the crux of the matter came at the Feast of the Tabernacles recorded in John's gospel, chapters 7 through 10. There are four great chapters dealing with this. And the burning issue was who **was** Jesus—who was He? All kinds of controversy broke out. Some said one thing and some another. Some said, "He's a good man." Others said, "He's a blasphemer. He's a Samaritan. He's illegitimate." All kinds of questions about Him. Even His own **family** call in to question His **identity.** But Jesus goes up in the middle of the Feast of Tabernacles, which would have been in October just about six months before His **final** arrival in Jerusalem, for that fatal Passover. And here the question breaks out, "Who is He?" And Jesus begins to explain to them in John chapter 8, verse 12, and here's what He said. Jesus spoke to them and said, *"I am the light of the world, he who follows me will <u>not</u> walk in darkness, but will have the <u>light of life</u>."* [5] Now, **I like that!** Just not the light of some distant world. You'll have the **light of life! You'll know who you are! You'll know what life is all about! And then He begins to establish His own identity. The Pharisee said to Him,** *"You're bearing witness to yourself and it's not true."* [5]

"Again Jesus spoke to them, saying, 'I am the light of the world; he who follows me will not walk in darkness, but will have the light of life.'" - John 8:12 RSV

You see the crucial thing, in any kind of a **witness,** is their rationality and whether or not they're going to bear witness to **themselves.** You take somebody and put them on the stand down here, you must know how **credible** their witness is. You could have somebody that gets on the stand and tell you that they're Napoleon. Well, that obviously wouldn't hold up. You would not trust their **identity.**

Only to the extent that they are **reputable,** that they are **rational,** are **you** going to believe their testimony. And so, *"Jesus says, 'Even if I do bear witness to myself, my testimony is true,' "*—because **I know who I am**—*" 'I know where I've <u>come from</u> and I know <u>where I'm going.' "* **I know what it's all about and that <u>establishes</u> my <u>testimony</u>. I—have a—self—understanding. I know the truth.** Now, He says, *" 'You judge according to the flesh, I judge no one.* **But even if I do judge,'** *"*—I want you to know that—*" 'my judgment is true, because it is not **I alone that judge** but **I and he who sent me.** Now, in your law it is written that the testimony of two men is true.' "* In other words, it must be corroborated or substantiated by two. *" 'I bear witness to myself' "*—because I'm a reputable witness. I know my identity—*" 'but also the **Father** who sent me he **bears witness to me.'" [6]* And so, here's this **witness bearing of God** to the person of the Lord Jesus Christ, and **subsequently, His** witness to us, as to our own self-identity.

At this Feast of Tabernacles, the Lord Jesus did one of His most notable miracles. You'll find it in John's gospel, chapter 9, where it has to do with the healing of the **blind** man. Now this blind man needed his **physical** sight, but he's a **living** illustrated sermon because Jesus was saying He was the light of life and these people at Jerusalem were **rejecting** His testimony. And they said, **"We can see. We don't need anybody to teach us anything."**

And so, the Lord Jesus took the blind man. You remember the story? I must tell it to you because it's associated with the most meaningful experience that I had on this trip this time. *(Don is referring to a trip to Israel)* This blind man came to Jesus, and Jesus did a very odd thing by our terms. Jesus simply took some of His own **saliva.** Now, in ancient times one's saliva was identified very closely with his own being or his spirit. So, to use His **saliva** meant His **own spirit,** His own **life.** He took some clay and made a little kind of an anointed-like salve. With that clay

He spread it on the **blind man's eyes.** I think meaning, **symbolically,** that this is **my** life in **human form,** the life of **God** identified with **clay.** That's meaningful to me. It's a nice devotional thought.

And then the Bible says, *"He anointed,"* literally—puts it on his eyes—the blind man's eyes. And He said, *"Go, wash in the pool of Siloam."* [7] Now, to understand this, which John says by the way, means **"Sent,"** He interprets it in John's gospel; **the word** *Siloam* [A] **means "Sent."**

Now, this goes back to an important prophecy in Isaiah. No doubt, **in connection with** the construction of the pool of Siloam. Back in the year 701 BC, the **Syrians** were laying **siege** to the city of Jerusalem. The king of Judah at that time was **Hezekiah,** and he **ordered** the famous **Hezekiah's Tunnel to be constructed.** [8] What this was, was the waters of the Gihon, [B] the most important source of water for the city of Jerusalem, is at the **nether** or the **lower foot** of Mount Zion. Now, the **water supply** was **vulnerable,** you see, to the attacking forces because it was outside the city gates. So, Hezekiah had two squads of men, to burrow quickly, an eighteen-hundred-foot tunnel, snaking its way down through the mountain and **bringing the water** out at another place at the pool of **Siloam.**

Now the Hebrew word Shiloach [C] [shee-lo'-akh] means "that which is **sent.**" And Isaiah says, *"they have refused the waters of Shiloach that are sent softly"* [9] —they go **softly** from God because the people were **in rebellion.** And in their **self-contained identity and autonomy, they were refusing these waters that became an illustrated sermon. At the feast of Tabernacles, it broke out! Who was Jesus? He says, "I'm sent from God!"** [10] **I am Shiloach! And so,** He says I want the **blind man** to go wash in the pool of Siloam.

That was a great experience for me. I had not been able to do this before. *(Don begins to describe, in a heartfelt manner, an experience he had during a trip to Israel)* So, one morning, Sandy, and Sam, and John

Wayne *(Three church members from Christian Assembly)* and I went down to the pool of Siloam. And Sam, and John and I decided to go through it. It was a tremendous experience. You can wade through that pool at the Gihon. You start down this path, you take a candle along, and you can make your way through Hezekiah's ancient tunnel. And it **was** just very delightful. Those waters come along cool, and sweet, and soft. It's a beautiful, beautiful experience. And when we got out, at the pool of Siloam, I just couldn't help but kneeling down right in those waters. And I got down on my knees, and I just put my face in that water, not believing in magic believe you me, but just with this thought, and I said, "Lord Jesus, open my eyes. Above all else help me to **see,** Lord. I want understanding." And I tell you just to stand in that pool of Siloam and to have a feeling that you know God is your Father, that your eyes have been opened, and you have a **self-understanding** that Jesus' self-consciousness is actually coming to you. **What a wonderful thing that is!**

I say, God open our eyes. More than **anything else man needs self-understanding. Man needs a self-consciousness. You need a <u>witness</u> of the <u>Spirit</u> that you are children of God. You need to <u>establish</u> your <u>identity</u>! How wonderful that Jesus Christ can actually come and do that <u>for you</u>. Jesus not only died <u>for</u> you, you're not only identified with Him as an ethical model, it's possible for Jesus to give you—His—own—self—identification. The self-consciousness of Jesus, as Son of Man, can be yours! The same <u>identical Spirit</u> that Jesus has, can be your Spirit as well.**

Paul makes this very clear in his great exposition of adoption. In Galatians, Paul describes it this way in Galatians chapter 4. He says, *"I mean that the **heir,** as long as he is a **child,** is no better than a **slave,** although he is the owner of all the estate; he is under **guardians** and **trustees** until the date set by the father."* He's under the **law.** *"So with* us; when we were **children,** we were, so to speak, just like **slaves** to the **elemental** spirits of the universe." Some people have an elemental spirit they're living out. They never come into a spirit of **adoption,** and a spirit of **sonship.** *"But when the time had fully come, God sent forth his Son."* Like those **waters** sent forth from the Gihon. He's the one **sent** forth. He was—*"**born** of woman, he was **born** under the law"*—and he kept the law and fulfilled the law—*"**to redeem those who are** <u>under</u> **the law, so that we might receive**—<u>adoption</u>—**as**—<u>sons</u>. **And** <u>because</u> **you are** <u>sons</u>, <u>God</u> **has sent the Spirit of** <u>his Son</u> **into your** <u>hearts</u>, **crying, 'Abba!** **Father!'** **So through God, you are no longer a slave but a** <u>son</u>, **and if you are a** <u>son</u>—**you**—**are**—**an**—**heir."** [11]

It's that same <u>Spirit</u> that indwelt the Spirit of the Lord Jesus. I believe that the Holy Spirit took on a <u>human</u> experience in the incarnation. The very <u>life</u> of <u>God</u> came into <u>Jesus</u> as Son of Man and <u>Jesus</u> <u>won</u> that <u>self-identity</u> for us. <u>His</u> self-consciousness can become <u>my</u> self-consciousness because it's the <u>same Spirit</u> that we have <u>together</u>. It's the Spirit of the <u>Son</u> in me crying, "<u>Abba</u>! <u>Father</u>!" God is my <u>Father</u> and I <u>know that</u> through Jesus Christ our Lord. What a great, wonderful, precious truth this is, to know who you are through Jesus Christ our Lord.

(Don begins speaking softly and tenderly) Oh, it's **wonderful** to know God. What a **joy** it is. The Spirit bearing witness with your spirit that you're children of **God.** That's the **deepest miracle** I know. That's the **most important truth** that can come to **you.** It seems so **natural** as you hear it through preaching or through the truth. **But I tell you what a wonderful, wonderful thing to know.** You don't have to look for some great ordinary experience. Because all you've got to do is submit your heart to Jesus Christ and be a blind man. Because if any man **wills** to do His will, he'll know the **doctrine,** whether it be of God or not. **The Spirit bears witness by that witness.** And if you have that **witness**—if

you have that witness—that **God** is your **Father,** I tell you, you have the greatest miracle that can possibly happen to the human heart, that you **belong** to God through Jesus Christ our Lord. It's **wonderful** that the Holy Spirit bears witness to us. That **same** identical Spirit that indwelt the Lord Jesus.

Are you willing for **His** self-consciousness to be **yours?** Now that means that you've got to totally **abandon** the **search** for your own **life** and **take on His.** This is a **deeper** consecration than anything I know. **There are many people who want Jesus as Savior. Many who are willing to be like Him just to come out good on the consequences of life. Are you <u>willing</u> for Jesus Christ to assume your self-identity?** Are you **willing** to take on His self-consciousness? So much that you can say, I don't know whether I live anymore or not. *"For me—to live—is—Christ! And the life which I now live in the flesh, I live by the faith of the Son of God who loved me and gave himself for me."* [12]

Well, all you blind people, would you like to come to the pool of Siloam? To the **Sent** One? That was the **main thing,** that the blind man **came** to the Lord Jesus. And have your eyes opened? You're going need an external life. You're going to need some divine, pardon me, **"saliva."** You're going to need that **anointed.** You're going to need it rubbed on your eyes so that you have a **self-awareness** and an **identity** by the Holy Spirit of God. That's what the Holy Spirit can do and that's what He **does** in the human heart. He lets us know who we are.

Who are you? Well, I'm a child of God. I belong to the King. I have that **same** Spirit that indwelt Jesus in my spirit. This is a great and awesome truth. We have **received—the Spirit**—of **sonship.**

Let's pray together, shall we . . .

We thank you, oh Lord, that we have received the **light** of life. Lord, we're not always certain how this is come about, but thank God, that it has been worked in us by the Holy Spirit. That there's that "set in rock" consciousness that God is our **Father,** and we **belong** to **Him.** Lord, what a tragedy it is, that some stand to miss the light of life, and they say, in effect, "We see." Therefore, **their sin remains.** Lord, we pray that we'll be like this blind man, even like his parents. We may not have **all** the answers but this one thing we know, for as we were blind, <u>**now we see.**</u> We **know** that we belong to **God,** and we know that God is like a Father because that Spirit within us cries, "Abba! Father!" That intimate, tender term of the family. That **same word** used by our Lord Jesus Christ, when He lifted up His Spirit and said, "God." He said, "Abba!" He said, "Father!" Thank you, Lord Jesus, that you've made the **big distinction.** You not only taught us that there was **a God,** but you taught us that **God is Father.** And you have worked that Spirit in our hearts this morning. We pray Lord, that you're going to send **us** to the pool of Siloam afresh. **That we're going to come back seeing!** Oh, open our understanding Lord! Enlighten our hearts and minds we pray. Give us eyes that can see. We're so grateful Lord, for what you can do. We're so grateful. And we look to you this morning for enablement and for help.

SERMON 21 ENDNOTES:

A   *Siloam,* a pool of Jerusalem, Strong's Greek Dictionary #4611. Of Hebrew origin #7975 *Shiloach.*

B   *Gihon,* proper name of stream shortened from *Giychown,* Strong's Hebrew Dictionary #1521. Also from John Wesley's Notes on the Bible for 2 Chronicles 32:30: Stopped, Isa 7:3, and the lower which was brought into another, called the lower pool, Isa 22:9. The former he diverted and brought by pipes into Jerusalem, which was a work of great art and labour.

C   *Shiloach,* proper name meaning: sent, a fountain just southeast of Jerusalem, Strong's Hebrew Dictionary #7975. Also, *apostello,* meaning: (by implication from John 9:7 gospel) to send out, Strong's Greek Dictionary #649.

SERMON 21 SCRIPTURE REFERENCES:

[1] Romans 6:14 (RSV)

For sin will have no dominion over you, since you are not under law but under grace.

[2] Romans 8:15-16 (RSV)

15 For you did not receive the spirit of slavery to fall back into fear, but you have received the spirit of sonship. When we cry, "Abba! Father!" 16 it is the Spirit himself bearing witness with our spirit that we are children of God,

[3] Romans 8:2 (RSV)

For the law of the Spirit of life in Christ Jesus has set me free from the law of sin and death.

[4] Romans 7:24 (KJV)

O wretched man that I am! who shall deliver me from the body of this death?

[5] John 8:12-13 (RSV)

12 Again Jesus spoke to them, saying, "I am the light of the world; he who follows me will not walk in darkness, but will have the light of life." 13 The Pharisees then said to him, "You are bearing witness to yourself; your testimony is not true."

[6] John 8:14-18 (RSV)

14 Jesus answered, "Even if I do bear witness to myself, my testimony is true, for I know whence I have come and whither I am going, but you do not know whence I come or whither I am going. 15 You judge according to the flesh, I judge no one. 16 Yet even if I do judge, my judgment is true, for it is not I alone that judge, but I and he who sent me. 17 In your law it is written that the testimony of two men is true; 18 I bear witness to myself, and the Father who sent me bears witness to me."

7 John 9:6-7 (RSV)

6 As he said this, he spat on the ground and made clay of the spittle and anointed the man's eyes with the clay, 7 saying to him, "Go, wash in the pool of Silo'am" (which means Sent). So he went and washed and came back seeing.

8 2 Chronicles 32:30 (ASV)

This same Hezekiah also stopped the upper spring of the waters of Gihon, and brought them straight down on the west side of the city of David. And Hezekiah prospered in all his works.

9 Isaiah 8:6 (ASV)

Forasmuch as this people have refused the waters of Shiloah that go softly, and rejoice in Rezin and Remaliah's son;

10 John 9:4 (KJV)

I must work the works of him that sent me, while it is day: the night cometh, when no man can work.

11 Galatians 4:1-7 (RSV)

1 I mean that the heir, as long as he is a child, is no better than a slave, though he is the owner of all the estate; 2 but he is under guardians and trustees until the date set by the father. 3 So with us; when we were children, we were slaves to the elemental spirits of the universe. 4 But when the time had fully come, God sent forth his Son, born of woman, born under the law, 5 to redeem those who were under the law, so that we might receive adoption as sons. 6 And because you are sons, God has sent the Spirit of his Son into our hearts, crying, "Abba! Father!" 7 So through God you are no longer a slave but a son, and if a son then an heir.

[12] Galatians 2:20 (KJV)

I am crucified with Christ: nevertheless I live; yet not I, but Christ liveth in me: and the life which I now live in the flesh I live by the faith of the Son of God, who loved me, and gave himself for me.

SERMON 22

THE PATH OF GLORY

"The way of the cross leads home. Are you willing to put your hands in the hands of the Spirit and say, 'Lord, I really want to be your son. I want that witness of the Spirit and I want the inheritance!'"

In one way I feel a great inadequacy to preach this sermon. It's always helpful if you can be more than just the postman delivering a message. It's **wonderful** if preaching can be truth through personality. Unfortunately, that's not always the case. And certainly, I feel woefully inadequate, as we talk about this rather sober and important profound passage. We're going to concentrate on Romans chapter 8, verse 17, [1] but I really invite your attention to the **rest** of this chapter.

Now, we've been doing a series of preaching from Romans chapters 6, 7 **and** 8, and now we have reached **chapter 8,** and we have underscored the **threefold** ministry of the Holy Spirit. The Holy Spirit has a Ministry of **Emancipation. He sets—us—free!** The Holy Spirit has a Ministry of **Enlightenment.** He establishes our identity by giving us a **spirit of sonship** and lets us know our relationship to **God.** And **thirdly,** the Holy Spirit has a Ministry of **Enablement,** as He **empowers** the **believer to face the realities of life.** He **helps us** in our infirmities or our weakness.

The great **key** to Romans chapters 6, 7 and 8 is what it means to be **"under grace."** That's the **main** theological truth—the **reign of grace**—the abundance of grace. The consequences of that, are that we might be super conquerors—<u>more</u> than conquerors—through Him that **loved us.**

But one of the **big problems,** that comes to every **believer, is a stern reality** that he bumps into. How can God be loving? How can you be certain of His **grace** and face such difficult trials? When you live amidst **death** and when you are facing **suffering** and feeling **pain,** how can you be assured of the love of God? And how can you **know** that God's grace is adequate **for you?** Can you be a super conqueror and **still live** in the reality that we are experiencing with your **eyes wide open?** Do difficult things happen to us? **Indeed, they do!** Is it **possible** amidst a **stern** reality to <u>still</u> be **more than a conqueror? Is—grace—adequate?** Will His grace be sufficient to make you <u>more</u> than a conqueror?

Well, **this chapter** attempts to discuss that issue. And so, we are rather **rudely** introduced to this and yet not **rudely** because Paul is very **tactful** as he closes off this first section of Romans chapter 8, by talking about the great benefits of our freedom, and our deliverance, and the witness of the Spirit.

And here's the way he puts it as we start reading with verse 15. Romans 8:15, *"You did <u>not</u> receive the spirit of <u>slavery</u> to fall back into fear,"*—glorious liberty emancipation—*"you have received the spirit of <u>sonship</u>. When we cry, "Abba! Father! It's the Spirit himself bearing witness with our spirit that we are children of God, <u>and</u> if we are children, then we are heirs."* Oh, what a glorious inheritance! What a <u>marvelous</u> tribute to grace! We are—*"<u>heirs</u> of God, fellow heirs with Christ,"*—**but**—now comes the interjection—now comes the introduction to the rest of this chapter—*"<u>provided</u> we <u>suffer</u> with him in order that we may also be <u>glorified</u> with him."* [2] Suffering is the pathway to glory. The Apostle is telling us that unless we, as it's translated, *"suffer with him"* we're not going to enter into **life,** and we're not going to go that royal pathway to **glory.** So **suffering** is God's way to bring us into life. And here's the acid test. **Will grace be sufficient to permit us to face all the realities of life as we have them?**

I think it's rather important for us to **know** that one cannot **really and truly** enter into life unless he experiences life in all of its depth. And that includes some **pain,** some **suffering,** and **some death.** Now, at first bloom, we would like to avoid that. Everything within us, within our carnal mind, tells us to avoid **suffering—not to suffer.** But according to **this** chapter and according to the teachings of the **scriptures,** it's **the way of a cross that leads <u>home</u>.** The cross, a pathway to suffering, that leads us to resurrection.

Elsewhere, the Apostle says in Romans, chapter 5, verse 3, he says, we **know**—*"That, we can rejoice in our <u>suffering</u>,"* Why? Because— *"suffering—produces—<u>endurance</u>, and endurance—produces—character."* [3] You know, people really aren't worth much until they've actually been **broken** and entered into all of the depths of the sufferings of life, anyway.

I was greatly impressed by the works of Michelangelo on this trip to Rome, and I was interested to see the various **levels** of his art as he grew in his experience. You almost can't believe that **Moses,** the **Pieta,** and the **Sistine Chapel. Those** were his **most experienced mature work.** And I understand that after Michelangelo, according to a tradition, had finished the statue of Moses, he said to the statue, "Why don't you speak?"— because it's so lifelike. And the little scratch on the knee is supposed to be where he **tapped** it and wanted the statue to speak. By comparison, all those statues alongside of his students, they don't look lifelike, they don't have much **life** in them. They look chalky and imitation. But if you're going to get <u>life</u>, it involves some **experience** and it involves some suffering and some maturity.

"For those whom he foreknew he also predestined to be conformed to the image of his Son, in order that he might be the first-born among many brethren." - Romans 8:29 RSV

The Apostle, in the rest of this chapter, actually explains to us what the purpose of life is. He describes it this way, in verse 28, *"We know that in everything God works for **good** with those who **love** him, who are called according to his purpose. Those whom he foreknew he also predestined,"*—now notice—*"**predestined to be conformed—to the image—of—his Son.**"* [4] Now that's the heart of predestination—not so much that **God** predestined some against the other—the elect versus the non-elect—the Bible doesn't go into the subject of the non-elect. **Predestination is your destiny! You were predestined to be conformed to the image of His Son. That's your destiny! Not your image, but His image. And if you're going to take on the family likeness, if you're going to glory in sonship and the witness of the Spirit and this marvelous inheritance, you have to take on the family likeness.**

Now it's very important that we become like the Father. That we are people after God's own heart because we are created in **His** image and likeness. And **I believe** that authentic **life—real life**—only comes as we take on the way of the cross. We're made for it. It's written in our destiny.

The cross is not something that was just lifted up on the hill of Calvary two thousand years ago. **The cross is the divine philosophy. It's the divine heart. It's the way of a cross.** And the cross, by the way, is primarily—sacrificial—self-giving, as you have learned basically to come out of yourself, your own **selfish fleshly life,** and into the life of the Spirit. That means, by the way, sometimes a negation of even what we call our **natural life.**

You know, I see it particular in Bible School, when we have some very, very, promising young pastors. And I see they do very well. They preach well, but I think to myself, they're going to be **much better** after they have suffered. After they have entered into a little bit of **life** and see where it really is. You know, sometimes we don't always make that distinction. We go about in our natural energies and sometimes, by the way, that can even become religious. Did you know it's possible just to take on religion, only to minister to your self-life and to further your own ego. You do it to salve your conscience a little. We're talking about a deep **involvement** in the **life of God. The way of the <u>cross</u>.** This is not a **profession.** It's not something that you can be assigned to in an office. It's something that happens **deep down** in your life.

And again, I say I'm reluctant to preach this sermon because who am I to **speak.** I feel so **inadequate** at this point. But I have seen pastors, who will even take a church, and as long as it's going **their** way, as long as something is happening to minister to their ego things are just **fine.** But you let them be out of that realm and all of a sudden, something happens to their spiritual life. I've seen youth pastors who build up a nice little youth group. It's **all** to minister to their ego. I've seen choir directors who only want that choir **their way,** and **not** for the unity of the church. So, I'm talking about people **involved** in the church. It may be a religious **activity** and **not** an involvement at all with the way of the cross. These are **very sober** things we're talking about.

I was impressed by Watchman Nee's book, <u>The Normal Christian Life</u>. Watchman Nee had this to say. I was **greatly** impressed by a comment or two in this book. He's **describing** what it means to **suffer** with Jesus. And he says, <u>"What does this mean? It simply means that I will not take any **action** without relying on **God.** I will find **no** sufficiency in myself. I **will not** take any step just because I have the **power** to do so. Even though I have that inherited power within me, I will not use</u>

it;" This is the kind of **suffering** that we're talking about. "I will put no reliance in **myself.** By taking the fruit, Adam became possessed of an inherent power to act,"—he did, he got knowledge—"but a power which played **right into** Satan's hands." He said, "You should **lose** that power to act when you come to know the Lord. The Lord cuts it off and you find you can no longer act on your own **initiative.** You have to live by the life of **Another.**" A

Now, remember we went so far last week as to talk about taking Jesus' self-consciousness. **He gives** us our inner identity, that Spirit of sonship. We take on the **self**-identity that Jesus established for us, and **now** we're asked to go **His way.** Take up **His life** and that's this life of suffering. "You have to live by the life of another. You have to draw everything from **Him.**" He says, "I think we all know ourselves in measure, but many a time we do not truly **tremble** at ourselves. We may, in a manner of courtesy to God, say: 'If the Lord does not want it, I cannot do it,' but in reality our subconscious thought is that really we can do it quite well ourselves, even if God does not ask us to do it nor empower us for it. Too often we have been caused to act, to **think,** to **decide,** to have power, **apart** from Him. Many of us Christians today are men with **over-developed souls.** We have grown too big in ourselves. We have become '**big souled.**' When we are in that condition, the life of the Son of God is confined and almost crowded out of action." A

And so, here's the kind of **suffering** we're talking about. Now, it's true that the suffering may involve these external things such as tribulation, distress, persecution, famine, nakedness, peril, and sword. That may be a part of the suffering too, **but I'm talking about a suffering that reaches down in your everyday life and means a no to your self-life, a no to your flesh life. That's suffering! When your will wants its own way, when your natural life wants to express itself for the glory of your own ego but you're willing to say no to that by the power of** the cross. That's pain! That's suffering! When you would answer back with harshness and with the critical way—when you would answer back in hostility—rather instead you crucify that! And out comes a gracious word and a comforting word. That's an inner pain to your ego. That's a death to your self-life. And that's the kind of suffering we're talking about. That's the real suffering.

Sometimes it would be a **nice** experience just to go **hungry** or to have some tribulation or distress. It's this **inner pain** of saying **no** to your **delicate little ego.** You know some people are like **living boils. They just walk around so sensitive. Every little thing offends them until the way of the cross comes home to them** and they tap in on sacrificial self-giving and living. That's the way of the cross, and that's what leads us truly home. Now **Jesus** lived that **way of the cross** constantly. So, when Jesus **went** to the cross at the end of His life, it was only the **logical** conclusion of the way He had lived. And **that's** the kind of life that we're to come to. That's the kind of thing that leads us to an authentic life and a true self-fulfillment.

The Apostle Paul elsewhere explains the **essence** of suffering. The **great** book of suffering in the New Testament, by the way, is 2 Corinthians. And in that wonderful passage of 2 Corinthians chapter 4, the Apostle tells us what it means in some of the purposes of suffering. I'd like to share that with you. 2 Corinthians chapter 4, beginning with verse 7, will you notice what he has to say. *"We have this treasure in **earthen vessels.**"* And that means, the kind of people that we **are.** Now why? *"To show that **the transcendent power belongs to God and not to us.**"*[5] **Why is it that sometimes difficult things happen to you, and you get thorns in the flesh? Why is it that life can be so frustrating and difficult? It's because you have** *"this treasure in earthen vessel."* **God does not want this earthen vessel to shine,** *"the treasure in the vessel."* No young man would give a diamond ring to his girl in a diamond studded box. She'd throw the ring away and keep the **box. God wants all the glory! And so sometimes these earthen vessels must be broken.**

Great pressures—great pains—great suffering comes upon us within and without. It's <u>God</u>, wanting to bring us to an end of our self-life. You have this treasure in earthen vessels. **God** does not want to glorify you primarily. He wants to glorify Jesus Christ **in** you and bring out that **Christ-life.** It's **Christ's life** that's meant to be lived in you. Your life is not much. It's a pretty sordid thing to tell you the truth. All your personalities don't sparkle like that. I don't know whether you knew it or not. We'd just as soon that you'd end all that and let Jesus Christ start living **through** you.

So, *"we have this treasure in earthen vessels."*[5] Now—*"we're afflicted in every way,"* Paul said. **But,** notice we're—*"not crushed."* **Now I want you to see this balance.** The Apostle has a **delightful** imagery here. It's probably like a man being **pursued** by a pursuer. *"We're afflicted in every way but we're not crushed."* We're *"perplexed"*—we don't know which way to go—*"but we're not driven to despair."* We are *"persecuted, but we are not forsaken."* We are *"struck down, but not destroyed."* J.B. Phillips translates that and says, 'We're knocked down, but we are **not** knocked out!' *(Don continues reading in RSV)* *"We are always carrying in our body the **death of Jesus,** so that the **life** of Jesus may be made manifest in **our bodies.** For while we live we are **always** being given up to **death** for Jesus' sake, so that the **life** of Jesus may be made manifest in our mortal flesh."*[6]

And so, you see, it's this pathway of **suffering** that leads us to glory. **Friends,** we're not to think it <u>strange.</u> I know every time I am, it's always strange to me again and again. But I think it was Sam Ervin [B] that said, "That we're like lightning bugs, you know our hindsight is better than our foresight." *(Don and congregation chuckle)* We've got lights behind us. But you can see **how** that some of those very, very, difficult experiences—very painful—that brought you to the brink of **death,** as it were, somehow God used that to mellow you and to soften you. And to let the life of the Lord Jesus become real **in** and **through** you.

Now there are two very important things to conclude from this chapter about suffering and I'd like to make them as plain as I can. Number one, **regardless** of the reality that we're in, regardless of **how trying,** regardless of how much suffering, regardless of how much persecution, regardless of what may be taking place, <u>**none of these**</u> **have the** <u>**power**</u> **to disturb your innocency before God. Paul puts that purposely right in this section. Because sometimes we** <u>**despair.**</u> **Your emotional life goes out of** <u>**kilter.**</u> **Your whole life seems like it's a very low point. That in** <u>**no way**</u> **disturbs your spiritual innocence before God.**

As the Apostle says, *"Who can lay anything to the charge against God's elect?"* [7] **You are not to imagine that the suffering and the pain coming to you in any way is disturbing your vindication before God. You still stand acquitted before Him.** <u>**Regardless**</u> **of what you may be experiencing.** <u>**None**</u> **of these powers can disturb your innocency.** That's what that chapter is saying.

And secondly, and here's this beautiful truth, if the **truth** were known, <u>**none**</u> **of those things** are **against** you. **God—is making— them—work—**<u>**for**</u> **you! All of those trials. All of those stresses.** *"All things are working together for* **good** *to them who love God and are the called according to his purpose."* [8] If your heart is yielded to Jesus Christ and if you have said, "Jesus is **my Lord,**" you've gone into **His** hands— there is **nothing** that can work against you. **All** of those things are really working **for** you. They're going to **redound** to your being conformed to the image of the Lord Jesus Christ. And so, you ought not think it strange, concerning the fiery trials that come to test you. Rather, you should **welcome** them as friends.

I don't imagine that Joseph was **very happy** when his brothers threw him down into that **pit.** But later, he learned some **great** lessons, and he says, *"You meant it to me for **evil**. **God** meant it to me for **good**."* [9] This chapter is **very** explicit, that if we enter into the sufferings of Jesus, it's **only the pathway to glory!** And so, what we **first** rejected—first bloom—is God's way of working something very beautiful and very precious in our lives. Well, I wonder, are you willing to come to an end of your **self-life**—your **natural life?** That's the way of the cross. I guarantee you, it's the **way** that leads home. If you ever tap in on the **way** of the cross and live sacrificial love, you're beginning to find the **real** essence of life and the pathway right to glory.

The **way** of the cross leads home. Are you willing to put your hands in the hands of the Spirit and say, "Lord, I really want to be your son. I want that witness of the Spirit and I want the **inheritance.** And if **that means** that I also **suffer** with You and become **involved** with You— **identified** with You—I'm willing to do that."

You know our Greek word translated "suffer with" is our English word "sympathy." That's the word. And **sympathy** means an identification with something—**closely** identified—an involvement—so that were **involved** with Jesus. **Not** just religious activity. It's an **involvement** with the **life** of Jesus and **His** way.

Well, that's my prayer. I'm **sorry** that I can only be a **postman** today. I can just deliver the message, but I can read it there in Romans 8. And I say, "Lord, let it happen to me." I know my flesh life **cringes.** I want **my way.** I don't want anybody **crossing** me. I want what I want **when I want it.** But how wonderful, you can be taught by the Spirit. And you can begin to **relish** the way of the cross that leads us home.

Let's pray together shall we:

Lord, we'll have to be taught this of You. Because the **natural man,** the **natural mind,** would not receive this message. I know that I wouldn't, Lord. Even though I've been converted, I **still resist** the way of the cross.

Lord, I'm asking that you'll teach me that way. I read this passage and it's so clear that we are heirs of God **provided** we **suffer** with Him in order that we may also be **glorified** with Him. Lord, we know that we're living in a world that suffers. And we're glad that Jesus Christ entered into this reality. He took it upon Himself with **all** aspects including the suffering and the death. And so, **Lord,** if that's really the **way** that we're constructed, if we're really **destined** to be **conformed** to the image of Jesus Christ, then Lord **hasten** that process. Open our eyes Lord, our understanding this truth that we'll see it properly, and we won't **shrink** from the **hand** of the Lord upon us.

Lord, I thank you for these two precious truths, that whatever **happens** to me cannot disturb my **innocency.** <u>Nothing</u> can come into my life that can cause me to lose my **acquittal** before God, because it is **God who justifies.** And Lord, sometimes there are deep groanings that go on within our breast. Sometimes Lord, there's an inner **war** that **breaks out**—a **Civil War.** Lord, we're **grateful** that it still doesn't disturb our standing before You. And then Lord, we thank you for this word that **breaks in** upon our consciousness this morning. That **all** of these things are not **really** against us, but they're **working** <u>for us</u> that we might be conformed to the image of God's dear Son.

And so, Lord, I ask that Your Holy Spirit will teach that this morning, and put us at peace in these things. Because Lord, we want to be more than conquerors through the grace of God. Lord, we're glad for this message of grace. How happy it made our hearts to know that you're not dealing with us after our sins. You're dealing **only in grace.** Lord, we're grateful for that glorious message. We **thank you** for the **freedom** that we enjoy. But now Lord, we're asking that we'll be taught that the grace of God will lead us into this **deeper** life. Lord, it not only leads us into Jesus' self-identity, but it leads us into being conformed to His life— **the way of the cross.**

<u>Oh</u>, **bring me Lord, bring me to an end of my self-life! Lord, help me to be in the Spirit.** And help that life to really be a life of **sacrificial love**—of **sacrificial self-giving.** Lord, will you broaden my horizons. So many times, Lord, I only want to serve just my **family** or just my local church. But Lord Jesus, You so **loved** the world. You had a **compassion** that went out to **all of mankind.** Lord, **teach me** to enter into the **sufferings** of humanity, of **all** mankind. **Lord don't let me narrow down my soul and become a little amoeba that just <u>dodges</u> every little trial. Lord, I want to have an <u>involvement</u>. I want to have a <u>deep</u> involvement with your people. Lord, if that means that I must <u>suffer</u>, then Lord I <u>welcome</u> that suffering in Your Name.** So, Lord, don't let me draw back and become a **narrow** little soul. But let me be **all** that I should be before You. Lord, I know that I pray on behalf of this congregation, and I do hold them up before You Lord. Help us to— learn—this—truth—of Romans chapter 8, we pray.

SERMON 22 ENDNOTES:

A   Nee, Watchman. (April 4, 1938). The Normal Christian Life.(p.94). Retrieved from Chapter 12 of WWW at https://tochrist.org/Doc/Books/Watchman%20Nee/The%20Normal%20Christian%20Life.pdf

B   Sam Ervin, US Senator 1954-1974 from North Carolina. He liked to call himself a "country lawyer," and often told humorous stories in his southern drawl. Retrieved from WWW at https://en.wikipedia.org/wiki/Sam_Ervin

SERMON 22 SCRIPTURE REFERENCES:

[1] Romans 8:17 (RSV)

and if children, then heirs, heirs of God and fellow heirs with Christ, provided we suffer with him in order that we may also be glorified with him.

[2] Romans 8:15-17 (RSV)

15 For you did not receive the spirit of slavery to fall back into fear, but you have received the spirit of sonship. When we cry, "Abba! Father!" 16 it is the Spirit himself bearing witness with our spirit that we are children of God, 17 and if children, then heirs, heirs of God and fellow heirs with Christ, provided we suffer with him in order that we may also be glorified with him.

[3] Romans 5:3-4 (RSV)

3 More than that, we rejoice in our sufferings, knowing that suffering produces endurance, 4 and endurance produces character, and character produces hope,

[4] Romans 8:28-29 (RSV)

28 We know that in everything God works for good with those who love him, who are called according to his purpose. 29 For those whom he foreknew he also predestined to be conformed to the image of his Son, in order that he might be the first-born among many brethren.

[5] 2 Corinthians 4:7 (RSV)

But we have this treasure in earthen vessels, to show that the transcendent power belongs to God and not to us.

[6] 2 Corinthians 4:8-1 (RSV)

8 We are afflicted in every way, but not crushed; perplexed, but not driven to despair; 9 persecuted, but not forsaken; struck down, but not destroyed; 10 always carrying in the body the death of Jesus, so that the life of Jesus may also be manifested in our bodies. 11 For while we live we are always being given up to death for Jesus' sake, so that the life of Jesus may be manifested in our mortal flesh.

[7] Romans 8:33 (KJV)

Who shall lay any thing to the charge of God's elect? It is God that justifieth.

[8] Romans 8:28 (KJV)

And we know that all things work together for good to them that love God, to them who are the called according to his purpose.

[9] Genesis 50:20 (RSV)

As for you, you meant evil against me; but God meant it for good, to bring it about that many people should be kept alive, as they are today.

SERMON 23

THE THREE GROANS

"The Holy Spirit is groaning with us. It's the groan of the Lord Jesus Christ who's identified with us in our predicament, and He's bringing us to "the glorious liberty of the children of God!"

Our Scripture reading this morning is taken from Romans chapter 8. We'll begin please with verse 18. We'd like to continue through verse 27. The point to Romans chapter 8 is established in verse 37, *"that we may be **more** than conquerors."* [1] We're trying to be **super conquerors.** Now we have seen that this comes by the grace of **God** and the **Reign of Grace.** When **grace reigns,** then **we reign in <u>life</u>.** But there are **terrific powers** that keep us from life and keep us participating in **death.**

The first great obstacle we have, of course, is our flesh. That spiritual thing within us, that ethical force, that gives us our great moral conflict so that we cannot do the things that we would. We contend with our flesh, the moral spiritual problem of sin.

In addition to that we have the **physical problem.** Not only the spiritual problem, but the **physical** one. And **that is,** we frankly, are living in the kind of reality that were living in, and **we bump into some hard facts.** We **suffer,** we have some **pain.** So **how** can you be **more than a conqueror?** How can you be a **super conqueror** amidst the kind of reality that were living in, and **especially** since it's not been fully **redeemed.**

Well, that's the **problem** and Paul is going to address himself **to that,** beginning with verse 18, as he tackles this great important subject of **suffering.** Now, I don't believe you can be a super conqueror, if you have your eyes **closed.** We're not **escape artists.** We don't go off in a metaphysical or philosophical **schemes** that don't account for the **whole of reality.** And that means some **stresses.** That means **pain** and that means **death.** How can we **cope** with that? How can you really be a **super conqueror** and **still live** in the kind of a world that we are experiencing?

One of the answers is given in the passage that were about to read. We're calling this sermon, <u>The Triple Groan</u> (<u>The Three Groans</u>). We're going to see that one of the solutions is in the **third groan.** The problem is the first **two** groans, and a part of the solution is in the **third** groan.

Alright let's share please with verse 18, *"I consider that the **sufferings** of this present time"*—Now we've seen how important **that phrase** is in **Romans.** It's a contrast between **this present time** and the **age to come,** the **age** of glory.—*"**I consider that the sufferings**"*—are they real? Yes, there here—*"of this **present** time there're not **worth comparing** with the glory that is to be **revealed** to us. **Creation** waits with **eager longing** for the revealing of the **sons of God; creation was subjected to futility"**—Notice that please—*"creation was subjected to <u>futility,</u>"*

That's where we get the **Doctrine of Emptiness.** The word means it's **empty, it's futile, it's vain.** It's been **subjected** to that, given over to **futility.** But now **notice**—*"**not of its own will, but** by the will of **him"**—God—*"who subjected it in <u>hope;</u>"*—That's an important point. A futile creation but subjected in **hope**—with **hope** written in to it—*"because creation itself will be **set free** from its **bondage to decay** and obtain **the glorious liberty** of the children of God."*—Now—*"We know that the **whole creation** has been <u>groaning</u>"*—That's the first groan—*"It's <u>groaning in</u> travail **together** until"*—right—*"now;"*—this very moment.

Now the second groan—*"not only **creation, but we <u>ourselves,</u>** who have the **first fruits** of the Spirit"*—and **only the first fruits,** by the way, it's very important to **know** the earnest of the spirit. **We also groan!** We—"**groan inwardly** *as we await for* ***adoption*** *as sons,*"—explained as the resurrection or—"*the redemption of* **our bodies.** *Now* **in this** <u>*hope*</u> *we*"—are—"**saved.** *Now hope that is* <u>*seen*</u> *is not hope*"—in other words, if you're experiencing something or possessing it or seeing it, you're not anticipating it or hoping for it. "*For who hopes for what he* ***sees?***" You'd no longer hope for something you **have.** "**But if we hope for what we do** <u>**not**</u> **see**"—do not **experience**—do not **possess fully in experience and that is our completed redemption.** We only have the earnest of it,—"*we wait for it with* <u>*patience.*</u>"

But now **how can** we wait for it with patience? Well, the solution **follows**—"*Likewise*"—you're to make **a parallel** and an illustration from what we've just **read** to the **third** <u>**groan.**</u> <u>**Likewise,**</u> **in the same** <u>**manner**</u> **on the same** <u>**principle**</u>—"*the* <u>*Spirit*</u> *helps us in* <u>*our*</u> *weakness;*"—our needs—our infirmities—"**We don't know** *how even to* **pray** *as we ought*"—we don't **understand** ourselves—"<u>**We don't know**</u> *how to pray as we* <u>***ought,***</u> *but the Spirit himself intercedes for us with* <u>*sighs*</u>"—the same word **with groans.** It's the third groan. The **Spirit** does it with **groans.** He groans too—"*with groans* **too deep for words.** *And he*"—God—"*who searches the hearts of men* **he knows what is the** <u>**mind**</u> **of the** *Spirit*"—that indwells the human heart—"*because* **the Spirit** *intercedes for the saints* **according to the will of God.**" [2]

So, this is the triple **groan,** and the third one is one of the **solutions** as to how we can be **super conquerors amidst** the kind of reality that we all experience.

Now, it's **very obvious** to us that the first groan is **creation.** And **creation** is groaning. And the best commentary on it is as read in <u>Tooth and Claw.</u> "Everywhere you look in creation, what we call the chain of **life** has become a chain of **death.** The big fish eat the little fish. And so, it goes on up the **chain of life** has become a **chain of death.** Before the fall and the advent of **sin** animals were not carnivorous. They were not given over to feeding on one another, but the entrance of sin has caused it to **groan.** And we talked on other occasions of how that all creation is in the **minor key.** If you record the sounds of nature, it's in a minor chord. It's waiting to come back to rest to the dominant chord." [A]

Everything you do has a way of turning to dust and ashes. Eventually it's going to be eaten up by **rust.** And I tell you it's a tremendous commentary on creation and human life to travel around the world and see all the great civilizations that have fallen, basically to decay and to corruption. Everything you put your hand to seems to be **possessed,** as it were, **by death.** So, creation is **groaning.** It's caught up in the **travail** as it were in the **pain** and in the **suffering.** It's just everywhere present.

Now we're participating in **that** as a part of creation. Even though we're also part of the **new creation,** we're **caught up** in this conflict, **and we also groan.** *"We groan too,"* the Apostle says, *"We groan inwardly."* [3] Now, we groan I think basically for two reasons.

The first is **obvious,** that we're living in physical **unredeemed bodies.** Our bodies are not redeemed. They are **touched** occasionally **by redemption** in the sense of the divine healing touch can **quicken us.** Which I think, is a foretaste of the resurrection **body.** But here and now our bodies are still subject to **decay** and all these processes. You get **cuts** on them. You get **calluses.** You get **aching backs.** You get things that go wrong. You're living in an **unredeemed body.** And as we have also pointed out, you are also contending with an **unredeemable flesh.** The flesh is **unredeemable!** The only thing you can do is not **walk** in it and **crucify** it. **But it's there!** And so, we have **this** kind of a **problem** that were **dealing** with.

In addition to that, we have the great problem of, let's just for a basic word call it, **ignorance.** And **by that,** I really mean an **uncertainty** about what kind of beings **we are.** Particularly when it comes to our unconscious processes, **down** in this area that's too deep for **words.** This area that's **unexpressible.** We have an uncertainty about our life. Most of us are **mysteries** to ourselves. And what's to **happen** when you have a **broken emotional** or **mental life.** How can it really be repaired, and **how** can you cope with that?

Solomon realized how difficult it was to face up to **emotional** and **spiritual personal problems.** Over in one of his Proverbs, he says *"A man's spirit will endure **sickness, but a broken spirit** who can bear?"* [4]

Give me a good old headache anytime. I don't mind them at all. Rather than those **internal <u>conflicts</u>.** Those **conflicts <u>inside</u>, deep within us that we can't <u>get at</u>.** And I really believe that we cannot **directly** affect our **emotional <u>life</u>.** It only comes **along** in the **train** of things. You cannot **directly control your <u>feelings</u>.** They're beyond your **control.** And that's true of **many** of our actions. To **will** is present with us. How to perform that which is good, we cannot find. We're **mysteries** to ourselves, and we have this psychological **depth** to us. **And I know that we're in trouble in our <u>depths</u>.** I'm in great sympathy depth psychology, that says that man in the depths of his being is **in trouble.** And we're acting out all these **unconscious processes** that you can't even **express,** you don't even **understand.**

That's what Paul is getting at here when he talks about our **hearts, our inner life. We don't know how to <u>pray</u> for us, even** *"to <u>pray</u> as we ought."* [5] We don't know what to **pray for** at times. And then *"we pray <u>amiss</u>."* [6] And it causes us to **groan.** It causes all kinds of **problems** to attend our way, **personally, emotionally, and psychologically.**

Someone wrote me a letter **this week.** I'm reading it, of course, with **permission.** This person said, "I **see** that I have **guilt** beyond my **farthest imagination** inside of **me.** I even feel guilty when I'm not even **involved.** I feel **guilty** for everyone **else.** You'd think I was the **Messiah."** *(Don chuckles)* The person says, "And that's not funny!" Of course, it's not. So, we have these **difficulties** that attend our way. Living our lives out in these physical bodies that are subject to death and corruption.

And also living our lives out in the **problems** that attend our **hearts** as it were. **Well, what a <u>problem</u> we have.**

Now, **how can you be more than a <u>conqueror</u>? How can you be a super conqueror and live in the kind of body you're living in** and the kind of **unredeemed reality** you're living in, this kind of **world? How** can you still have peace and be <u>**more**</u> **than a conqueror?**

Thank God the solution is in the third groan. **I know creation is groaning and I know that I'm groaning.** By the way, I have very little use for a **gospel** that doesn't preach a **groan** in it. If you don't see a **cross <u>embedded</u>** at the heart of our faith, that this thing is just like tripping the **light fantastic. Somethings wrong with your kind of gospel. We're talking about a kind of reality we live in that causes <u>pain and suffering</u> and involves us in death.**

In one way my Christian life has been one **long groan. Does that <u>mean</u>** that we're **defeated, that were passive? On the <u>contrary</u>, <u>it doesn't mean that whatever</u>.** Because, you see, God the Holy Ghost is also **groaning too,** amidst all these very **difficult** circumstances that we're living in. **He groans right along with us. It's a <u>very</u> sympathetic groan.**

We're asked to identify with Jesus in His sufferings. As a matter fact, it's a rather strong condition. *"We are **heirs,** provided we **suffer with him** in order that we might be also glorified with **him.**"* [7] **Likewise, the Spirit also suffers with us.** Now, it's one thing to **suffer with Jesus.** I tell you it's another thing to know that Jesus is **suffering** with **you.**

"Likewise the Spirit helps us in our weakness; for we do not know how to pray as we ought, but the Spirit himself intercedes for us with sighs too deep for words. And he who searches the hearts of men knows what is the mind of the Spirit, because the Spirit intercedes for the saints according to the will of God." - Romans 8:26-27 RSV

Let's call that the groan of the Christ within us. As long as Jesus Christ is groaning too, **I tell you** I can be a super conqueror. I can be **more** than a conqueror, because I know that he's groaning right along with me. Now, I don't understand how that works out altogether. But I **do know** that it makes a **difference**.

I know when I went to see Adela this week in the hospital, she says, "Oh, I know everything will be alright, now that you're here, and you just **know**." Well, I was just sitting in the chair. *(Don chuckles)* I just went down to sit **by** her. But Adela says, "Now that **you're here and you know**."

So, it's <u>something</u> to <u>know</u> that God the creator of the universe, who <u>subjected</u> the world in <u>hope</u>, has come among us, and <u>He also</u> has taken up our groaning. *"Likewise, the Spirit also groans. He intercedes for us with <u>groans</u> too deep for words."* [5] He suffers with us. He understands our lot. *"He's **touched** by the feeling of our infirmities."* [8]

Now many times, we ask the question, **"Why? Why** Lord is this happening? **Why** is that happening? **Why** am I going through this? **Why** don't I get an answer to my prayer?" I tell you; I don't have an **answer** to all those **why's.** I don't have any **glib** answers anyway. **But as long as I know that a** *"<u>why?</u>"* [9] **came roaring out of the throat of the Lord Jesus <u>Christ</u>, I tell you it gives me a <u>compassion</u>, and a <u>sympathy</u>, and a <u>comfort</u> to <u>know</u> that Jesus also said, "<u>Why</u>?" right in the midst of all my sufferings. And if <u>God himself</u> can say <u>why</u> in my <u>boots</u>, as it were, I tell you I can be a super conqueror.**

But I think the most **beautiful thing** about this groan of the **Spirit,** is **not only** is it a **sympathetic groan,** it's **a groan** identified completely **with us** as He has entered into our **creation** and taken His place **with us.** **But this groan also is a highly successful groan.**

You see, we don't know how we should pray as we <u>ought</u>. <u>I don't</u> know what to ask for in the <u>depths</u> of my emotional subconscious life.

But thank God in the <u>depths</u> of my <u>being</u>, in the area where it <u>really counts</u>, the <u>Holy Spirit of God</u> has taken <u>possession</u> of my being and there in my <u>depths, He groans according to the will of God</u>!

I tell you I'm right on <u>target</u>! I'm <u>moving</u> in the direction of <u>glory</u>! <u>I'm</u> not headed <u>only</u> for <u>suffering</u>. <u>That suffering</u> is leading me right on <u>target</u> to <u>glory</u>. <u>I can't</u> understand all the things that are happening to <u>me</u>, but the Holy Spirit of God, *"who's the <u>author</u> and the <u>bishop</u> of my soul,"* [10] is <u>moving me</u> <u>right</u> in the direction of the will of God. I will not <u>live then by</u> these things. I will not draw my <u>energy</u> from these <u>lies</u> round about me. Rather, I know that the Holy Ghost is causing me to be a super conqueror. As a matter fact, these things that are happening to me, are turning out for a <u>testimony</u>! They are <u>redounding</u> to the glory of God! <u>None</u> of these things can be against me!

Do I <u>suffer</u>? <u>Of course, I do</u>! I <u>groan</u>. I have <u>pain</u>. I have <u>conflicts</u>. But thank God, there's a deeper way that lets me embrace that <u>way of the cross</u> and <u>know</u> that by the Holy Spirit of God I'm right on target.

You know, it's a **great** important truth **to know** that the **things** that are **happening** to you are **falling out** for your **advancement,** because the Holy Spirit is **groaning** within you **according** to the will of God. Aren't you **glad** to know that God Himself prays according to His will as He searches **your** hearts and **your** emotional life? And **there** down in a way that you can't **understand or interpret,** there's the Holy Spirit of God at work, **way down** in the depths of your **being** and **causing** you to move off **to glory.**

So, what are you going to **live by** then? Are you going to live by these things that cause you to go **up and down** and **vacillate** and **move you all around? Are all of these things going to move you? Or like Paul are you are going to say,** *"None of these things move me, because I know that the Holy Ghost of God is working in me and praying right according to his will."* [11]

Now, **the world** is designed, I think, in every way to avoid pain and suffering. In the most **significant way** though, as far as this sermon is concerned, it's called **defensiveness. I don't like to suffer.** I want to avoid **pain** in the natural. My carnal mind would like to avoid **pain** and **suffering,** and so I become **defensive.** What is defensiveness? **It's just a self-protective device that** won't **let you enter into pain and** suffering. **Where you become** critical **of others and when you begin to** blame **others and you won't** get involved **with others. It's a** protective device, **and it's the** way **of the world. It is** not **the way of the cross!**

We have a way of absorbing that cross **to us. And that can only be taught to us, I believe, by the Spirit. Where that** suffering **becomes** redeemable. Redeemable **as it were. And it falls out for our glory and** *"works together for our good."* [12]

And so, we enter into **suffering.** We know that the **Holy Spirit** has entered into our **suffering.** It's by this **third groan** that we become **super conquerors.** *"We are* more *than conquerors through him that loved us."* [13] Do we live in this reality with eyes wide open? Indeed, we **do. Do we groan?** Indeed, we do**! Are we defeated?** We are not**! We are** more than conquerors **through Him that loved us. Do we have to be defensive about** pain **and** suffering**? No, we don't.**

By the way of the cross we **absorb it. We welcome it.** We **receive it** unto ourselves only to be **transformed** and **redeemed** by the way of the cross of our Lord Jesus Christ. *"*I reckon *that the sufferings of this present time, why they're just not* worthy *to be compared with the glory that is going to be revealed in* me.*"* [14]

And so, I've got my eye on that **Celestial City.** Do I have to rake the **muck** down here? No, I **don't!** Not as long as I'm **seeing** the Celestial City. I've got that **gleam** in my eye. That faraway look. Do any of these things **move me? Oh, no! They don't!** Not when seen in proper perspective and **knowing that the Holy Ghost** is **deep** at work in **my** life. In my

subconscious life. **Groaning** within me with inexpressible sighs to the Lord.

I might add, by the way, that **none** of these **groans** are the **death rattle,** because the **word** is the **birth pang. Creation** is in **pain, but it's a birth pang. I'm in <u>pain,</u> <u>but it's a birth pain.</u>** I'm just anticipating to give **birth,** as it were, to that **glorious inheritance** that belongs to the children of God.

So, the Holy Spirit is groaning with us. **I can make it,** as long as I know about the **third** groan. When I hear the awful language of **nature,** and **creation,** and **society,** and when I hear my own **inner pain, thank God,** I can also hear a third groan. It's the groan of the Lord Jesus Christ who's **identified with us** in our predicament, and he's bringing us to *"the glorious liberty of the children of God."* [15]

Let's pray shall we:

Our Father, we really truly want to be **super** conquerors. **We** want to live life with **patience.** We want to be **steadfast.** We want to be **grounded.** We want to be **established.** Not tossed about by every little wind of doctrine and experience. And, so often Lord, we draw our energies from these things round about us. It's these **things** that take their **stand about us.** These **circumstances** that **cause** us to be so **moved.** But Lord, we're praying that we won't be **moved** by our **physical man, by our emotional life** or **subconscious life.** We're going to be moved only by the truth of the Spirit of God. **Lord,** we with **patience** can **wait** for this redemption, **full redemption,** to catch up with us if we'll just **know** that God Himself is groaning with us. He's not only groaning **sympathetically,** but He's also groaning **successfully** as **He** has written **hope** into our hearts.

Thank you, Lord, that it's not a **death rattle.** It's a **birth pang.** We're about to give birth Lord, to the new creation. Our spirits Lord are sometimes in conflict as we **feel** the **tug** of the first fruits of the Spirit. They keep calling us up **higher.** We know that we're made for

better things. But Lord, we pray that during this present time, we'll be **grounded, established; <u>right</u> in the midst of it all,** we'll still be **super conquerors** through Him that loved us.

Lord don't let us be **defensive** then about the **pain.** Let us **redeem it** and **transform it** and turn it all to a **testimony.** Lord, we know that we're **assigned to suffering.** And unless we suffer with you, we **cannot** be **glorified.** And so, Lord **forgive us,** because in our **worldly way** we've thought **not** to involve **ourselves** with **pain** and **suffering** of others and with the **sins** of the world, but Lord we've tried to **escape** it. So, Lord we're going to take our **stand** with You in the way of the **cross** today. But we can only **do that,** if the Holy Spirit will say that He is leading us to glory. So, Lord, will you come and talk to our hearts now through this **Word** and **through this message.** Speak to us Lord, in the way you want to. We ask this in Jesus' name, Amen.

SERMON 23 ENDNOTES:

^A Jo Walton. (November 1, 2003), *Tooth and Claw* (Tor Book, New York City, NY)

SERMON 23 SCRIPTURE REFERENCES:

¹ Romans 8:37 (RSV)

No, in all these things we are more than conquerors through him who loved us.

² Romans 8:18-27 (RSV)

18 I consider that the sufferings of this present time are not worth comparing with the glory that is to be revealed to us. 19 For the creation waits with eager longing for the revealing of the sons of God; 20 for the creation was subjected to futility, not of its own will but by the will of him who subjected it in hope; 21 because the creation itself will be set free from its bondage to decay and obtain the glorious liberty of the children of God. 22 We know that the whole creation has been groaning in travail together until now; 23 and not only the creation, but we ourselves, who have the first fruits of the Spirit, groan inwardly as we wait for adoption as sons, the redemption of our bodies. 24 For in this hope we were saved. Now hope that is seen is not hope. For who hopes for what he sees? 25 But if we hope for what we do not see, we wait for it with patience. 26 Likewise the Spirit helps us in our weakness; for we do not know how to pray as we ought, but the Spirit himself intercedes for us with sighs too deep for words. 27 And he who searches the hearts of men knows what is the mind of the Spirit, because the Spirit intercedes for the saints according to the will of God.

[3] Romans 8:23 (RSV)

and not only the creation, but we ourselves, who have the first fruits of the Spirit, groan inwardly as we wait for adoption as sons, the redemption of our bodies.

[4] Proverbs 18:14 (RSV)

A man's spirit will endure sickness; but a broken spirit who can bear?

[5] Romans 8:26 (RSV)

Likewise the Spirit helps us in our weakness; for we do not know how to pray as we ought, but the Spirit himself intercedes for us with sighs too deep for words.

[6] James 4:3 (ASV)

Ye ask, and receive not, because ye ask amiss, that ye may spend it in your pleasures.

[7] Romans 8:17 (RSV)

and if children, then heirs, heirs of God and fellow heirs with Christ, provided we suffer with him in order that we may also be glorified with him.

8 Hebrews 4:15 (ASV)

For we have not a high priest that cannot be touched with the feeling of our infirmities; but one that hath been in all points tempted like as we are, yet without sin.

9 Matthew 27:46 (RSV)

And about the ninth hour Jesus cried with a loud voice, "Eli, Eli, la'ma sabach-tha'ni?" that is, "My God, my God, why hast thou forsaken me?"

10 1 Peter 2:25 (KJV)

For ye were as sheep going astray; but are now returned unto the Shepherd and Bishop of your souls.

11 Romans 8:26-27 (RSV)

26 Likewise the Spirit helps us in our weakness; for we do not know how to pray as we ought, but the Spirit himself intercedes for us with sighs too deep for words. 27 And he who searches the hearts of men knows what is the mind of the Spirit, because the Spirit intercedes for the saints according to the will of God.

12 Romans 8:28 (RSV)

We know that in everything God works for good with those who love him, who are called according to his purpose.

13 Romans 8:37 (RSV)

No, in all these things we are more than conquerors through him who loved us.

14 Romans 8:18 (KJV)

I am crucified with Christ: nevertheless I live; yet not I, but Christ liveth in me: and the life which I now live in the flesh I live by the faith of the Son of God, who loved me, and gave himself for me.

[15] Romans 8:21 (RSV)

Because the creation itself will be set free from its bondage to decay and obtain the glorious liberty of the children of God.

SERMON 24

THE ETERNAL PLAN OF GOD

"Brother WE CAN TAKE IT! We can be super con-
querors through Him that loved us because we're
involved in the great eternal plan of God!"

Our attention has been drawn to Romans chapter 8 today. This is a very long series that we've been **pursuing** in Romans chapters 6, 7 and 8. And this evening our text is found in Romans chapter 8, beginning with verse 28. We're going to read some of the most **loved** and **famous words** in all the New Testament. We'd like to go through verse 30 and then there's a **very important** passage that we need to pick up in **chapter 9.**

Romans chapter 8 verse 28, *"We know that in **everything God** **works for good** with those who **love him,** who are **called** according to his **purpose.**" "**For**"*— this is **why** everything works together for **good**— *"**For** those whom he **foreknew** he also **predestined.**" "He predestined to be **conformed** to the **image of his Son,** in order that **he**"*—**Christ**—*"might be the **first-born** among **many** brothers"*—just the **first one, that's all,** among an **entire family**—a very large family of **brothers**—brethren—*"**And** those whom he **predestined** he also **called; and** those whom he **called** he also **justified; and** those whom he **justified** he also **glorified.**"* [1]

Now while we're reading Scripture, we'll go on to look at Romans chapter 9 and let's pick up, please, with verse 6. I'd like to read to about verse 24, a **very key passage** for understanding what Paul is establishing in that section of Romans chapter 8 about the eternal purposes or the

eternal plan of **God.** *"It's **not** as though the word of God had **failed"**—* Israel's unbelief and rejection of the gospel. Not as though **God's word or plan,** promise, will had **failed**—*"**For not all** who are **descended** from **Israel** belong to **Israel,** and **not all** are children of Abraham because they are his descendants;"*—**physically**—*"**but** 'Through Isaac shall your descendants **be named'** "*—in view of the **call.** Now—*"This means that it is **not** the children of the **flesh** who are the children of God, but the children of the **promise** who are **reckoned as descendants.** "This is what the promise **said,** 'About this time I will return and Sarah will have **a son.'** And not only so, but also when **Rebecca** had conceived children by one man, our forefather Isaac, though they were **not yet born"**—they—*"had done neither **good nor bad,** in order that **God's purpose of election** might continue, **not because of** <u>works</u> but because of **his call,** she was told, 'The elder will serve the younger.'** As it is written 'Jacob I have **loved,** but Esau have I **hated.'** "* [2]

"For all who are led by the Spirit of God are sons of God."
- *Romans 8:14 RSV*

(Continue reading at verse 14) *"What are going to say then? **Is there injustice"**—with God?—*"Injustice on God's part? **By <u>no</u> means!"**—*Don't even entertain the thought. That's not what we're talking about, God's injustice, that could **not** be. It couldn't follow. *"He says to Moses, '**I will have <u>mercy</u> on whom <u>I</u> <u>will</u> <u>have</u> <u>mercy</u>,** and I will have **compassion** on whom <u>I</u> have compassion.'* **So it depends <u>not</u> upon man's <u>will</u> or on exertion, <u>but</u> <u>upon</u> <u>God's</u> <u>mercy</u>.** For the scripture says to Pharaoh, 'I have raised you up for the very purpose of showing <u>my power in you</u>, so that my name'*—my <u>character</u>, my <u>being</u>, my <u>attributes</u>, or my <u>glory</u>—*'may be <u>proclaimed</u> in <u>all</u> the earth.'* **So then he has <u>mercy</u> upon whom <u>HE</u> wills, and he <u>HARDENS</u> the hearts of whomever <u>HE</u> <u>WILLS</u>."* [2]

(Continue reading at verse 19) "You'll say to me then"—you can anticipate the human argument—" *'Why does he still find fault?' "*—in other words, how can anybody be **good or bad?** " *'For who can resist his will?' "* Some might draw that false conclusion. ***"But who are you, a <u>man</u>, to answer back to <u>God</u>?** Will what is **molded** say to the **molder**, 'Why have you made me thus?'* Has the **Potter** no right over the **clay**, to *make out of the same lump one vessel for **beauty** another for menial use?* <u>**What if God**</u>, <u>**desiring**</u> *to show his <u>**wrath**</u> and to make <u>**known**</u> his power, has <u>**endured**</u> with much patience"*—notice that—*"**the vessels of wrath** <u>**made**</u> for destruction."*—Now, please note verse 23—*"<u>**in order to make**</u> <u>**known**</u> the <u>**riches**</u> <u>**of**</u> <u>**his glory**</u> for the vessels of mercy,"*—What if He's willing to take **some** as **vessels of wrath in order to make** <u>known</u> the **riches of His** <u>glory</u> **for the vessels of mercy**—*"whom he has prepared beforehand **for glory, even us,** whom he has <u>called,</u> not from Jews only, but also from the Gentiles?"* [2]

Now that's a very **profound,** a very **humbling awesome passage of Scripture.** One ought really to read that on their **knees,** with a **humble broken heart.** What **awesome** tremendous words, we have just read.

Now, I **remind you** that Romans chapter 8, is taken up to a large extent with the subject of **suffering.** And we have said **over and over again,** the great point to this chapter, is that we might be **super** conquerors—<u>**more**</u> **than conquerors** through the **reign of grace** as grace **reigns** in our lives. **But** we find all this very **stern reality,** all these **difficult things** that happened to us, and they throw us off **balance.** They seem to keep us off **base,** as it were. And so **how** are we going to have **assurance** that we're going to **make it** in this kind of reality, when we **suffer?**

We have seen several important things, so far. We established, **first of all,** that **suffering** is **absolutely** <u>**essential.**</u> Suffering is not something incidental. If we **suffer** with Him, we're also going to be **glorified** <u>with</u>

Him. **Suffering** is an **essential** part of our **glorification.** We ought not think it **strange** then when we suffer as though it were **out** of the will of God, because it can turn to a testimony and **redound** to God's glory.

Now the **second reason,** we saw this morning, was in what we call the third **groan.** There are **triple groans** in this chapter. There's the **groan of creation** as it travails in **pain.** There's the **groan of the Christian** as he has the first fruits of the Spirit in **groans,** but there's also the **groan of God Himself by the Holy Spirit as He groans internally within us directly on target for His will.** So, when we **know** that God has identified with us, and He **groans** with us, we find this **enablement** coming from Him that helps us in **our weakness.**

And **now** we have this **next great reason** why Christians can be **super conquerors** amidst all of the reality that we're experiencing. And it is simply this: When we have an **understanding** of how **valid** and of how **good** is the **eternal plan** and **purposes of God;** When we see the **eternal purpose of God and understand the divine plan from creation, it's then that we don't lose heart during this present time. For I consider that the sufferings of this present time are not worthy to be compared with the glory that's going to be revealed to us in light of the eternal plan.**

Occasionally, in a classroom, I'll put a little **dot** on a board. And then I'll draw, in contrast to that, a **great line** all across the board and extend it as far as I possibly **can. That little dot represents this present time. It shows our momentary existence in the plan of God. That little dot is not the whole picture. You've got to see the long line. You have to have that eternal look in your eye in order to properly cope with any given thing that's going to happen. When you understand the eternal purpose, when you see the eternal purposes of God, it's then you can cope with anything that happens, when you understand that we're involved in an eternal design.**

So, the apostle is giving us the <u>five steps</u> of the great eternal plan, and he's making a <u>commentary</u> about that purpose. I'd like to briefly notice these <u>five steps</u> in the eternal plan, and then were going to notice in closing the **nature** of this plan.

Notice the five steps. **We know that everything is working for good.** We know that God is <u>working</u> with us <u>for</u> good, because of these five things: Number one—His foreknowledge, His predestination, His election or call, His justification, and His glorification.

Now those are five inseparable links. **Two of them** go to eternity past, **two of them** are at work in the present time, and **one of them** has to do with the future. **You cannot separate, <u>past</u>, <u>present</u> and <u>future</u>.**

Now, let's ask first of all, what **is** the eternal plan of God? At **essence,** what are the purposes of **God?** What is He **primarily up to?** What's creation and history all about? Now, if you imagine it's the plan of salvation, you're **wrong!** The plan of salvation is not **basically** the eternal purpose of **God. That's not what God is primarily doing. Salvation is** a <u>negative</u> thing. I tell you the purposes of God are far more than a fire escape from <u>hell</u>! God has something <u>positive</u> in mind. And when some young man marries a young lady, he <u>keeps</u> her from being an old maid. **That isn't why he married her.** He had something else in mind. *(Don chuckles)* Now the old maid shift incidentally, comes along. It is wonderful to **know** that you're **not** going to **hell.** But it's a **wonderful** thing to know what the eternal purposes of God **are.** They are very, very, clearly **established** in Scripture.

 "For from him and through him and to him are all things. To him be glory for ever. Amen." - Romans 11:36 RSV

I suppose the **best** single **summary** of what the great eternal purposes of God are Romans 11:36, *"From him, through him, and to him are all things to him be glory for ever. Amen."* [3]

The great eternal purpose of God is to manifest His glory. The most singly important thing in the universe is God and His glory. So, if God created us to share in His glory, to participate in His glory, then God, you see, wants to get greater and greater glory. He wants us to enlarge His glory and magnify His name. God wants man to know what He's like. All of creation has been a revelation of Himself and hence history and divine providence. It's all designed to reveal something of the name—the characteristics—the being of God.

All of history is a great commentary, if you please, on **theology.** And so, we have these **five steps,** that God is trying to lead us to **glory.** Now, the first one is His **foreknowledge.** Those whom He **foreknew.** Now I like to think of foreknowledge, really, as **just** the **design** or the eternalness of the eternal **plan.** The fact that God has **foreknowledge** means that He knows everything. He has a **purpose,** and He has a **plan.** Some people **mistakenly** think, by the way, that God could look ahead, and He could see who was **good or bad,** and thereby He decided to form His plan on the basis of His **foreknowledge,** knowing who was **good and bad. I** reject that **at once.** That is not good Bible doctrine!

The grounds of election are not in man. The grounds of election are in God Himself for His glory. There is none good, no not one. Romans chapter 9 makes this very clear, *"They were not yet born. They had not done good or bad, in order that God's purpose of election might continue, not because of works but because of his call."* [4] Verse 16 says, *"It depends not on man's will or exertion, but upon God's mercy."* [5] God's foreknowledge is simply His marvelous wisdom—His insight to decree this eternal purpose and plan. I tell you it's wonderful to know that creation and history is not running "willy-nilly." Nothing is off course! God has His mighty eternal hand upon creation and His foreknowledge foresees that. There's great wisdom. A great eternal plan that's unfolding down through creation and history. And I tell you, thank God, I'm a part of that!

So, by **His foreknowledge, He also predestined.** *"Those whom he foreknew, he also **predestined.**"* [6] Now predestination, **basically,** means that God is going to guarantee **the plan.** He not only **sees** the **plan.** He not only **knows** that eternal purpose. But **God is going to see that it's carried out. Hence** the word **predestination.** It happens to be in the Greek New Testament, our word **horizon.** It means that God has put down **limits.** I like to say He's driven great **stakes** in history. And brother it can go **thus** far and **no farther. God has determined the times before appointed. God is sovereign. God is the eternal God. Man is not the center of the universe. It's God! And God has predestined us.**

Now, I know it's a very difficult doctrine for some. I know that it's **hard** to understand, how that **some** could be **vessels** of His **mercy** and others could be vessels of His **wrath.** You say, **"How can God do that and be just?"** I don't <u>know,</u> except to say <u>this, that God is perfect!</u> And if <u>God</u> wants to <u>ordain</u> something as a means to His greater glory, <u>God</u> has the right to do that.

And Paul is saying in effect, <u>"Don't you be a 'smart aleck' and ask God, 'Why?'"</u> <u>You just fall on your knees and say, "Thanks be unto God that I'm a 'vessel of his mercy!'"</u> [7] I would like to add, by the way, that the New Testament and the **Bible** does not go into the subject of the **non-elect.** That's Calvin's so-called **horrible** decree [A], that's **speculation** on the other side of this theology. But we know very little about that part of it, if any.

We **do know** however, that **God** has **predestined** us as *"vessels of his mercy."* [7] I **would** like to point out, however, that **all** the way through Scripture, the **emphasis** upon predestination is a thing that's written in our **destiny.** Not that God, blindfolded, reached down, and says, "You're the **elect** and you're the **non-elect.**" That's not the way of God, whatever. We know that. But we are *"predestined to be conformed to the image of his <u>Son</u>."* [6]

That's what's written in our destiny. God has predestined us to that. Isn't that a glorious destiny? <u>That it's all going to work out!</u> <u>That's a PART OF THE PLAN!</u> <u>I'm going to wake up in Jesus' likeness!</u> I'm going to be <u>conformed</u> to the <u>image</u> of His <u>Son!</u> I tell you, <u>that does my heart GOOD!</u> While I'm <u>suffering</u>—and <u>disturbed</u>—and <u>confused</u>—and <u>bewildered</u> down here, <u>God</u> by the Holy Ghost is still **moving me right on target.** And that is to be conformed to the image of His Son.

God's foreknowledge is going to **see** that I'm going to be **predestined** to the image of the Lord Jesus Christ. That's going to happen to me. You never thought it would? You thought there was **no hope** for me? *(Don chuckles)* But I tell you I'm going to be **conformed** to the image of His Son. **And I've got news for you,** so are **you**—and **you**—and **you**—and **you**—and <u>you</u>! You are **predestined** to be conformed to the image of His Son. **That destiny** is going to be fulfilled through our Lord Jesus Christ.

Now the **third step is the call.** *"And those whom he **predestined** he also **called.**"* [8] Now this is the temporal execution of the eternal plan. **In history—in this present time—**He **calls** us. Now the **call** is basically the **definition** that comes to us. You see it's a definition of our **condition.** It's what God <u>calls</u> you that **counts.** And *"let God be true and every man a liar."* [9] <u>God</u> calls me a <u>saint.</u> I am called *"<u>saint.</u>"* [10] I'm a saint, **in virtue of my <u>call</u>. It's the definition <u>God gives to me</u>. And God looks at me and says, "Hello saint." <u>That's me, I'm a saint, in virtue of the CALL!</u> <u>I'm called that!</u> The <u>call</u> is what establishes my condition. It's because of what God <u>thinks about me</u> and what He <u>calls</u>.**

I believe, incidentally, that that call is *efficacious*. [B] I don't understand **this,** but I believe that behind that divine **call** is that marvelous power of the Holy Spirit that goes out and **draws** your hearts. I think it has an irresistible **quality** about it. There's something about that **divine call** that **woos** you and **brings** you to Himself. It's **wonderful** when **God** calls you and reaches out and calls you to Himself. **Thank God that Jesus Christ calls me by the Spirit.** *"I haven't chosen him, but he chose me."* [11] *"And he ordained me that I should bring forth fruit and be conformed to the image of his dear Son."* [6] And so we have **the call,** step number three. That's where we are at this particular point.

Step number four, *"those whom he called, he also justified."* [8] Now **justification,** in a way, is the **essence** of this eternal plan and purpose. **Justification basically means that God has** reversed everything **that's against us.** Justification means **acquittal.** You **stand** in a **right relationship** with God. The word **righteousness** is a **noun. Justification** is the **verb.** They are the same identical words. Justification means you **stand** in a **right relationship with Him. You have been made accepted in the beloved. You are acquitted. You are** justified! **There is nothing against you! And as we have seen in this chapter there is** nothing **that can disturb your** innocency. If God is for you, who can be against you! And justification is the divine decision of the JUDGE of the universe that he's FOR you. **I tell you; the Judge became our** Advocate. Can you see him taking off His judicial robe **and coming down and being our** lawyer **and standing at our side and being our advocate? That's the glorious Paraclete. The wonderful Holy Spirit. The comforter who comes among us and represents our cause.**

We—stand—justified—before the throne of God. Now that sentence, the word of that justification, I am receiving right now. Am I in fact justified? Am I a righteous person inside? I'm not! Justification is an evangelical doctrine. That means it's a sentence of God upon me.

It's God's divine decree. And it's what God <u>says</u> about me that counts. God looks at me and says, "You are justified in <u>terms of Jesus Christ!</u>" <u>It's on the basis of Jesus' work</u> that I stand justified. And I tell you, that's the <u>sentence</u> of the <u>last</u> judgment.

Don't forget that! Justification has reference to the <u>final judgment seat of God</u>. That final judgment seat has already <u>rendered</u> the verdict and has come back on me and said, "Justified." That's why I feel so <u>good</u>! That's why I'm a super <u>CONQUEROR</u>! <u>NONE OF THESE THINGS ARE AGAINST ME!</u>

Now, they would like to make me feel guilty. They would <u>like</u> to bring me under condemnation. They would <u>like</u> to say, "<u>You</u> don't belong to God. <u>You're</u> not worthy." But I tell you I disown all that in the name of the Lord Jesus Christ, and I tell you His divine decree has said, "I have <u>foreseen you</u>. I have <u>predestined you</u>. I have <u>called you</u> and I have pronounced <u>justification</u> upon you. You are justified."

The **fifth** glorious step **is**, "*them whom he justified he also glorified.*" [8] Now the most interesting thing about **glorification** is that it's in the past tense. He **has** glorified, **past tense. Why is that so? Because** God is <u>eternal</u>. There is no beginning or end with God. He is **Alpha and Omega.**

Now **I am, by experience,** passing through these various stages, you see. I'm at the point of the **call** and justification **now.** But because I stand justified, I can **guarantee** you in terms of the eternal plan, I'm **already glorified** in God's mind. I'm just **waiting** for it to catch up.

Can you **see** that? **He <u>has</u> glorified. You can't separate any one of the five of those links. You <u>cannot</u> <u>separate</u> the foreknowledge—** with the **predestination**—with the **call**—the **justification**—and the **glorification.** That's why, bless your heart, "*I <u>reckon</u> that the sufferings of this present time, they're just <u>not worthy</u> to be compared with the* *glory that's going to be revealed in me."* [12] I've already got it, in God. It **belongs** to me. Can you see that?

Well, glorification is the GOAL of the plan! That's what God had in mind all the time. That's why from **eternity**, God created **a world**. Did He need the **world?** Did God need creation? No, God was perfect, not as though He **needed** anything. Creation **added nothing** to His glory. You don't add anything to the glory of God.

But God in His love created the world, that **man** might share in His glory, and primarily that He could *"show the riches of his mercy to all."* [13] So God wants to reveal His glory, and He has that eternal plan. Now I tell you, if you know something about that eternal plan, if you know what you're in on, if you know how **big** this program is, I tell you, these little bumps that come along the way, they don't amount to a hill of beans! But if you're only looking at that dot, if that's all you can see, then all these things just look like huge mountains. But I tell you, if you can see them in light of the eternal plan and know that they're just leading you off to glory.

Now, I've got news for you. There is **nothing** that can **work** against you! It's all working together for your **good**! That's the eternal plan. Can you see that God is essentially **good?** Now, if **He permitted evil to come into the world, ONLY to further reveal His glory.**

Now, I don't understand how that can be at the divine level. How can a **bad means** justify an end? I'm not sure of that from a human level. Like the Watergate people had their problems, thinking that the **means** justified the **end**. But according to Romans chapter 9, **GOD can reveal His POWER** and raise up a man like **Pharaoh**. I might add by the way, for very just reasons, to reveal his lack in order that the vessels of mercy might see how marvelous is the grace and the goodness of God when contrasted with His awful wrath. I tell you, if any of us got our "just desserts" we'd all come under His wrath.

Aren't you glad to know that God is good? That God is full of love and mercy? And you are vessels of His marvelous mercy. You are in on that great plan. Did you know that God foreknew you from the foundations of the world? Do you know that He is predestined you to be conformed to the image of His Son? And did you know that there's been a call that's gone out by His Spirit and has given you a self-identification and described your condition? Did you know that you stand justified before God right now and that you are glory bound, you are bound for eternal glory?

If you know all of that, then I tell you, I reckon, that the sufferings of this present time. *(Don speaks with a non-caring attitude)* "Ho-hum. What do they matter?" *(Don changes to a compelling tone)* Brother WE CAN TAKE IT! We can be super conquerors through Him that loved us because we're involved in the great eternal plan of God.

One more time: There is nothing that can come into your life that God will not ordain for good. He will turn it to a testimony and cause it to redound to His glory and for your good. You thought all that suffering was to squash you. It wasn't! It was God's way of turning something for good. You don't always understand it at the present moment.

"No chastening for the moment seems very good, but grievous." [14] Have you ever been spanked? It doesn't seem very pleasant, but it's all redounding says the Bible for the development of our life in this great schooling that were experiencing here now. Thank God for that eternal purpose and plan. And I tell you, it's good. Everything is working together for your good.

Do you feel happy to know that? Are you going to gripe so bad the next time something happens? *(Don chuckles)* Yea, I know you are. Don't answer that! *(Don chuckles harder)* I know what you're going to do. But I hope this great truth will come into our hearts.

Remember the **triple groan.** The Holy Spirit is involved with us in this groaning experience. And **remember** to keep sight of the eternal purpose. *"I know that everything works together for good to them that love God and are the called according to his purpose."* [15] **I'm glad** that He's opened up my heart to love Him, and I want to love Him **all** the more.

SERMON 24 ENDNOTES:

A John Calvin. (1509-1564), *Institutes of the Christian Religion, book 3 ch. 23.* Translator (Henry Beveridge) 2002-08-01. Located online at http://www.ntslibrary.com/PDF%20Books/Calvin%20Institutes%20 of%20Christian%20Religion.pdf

B *efficacious,* meaning effectual; productive of effects; producing the effect intended; having power adequate to the purpose intended; powerful; as an efficacious remedy for disease. Online Webster's Dictionary of 1828, located at http://webstersdictionary1828.com/ Dictionary/efficacious

SERMON 24 SCRIPTURES REFERENCES:

1 Romans 8:28-30 (RSV)

28 We know that in everything God works for good with those who love him, who are called according to his purpose. 29 For those whom he foreknew he also predestined to be conformed to the image of his Son, in order that he might be the first-born among many brethren. 30 And those whom he predestined he also called; and those whom he called he also justified; and those whom he justified he also glorified.

2 Romans 9:6-24 (RSV)

6 But it is not as though the word of God had failed. For not all who are descended from Israel belong to Israel, 7 and not all are children of Abraham because they are his descendants; but "Through Isaac

shall your descendants be named." 8 This means that it is not the children of the flesh who are the children of God, but the children of the promise are reckoned as descendants. 9 For this is what the promise said, "About this time I will return and Sarah shall have a son." 10 And not only so, but also when Rebecca had conceived children by one man, our forefather Isaac, 11 though they were not yet born and had done nothing either good or bad, in order that God's purpose of election might continue, not because of works but because of his call, 12 she was told, "The elder will serve the younger." 13 As it is written, "Jacob I loved, but Esau I hated."

14 What shall we say then? Is there injustice on God's part? By no means! 15 For he says to Moses, "I will have mercy on whom I have mercy, and I will have compassion on whom I have compassion." 16 So it depends not upon man's will or exertion, but upon God's mercy. 17 For the scripture says to Pharaoh, "I have raised you up for the very purpose of showing my power in you, so that my name may be proclaimed in all the earth." 18 So then he has mercy upon whomever he wills, and he hardens the heart of whomever he wills.

19 You will say to me then, "Why does he still find fault? For who can resist his will?" 20 But who are you, a man, to answer back to God? Will what is molded say to its molder, "Why have you made me thus?" 21 Has the potter no right over the clay, to make out of the same lump one vessel for beauty and another for menial use? 22 What if God, desiring to show his wrath and to make known his power, has endured with much patience the vessels of wrath made for destruction, 23 in order to make known the riches of his glory for the vessels of mercy, which he has prepared beforehand for glory, 24 even us whom he has called, not from the Jews only but also from the Gentiles?

[3] Romans 11:36 (RSV)

For from him and through him and to him are all things. To him be glory for ever. Amen.

[4] Romans 9:11 (RSV)

though they were not yet born and had done nothing either good or bad, in order that God's purpose of election might continue, not because of works but because of his call,

[5] Romans 9:16 (RSV)

So it depends not upon man's will or exertion, but upon God's mercy.

[6] Romans 8:29 (RSV)

For those whom he foreknew he also predestined to be conformed to the image of his Son, in order that he might be the first-born among many brethren.

[7] Romans 9:22-24 (RSV)

22 What if God, desiring to show his wrath and to make known his power, has endured with much patience the vessels of wrath made for destruction, 23 in order to make known the riches of his glory for the vessels of mercy, which he has prepared beforehand for glory, 24 even us whom he has called, not from the Jews only but also from the Gentiles?

[8] Romans 8:30 (RSV)

And those whom he predestined he also called; and those whom he called he also justified; and those whom he justified he also glorified.

[9] Romans 3:4 (KJV)

God forbid: yea, let God be true, but every man a liar; as it is written, That thou mightest be justified in thy sayings, and mightest overcome when thou art judged.

[10] 1 Corinthians 1:2-3 (RSV)

To the church of God which is at Corinth, to those sanctified in Christ Jesus, called to be saints together with all those who in every place call on the name of our Lord Jesus Christ, both their Lord and ours: Grace to you and peace from God our Father and the Lord Jesus Christ.

[11] John 15:16 (RSV)

You did not choose me, but I chose you and appointed you that you should go and bear fruit and that your fruit should abide; so that whatever you ask the Father in my name, he may give it to you.

[12] Romans 8:18 (KJV)

For I reckon that the sufferings of this present time are not worthy to be compared with the glory which shall be revealed in us.

[13] Ephesians 2:7 (RSV)

that in the coming ages he might show the immeasurable riches of his grace in kindness toward us in Christ Jesus.

[14] Hebrews 12:11 (KJV)

Now no chastening for the present seemeth to be joyous, but grievous: nevertheless afterward it yieldeth the peaceable fruit of righteousness unto them which are exercised thereby.

[15] Romans 8:28 (RSV)

We know that in everything God works for good with those who love him, who are called according to his purpose.

SERMON 25

THE LOVE OF GOD

Well, I say, 'Hallelujah.' I say, 'Praise the Lord Jesus that nothing can disturb my innocency.' The Supreme Court has ruled, and the law of the kingdom says, 'Justified,' right in the midst of this present time!"

Our Scripture reading for this morning is taken from Romans chapter 8, beginning with verse 31, and we'll go, please, to the end of the chapter. Romans chapter 8, verses 31 to 39. Those of you who've been in attendance over these past few months will know that we are **now** reaching the **conclusion** of a **long series** based upon Romans chapters **6, 7 and 8,** one of most **significant** parts of our Bible. The theological statements here are **absolutely essential** to the Christian life.

We have **seen** that this is a **commentary** on what it means to **be,** *"not under law but under grace."* [1] That's the **main** theological statement. **You are—not—under—law—but—under grace.** Romans chapters 6, 7 and 8 shows the implications of that. What's **implied** in being under grace. Now, we noticed also, that there **are** some things that tend to **keep us** from entering into **life** with its **abundance** and its fullness. The **object** of **grace** is that it **might reign,** so that we might be **conquerors.** Not just **conquerors** but, *"more than conquerors."* [2] Or, we like to say, **super conquerors.** That we might be **super** conquerors with a very **decisive** and a significant victory in our life through the Lord Jesus.

We noticed the **two great obstacles.** There is, first of all, what the Bible calls the **flesh.** That means that **power** at work with**in** you that answers to **death** and brings you to **bondage, condemnation, and despair. Outside you,** is what the Bible calls **the world.** And we mean that **complex of unredeemed forces** that <u>impinge</u> upon us and want to bring destruction to our lives.

One of the **big** problems we all face, of course, **is—suffering.** We run into **tests,** and to **strains,** and to **pressures.** And they cause us to **groan.** And we **wonder** at times **how God** can really **love** us. Don't all these difficult circumstances belie the love of God? How can we be **sure** of the love of Christ?

This passage that we're about to read is the **final summary,** the **final conclusion** and **argument** of the Apostle Paul to show us how **in—all—these—things,** we can still be **more** than conquerors. I might say, by way of a refreshment of our **memory,** we've seen several things about **suffering.**

The first thing is that it's **necessary—and—it—is—purposive—** that **suffering** is **causing** us to be conformed to the **image** of Jesus Christ. It's **causing** us to see that our life is **normative in <u>Him</u>** and not in ourselves. We're slow to learn that. Most of us, I believe, are **persuaded** that if we can find life **within** ourselves, **we will.** By our **energies,** by our **strength, our** resources <u>we</u> **will try** to find the significance of life. But somehow that has to be broken and brought to a point of **death.** This natural life in a sense has to **end** for us before were born into the life of the **Spirit** and find that life which is **really life** and **peace.**

Then we also noticed that the **Holy Spirit** is very **deeply <u>involved</u>** with us. We talked about, you remember, the **triple groan.** That **creation groans. We <u>groan</u>.** But also thank God the Holy Spirit <u>**groans**</u> and that's a **successful groan.** He's groaning according to the will of **God.** He's **involved** with us. He's **groaning** with us amidst this present time and amidst our trials.

Then we also looked at that un**changing good** will of God. *"All things are working together for good to them that love God and are the called according to His purpose."* [3]

And now the **last** great thing that <u>sustains</u> us and gives us the **victory** and the **assurance** is the **greatest** thing in the world, of course, and that's **knowledge of God's love.** And if we can just but **know that.** And I've found this to be true, many times, that a Christian can go through anything and **will,** if he just says, **"Is the Lord with me?"** But **you let a person begin to wonder, <u>if God</u> is <u>for</u> them or <u>against</u> them,** then all of a sudden that's a despair they cannot **endure.** If they feel that God has <u>**abandoned**</u> **them** and given them **over,** you see, to the forces of the flesh in the world, <u>**that**</u> **they cannot stand,** and often times we're brought to the point of **tears.**

I know only this week some **wept** with me to say, **"How can it be that I serve Christ,** and He has all of my life, yet that these <u>**terrible pains**</u> are coming into my life? **Does—God—love—me?** And what are the **assurances of this?"** Well, we have to have these **assurances.** And the Apostle is going to **tell us** upon **what grounds** we can be a <u>**super conqueror,**</u> and **still** have our eyes **wide open.**

As you know I have **very little use** for any kind of a religion, that means you have to metaphysically close your eyes and deny reality. If you can't be **wide open** and **live in this life** as it presently constituted, and **still be a victor, we've got the wrong thing. We've got to go on** <u>**looking.** If this won't hold up in <u>life,</u> I mean <u>real life, life as we now know it,</u> with these unredeemed <u>bodies</u> and an unredeemed <u>society</u>, then we've got to find something **else** that will **hold us up.** But thanks be unto God, we are becoming **more** than conquerors through Him that loved us.

I think Romans chapter 8, verse 31 to 39, is **best studied** by answering the two questions of **Paul.** The two **key** questions. The first question is verse 31 to 34. It's found in verse 31, when he says, *"If God is for us **who is** against us?"* [4] That's his key question. He'll go on to develop this in various ways in verses 31 to 34, and he will **show the <u>proof</u> of the grounds of assurances** as to **knowing** that God is **for us,** not against us.

His second key question is in verse 35, *"**Who can <u>separate</u> us from the love of Christ?"** [5] **What** can separate us? And then he'll go on to give assurances that **nothing <u>can</u>** and the proof for **that.** So as time permits, now, we'll look at these **two questions** and this beautiful passage of Scripture. I'm rather confident that **this** particular passage has meant **<u>more</u>** probably to the people of God than any other part of our New Testament. How many have read into Romans chapter 8, amidst all their condemnation, and amidst their **despair,** and yet they have been **uplifted** and **renewed** and discovered that Jesus **loves** them all afresh in a brand-new way.

Let's take a look please, shall we, at the first question in chapter 8, verse 31, *"What then shall we say to **this?"**—Everything that's been developed and discussed up to this point—*"If <u>God</u> is for us,"*—Question—*"<u>who</u> is against us?"* Who **can be?** That is, with any degree of **success.** If <u>God</u> is for you, <u>who</u> can be against you? Now, just let those words sink in for a moment. I just love to say that, **with the knowledge that <u>God is for me</u>—and if <u>God is for me</u>—who can be against me? *"He who did not spare his own <u>Son</u> but gave <u>him</u> up for us all,** will he not also give us <u>all things</u> with <u>him</u>?"*—of our eternal inheritance and the guarantee of our salvation—*"will he not give us **all things** with <u>him</u>?"* The argument from the greater to the lesser. **If** He gives us Jesus Christ, the greatest of all, will He give us these **lesser** things? *"**Who shall bring any charge against <u>God's elect</u>?"*** Who can? You see, because *"It is <u>God</u> who justifies; so, who is to condemn? **Is it** Christ Jesus, who **died**,"*—Is it the Messiah, the Son of God, Christ Jesus who **<u>died</u>?** — *"**Yes, who was raised** *from the dead, who is at the right hand of God, who indeed intercedes for us?"* [6]

And so, here's this marvelous passage of Scripture saying, there is **nothing** in **this** creation that can disturb your innocency before God. Can sin? <u>NO</u>! Because you stand <u>justified</u> before God! The essential issue in life is <u>not</u> sin! The main basis of life is <u>not</u> morality! That's legalism <u>pure and simple</u>! Some people think that they're <u>good</u> or <u>bad</u>, <u>right</u> or <u>wrong</u>, they're in a right relationship with God. It's <u>faith</u> that puts you in a relationship with Jesus Christ and <u>not</u> <u>your</u> <u>works</u>, good or bad!

We're talking about a <u>grace</u>—that is—<u>greater—than—our—SIN</u>! And if we have a relationship with God that's based upon our <u>works</u>, then we've had it. It's either going to be by <u>grace</u> or it's going to be by <u>faith</u>. And thank God, the Supreme Court of the universe, has said you're <u>justified</u>. There <u>is no higher Court of Appeal</u> and all the adversaries of life, including my conscience and Satan, can go no higher than <u>God</u>. And the Supreme Court has looked at me and said **justified.** Who can condemn me?

Now, I know **very well** that we should constantly feel unworthy for our sins and in need of <u>**forgiveness.**</u> Mankind is **neurotically** and **chronically** taken up with a sense of **condemnation.** But I tell you, as believers, according to the scriptures we are **not condemned. I'm looking at God's sentence upon me. I'm not looking at my sins. I'm looking at His grace,** His **marvelous grace** that gives me this **glorious liberty** and lets me know that I'm justified in His sight.

So, who can **condemn you?** There is **nothing** that can disturb your **innocency.** That's **exactly** what the Apostle is saying. Because God is **greater** than your sin. Thank God were talking then about this relationship that we have with Him through Jesus. How important that is.

Now what proof do we have of this? How can we know this? Well, the first thing is because of what God Himself has **done.** What **has** God done? **He did not—spare—His own Son, but He gave Him up for us all.** Like Abraham, He did not **spare** His son. He gave Him up. Gave Him up to **what? Gave Him up to the full processes of judicial wrath.** He did not spare His own son.

And here's the burning issue. Was the sacrificial death and the shed blood of the Lord Jesus Christ adequate to put your conscience and the judicial processes of God at peace? I tell you; God is at peace, in the blood of His Son. He does NOT impute your sins to you. "_Blessed is the man_ to whom the Lord does not impute sin." [7] He imputes **righteousness to you. And you'll never know the full glorious bit of the grace of God until you understand that marvelous Doctrine of Imputed Righteousness.**

I stand justified in the sight of God. You could find a lot of things wrong with me. My **conscience** would like to keep me under condemnation. But as far as **I'm** concerned God doesn't see anything wrong with me. He says **I'm right.** That's the gift of righteousness. **I'm right!** You say, "Oh, you're not all that hot." **I am too!** (Congregation laughs) Because I have a relationship with **Jesus.** I trust the Lord Jesus Christ, and I have peace with God through Him.

Can you see that? **That He did not spare His own son.** So consequently, I'm not going to try to do a penance for my sin. I'm just going to run to Jesus and **confess** them and know that I stand justified in His sight because I have **faith** in the Lord Jesus. He did **not** spare His own Son. He **gave** Him up for us all.

Now if He did that, going from the **greater** to the **lesser,** if **He** gave us **Jesus** and thereby validated His love and illustrated His love, won't He give you everything else? What would He **withhold** from you? Would

He want you to have **bad?** No, He wouldn't. Not if He has validated how much He loves you by giving you the Lord Jesus Christ. So, who's going to bring any charge against you? God has no charge against you. You've been **made** accepted in the Beloved.

Now not only **that,** but can you see what **Jesus** is also **doing** for us that **further** validates **His love** and lets us know that **nothing** can disturb our **innocency** and our **standing** before God. **Is it Christ Jesus who died? <u>Yes</u>! Not only who <u>died,</u> but who is <u>alive</u>!** It's a wonderful thing to know that Jesus Christ not only **<u>died,</u>** but He's also **living. Jesus Christ was raised for our justification. And as long as my elder brother, my <u>substitute,</u> is there in the presence of God for me, He's alive in the presence of God, I tell you that's all I need to know, because He's my federal head. He acted on my behalf. And there is a <u>man</u> in the Godhead.** A **man** has become **God,** through Jesus Christ our Lord. There's that perfect atonement as God and man became **one** through Jesus Christ.

I **know that truth** and that **truth** holds me, oh so wonderfully. How **nice** to **know** that there is a **<u>Lamb</u>** at the heart of the throne. That's the great **key** of the book of Revelation, I think, that the **processes** of the divine government are being **ordered** by redemptive things like sacrificial love. A **Lamb** is at the **heart** of the throne. That's the great picture in the book of Revelation. To know that the **wheels of justice— that the kingdom of God is being administered by our Lord Jesus. He's at the right hand of the Father. He's not only <u>alive</u>, but he's at the right hand of <u>God</u>. That means that <u>He administers</u> the <u>things</u> of God. He has all <u>power</u> invested in Him,** and that's all I need to know.

All power is given to the Lord Jesus Christ. **<u>He's</u> administering** the **kingdom,** and like I like to say, "The **burning question** is **not** that Jesus is **like God, is God <u>like</u> <u>Jesus</u>?** I tell you; **God is <u>like</u> <u>Jesus</u>!** He loves us! **He loves us** with an undying love, and He gives Himself for us, as witnessed by His marvelous cross.

Now, not only <u>that</u>, He's not only <u>alive</u>, He's not only <u>all-powerful</u> in administrating the kingdom, but bless your hearts, He's a **high priest** up there who's **interceding** for you and for me. **Is He against me? No, He's <u>interceding</u> for me! When I do wrong, does He pray against me? He prays <u>for me</u>! He <u>intercedes</u> <u>for me</u>!** Do you think His prayers will be unavailed? I tell you it's wonderful to **know** that **God—is—for me.** He has **witnessed** that through what He has done in Christ, and through what Jesus Christ is presently doing **for me.**

<u>Well</u>, **what shall we say to <u>this</u>?** What are **you** going to say? Think, what you're going to say? **<u>What shall we say to this</u>? If God is for us, who can be against us?** Well, I could say a **whole lot,** but I just know that something down deep within me says, "**Thank God** for that great truth. **Praise God** for that truth." I just want to **rejoice** that **God is for me,** and that's **all,** and will **never** be against me. He's **for me—constantly—**as revealed to the Lord Jesus Christ.

Next question, but **what about life?** Isn't it possible that there are other conflicting powers that **might** be able to separate us from the love of God? Now, it's **clear** that nothing is against us. **Nothing** in creation can disturb your innocency. **Maybe** there's something though that can **break** the power and **break** that loving embrace of God. **What** or **who** shall be able to **separate** us from the love of Christ?

Now, don't answer too quickly. Because I tell you, life can throw some mighty hard curves your way. And sometimes you **wonder** if that rope will **break. You wonder,** how can you be **going** through this thing, and **enduring** this thing, and **still harmonize** that with a God of love **who loves you?** How can you do that when these <u>awful</u> **tests** come into our lives? Well, sometimes they can get pretty **stressful.**

The Apostle enumerates **seven** things in verse 35. *"Tribulation"*[5]— does it come our way? **Yes, it does!** Tribulation, by the way, just means **affliction or pain,** things that **afflictions** come into your life and <u>pain</u> comes into your life. Can **tribulation?** Sometimes you **wonder** if it's not **greater** than God's love.

How about **distress?** *"Distress,"*[5] means, we'd call it today, **stress.** **Pressures, within and without,** all kinds of **emotional mental pressures** sometimes that you think, I think I'm going to lose **my <u>mind</u>. <u>Pressures!</u> <u>Distresses!</u>**

"Persecution,"[5] and that is external pressures **against** you which can make life stressful for you and **especially** when you feel **rejected** by others. Those that **love you,** particularly in the church. You have the feeling that **people** aren't **for you. God** is for you. Are people always for you? No, they're not. Sometimes they're not sure whether they **like** you or **not.**

"Famine,"[5] **physical needs,** lack of food. **See! Surely,** we sometimes can be rash Christians. **As long as the Lord is meeting our needs, and perfect health, perfect wealth, perfect happiness, who <u>can't</u> go to heaven under those kinds of conditions?** But you let those blessings essentially be withdrawn, **then** we wonder where is the love of God? We're talking about famine.

"Nakedness,"[5] that would mean a lack of adequate housing and clothing. Or *"Peril,"*[5] dangers, all kinds of things that can loom up on the horizon. **Or the worst of all** is the *"Sword,"*[5] **that** would be **death.** And **sometimes** that's the most **testing point** of all. The Christian martyrs, all those who, in a sense, under Jesus, **do** come to a premature death. **Tiny babies.** Every time I have a funeral with a little **baby** and see the **anguish** of those **parents,** it always calls greatly into **question** the love of God. How can it **be** that He could have ordered the universe like this and still permit that?

Isn't it amazing though, that if you can **solve** this problem at the highest level that would be **death?** You can **solve it all the way down the line. If you know that Jesus Christ is risen from the dead, and He has redemptive designs upon our bodies,** isn't it wonderful to know that whatever happens all the way, you **still** know that He's designing good for you and He's working all things out for good.

The Apostle Paul goes on to give us **four parallels** here, **four pairs of contrast** in verses 38 and 39. And as he **thinks it through** and as he **knows** God, *"I am fully persuaded,"* [8] *"I am **sure** that neither **death, nor life,**"* [9] —and like **I like** to say, I've known people who wanted to **die.** They weren't afraid of **death,** but they were afraid of **life. Life overwhelmed them. I'm glad that neither death NOR life** can separate me from the love of God, which is in Christ Jesus, our Lord.

"...nor angels, nor principalities, nor powers," —anything in the **spiritual realm** whether it be **good or bad. There is no created thing** in the supernatural realm that can *"**separate** me from the love of God in Christ Jesus, our Lord."* [9] *"...nor things present, nor things to come."* [9] This word **present** might mean anything **impending** just right on the horizon I see and I'm facing it. Will I be able to make it through? And also, sometimes the future can be **so foreboding** and so **threatening. Will I make it through? Will we make it?** And I think most of us **can** live one day at a time, but we're so concerned about the future. **Will— it—come out—all right?** Well, thank God, the Apostle Paul says, *"things present or things to come."* [9] Is **God** the author of the future? *(Don begins speaking softly and gently)* I know—who holds the future. He has it right in His hand. The eternal God—is working all things out for my good.

"...nor height, nor depth," [9] —probably a poetic expression meaning anything you could **imagine.** We're not sure **what all** Paul includes there but any **deep** thing any **high** thing, anything that seems **insurmountable** to you. Well, let's just have done with it by saying,

nothing <u>in</u> creation, *"anything else in all creation,"* <u>no</u> created thing, *"will be able to separate you from the love of God"*—which is—*"in Christ Jesus our Lord."* [8]

Now, how do we know that? How can we be sure of it? What's the proof? Well, Paul gives us two basic reasons that lets us <u>know</u> that **nothing** can separate us from the love of God. The first clue is in verse 36, when he **quotes** from Psalm 44, verse 22, and says, *"As it Is <u>written,</u>"* in this **beautiful** passage from the Psalms, *"For <u>thy sake</u> we are being killed all the day long;"* That means during this entire age and throughout all aspects of our life, *"We are regarded as sheep to be slaughtered."* [10]

"For thy sake," now, that's the clue. It's *"For **thy sake**"* [10] that all these things are happening. <u>Is God</u> divorced from this action, from all the suffering? No—it's—for—<u>His</u>—sake. Now, I can believe this, that when I make a surrender and a commitment of my life to God that that necessarily <u>involves</u> Him <u>then</u> in my life. I become His charge. It's for <u>His</u> <u>SAKE</u> now! I am asked to suffer <u>with</u> Him. If I'm to be a fellow heir, and a son of God, I want to <u>suffer</u> with Him in order that I might also be glorified with Him.

And so, if I say, "I'm going into God's hands. I'm putting my life in the hands and trust Him." Then I have become God's charge. I belong to <u>Him</u>. And <u>now</u>, it's for <u>His sake</u>! Alright! Is the God of the universe concerned about <u>His sake</u>? About <u>His name</u>? Or <u>His character</u> or <u>His cause</u>? <u>I tell you He's</u> <u>concerned</u>, because He's going to glorify <u>only</u> His name. What's done for <u>His</u> sake involves His <u>honor</u> and His <u>dignity</u> and His <u>name</u>. And so, <u>God</u> is going to <u>see</u> to it, that nothing comes into my life that He's not going to bring about for good. **Nothing** can separate me from the love of God, because this is for His sake.

It makes a **difference** whether it's done for **His sake** or not. And if you **love God,** you can be **assured** that you're going to be loved **back**

continually. And that **right early** is going to happen **all** through your life. For **Thy sake.** That makes the difference. **God** knows what you're going through. It's for **His** sake. He knows **just** how much you can bear. Do you think there is **anything** going through your life that God doesn't understand and is involved in? It's for **His sake** that you're committed to Him. He's **going** to see you through.

But now, the second reason, is a beautiful one, and **that's** verse 37. The Apostle began to learn something about **life** and experiences when he says, *"In all these things we are more than conquerors through him that loved us."* [11] I'm glad he didn't say **out** of them. It's not always the grace of God that **delivers you.** There is a deliverance faith. There's also an enduring faith. Both of those have to be harmonized in Scripture. Sometimes you get a great **deliverance** out of a trial. **Sometimes** you get **grace** to go through— *"my grace is sufficient for you."* [12]

The thing about this, I believe, is that you **discover** that **amidst these stresses,** these pressures, **amidst** all these things that are happening to you, you begin to **discover that God transmutes them and makes you into a conqueror. You find that amidst your weakness, you become strong. Life has a way of teaching you that those things that come into your life are falling out for your good. You are turning them to a testimony. They are working on your behalf for good.**

I know that our **hindsight** is always better than our **foresight.** And at the **moment,** you can't **see it.** We can't see the forest for the trees. We get **blinded** to what's happening to us. But when you look **back,** you can say, "Lord, I know it was that **crisis** that **really** brought me to **reality** and started making me a little bit authentic in the Spirit. It was that **breaking point,** and **now I see that You worked good for that,** didn't You Lord? Now, I don't see the **eternal** consequences of that, **but as I look back, I see You are making me more than a conqueror."**

So, we have the assurance even in this life that God starts taking these difficult things and working—them—out—for—a—testimony, transmuting them to His glory so that IN these things we become super conquerors.

Now, that lets us know if God is doing it in this present time, while the full processes of redemption are not among us, how much more will be the eternal outlook? What will God do in eternity? I tell you we can rest assured that God is going to take all of these things and give glory to His name and cause us to be conformed to the image of His Son the Lord Jesus Christ.

Now, I **know** that **I** can see that at least at the human level. Even in the area of human love, when love gets **tested** at the **personal** level, but **love triumphs** and there is a reconciliation and a **forgiveness** and a **restoration,** there's always something won that's deeper than if it had not happened before. You live in your **family life** and your **marriages** and so on, and there are often great **stresses** that can come **especially,** by the way, at that **point.** Those are the closest things to all of us.

But I like the way that Tennyson put it, **poetically,** when he said, talking about this,

"And **blessings** on the **falling out**

That **all** the more endears,

When we fall **out** with those we love

But kiss again with tears!" A

So, what we might **think** is a falling out, can be **turned** to a **testimony** and bring about a **restoration** and a **reconciliation** that is **far** deeper than anything we had known. Would we **truly appreciate** the love and the grace of **God,** if we didn't have a **background** of stress against it? **I doubt it!** But when God brings us **through** and **rescues** those things, it's **then** we are **confident** that His **grace triumphs.** And it will go on doing so **and there is <u>nothing</u>—is it possible to get to the point where you'll say I am <u>persuaded</u>, there is <u>NOTHING</u>, there <u>isn't</u> <u>ANYTHING</u>, that can separate me from the love of God.**

Are you now endeared to the love of God? Do you know that it's greater than all creation? Oh, thank God for that marvelous truth! You begin to understand something about our heavenly Father and His unchanging **marvelous, wonderful infinite grace** and love.

What shall we say to these things? What are you going to say to this? Well, I say, "Hallelujah." I say, "**Praise the Lord Jesus** that **nothing** can disturb my innocency." **The Supreme Court has ruled,** and the **law of the kingdom** says, "**Justified,**" right in the midst of this present time. I stand acquitted before the throne of God. **Thank God** that His marvelous love is showing me that **nothing** can make that rope to break. **Nothing** can break His marvelous clinch, that loving embrace, that is about me. Jesus loves me. That's **all** I need to know. I can be a **<u>super conqueror</u>** through Him that loved us.

SERMON 25 ENDNOTES:

A   Alfred, Lord Tennyson. (1809-92) English Poet, (89). Retrieved online WWW: https://www.oxfordreference.com/view/10.1093/acref/9780191866692.001.0001/q-oro-ed6-00010677

SERMON 25 SCRIPTURE REFERENCES:

1   Romans 6:14 (RSV)

For sin will have no dominion over you, since you are not under law but under grace.

2   Romans 8:37 (RSV)

No, in all these things we are more than conquerors through him who loved us.

3   Romans 8:28 (KJV)

And we know that all things work together for good to them that love God, to them who are the called according to his purpose.

4 Romans 8:31 (RSV)

What then shall we say to this? If God is for us, who is against us?

5 Romans 8:35 (RSV)

Who shall separate us from the love of Christ? Shall tribulation, or distress, or persecution, or famine, or nakedness, or peril, or sword?

6 Romans 8:31-34 (RSV)

31 What then shall we say to this? If God is for us, who is against us? 32 He who did not spare his own Son but gave him up for us all, will he not also give us all things with him? 33 Who shall bring any charge against God's elect? It is God who justifies; 34 who is to condemn? Is it Christ Jesus, who died, yes, who was raised from the dead, who is at the right hand of God, who indeed intercedes for us?

7 Romans 4:8 (KJV)

Blessed is the man to whom the Lord will not impute sin.

8 Romans 8:38-39 (KJV)

38 For I am persuaded, that neither death, nor life, nor angels, nor principalities, nor powers, nor things present, nor things to come, 39 Nor height, nor depth, nor any other creature, shall be able to separate us from the love of God, which is in Christ Jesus our Lord.

9 Romans 8:38-39 (RSV)

38 For I am sure that neither death, nor life, nor angels, nor principalities, nor things present, nor things to come, nor powers, 39 nor height, nor depth, nor anything else in all creation, will be able to separate us from the love of God in Christ Jesus our Lord.

[10] Romans 8:36 (RSV)

As it is written, "For thy sake we are being killed all the day long; we are regarded as sheep to be slaughtered."

[11] Romans 8:37 (RSV)

No, in all these things we are more than conquerors through him who loved us.

[12] 2 Corinthians 12:9 (RSV)

but he said to me, "My grace is sufficient for you, for my power is made perfect in weakness." I will all the more gladly boast of my weaknesses, that the power of Christ may rest upon me.

Introducing an Interactive Website

It is our desire to build a Reign of Grace Community with people around the world, who read this great book, who desire to learn more and more about Grace.

We hope to gather personal testimonies of how the truths taught by our author have affected our readers.

Keep checking back to the website as resources will be added and the information will be updated.

There are email addresses below for you to use to communicate directly with the author, Donald R. Pickerill, Pastor Ron Isam, and others.

We will also be sharing information about our wonderful publishing company, Beyond Publishing. If you are interested in writing a book, we highly recommend this company.

www.reign-of-grace.org

Use the following email addresses to connect with some of our team.

Pastor Don Pickerill   Author
                        pastordon@reign-of-grace.org

Pastor Ron Isam   Pastor
                        pastorron@reign-of-grace.org

Johnny Fowler   Technical Advisor
                        johnnyjfowler@reign-of-grace.org

Michael Butler   Publisher/CEO
                        michael@beyondpublishing.net

Printed in the USA
CPSIA information can be obtained
at www.ICGtesting.com
JSHW060739070224
56314JS00017B/21

9 781637 923580

" I had the privilege of sitting under Pastor Don's original presentation of The Reign of Grace sermon series and it changed my life. For over forty years, I have also used it in transcribed manuscript format to teach hundreds of believers world-wide..."

Gary Matsdorf
Global Education Coordinator
International Church of the Foursquare Gospel

"Words carry weight and when a respected leader uses them wisely, they become a foundation for life. Pastor Don Pickerill is a gifted communicator, thinker, pastor, and visionary.."

Dr. Glenn Burris
Former President of The Foursquare Church

DONALD PICKRELL

Read this short and exciting book on a passage of Scripture that is unfortunately little taught and less understood, but is absolutely vital to understanding and living the Christian life as Christ means for us to live it...Thank you, Pastors Don and Ron for making this little gem available to a wider audience!

Rev. Dr. Valson Abraham, *President,*
India Gospel Outreach & India Bible College and Seminary.

"The Reign of Grace series opened up the love of the Father to me. Also, my husband Russ listened to the series 18+ times and then truly grasped what grace was all about, so we named our daughter, Raina Grace in honor of 'The Reign of Grace.'"

Robin McGregor-Wit

"...These truths have fueled spiritual balance and growth in my life over and over through the years." **Mike McGregor**

"The Reign of Grace has been the most transforming study of my life, and my ministry life. I have taught it and preached it... I wholeheartedly endorse this book... that is the character of Don Pickerill, that anything he has written or said is simply to be given away. **Jim Cosby**

BEYOND

ISBN 978-1-63792-358-0

90000

9 781637 923580